Clothing Construction

Clothing

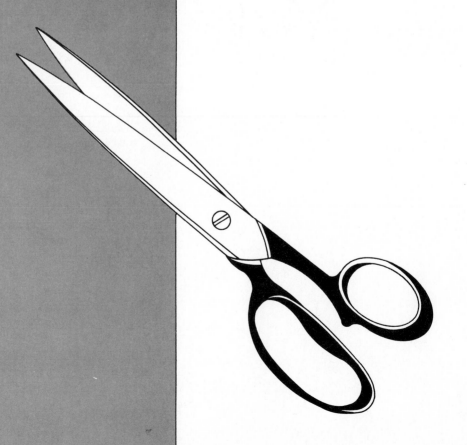

Construction

Mary Jo Kallal

University of Delaware

Macmillan Publishing Company
NEW YORK

Collier Macmillan Publishers
LONDON

Macmillan Publishing Company
866 Third Avenue, New York, New York 10022

Collier Macmillan Canada, Inc.

Library of Congress Cataloging in Publication Data

Kallal, Mary Jo.
   Clothing construction.

   Bibliography: p.
   Includes index.
   1. Dressmaking.   2. Tailoring.   I. Title.
TT518.K32   646.4   81-8426
ISBN 0-02-361640-7   AACR2

Printing: 1   2   3   4   5   6   7   8   Year: 5   6   7   8   9   0   1   2   3

ISBN 0-02-361640-7

Preface

Clothing construction can be likened to erecting a building. But unlike carpentry, and its stable, cube-like structures, the garment structure must be built to fit over an animate, three-dimensional body. The components of the medium—pattern, styling, and fabric—must be manipulated so that they begin to interrelate with the physical color and texture of the body as well as its form. Thus the garment and body become unified. The garment form corresponds with the body form in *fit*. The fabric is cut, manipulated, and controlled by the sewer through a sequence of *construction processes*. Garment surfaces are smoothed, creased, and molded by careful *pressing*. The ultimate goal of creating harmony among body, fabric, and styling has been achieved.

The format of *Clothing Construction* has been designed to contribute to achievement of the above goals. Subgoals are stated as objectives. To meet each subgoal, comprehension of the theory and rationale behind each process is essential. Therefore, each of the following chapters is introduced by an objective. Theoretical material and general construction procedures for performing each process follow. In addition,

variations of the general procedures are provided. Students are then provided with criteria to enable them to self-evaluate their performance. Thus, the student striving for conceptual understanding and quality workmanship can work toward meeting the stated objectives.

This arrangement should foster independent study as well as simplify the instructional process. Students are first familiarized with the concepts and general procedures before they apply them to a construction process. Positive relationships—rather than differences—among construction techniques are supported through theoretical rationale. Such an organization enables the professor to cover a single theory and process in each lecture-demonstration. Possible construction alternatives to meet a range of skill levels can then be demonstrated and discussed. If the professor prefers, construction may also be taught following a sequence organized by garment units: (e.g., sleeve, collar, pocket, hem, cuff, etc.) by drawing the needed topics from each chapter.

As you can see, the text can be used to meet the needs of students at two major skill levels. Basic theory and general construction procedures challenge the beginning sewer, while more complex fitting and construction processes are designed to challenge the more advanced sewing student.

The male student has not been ignored. The sizing chart and a majority of the line drawings throughout the text illustrate garments that may be worn by both males and females. Chapter 1, "The Body-Garment Relationship," discusses line, texture, and color as these elements pertain to the attire of both sexes. Although most techniques are applicable to either gender, some are designated specifically for males. These items, designated "man-tailored," may be used in the construction of garments for males or females.

The fitting component is closely examined. Special tables have been designed to enable the sewer to analyze sequentially a variety of fitting problems by using survey, diagnosis, and pattern manipulation. Both two- and three-dimensional misfit can be eliminated or minimized. Correlations between two- and three-dimensional fitting methods are clearly illustrated and compared in the set of tables as well as in another set of charts that show how to adjust and alter the pattern. The sewer must select a fitting method based upon individual skill level, complexity of individual body contours, and the ultimate quality desired.

Students are shown how to incorporate fitting into one of two construction plans. Unit and Process Construction Plans enable the student to organize the construction sequence before beginning to sew. Three fittings are incorporated into each sequence. Organizational strategies for construction are illustrated in a set of charts for basic garment types. Readers are encouraged to select and develop a plan that matches both their skill level and time schedule.

Throughout the text, students are encouraged to make decisions regarding their individual sewing situation. After first examining their goals, they must make choices based upon the garment quality-level desired, time allotted to the project, their sewing skill level, fabric characteristics, pattern styling complexity, and garment function.

Additional features of the text include:

· Metric and English measurement and sizing charts. All measurements are presented in metric increments followed by the equivalent in inches.
· Charts are utilized throughout the text to illustrate theoretical categorization of the construction processes for better comprehension.
· Key terms are highlighted throughout the text.

Acknowledgments

I especially thank my students who have been marvelous teachers and critics; particularly Kim Bartgis, Faith Brewington, Debra Brorsen, Leslie Genzlinger, and Leigh Mekanik, for critiquing portions of the text from a student's viewpoint; and Gina Centurione, Peggy Ferri, and Anne Perrella, for illustrating small portions of the text. I appreciate the support I received from the Textiles, Design and Consumer Economics Department at the University of Delaware and the Division of Comprehensive Planning and Design while I was on the faculty at

Southern Illinois University, Carbondale. Both Carol Mosher and Kathy Starks performed wonders on the typewriter. I thank my colleagues and friends, Ellen Ahrbeck annd Amy Sinclair, who helped get the book off the ground and provided encouragement, input, and support since that time. I thank Elva Berryman (Louisiana State University), Ellen Goldsberry (University of Arizona), and Amy Sinclair (University of Puget Sound) for the long hours they spent reviewing the manuscript. And finally, a very special thanks to my family and close friends for their love and support.

MJK

Contents

Part One

THE PRELIMINARIES   1

1   **The Body-Garment Relationship**   5

2   **Fabric Selection**   14

3   **Measurements for Pattern Size and Fit**   28

4   **Decoding the Pattern**   38

Part Two

HANDLING MAJOR SEWING EQUIPMENT   45

5   **Sewing Tools**   49

6   Sewing Machine   55

7   Pressing   55

Part Three

GETTING READY TO SEW   71

8   Components of Fit   73

9   Fabric Preparation   106

10 Pattern Layout and Cutting   110

11 Marking Techniques   123

Part Four

STRATEGIES FOR CONSTRUCTION   129

12 Organization and Fitting Strategies   131

13 Stitching Strategies   143

14 Contouring Strategies   161

Part Five

GARMENT CONTOURING AND STYLING: SEAMS 179

15 Creating Contour Within Fabric
    Sections   183

16 Joining Seam Lines of Equal Length   187

17 Joining Seam Lines of Unequal
    Length   194

18 Joining Circumference Seams   199

Part Six

STRUCTURAL SEAMS: PROTECTIVE AND DECORATIVE FUNCTIONS 213

19 Protective Raw-edge Treatments   215

20 Protective/Decorative Enclosed
    Seams   220

21 Decorative Seams   223

Part Seven

ENCLOSED SEAMS: CONCEALING AND FINISHING GARMENT PERIMETERS   227

22   Facings   239

23   Bindings and Bands   255

Part Eight

CLOSURE SYSTEMS AND POCKETS   277

24   Major Closures   279

25   Fasteners   305

26   Pockets   313

Metric Equivalency Chart   328

Bibliography   331

Index   333

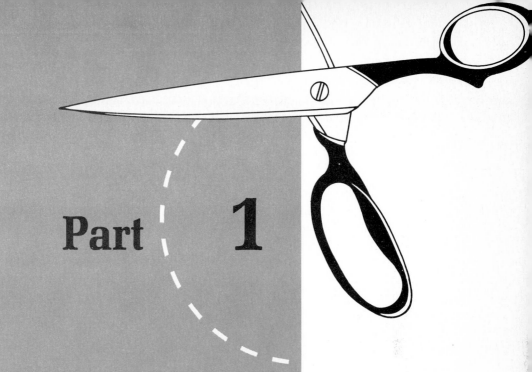

Part 1

The Preliminaries

Constructing apparel for yourself and your friends enables you to utilize both your aesthetic and your technical skills. YOU select the design. YOU select the fabric colors and textures. YOU select the trim. YOU determine the pattern size. And YOU fit the pattern—and prepare the fabric—and construct the garment. YOU create a unique new dress—or shirt—or pants. The preliminary selection steps are just as critical to the success of your completed garment as are your construction skills. A beautifully constructed shirt with mismatched buttons is as much a disappointment as a poorly constructed shirt with perfectly matched buttons.

Design and fabric coordination are critical. Yet if the garment does not enhance the wearer, it is still not a successful garment. During the preliminary selection process you are dealing with three interrelated components which condition the ultimate appearance of the garment: body, pattern, and fabric.[1]

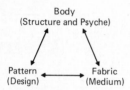

The human *physical structure* is the structural framework foundation for all your designs. You have observed that all human structures feature basic characteristics: a series of complex concave and convex curves and planes; length, width, and depth. The constant movement of the body forces these curves and dimensions to continually change . . . so that the garment must flatter the figure while it is both stationary and mobile. Thus the body forms the structural framework for any garment design. Body dimensions directly determine pattern size. Specified measurements are later used to fit the pattern to your specific contours, lengths, and widths.

In addition to the physical structure of the body, you must also consider any *socio-psychological needs*. Will the design and fabric coordinate with your lifestyle, including work, leisure, and social activities? Will it suit your individual taste? Will it enhance your figure? Will the garment be both psychologically and physically comfortable? Will you feel good when you wear it? If not, it may not be worth the time, dollars, and energy you will expend constructing it.

The *pattern* forms the decorative design. Since this design will cover the human form, it should relate to the anatomical structure and permit comfortable movement. You can utilize the design elements in your design to enhance your figure assets and to camouflage any irregularities. As you begin to consider various pattern designs, try not to be overly careful

[1] Meshke, *Textiles and Clothing Analysis and Synthesis* (Minneapolis: Burgess Publishing Company, 1961), pp. 28–29.

Predicting Construction Complexity

Component	Less Complex	More Complex
FIT	Loose Skims	Fitted
FABRIC	No fraying, minimal fraying	Frays readily
	Closely woven	Loosely woven
	Slightly textured, tweedy	Smooth, slippery, shiny
	Medium thickness	Bulky, very thin
	Medium value	Very light, very dark
	Stable	Stretchy, stiff
	Responsive (easily manipulated)	Non-responsive
	Small, all-over prints; solids	Checks, plaids, stripes, large print
CONSTRUCTION:		
Silhouette	Straight, slightly flared	Circular, pleated, gathered, underlined, lined
Style Details	Darts, dart-tucks, ease, gathers	Ruffles, pleats, pin-tucks, draping
Quantity	Few seams	Many seams
Style Seams	Simple, straight, slight curve	In-set corners, circular, angular
Function	Seams of equal length	Seams of unequal length: ease, gathers, tucks, pleats
Details	Plain structural seams	Decorative seams, top stitching
Edge Treatments	Zig-zag, overcast, Hong Kong	Bound
Inner Support	Simple interfacing, stays	Padded, contoured
Perimeter Finishes:		
Edges	Facings, bindings	Appendages (sleeves, collars, cuffs, waistbands)
Sleeves	Cut-in-one: Dolman, Kimono	Mounted: Raglan, Set-in, Man-tailored
Collars	Flat, band, shawl	Rolled, band, tailored
Cuffs	Band with no closure	French, man-tailored
Waistlines	Straight band, casing	Seamed, shaped, contoured bands
Hems	Straight, slightly flared	Circular, pleated, rolled
Closures	Zippers, snaps, hooks and eyes, velcro	Button and buttonhole
Pockets	Patch, in-seam	Welt, side hip pocket

about what may seem to be overwhelming physical deficiencies (oh—those broad hips! that rounded tummy!). If you are too careful, your wardrobe may become rather boring and dull. Use the design elements to spark up your wardrobe—and to have fun manipulating lines, colors, and textures.

Analyze potential patterns: Where are seams, darts, or tucks located? Are they primarily vertical or horizontal? Has style fullness been added through flare, gathers, pleats, smocking, or pin-tucks? Do collars, cuffs, and pockets form predominantly rounded or angular shapes? Where are closures located? What type of closure is used?

The body is your framework and the pattern is your applied design. Your *fabric* thus becomes the medium through which the two are inter-related. The garments may be composed of one or more fabrics. These fabrics support the garment silhouette and style features and also add the design elements of color and texture to your design. The fabrics used must harmonize with one another through color, pattern, or texture.

Consider how the fabric behaves. Pick up many different fabrics and observe how they fall. Fabrics which fall in soft folds will work best in soft, gathered designs; fabrics which stand out crisply will work best in tailored, structured styles.

At the same time you are analyzing designs and fabrics, also consider how difficult the design will be to construct. The chart, "Predicting Construction Complexity," on page 3 will help you to estimate the construction complexity of your design. If you are just learning to sew, choose a design with many less complex features in it. If you have sewing experience, you may wish to challenge yourself with a more complex construction technique or a more difficult fabric. The choice is yours.

Chapter 1, "The Body-Garment Relationship," and Chapter 2, "Fabric Selection," will assist you in analyzing physical and psychological needs and with making pattern and fabric selections. Chapter 3, "Measurements for Pattern Size and Fit," describes how to take strategic measures of body dimensions.

Turn to Chapter 4, "Decoding the Pattern," for assistance in interpreting the information supplied on the pattern envelope, instruction sheet, and pattern. Consider the fabric choices suggested on the back of the envelope when shopping for potential fabrics. Precise garment dimensions are listed on the pattern envelope which may help you to choose between the pants with the narrow or the fuller pants legs. Fabric yardage can also be a factor in choosing fabrics—compute the total cost of different fabrics for different designs. Which is really more economical?

Try to envision the completed garment before you start. How will the striped cotton appear in the shirt? Will the fabric have enough body to support the collar? Is the fabric so sheer that you will see many inner construction details? Your ability to foresee the design in a particular fabric and on a particular body are critical to your success.

1 The Body-Garment Relationship

OBJECTIVE

To select a pattern design (silhouette, line) and fabric (texture, color), harmonizing with a) the body form and proportions and with b) one's personal lifestyle.

In order to choose distinctive clothing that is in harmony with personal physical characteristics and personal taste, one must coordinate garment lines and proportion as well as fabric color, texture, and hand. Clothing can create the illusion of a well-proportioned figure even when the dimensions of that figure deviate from the standard.

The freedom to select each of the materials needed to construct a garment allows the designer to exercise great personal creativity but also calls for the making of many decisions. Choice of design, color, texture, and proportion must be considered in relation to individual body proportions and coloring as well as in relation to one another.

Analysis of Physical Characteristics and Personal Taste

Although garment design and fabric coordination are of primary importance in clothing con-

PHYSICAL PROPORTIONS

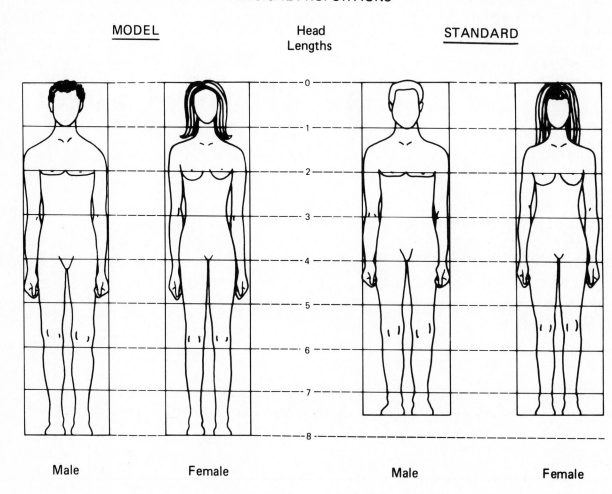

MODEL

Head
Lengths

STANDARD

Male   Female   Male   Female

struction, the design and fabric cannot be selected without first analyzing personal body proportions and coloring. Choice of garment styling, color, and fabric also depend upon individual life-styles, including work and leisure activities.

Proportion refers to the ratios of height to body width and body depth. In addition, the levels of the waist, hips, and knees influence physical proportions. Currently, the tall, slender, long-legged figure of the model is the ideal

for both sexes. The ideal figure differs from the *standard* figure, which represents the average male and average female proportions. Standard male and female figures are 7½ head lengths tall, whereas the model's figure is at least 8 head lengths tall. The model figure is also narrower in relation to height than is the standard figure. Refer to the illustrations of model and standard figures showing the body levels that indicate good proportion.

Patterns and ready-to-wear are fitted to standard figure proportions. Due to variations in height, circumference, and body levels, however, very few people correspond precisely to these standards. Individuals of equal height and circumference may differ in other ways. One may have a higher waist level and long upper legs, whereas another may have longer-than-average arms, shorter legs, and a long torso.

Steps can be taken to camouflage variations in proportion so as to create the illusions of greater leg length, a longer waistline, narrower hips, and so on. By manipulating the design elements of line, color, and texture, one may produce optical illusions or fool the eye of the viewer. For example, subdued color, crisp fabric, and a flared or trapezoid silhouette that does not cling to the figure can disguise hip bulges and a thick waist. A contrasting collar or trim at the neckline can lead the eye upward and away from lower torso problems. When a man's tie and shirt contrast with his jacket in both texture and color, they guide the eye upward toward the face.

As a result of these and other physical variations, care must be taken to select clothing that suits individual proportions and contours. In constructing a garment, it is usually impossible to "preview" the garment design, fabric, and fit, as one may do when purchasing ready-to-wear. The ability to *visualize* style and fabric design on various figures can be developed by studying ready-to-wear, fashion magazines, and actually sewing garments using a variety of patterns and fabrics. By trying on ready-to-wear in many styles and fabrics, the sewer can analyze compatibility of fabric, garment design, and figure before purchasing sewing materials. It is also important to remember that not all ready-to-wear is well designed.

Pattern silhouette and design lines, fabric color and texture, and body proportions can be coordinated by:

1. *Analyzing individual body proportions* to de-termine which physical characteristics are assets to emphasize and which might be visually camouflaged through choice of garment design. Refer to the chart entitled "Analysis of Figure Characteristics" on page 8 to analyze body proportions.
2. *Studying the design elements* to determine how they can be utilized to emphasize or deemphasize the desired body proportions. A description of the elements of silhouette, line, color, and texture are described beginning on page 9.

ANALYSIS OF PHYSICAL CHARACTERISTICS

How do individual body proportions differ from average?

Proportion = ratios of height: width/depth

Check the points on the continuum (page 8) that best describe a given individual's personal characteristics.

Personal taste refers to individual preferences in garment styling, fabrics, colors, textures, and ease of care. These preferences develop over time, reflecting the following influences:

Community size, location
Peers
Family
Job/school
Age
Activities
Media; current fashion predictions
Prevailing local fashions
Clothing, pattern, fabric choices available
Time, money available to care for clothing
Income

As each of these factors changes, personal taste as expressed in clothing choices is modified.

Analysis of Figure Characteristics

	Less than Average	Average	Greater than Average
Height:	short		tall
Overall size:	small		large
Length:			
Neck length	short		long
Bust level	high		low
Waist level	high		low
Hip level	high		low
Leg length	short		long
Arm length	short		long
Width:			
Shoulders	narrow		broad
Waist	narrow		broad
Hips	narrow		broad
Depth:			
Bust/Chest	flat		prominent
Abdomen	flat		prominent
Seat	flat		prominent
Circumference:			
Neck	thin		thick
Bust/Chest	small		large
Waist	small		large
Hips	small		large
Thighs	thin		heavy
Calves	thin		thick
Arms	thin		heavy

Features to emphasize:

Features to camouflage:

Design Elements

Color and silhouette are the first aspects of the garment to be noticed. They influence apparent body size and proportion most directly. Usage of line and texture work subtly to influence the way in which physical characteristics are perceived. In all cases, these design elements draw the eye to the area of greatest contrast. When selecting a pattern and fabric combination, use the following design elements described to carefully analyze the potential garment as it will relate to various physical characteristics.

SILHOUETTE

The silhouette or outline shape of the garment directly influences apparent physical proportion when the figure is seen from a distance. The eye uses the outer shape created by the garment silhouette to assess the body's proportions; it can be deceived by the location of areas of fullness or areas of close fit. Men's clothing generally combines the bifurcated silhouette with the wedge- or T-shaped silhouette.

LINE

The lines within the silhouette are created through the use of seams, trims, color or texture contrasts, rows of buttons, and garment cut. The greater the contrast created, the more visible the lines are and the greater their ability to lead the eye directionally to or from various areas of the body. Long, thick, or repetitious lines are also more forceful in carrying the eye. As the number of lines in the fabric pattern increases, the number of seams within the pattern should be reduced.

Refer to the examples illustrating the use of line in various garments. Notice how the location and strength of the line influence body proportion.

Garment Length

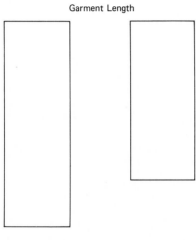

Which length makes the body appear longer?

Vertical Seams

Which figure looks thinner?

Vertical Seams, Darts

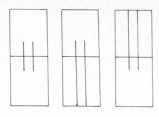

Which section of the body appears more slender?

Horizontal Seams

How do horizontal lines influence height? Which figure appears shorter?

Buttons

Note button location, size, spacing, and contrast

Trims

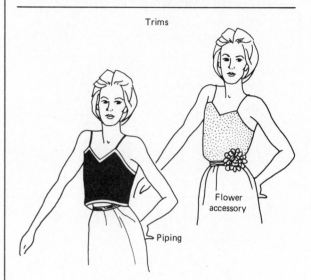

Piping

Flower accessory

How do these trims draw the eye to various parts of the body?

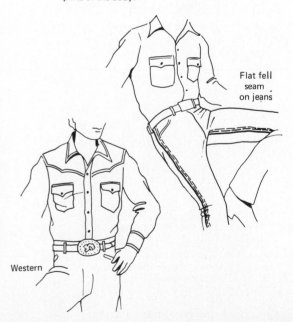

Flat fell seam on jeans

Western

Stripes

How does line spacing influence
eye movement?

Which jacket creates greater width?

COLOR

Color draws the eye to the garment and can enhance the natural coloring of the wearer, influence the apparent size of the body, and also draw the eye to a desired focal point.

The three primary colors of red, blue, and yellow are combined to create the secondary colors of violet, green, and orange. Intermediate colors are the result of primary and secondary color combinations, forming colors such as blue-green, yellow-orange, or red-violet. The color derived is influenced by the proportion of the color quantities used.

Color has the three dimensions of hue, value, and intensity:

- *Hue* is the name of a color. Red, orange, and yellow, the colors of the sun and fire, are associated with warmth, excitement, and motion. Blue, green, and violet are the restful, cool colors of the sea and forest.
- *Value* refers to the lightness or darkness of any hue. Orange is lightened to peach and darkened to rust and brown.
- *Intensity,* the brightness or dullness of a hue, refers to its clarity or its grayness.

Consider the following when choosing color:

1. The natural coloring created by the skin, hair, eyes, and teeth may be predominantly warm or cool. As the largest body color area, the skin is either yellow- or blue-toned. Hair, eyes, and teeth pick up skin tones while simultaneously contrasting in lightness or darkness.

   Use clothing colors to emphasize natural coloring. Yellow-toned skins look best in warm colors or in cool colors that have been mixed with warm hues, such as blue-green or maroon (red-violet). Cool hues will enhance blue-toned coloring.

2. When using one color, consider whether the color advances or recedes.

   These colors advance, increasing apparent body size:

   Warm hues: red, yellow, orange

   Light values, such as pink, yellow, lavender

   Bright intensities, such as blue, green, red

   These colors recede, optically decreasing body size:

   Cool hues: blue, green, violet

   Dark values, such as navy (dark blue), maroon (dark red), and rust (dark orange)

   Dull intensities, such as gold (yellow), maroon (red), avocado (green)

3. When using two or more colors, consider their proximity on the color wheel.

   Hues near one another on the color wheel are related. When they are used together, the effect is easily unified and harmonious.

   Colors positioned on opposite sides of the color wheel contrast with one another. As a result, their combined use can create bold effects, strong divisional lines, or intensification of color. The eye can be drawn away from problem areas by using bright or light colors with large areas of dull or dark colors. To draw the eye away from a prominent abdomen, place the more intense color near the face.

4. If the fabric is patterned, consider the degree of color contrast and the pattern size. When colors are muted, one overall warm or cool color is apparent. Large-scale patterns high in color contrast will increase apparent body size more than if the same pattern is low in color contrast.

TEXTURE

Fabric texture is created by inherent fiber characteristics, yarn ply and twist, and the fabric construction. Texture relates to both the *visual* and the *tactile* senses. The roughness or smoothness of a fabric can be seen as well as felt because of the light reflected from it. Smooth fabrics reflect more light than rough ones do.

Textural Characteristics

Increase apparent body size			Reduce apparent body size
Rough	⟵	⟶	Smooth
Hard	⟵	⟶	Soft
Coarse	⟵	⟶	Fine
Heavy	⟵	⟶	Light
Thick	⟵	⟶	Thin
Shiny	⟵	⟶	Dull
Stretchy	⟵	⟶	Stiff

Texture also involves the fabric's *hand. Hand* refers to drape as determined by a fabric's flexibility, weight, and thickness. These characteristics also influence visibility of body contours. A soft, weighty, and lustrous fabric, such as jersey, emphasizes body contours more than a crisp, medium-weight fabric, such as glazed cotton.

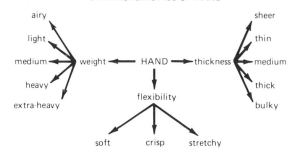

CHARACTERISTICS OF HAND

Texture-selection considerations:[2]

1. Clingy, stretchy fabrics reveal body contours.

How do these textures influence body size?

2. Crisp to stiff fabrics are less flexible; thus they fall away from the body and can hide figure irregularities.
3. Stiff fabrics may overwhelm a small figure or add the illusion of greater size to a larger figure.
4. Rough, thick fabrics add bulk to the apparent body size.
5. Shiny and lustrous fabrics reflect light, emphasizing body contours and enlarging the figure.
6. Dull textures absorb light. As a result, they do not enlarge the body size.

2 Fabric Selection

OBJECTIVE

To use a basic knowledge of fabric structures, general fiber properties, finishes, and care requirements to evaluate and select fabrics compatible with the pattern design and planned end-use.

The ultimate appearance of any garment is influenced by compatibility of fabric hand with the desired garment structure. Not all fabrics are suitable for all garment styles. For example, a drapable fabric cannot be forced to hold the structured lines of a suit. Generally, final results are best when the innate character of the fabric is compatible with the styling of the garment. Soft fabrics work well with soft, full designs; crisp fabrics hold straighter, tailored design lines.

Many factors must be considered in the selection of both the outer and inner fabrics needed to construct a garment. Analyze garment styling and function in relation to the fibers and fabrics available on the market. Review the sections on color, texture, silhouette, and line in Chapter 1. To make a wise choice of fabric for a specific design and end use, insight into the various fiber and fabric structures available is necessary. Does the fabric pattern and texture suit the garment structure? What are the cost and time expenditures needed for upkeep? What quality points must be appraised to determine performance capabilities?

Fabric Characteristics

The fabric chosen for garment construction greatly influences the success of the sewing endeavor. The fiber or blended fibers, yarn structure, fabric structure, dyes, and applied finishes combine to create the final fabric structure. Infinite combinations ultimately influence fabric drapability, texture, weave, and care as well as quality and performance characteristics.

FIBER CONTENT

In 1960, the Textile Fiber Products Identification Act became effective. This legislation requires almost all textile products sold at retail to carry labels stating the textile fiber content. The percentage of fiber content must be stated on the bolt-end labels of yard goods and on labels attached to ready-to-wear garments.

Consumers must be able to interpret the fiber-content label. Extensive availability of natural and synthetic fibers as well as numerous fiber blends increases the need for consumer knowledge. Fortunately, categorizing general fiber properties and care requirements of the many brand name fibers under generic groups simplifies the learning process. Become familiar with the fiber properties and care requirements for each of the natural and synthetic fiber groups listed on the chart beginning on page 16.

YARN STRUCTURE

Yarn is the medium of fabric construction. The character of the fabric it forms is determined to a great degree by the nature of the yarns used. Before they are formed into yarns, fibers are referred to as *staples* or *filaments*. Silk and all the synthetic fibers originally existed as long continuous strands or filaments. These fibers require only a small degree of twist to form a yarn. The remaining natural fibers exist in short-length or staple form. Synthetic fibers may also be cut into short, staple lengths to imitate the natural fibers. Staple fibers require more complex yarn twisting techniques to hold them together.

Yarn variations exist as a result of the fiber length, the twist of each yarn strand, and the number of strands twisted together. Generally long, smooth, tightly twisted fibers are stronger and form a more durable yarn. Slubbed or loopy yarns tend to snag more readily than smoothly twisted yarns.

FABRIC STRUCTURE

Fabrics may be woven by interlacing the yarns or knitted by interlooping them. Variations in yarn character, fiber content, and the method for intertwining the yarns influence the fabric structure. Woven and knitted fabric structures are briefly discussed below to provide a general background.

Woven Fabrics

Basic weaves formed by interlacing yarns include the plain, twill, and satin weaves. Woven fabrics are derived from these weaves or from variations of them. The plain and twill weaves

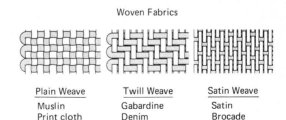

Woven Fabrics

Plain Weave	Twill Weave	Satin Weave
Muslin	Gabardine	Satin
Print cloth	Denim	Brocade
Voile	Whipcord	Damask
Gingham	Calvary twill	Brocatelle

are most durable. The satin weave, however, may snag easily if the float yarns are long. Loosely woven fabrics made from novelty yarns are usually less durable and may snag or stretch. A characteristic of all woven fabrics is that they fray at cut edges and should be protected. Loosely woven fabrics made from smooth, slippery yarns fray most readily.

Natural Fibers

	Fiber	Characteristics and Apparel Uses	Properties	Care
Cellulose Fibers	COTTON From cottonseed pod	Light to medium-weight apparel. Found in broadcloth, poplin, terry, corduroy, seersucker, denim, etc.	*Advantages:* Wide selection of weights and colors. Versatile, durable, can withstand frequent laundering. Absorbent, dyes well, stronger when wet. *Limitations:* Untreated cotton wrinkles easily, is flammable, shrinks. (Finishes reduce these problems.)	Can be washed and dried at regular washer setting. Bleach can be used on white cottons. Cotton may be pressed with hot iron while damp or steam-ironed.
	LINEN From flax plant	Women's and children's blouses and dresses. Men's and women's summer suits and sportswear; toweling, tablecloths, spring and summer wear, linen handkerchiefs, damask.	*Advantages:* Extremely strong. Comfortable to wear because of high moisture absorption. Moth resistant. Natural luster and stiffness. Cool. *Limitations:* Poor affinity for dyes. Wrinkles easily if not treated. Press crease retention is poor.	Usually dry-cleaned to retain crispness; launders well if preshrunk and softer look is desired. For smooth appearance, it should be ironed damp at a high temperature.
Protein Fibers	SILK From silkworm cocoon	Various weaves and weights used for dresses, shirts, suits, scarves, and linings.	*Advantages:* Luxurious in hand and feel. Adaptable to a variety of constructions. Strong, absorbent; cool in summer and warm in winter. Moderately resilient. *Limitations:* Sunlight and perspiration weaken the fabric. Some fabrics water-spot. Silk generates static electricity.	Usually dry-cleaned. Hand-washable in mild suds and lukewarm water; avoid chlorine bleach. Should be ironed with low heat on wrong side while damp or steam-ironed.

Natural Fibers

	Fiber	Characteristics and Apparel Uses	Properties	Care
Protein Fibers	WOOL From sheep fleece	Versatile in weight, texture, weave, and color—used for tailored garments because it can mold into shape; also dresses, sweaters, and blouses. Found in gabardine, flannel, crepe, jersey, tweed, etc.	*Advantages:* Warm and absorbent. Can be cool in lightweight fabrics. Wool resists wrinkling. Naturally water and flame-resistant. Dyes readily. *Limitations:* Shrinks, needs to be mothproofed.	Usually dry-cleaned. Can be hand-washed, but avoid agitation. Do not tumble dry. Block into shape on flat surface. To avoid stretching and shine, press on wrong side using damp cloth or steam. Do not use chlorine bleach. Machine wash only if care instructions are followed.

Synthetic Fibers

Fiber	Characteristics and Apparel Uses	Properties	Care

The synthetic fibers have been subdivided into "generic" or family names. In general, the fibers within a specific generic group possess the same essential properties and require the same basic care. Under the *generic* name, a *trade name* or *brand name* is included. The trade name tells the ownership or origin of the particular fiber. These trademarks advertise the company as well as indicate the type of fiber. The list of trade names under each generic category is not complete due to the tremendous number of trademarked fibers available.

Fiber	Characteristics and Apparel Uses	Properties	Care
ACETATE Celanese Chromspun Estron	Silklike appearance, soft feel, deep luster, excellent drape. Used in lingerie, blouses, dresses, linings.	*Advantages:* Takes colors well. Resistant to stretch and shrinkage. Resistant to moths and mildew. Moderately absorbent. *Limitations:* Wrinkles easily. Weakened by light. Low strength. Holds in body heat; holds static electricity.	Usually dry-cleaned. If washed, use warm water and gentle cycle. Tumble-dry at cool setting. Iron while damp with low temperature and light pressure on wrong side.

Synthetic Fibers

Fiber	Characteristics and Apparel Uses	Properties	Care
ACRYLIC Acrilan Creslan Orlon	Commonly light, soft, fluffy. Used for sweaters, dresses, suits, and sportswear. Found in knits, fleece, fake fur.	*Advantages:* Bulk without weight. Good wrinkle resistance. Strong. Quick-drying. Moth and mildew resistant. Warm. Dyes well. Woollike. *Limitations:* Heat-sensitive. Accumulates static electricity. May pill in some yarn constructions due to low absorbency.	Remove oily stains before cleaning. May be dry-cleaned or laundered. Chlorine bleach may be used on white fabrics. Machine wash (warm) and tumble-dry. Use fabric softener. Seldom requires ironing, but if so, use a low heat setting on the wrong side. Pleats and creases can be heat-set.
MODACRYLIC SEF Elura Verel	Available in deep pile, fleece, and furlike fabrics. Used chiefly for heavy coats and linings.	*Advantages:* Wrinkle-resistant. Flame-resistant. Retains shape well. Excellent elasticity. Warm. Resilient. *Limitations:* May accumulate static electricity. Heat-sensitive. Low absorbency. Low strength.	Furlike fabrics are most safely dry-cleaned. If washable, follow same directions as for acrylic. Avoid ironing, as they melt easily.
NYLON Antron Blue C Celanese Enkalure Qiana	Available in many textures and weights. Often found in blends. Used for lingerie, dresses, and stretch fabrics.	*Advantages:* Wrinkle-resistant. Exceptional strength. Can be heat-set to retain pleats. Stable. Colorfast. *Limitations:* Accumulates static electricity. Holds in body heat, oils, and perspiration. Tends to pill. Low absorbency.	Remove oily stains before cleaning. Machine wash regular; use fabric softener. Tumble- or drip-dry. Use low pressing temperature on wrong side if needed.
POLYESTER Dacron Fortrel Kodel Trevira	Available in many weights, textures, and weaves. Used mainly for permanent-press and knit fabrics. Often blended with cotton, wool, rayon.	*Advantages:* Excellent wrinkle and abrasion resistance. Wash and wear. Quick-drying. Resistant to stretching and shrinking. High strength. Pleats can be heat-set.	Remove oily stains before cleaning. Machine wash and dry, regular temperature. Use fabric softener. May not require ironing; otherwise use medium setting.

Synthetic Fibers

Fiber	Characteristics and Apparel Uses	Properties	Care
POLYESTER (continued)		*Limitations:* Low absorbency; may hold in body heat. May pill and pick up lint. Accumulates static electricity. Affinity for oily stains.	
RAYON Avril Beau-Grip Coloray Fibro	Comes in a wide range of qualities. Can be made to resemble natural fibers. Used for dresses, suits, coats, lingerie, linings. Often woven to resemble linen.	*Advantages:* Soft and comfortable. Good affinity for dyes. Colorfast. Absorbent. *Limitations:* Low strength. Wrinkles, shrinks, stretches if not finished. Holds in body heat.	Usually dry-cleaned. If wet, may wrinkle, ravel, or shrink. If washable, use mild suds. Iron when damp at a moderate setting to avoid shine.
SPANDEX Lycra	Elastic fiber, often used with other fibers to incorporate stretch. Used in swimwear, foundations, and active sportswear.	*Advantages:* Elastic, lightweight, strong. Resistant to body oils, cosmetics. Nonabsorbent, so dries quickly. *Limitations:* Low absorbency. Yellows with age. Heat-sensitive.	Hand- or machine-wash on gentle cycle; tumble-dry at low setting. Avoid chlorine bleach. Iron only at low temperatures.
TRIACETATE Arnel	Often found in blends such as tricot, sharkskin, flannel, and taffeta. Used for garments that require pleat retention; sportswear.	*Advantages:* Good wrinkle and shine resistance. Good affinity for dyes. Can be permanently pleated. *Limitations:* Low strength.	Machine-wash, tumble-dry. Usually requires ironing. Can take higher temperature than acetate.

Pile Fabrics

The pile weave produces a thick, textured fabric by incorporating an additional yarn in the weaving process. Corduroy, velvet, and other pile fabrics must be cut with the pattern pieces lying in one direction due to lengthwise (up-and-down) color variations. Light is reflected

Pile Fabrics

Loop Pile
Terrycloth

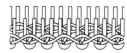

Cut Pile
Velvet
Velveteen
Corduroy

differently by the yarns and, if the pattern pieces are reversed, may cause the back panel of a constructed skirt to appear darker than the front panel. Yardage must be purchased following "with nap" requirements.

Knitted Fabrics

Created by interlooping yarns, knitted fabrics are characterized by their stretch. The degree and direction of stretch vary according to the knitting process. Knitted fabrics may be purchased in tubular or flat format. Basic knitting processes include production of *weft* and *warp* knits.

Weft knits are made by using a single yarn to form loops across the fabric width. As a result, these knits stretch more in the width than in the lengthwise direction. Weft knits tend to run vertically if a loop is broken. Single and double knits are both weft knits. *Single knits* can be made using one of three basic stitches:

1. A flat jersey knit is used to make hosiery, sweaters, and sportswear. Since these fabrics tend to run, a variation of the flat knit can be used to improve run resistance.
2. Purl knits look the same on both front and back and have nearly the same degree of stretch in both the lengthwise and crosswise directions. They are commonly used to make bulky sweaters or children's wear.
3. Rib knits are warm and exhibit a high degree of elasticity, making them excellent for sweater ribbing. The ribs are formed by alternating rows of plain and purl stitches.

Weft knits

Jersey knit

Purl knit

Rib knit

Double knits are made using an interlock stitch or by binding two weft knits together periodically. They are firmer, heavier, less stretchy, and more resilient than single knits. They also resist runs and are dimensionally stable.

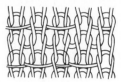
Double knit

Warp knits are created by loops formed in a lengthwise direction. They have less stretch and tend to be runproof. Tricot and raschel knits are common examples. *Tricot knits,* used primarily in lingerie and lounge wear, may vary from sheer and filmy to firmer and opaque. They feature good air and water permeability, crease resistance, drape, run resistance, and elasticity. *Raschel* knitting is a versatile technique for creating patterned knits ranging from crochet effects and laces to power nets for foundations and swimwear as well as drapery fabrics.

Warp knits

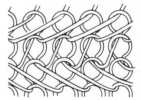
Tricot knit

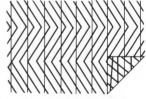
Raschel knit

Descriptive Terminology: Wovens

Once the yarns have been woven to form a fabric, the length of goods can be described using the terms listed below. An understanding of the fabric structure is essential to fabric preparation, cutting, pattern layout, fitting, and construction. Refer to the corresponding point on the fabric diagram when reviewing the descriptions.

Grain refers to the direction of the yarns forming the fabric. Lengthwise grain (warp yarns) is parallel to the selvage and crosswise grain (filling yarns) is perpendicular to the selvage.

Selvages are firmly woven edges formed along each lengthwise edge.

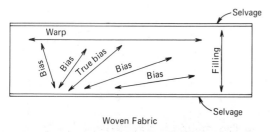

Woven Fabric

Warp yarns form the lengthwise grain of the fabric. This direction has the least stretch and is generally cut to hang vertically on the body.

Filling yarns make up the crosswise grain of the fabric. This grain direction has slightly more stretch than the lengthwise grain and usually lies parallel to the floor in the constructed garment.

True bias does not follow a grain direction but bisects the right angle created by intersecting crosswise and lengthwise yarns. The true bias direction has the maximum amount of stretch found in a woven fabric. Garments cut with the true bias hanging vertically tend to cling to and follow body contours closely. Bias stretch can be utilized to fit woven fabrics over body bulges without using darts.

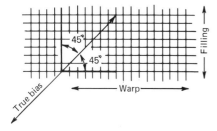

Bias refers to any angle direction intersecting the fabric grain lines except the true bias. Each bias

direction varies in stretch from minimal (near a warp or filling direction) to nearly maximal (close to the true bias direction).

Descriptive Terminology: Knits

The structure of the knitted fabric varies from the woven fabric and thus requires other descriptors. These terms include the following:

A *wale* follows the direction of the lengthwise yarns in a knitted fabric. This direction will usually have less stretch than the crosswise direction.

Courses form the rows of loops making up the crosswise direction of knitted fabrics. This direction may be quite stretchy.

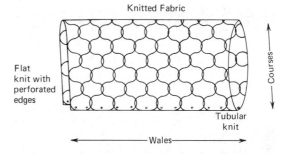

Flat-knitted fabric edges are often perforated, forming an edge comparable to the selvage found on woven fabrics. Tubular knits have no corresponding edge but can be cut along a wale yarn, if necessary, to open them out flat.

Functional Fabric Finishes

Fabrics may be treated to secure improved performance characteristics, such as wrinkle resistance, to minimize ironing. Functional finishes influence fabric behavior, often making the fabric more suitable for a specific end use. Several finishes can be incorporated into one fabric.

They may also lower abrasion resistance and prevent straightening of off-grain fabrics. The finishes described below will be identified on the bolt-end label if the fabric has been treated.

Antibacterial finishes resist bacteria, thus inhibiting odors, reducing damage from mildew-producing fungi or rot-producing bacteria, and controlling the spread of disease.

Antistatic finishes reduce static buildup, thus eliminating fabric cling and "sparking." Fabric softeners may impart this finish during laundering, or the finish may be durable.

Durable-press and minimum care finishes enable the fabric to shed wrinkles during wear and allow its surface to remain smooth and wrinkle-free after laundering. These finishes are effective only on cellulose fibers. Synthetic fibers will not accept such finishes, but are often used in blends with cellulosics (e.g., polyester with cotton) to impart their built-in wrinkle-resistant characteristics.

Generally, fabrics with this finish are also dimensionally stable for the life of the finish. The finish has low abrasion resistance, so garments should be laundered inside-out on a delicate or perma-press cycle.

Flame-retardant fabrics are self-extinguishing when the flame source is removed. Wool, silk, modacrylic, polyvinyl chlorides, and special formulas of acetate, triacetate, rayon, polyester, and nylon are inherently flame-retardant. Flame-retardant finishes resist flaming once the source is removed; if the source is not removed, these fabrics may be consumed by flames. Synthetic fibers may melt, drip, and produce toxic flames; finishes may increase smoke output.

Mercerized fabrics have increased strength, improved dye affinity, and greater luster. Only cotton and linen are mercerized.

Mildew-resistant finishes resist the growth of molds and mildew.

Mothproof fabrics resist attack by moths and carpet beetles.

Stain- and soil-resistant finishes reduce soil deposition and penetration of stains into the fibers. They may resist water-borne and/or oil-borne stains.

Soil-release finishes are used on synthetic fibers with durable press finishes to permit release of soil- and oil-borne stains. They also prevent soil redeposition, add antistatic qualities, and improve the soft hand of the fabric. In addition, they may cause some color loss and reduce the durable-press characteristics of the fabric.

Stabilization finishes maintain the fabric dimensions by minimizing shrinkage. *Residual shrinkage* refers to shrinkage that occurs progressively each time the fabric is laundered. Fabrics should be labeled according to the maximum percentage of shrinkage remaining.

Sanforized indicates a maximum residual shrinkage of 1 to 2 percent when flat-dried. Fabrics with 2 percent or more residual shrinkage may shrink 2.5 cm (1 in) or more per yard. Many fabrics labeled "preshrunk" or "supershrunk" may continue to shrink if residual shrinkage remains; they should be tested before use.

Fabrics with shrink-resistant finishes may create problems during construction. If the weave is compact, it may be difficult to ease out fullness, thus necessitating modification of the pattern. Synthetic fibers are considered highly stable but should still be tested before cutting.

Water-repellent and waterproof finishes influence water penetration. Water-repellent fabrics are relatively porous yet resist wetting. Water-repellent finishes do not alter the fabric appearance and should be used on closely woven fabrics. *Waterproof* fabrics are nonporous, thus sealing out all moisture as well as holding in body perspiration. Waterproof garments are uncomfortable to wear under humid conditions. *Micro-porous* fabrics enable perspiration to evaporate, but prevent larger water droplets from penetrating the fabric.

Fabric-Garment Compatibility

Successful garment construction results from more than the skillful performance of fitting, construction, and pressing techniques. Selecting a fabric compatible with the garment structure and details is also essential.

The final fabric choice must be capable of supporting the garment silhouette and the shapes within, such as pockets, flaps, or collars. Consider also whether the fabric can be manipulated successfully into design details requiring easing or stretching, gathering, or pleating.

FABRIC AND GARMENT STRUCTURE COMPATIBILITY

Note the types of fabrics suggested on the pattern envelope. These fabrics will best hold the lines of the garment. Study similar ready-to-wear garment designs representative of all price levels. Which fabrics, including inner-support fabrics, most successfully hold the garment lines? Study the hand of potential fabrics by draping each over your arm. Consider their stiffness, softness, thickness, and weight in relation to the design silhouette and shapes to be formed. Soft silhouettes should be constructed of soft, supple fabrics, whereas tailored silhouettes require greater body and weight. Stretchy knits cling to body contours, creating a personal silhouette.

FABRIC MANIPULATION

Garment design details call for varying degrees of fabric manipulation capabilities. Easing in the cap of a set-in sleeve requires compression of the sleeve cap yarns to enable it to fit smoothly into the armscye. Firmly woven, flat-surfaced fabrics and those with a crease-resistant finish resist compression and stretching, making eased construction difficult. To lie taut over body hollows (i.e., the curve below the buttocks on pants), the fabric is sometimes stretched; it must therefore have some elasticity. Pleated designs must incorporate fabrics that can be heat-set to hold the creases. Gath-

ered design silhouettes are influenced by the bulk and stiffness of the fabric. Soft, supple fabrics gather more readily.

INNER SUPPORT

To retain shape and support the desired garment contours, inner fabric layers are incorporated into the garment structure. *Interfacings* provide support and shape retention to isolated areas such as necklines, lapels and button closures, collars, cuffs, and waistbands. *Underlinings* lend light body and shape retention to limp, loosely woven, or stretchy fabrics by completely backing the outer fabric layer. They support without changing the fabric's character. They also provide opacity to sheer or translucent fabrics. The entire garment or major garment sections can be underlined.

The inner contouring fabrics must be compatible with both the outer fabric and the intended garment structure. Usually, the more structured and detailed the garment design, the greater the need for inner support. Consider current styling and construction practices, which may vary from minimal use of inner contouring to extensive use of underlinings, interfacings, and padding. Inner fabrics must supply needed support without loss of flexibility or the creation of excess stiffness.

Before attempting to select a suitable fabric, refer to the pattern instruction sheet (pattern layout) to see which sections of the garment are to be supported. One or more interfacings varying in flexibility and stiffness may be used in one garment. Consider the area to be supported. For example,

1. Waistbands require greater stiffness and flexibility to maintain their shape at a body flex point and to support the fabric hanging from them.

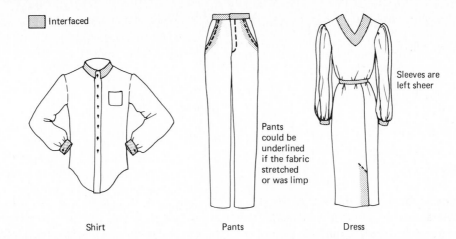

Interfaced

Shirt

Pants

Pants could be underlined if the fabric stretched or was limp

Dress

Sleeves are left sheer

2. Collars and cuffs must maintain their shape in addition to curving smoothly around the body. Interfacings for these or other curved areas can be cut on the true bias to improve their flexibility.
3. Button-closure edges must support the closure system without drooping or being overly stiff. Neckline needs are similar.
4. Sometimes the entire garment or a major garment section requires additional body to help it retain its shape or to provide opacity. Underlining fabrics should be lightweight yet dimensionally stable.

Selection of an inner fabric is essentially a process of elimination:

1. Consider only those inner fabrics with care requirements like those of the outer fabric.
2. Generally, *woven* inner fabrics are most compatible with *woven* outer fabrics. Knitted outer fabrics are *not* underlined but are best interfaced with all-bias nonwoven or true-bias-cut woven under fabrics. Unstructured knit garments are not interfaced.
3. Interfacings may be applied by stitching or fusing them to the wrong side of the outer fabric. Stitchables change the character of the outer fabric only by the degree of support

added. The adhesive binding of the fused interfacing tends to reduce flexibility and increase stiffness of the outer fabric.
4. From among the remaining interfacing choices available, choose possibilities similar in hand to the outer fabric. If a fusible interfacing will be used, choose one *lighter* in hand than the outer fabric to compensate for the increased stiffness that results from the fusing process.
5. Hold the inner and outer fabric layers together so as to simulate their arrangement in the constructed garment. Choose the inner support fabric that provides the degree of body and flexibility needed without overwhelming the outer fabric.
6. Whenever possible, use a dark interfacing fabric with dark fabric colors and white with light-colored fabrics. Match underlining and outer fabric colors as closely as possible.

Care and Maintenance

Fabric care and maintenance are based upon the fiber(s) used, yarn and fabric structure, dye type, dyeing and printing method, and finish applied. Each garment and fabric available on

Carter Fabrics, Inc.	3.99	SOHO 50% Fortrel Polyester 35% Cotton 15% Wool 44/45" wide crease resistant Machine wash, warm, tumble dry. Remove promptly METHOD ⚠3	Style *5399* Pattern *6476* WATER - B - GNVY *20* Color Color # Yds.

FIESTA *By Hi-Fashion Fabrics*	Yards *25* ⚠	100% POLYESTER *4.50* Machine wash, warm, tumble day, remove promptly.	Style Color *392*

Bolt-end Labels

the market must be supplied with a permanently attached *care label*. The care label indicates the most desirable method to use to maintain the original fabric and construction characteristics during the garment's life. The time and expense involved in care and maintenance can then be anticipated prior to purchase.

The nine care labels commonly supplied with yard goods are the following:

1. Machine-Wash, Warm
2. Machine-Wash, Warm—Line-Dry
3. Machine-Wash, Warm—Tumble-Dry—Remove Promptly
4. Machine-Wash, Warm—Delicate Cycle—Tumble-Dry, Low—Use Cool Iron
5. Machine-Wash, Warm—Do Not Dry Clean
6. Hand-Wash Separately—Use Cool Iron
7. Dry-Clean Only
8. Pile Dry-Clean—Pile-Fabric Method Only
9. Wipe With Damp Cloth Only

If a care label is not provided when the fabric is purchased, request the appropriate label from the salesperson. During garment construction, the label can be sewn inconspicuously into a seam as a reminder of the fabric's care requirements.

Notice that each care method is coded with a triangle enclosing a number, ⚠. The triangular code and care instructions are located on the fabric *bolt-end label* with other information useful in fabric selection and maintenance.

Sample-fabric bolt-end labels appear above.

Basic information supplied by either the bolt-end label or an attached hangtag includes:

1. Fiber content by percentage.
2. Finishes used, if any.
3. Fabric width. This may not always be accurate so double check.
4. Triangular number code with care method.
5. Style, color, and pattern-code numbers.
6. Bolt yardage.
7. Manufacturer, trade name.
8. Special care or stitching instructions—sometimes included on hangtag.

Quality Considerations

The final choices of outer and inner fabric must be based upon quality. Excellence of fabric structure and suitability to end use are based upon quality fabric criteria and performance requirements.

FABRIC QUALITY CRITERIA

Before purchasing any fabric, evaluate its structural quality. This check to determine quality level should be performed *before* the fabric is cut and purchased and should include:

1. *Examination of Fabric for Flaws.* Any irregularities within the fabric—such as uneven color or printing, soiling, pulled yarns or runs, uneven weaving, loose yarns, or fading at a folded edge—should be examined closely to determine the degree of the problem. In some instances, the fabric shop may provide additional fabric at no cost. Consider fitting the pattern layout around a flaw. Generally, flaws should be avoided.

2. *Tentering Quality.* Tentering is the process by which fabrics are dried under pressure while stretched across a tentering frame. If the lengthwise or crosswise yarns are not aligned at right angles during this process, several problems may arise during pattern layout.

   a. Several inches of purchased fabric may be lost when the ends are straightened by pulling a crosswise yarn. In some cases, so much fabric is lost that more fabric must be purchased in order to cut out all the required pattern pieces.

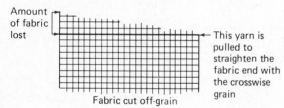

Amount of fabric lost

This yarn is pulled to straighten the fabric end with the crosswise grain

Fabric cut off-grain

   b. Heat-set fabrics or fabrics with a resin finish cannot be trued to realign the crosswise and lengthwise yarns at right angles to one another. If the fabric design is

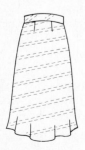

Skirt cut on lengthwise grain. Horizontal grain was heat-set out of alignment; therefore, print hangs unbalanced.

printed on grain but the fabric was poorly tentered, the design will appear unbalanced once the garment is constructed.

To check the tentering quality, examine the fabric ends. The crosswise yarns should be nearly perpendicular to the fold and selvage edges.

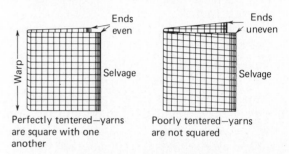

Ends even

Warp

Selvage

Ends uneven

Selvage

Perfectly tentered—yarns are square with one another

Poorly tentered—yarns are not squared

Very few fabrics are perfectly tentered, but variations greater than 2.5 cm (1 in) should be avoided, particularly if the fabric cannot be trued. Sometimes the fabric ends will be cut evenly, but a closer look may show the tentering to be poor. Natural fiber fabrics with *no* finish can be trued, but if the fabric ends are cut unevenly with the crosswise grain, extra yardage may be needed to compensate for the loss.

3. *Wrinkle Resistance (Resiliency).* Fabric resiliency can be determined by crushing a section of the fabric in the palm of the hand for about five seconds. Release the fabric and notice if the wrinkles fall out. If they do not, the garment will rumple easily during wear.

4. *Firmness of Weave.* Use the *thumb test* to determine how easily the yarns will slip back

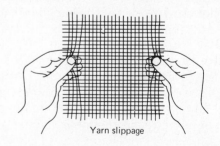

Yarn slippage

from one another. Try to pull the yarns back between the thumbs and forefingers. If the yarns shift easily, the fabric may pull at stress seams, possibly developing holes. Loosely woven fabrics or fabrics made from long, smooth, lustrous yarns slip most readily.

5. *Elasticity.* A fabric's ability to stretch and return to its original size is of particular importance when knitted or loosely woven fabrics are used. Pull the fabric using the thumb test described in paragraph 4, above. If the fabric stretches and does not recover within a few seconds, the garment may bag in stress areas. Firm knits and wovens and heavier fabrics retain their size best. Double knits are better than single knits, wovens are better than knits, and synthetics will hold their shape better than natural fibers.

6. *Pilling.* Short staple fibers that are low in absorbency will hold static electricity. They tend to pill more as they are subjected to friction during wear. Rub the right sides of two layers of the fabric together briskly. If the nap rolls up into fiber balls (pills), satisfactory wear cannot be expected.

PERFORMANCE REQUIREMENTS

How must the garment perform once it is constructed? How well will the fabric meet personal needs for fashionability, comfort, and durability?

Psychological comfort factors, including fabric color, texture, and hand, influence fabric choice. Personal feelings about work or sports activities are also subtly related to fabric and apparel styling. Indoor or outdoor activities may affect the degree of warmth or coolness needed as well as durability requirements. How comfortable will the fabric be under various temperature, humidity, and wind conditions?

Each fabric has an *anticipated product life* based upon its strength and flexibility as well as its ability to withstand abrasion and soil wear. Durability is influenced by inherent characteristics of fiber, yarn, and fabric structure. Review the general characteristics of each fiber and consider how they will interact in various blends found on the market (see fiber chart, page 16). Polyester and cotton blend fabrics take advantage of cotton's absorbency and polyester's wrinkle resistance. Yarn structure also influences fabric durability. Complex and loopy yarn structures tend to snag more readily than smoothly twisted yarns. Slubbed yarns wear more quickly where the yarn is thicker.

Fabric structures based upon plain and twill weaves are more durable than satin or novelty weaves, which snag or abrade more readily when the float yarns are long. Weft knits may run if a yarn is broken, especially if the yarns are smooth rather than rough. *Basic-weave or plain-knit fabrics are generally more durable than complicated fabric constructions.* Firmly woven fabrics are also considered more durable than loosely woven fabrics.

CRITERIA FOR EVALUATION

FABRIC SELECTION

Check to insure quality performance:

___ **1.** Outer fabric suitable for garment structure (suggested by pattern company or similar hand to suggested fabric).

___ **2.** Fabrics appear to meet performance requirements after evaluating fiber, yarn, and weave characteristics.

___ **3.** Fabric quality examined; meets needs of garment to be constructed.

___ **4.** Inner fabric(s) provide the support needed by the outer fabric and garment structure.

___ **5.** When two or more fabrics are used, care requirements are compatible.

3 Measurements for Pattern Size and Fit

OBJECTIVES

1. For any garment type, accurately take the needed body measurements and select the figure type and size with the most closely corresponding measurements from those given in the sizing charts.

2. For two-dimensional fitting (if chosen fitting method, Chapter 8), accurately take the needed body measures, add ease, and compare with the pattern measures described in Chapter 8.

A pattern that conforms closely to body dimensions and contours will provide the best fit and comfort. Because ready-to-wear sizes do not always correspond with pattern sizes, it is essential that you be measured, evaluate the size charts, and choose a *pattern* size. If you already know your pattern size, reevaluate it periodically to check for dimensional and proportional changes due to weight fluctuation or redistribution.

Pattern size is determined by comparing specified individual body measurements with matched standardized body measurements. The best pattern size will enable the final garment to fit any figure close in size and proportion to the standard. Figures varying in proportion or contour (with extra bulges or hollows) but close in dimension will require pattern alterations for a good fit.

Body measurements are taken at important anatomical structures or in relation to body joint locations. They include length, circumference, and width measures. Length measurements indicate vertical proportions of body segments, including the upper and lower torso (back waist length, crotch depth), arm and leg lengths, and shoulder-to-apex length. Bust, waist, and hip levels are thus indicated. Circumference measures provide girth dimensions of important anatomical structures: bust or chest, waist, and hips. Width measures provide horizontal fitting dimensions for back width and shoulder length.

Pattern measurements are somewhat larger than their corresponding body measures. The pattern is cut larger than the body to provide *ease* for comfortable movement. The pattern is measured only when its dimensions will be used for two-dimensional pattern fitting. Pattern measurement procedures are described in Chapter 8.

Body Measurement Guidelines

Although accurate measurements are essential, they may be difficult to acquire, since measurements are generally taken quickly and haphazardly. Even when measurements are taken carefully, it is nearly impossible for one fitter to get the same figures twice from the same individual. Precision and care cannot be emphasized enough. Guidelines for measuring follow:

1. Ask a competent friend to take your measurements, since it is nearly impossible to take your own measurements accurately.
2. Stand with feet together in a *normal* posture.
3. Take the measurements over the undergarments to be worn with the completed garment. Different lingerie styles can create dimensional variations, resulting in pattern size or fit variations.
4. Use a nonstretchy tape measure to take the measurements described on the next few pages. Pull the tape taut, but not too tight. Be honest, or the finished garment will not fit.

5. By standing in front of a mirror, you can make a visual check of the tape position as each measurement is taken. Vertical measures should be taken perpendicular to the floor; circumference measures should be taken parallel to the floor.
6. Body locations can be marked to maintain a more precise point of reference for several interrelated measurements. The marking of body points also ensures that the measurement can be double-checked with accuracy.

   a. Adjust a fine chain around the neck so it lies at the base. Neck-base location is important for determining shoulder length and back and front waist-length measurements.
   b. Tie a string or narrow elastic around the natural indentation of the waistline to identify its position for length measurements, including back and front waist lengths, waist-to-hip, waist-to-floor, and crotch level and length measurements.
   c. Tie a narrow elastic around the armscye, positioning the elastic at the top of the shoulder joint where the sleeve will join the garment. From front and back, the elastic should appear to fall perpendicular to the floor. The armscye elastic is used to measure shoulder length, arm length, and back width.

Procedures for taking women's and men's body measurements are outlined on the next few pages. Follow the instructions precisely so that the pattern size corresponding most closely with *actual* body measurements will be chosen. The measurements are divided into two groups: (1) those needed to determine figure type and size and (2) those needed to adjust the pattern for two-dimensional fitting. Pattern measurement procedures are described in Chapter 8 but for convenience are recorded with body measurements determined in this chapter.

BODY MEASUREMENT
PROCEDURES: WOMEN

Sizing Measurements: Women

Record measurements on the chart on page 33 under column one, labeled "Body Measurements." To determine *figure type*, take measurements one and two.

1. *Height.* Stand barefooted, with posture normal, against a wall. Place a ruler on your head, parallel to the floor, and mark the point where it touches the wall. Measure the distance from the mark to the floor.
2. *Back waist length.* Measure from the top of the prominent back neck bone (neck chain) down the center back to the waistline string (determines waist level).

To determine *size,* take measurements three through six.

3. *High Bust.* Measure under the arms, above the bust, and straight across the back. Also called scye level.
4. *Bust.* Measure around the fullest part of the bust with the tape straight across the back. Proceed to measurement 7 before removing tape.
5. *Waist.* Measure around the waistline at the string position.
6. *Full Hip.* Measure around the fullest part of the hip, usually 18 to 23 cm (7 to 9 in) below the waistline. Proceed to measurement 13 before removing tape from around hips.

Fitting Measurements: Women

Measurements seven through nineteen are used in addition to the previous measurements to fit the pattern more closely to individual figures.

7. *Shoulder to Bust Point.* Measure from the neck base at the shoulder to the apex of the bust (determines bust level).
8. *Shoulder.* Measure from the base of the neck (neck chain) to the prominent shoulder bone (armscye elastic).
9. *Front Waist Length over Bust.* Measure from the neck base (neck chain) at the shoulder, over the bust point, and to the waistline string below the bust. Tape is parallel to center front.
10. *Front Waist Length.* Measure from the neck base or hollow just above the collar bones (neck chain) down the center front to the waistline string.
11. *Arm Length.* Bend the arm slightly so that the elbow position can be determined for dart location. Measure from the shoulder-armscye string intersection to the elbow and from the elbow to the wrist bone. Record both measurements as well as the total length.
12. *Biceps.* Measure the arm circumference 2.5 cm (1 in) below the armpit. (Also called the sleeve scye level.)
13. *Waist-to-Hip.* Measure from the waistline string to the full hip level (determines hip level).
14. *High Hip.* Measure around the high hip over the hip bones about 7.5 cm (3 in) below the waist.
15. *Crotch Level.* Sit erect on a hard, flat surface. Measure from the waistline string at the side over the hip curve to the surface (determines crotch level).
16. *Crotch Length.* Position the spline between the legs with one end beginning at the center front waistline string and the other end at the back. *The spline position should be comfortable, as no ease is added.* Mark the center front and back waistline levels on the spline. Mark a midpoint between the legs to separate the measurement into *front*

and *back crotch lengths*. Carefully remove the spline from between the legs; trace the shape of the inside of the spline on paper for future reference. Mark the front and back waistline points and the crotch point. Measure the front and back crotch lengths. (The back crotch length is usually longer.)

17. *Back Width*. Measure 12.5 cm (5 in) below the prominent neck bone (neck chain). At this level, measure across the back, with the arms slightly forward, from arm hinge to arm hinge (between elastic armscye markers).

18. *Skirt Length*. Measure from the waistline

Sizing and Adjustment Chart: Women

Determine	Body Measurements	For Size:[1]	For Pattern Adjustments:			
		1 Body Measurements	2 Minimum Ease	3 Body + Ease	4 Pattern	5 Change Needed
Figure Type	1. Height		—	—	—	—
	2. Back Waist Length		0.0–0.6 cm			
Size	3. High Bust		3.8–7.5 cm			
	4. Bust		5.0–10.0 cm			
	5. Waist		1.3–2.5 cm			
	6. Full Hip		5.0–7.5 cm			
Additional Pattern Adjustments	7. Shoulder-to-Bust Point		—			
	8. Shoulder		0.0–1.0 cm			
	9. Front Waist Length Over Bust		0.0–0.6 cm			
	10. Front Waist Length		0.0–0.6 cm			
	11. Arm Length: Total		—			
	11a. Arm Length: Shoulder-to-Elbow		—			
	11b. Arm Length: Elbow-to-Wrist		—			
	12. Biceps		5.0–7.5 cm			
	13. Waist-to-Hips		—			
	14. Hip High		2.5 cm			
	15. Crotch Level		1.3–2.0 cm			
	16a. Crotch Length: Front		—			
	16b. Crotch Length: Back		—			
	17. Back Width		1.3–2.0 cm			
	18. Skirt Length		—			
	19. Pants Length		—			

Figure type:

Pattern size:

Record measurements in centimeters.

[1] Instructions for determining pattern size begin on page 33.

string at center back to the desired skirt length.

19. *Pants Length.* Measure from the waistline string at the side to the desired pant length. Wear the shoes to be worn with the finished pants, since heel height may influence the final pants length.

BODY MEASUREMENT PROCEDURES: MEN

Sizing Measurements: Men

To determine pattern *size,* take measurements one through six. Record all measurements under column one, labeled "Body Measurements" on page 33.

1. *Height.* Stand barefooted, with posture normal, against a wall. Place a ruler on the head, parallel to the floor, and mark the point where it touches the wall. Measure the distance from the mark to the floor.
2. *Neckband.* Measure around the base of the neck at the neck chain. Add 1.3 cm (½ in for comfort).
3. *Chest.* Measure around the fullest part.
4. *Waist.* Measure around the waistline over the string.
5. *Hip/seat.* Measure around the fullest part of the seat about 20.5 cm (8 in) below the waist.
6. *Shirt Sleeve Length.* Slightly bend and raise the arm. Measure from the prominent back neck bone (neck chain) across the shoulder, around the elbow, and to the wrist bone.

7. *Shoulder.* Measure from the base of the neck (neck chain) to the prominent shoulder bone (armscye elastic).
8. *Back Width.* Measure 15 cm (6 in) below the prominent neckbone (neck chain). At this level measure across the back, with the arms slightly forward, to arm hinge (between elastic armscye markers).
9. *Arm Length.* Bend the arm slightly. Measure from the prominent shoulder bone (armscye elastic) to the elbow and from the elbow to the wrist bone. Record both measurements, as well as the total length.
10. *Biceps.* Measure the arm circumference 2.5 cm (1 in) below the armpit. Also called sleeve scye level.
11. *Crotch Level.* Sit erect on a hard, flat surface. Measure from the waistline string to the surface with a ruler.
12. *Crotch Length.* Position the spline between the legs with one end beginning at the center front waistband string and the other end at the center back waistline string. *The spline should be comfortable, as no ease is added.* Mark the center front and back waistline levels on the spline. Mark a midpoint between the legs to separate the measurements into *front* and *back crotch lengths.* Carefully remove the spline from between the legs; trace the shape of the inside of the spline on paper for future reference. Mark the front and back waistline points and the crotch point. Measure the front and back crotch lengths. (The back crotch length is usually longer.)
13. *Outseam.* Measure down the side of the body from the waistline string to the desired pants length.
14. *Inseam.* Measure the inside of the leg from the crotch level to the desired pants length.

Sizing and Adjustment Chart: Men

Determine	Body Measurements	For Size:[2]	For Pattern Adjustments:			
		1 Body Measurements	2 Minimum Ease	3 Body + Ease	4 Pattern	5 Change Needed
Figure Type and Size	1. Height		—	—	—	—
	2. Neckband (includes ½ in ease)		—			
	3. Chest		5.0–2.5 cm			
	4. Waist		2.5 cm			
	5. Hip/seat		5.0–7.5 cm			
	6. Shirt sleeve length		—			
Additional Pattern Adjustments	7. Shoulder		0.0–1.0 cm			
	8. Back width		1.3–2.0 cm			
	9. Arm length: total		—			
	9a. Arm length: shoulder to elbow		—			
	9b. Arm length: elbow to wrist		—			
	10. Biceps		5.0–7.5 cm			
	11. Crotch level		1.3–2.0 cm			
	12a. Crotch length: front		—			
	12b. Crotch length: back		—			
	13. Outseam		—			
	14. Inseam		—			
Figure type:						
Pattern size:						

Record measurements in centimeters.

[2] Instructions for determining pattern size begin on page 36.

Determination of Pattern Figure Type and Size

Correctly calculating the pattern *figure type* and *size* is essential to achieving a well-fitting garment. A wise sizing choice can eliminate many adjustments that might otherwise be needed later to perfect the garment fit. Figure type is determined before size. Compare individual body measurements with the sizing charts on page 34.

FIGURE TYPE

From general observation, it can be seen that women's figures vary more in contour, proportion, and build than do men's. To better fit these many body types, women's patterns have been classified into seven *figure types*.

Junior Petite, Junior, Miss Petite, Misses, Half-Size, and *Women's* figure types are designed for developed figures. *Young Junior/Teen* is designed for the young developing figure. The Misses figure type is considered aver-

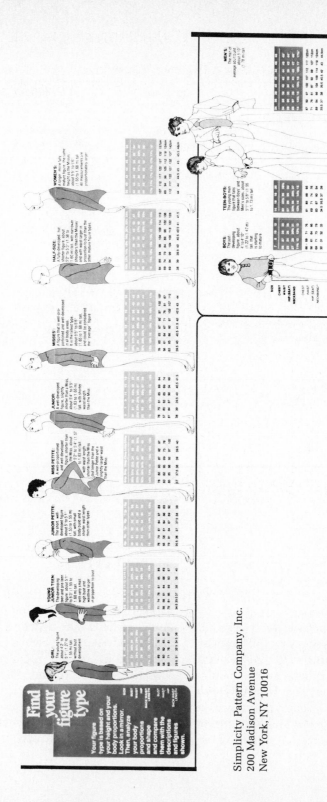

Simplicity Pattern Company, Inc.
200 Madison Avenue
New York, NY 10016

age, so there are many more pattern styles available for it.

Before the correct pattern size can be determined, each figure must be analyzed so a figure type can be selected. *Figure type* is based on three factors:

Height
Back waist length
Individual body proportions

Analyze both the front and side views of your figure in front of a mirror while wearing undergarments. Consider torso length as well as the bust, waist, and hip levels. Compare your body build with the figure type illustrations and descriptions found on page 34 or with the measurement charts in the back of the pattern book. Figure types are intended to describe body proportion, not age.

Select those figure types that most closely describe your figure, then compare your high bust, waist, and hip measurements with those on the size charts. The figure type with a size corresponding to both the back waist length and the circumference body measurements will provide the best fit, thus requiring fewer alterations later.

PATTERN SIZE

To select the best size, compare your body size measurements with those provided for the figure type chosen. If the measurements fall between sizes, several factors must be considered. Decide which size will require fewer or simpler pattern adjustments. If pattern adjustment difficulty is not a factor, a small-boned individual might select the smaller size and a large-boned person, the larger size. Also, consider the type of fit desired: snug or loose? Different pattern sizes may be required for the upper and lower

portions of the body. Consider any key measurements needed to make the best sizing decision.

Key Size Measurements

Certain measurements are pertinent to size determination for different garment types.

For Women.
Garments fitting the upper torso. The *bust* and *high bust* measurements are keys to pattern size selection for any garment fitting the upper body, such as a dress, blouse, jacket, or coat. The bust-shoulder-armscye portion of the body can be difficult to fit because of the combination of convex and concave body curves located here. The more closely the pattern size matches this area, the simpler fitting should be later. Purchase coat, jacket, and maternity patterns by the same size as the dress, as additional ease or size has already been added to these patterns for correct fit.

To *accurately determine bust size,* compare the bust and high bust measurements. If there is a difference of 5 cm (2 in) or more, the bust is full. Select the pattern size by the *high bust* measurement and be prepared to adjust the bust portion of the pattern. Using the high bust measurement ensures better fit through the shoulder-armscye area for women with larger- or smaller-than-average bust curves. The bust area is easier to adjust than the shoulder area.

Garments fitting the lower torso. The *hip* measurement is used to select the correct pants or skirt size. If the body circumference is larger at the thigh or abdomen level than at the hip level, use that larger dimension for the hip measurement.

Garments fitting both the upper and lower torso. If the pattern chosen includes several coordinating garments and the individual bust and hip measurements require different sizes, purchase the pattern by the *bust* size. The hip and waist areas are easier to adjust than the bust areas.

For Men. Men's patterns are designed for two figure types: *Men's* and *Teen Boys'*. Select your figure type by age and similarity of measurements.

Garments fitting the upper torso. Use the *neckband* measurement to determine the classic shirt size and the *chest* measurement for jacket or coat size.

Garments fitting the lower torso. Unless the hips are out of proportion, use the *waist* measurement to determine pants size. If the hips are large, use the hip/seat measurement to select pants size and adjust the waist to fit.

Pattern Ease

COMFORT EASE

In addition to the standard body dimensions, patterns include extra size to permit the body to move freely in the finished garment. Without this *comfort ease,* clothing would fit skin-tight, hindering basic body movement.

The comfort ease provided will vary among figure types, pattern companies, and garment or fabric type. The ease provided under column 2 of the sizing and adjustment charts on pages 31 and 33 is the minimum needed for a basic fitted garment constructed of medium-weight woven fabric.

Fabric Type. Patterns designed to be constructed from knits or stretch wovens may have less ease, since they stretch as the body moves. Bathing-suit dimensions may be less than body dimensions to allow for a snug fit.

Figure Type. Ease will also vary according to figure type. Patterns designed for larger figures include more ease than do patterns for smaller ones. Larger figures usually expand more during movement.

Garment Type. Comfort ease varies considerably according to garment type. Some close-fitting evening wear is stabilized by minimal ease beyond actual body measurements. In contrast, jackets and coats need enough ease to let them fit comfortably over blouses, dresses, and sweaters. Although patterns usually illustrate the jacket or coat over the bulkiest garment for which ease has been allotted, it is wise to fit the pattern over the thickest inner garment to be worn. The table on page 37 can serve as a guide.

STYLE EASE

Many garments have additional size added beyond the comfort ease. This is known as *style ease* and provides various fashion effects. Examples include gathered skirts or sleeves, the tent dress, raglan and kimono sleeves, flared pants or skirts, and so on. Virtually all garments have some style ease.

Study the pattern illustration or photograph of your chosen design. How closely does the garment fit the body? Darted garments tend to fit closer than gathered or pleated garments. Where are major seams placed? How straight or flared are pants and skirts? Is the jacket lined or unlined?

Study the finished garment dimensions on the back of the pattern envelope. These will let you make comparisons between patterns to check skirt or pant leg widths and lengths. Lower-edge widths and finished lengths are provided for pants, skirts, dresses, tops, jackets, and coats. The garment description often begins with "fitted," "semi-fitted," "loose-fitted," or "very loose-fitted," which gives a good idea of the

Ease Allowances for Women's and Men's Garments*

Misses' Garments

	Bust	Waist	Hip
Strapless dress	3.0 mm (⅛ in)	6.0 mm (¼ in)	6.5 cm (2½ in)
Evening dress	2.5 cm (1 in)	6.0 mm (¼ in)	6.5 cm (2½ in)
Basic dress	7.0 cm (2¾ in)	2.5 cm (1 in)	6.5 cm (2½ in)
Jacket	10.0 cm (4 in)	10.0 cm (4 in)	9.5 cm (3¾ in)
Coat	12.5 cm (5 in)	12.5 cm (5 in)	12.5 cm (5 in)

Men's Garments

	Chest	Waist	Hip
Vest	0.0 cm	5.0 cm (2 in)	0.0 cm
Shirt	10.0 cm (4 in)	18.0 cm (7 in)	5.0 cm (2 in)
Jacket	12.5 cm (5 in)	19.3 cm (7½ in)	11.5 cm (4½ in)
Coat	15.0 cm (6 in)	20.5 cm (8 in)	15.6 cm (6¼ in)

* Courtesy Butterick Fashion Marketing Company.

fit provided. Loose-fitted garments are easier to fit than close-fitted garments, since they skim body contours rather than following them closely.

To improve pattern fit two-dimensionally, compare your body measurements plus ease (column #3) with the corresponding pattern measurement under column four. To determine if the pattern must be adjusted, subtract the pattern measurement from the body ease measurement. A negative score indicates that the pattern must be enlarged by the amount indicated; a positive score indicates that the pattern may be too large or that the design includes additional style ease. Refer to Chapter 8 for instructions on pattern adjustments.

4 Decoding the Pattern

OBJECTIVE

To interpret and utilize the information supplied by the pattern envelope and instruction sheet.

A wealth of information is stored within the pattern packet. Facts, symbols, terminology, and instructions necessary to compare, select, and construct the garment are compactly presented.

The *pattern envelope* presents comparative and descriptive information needed to choose the pattern and to purchase the materials with which to construct the garment. The *pattern instruction sheet* describes how to use the *pattern* to cut out the fabric and to construct the garment.

Pattern Catalogs

To choose a pattern, study the pattern designs illustrated in pattern catalogs available at fabric stores or other sewing centers. The four major pattern companies, featuring patterns widely available, include Butterick, McCall's, Simplicity, and Vogue. The first three companies offer complete collections of designs for both sexes and for all figure types and ages. Vogue emphasizes a wide selection of patterns for misses as well as limited groups of patterns for men, children and toddlers, women, and half-sizes. Pattern catalogs include:

Special sections featuring dresses, sportswear, coordinates, suits and coats, active sportswear, evening and bridal, lingerie, at-home wear, maternity, etc.

Fashions for men and teenage boys, including suits, sportswear, and loungewear.

A wide range of children's designs for boys and girls in children's, toddlers', babies', and boys' and girls' sizes.

A majority of the patterns devoted to the misses' figure type as well as a wide selection for the remaining women's figure types.

A selection of "designer" patterns, originally available only from Vogue and now offered by several other major pattern companies also. Many young American designers are featured in Butterick, McCall's, and Simplicity, and well-established designers are featured in Vogue.

Television personalities are often utilized to lend credibility to the featured designs.

A selection of "easy-sew" patterns, often including quick-sewing tips.

A small selection of multisized patterns featuring two or three sequenced sizes marked on one pattern and designed to simplify fitting procedures. Seam lines, however, are not marked.

Craft sections including home accessories, costumes, needlework, dolls and doll clothes, toys, and clothing accessories.

Each pattern catalog contains all the patterns currently available and provides much of the same basic information that is on the pattern envelope. The data provided permit the shopper to make comparisons between patterns regarding finished garment dimensions, styling features, fabric suggestions, and yardage and trim requirements.

Pattern Envelope

Once the pattern style has been chosen, the pattern envelope provides a convenient way of keeping purchasing data at one's fingertips. With pattern in hand, the shopper can study suggested fabrics to determine their compatibility with the garment design. Notions can be checked for availability and closeness of color match. Cost of fabric and notions can be figured before purchase with the help of the yardage and notions specifications.

ENVELOPE FRONT: BASIC INFORMATION

1. *Pattern Company.* The name of the pattern company—Butterick, McCall's, Simplicity, Vogue—is prominently displayed. A designer's name may also be provided.
2. *Pattern Number and Price.* The pattern number (styling code) and price can be found in the corner or along the side of the envelope.
3. *Pattern Size.* The size of the pattern will be stated in a prominent spot for quick reference when the pattern is being purchased. In addition to the size, the corresponding bust or chest measurements are often stated for shirts, blouses, dresses, jackets, and coats. The waist or hip measurement may be stated on a pants or skirt pattern.
4. *Pattern Style Views.* Many patterns show alternate views of the basic design style chosen. Variations may include a choice of collar or sleeve styles or hem lengths. Each view has an identification letter (e.g., View A, View B) to aid in computing yardage and selecting notions.

ENVELOPE BACK: BASIC INFORMATION

5. *Pattern Number, Price, and Size.* This information is not presented in exactly the same way by each pattern company.

6. *Garment Description.* A concise description of each garment supplies details about fit and design lines that may not be visible in the garment illustration.

7. *Back Views.* Small line drawings of the back view of each garment indicate style lines and construction details of the garment as seen from the rear.

8. *Number of Pattern Pieces.* The number of pattern pieces included in the pattern is indicated. Some pattern companies also include the name and a diagram of each pattern piece.

9. *Suggested Fabrics.* Well-known fabric types suitable for this particular garment are listed. Note whether the fabrics suggested are primarily soft, crisp, heavy, or light. Use these categories to determine whether an unlisted fabric might also be suitable for the style.

10. *Knit Stretch Gauge.* Many patterns are designed for use only with knit fabrics. Such patterns have less wearing ease because they rely upon the natural elasticity of the fabric to provide comfortable fit. A stretch gauge provided on either the front or back of the pattern envelope helps the shopper to determine the degree of stretch needed for that particular garment design.

    To use a knit stretch gauge, fold the fabric parallel to and about 5 cm (2 in) from the crosswise edge of the knit fabric. Hold the fabric against the left edge of the gauge. Take hold of the knit at the 10-cm (4-in) mark and stretch gently to the point indicated by the gauge.

    The knit should stretch easily to the point indicated to ensure comfortable fit. The fabric should then return to its original size. If it remains stretched, the knit may bag or stretch out of shape during wear.

11. *Advice about Special Fabrics.* This section lists fabric types that are unsuitable for the pattern style. Examples of what to avoid may include striped, plaid, or napped fabrics, one-way designs, or diagonally printed

How to Use Simplicity's PICK-A-KNIT Rule™ *

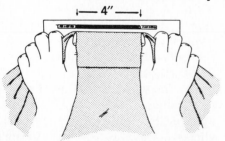

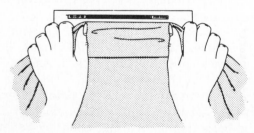

|← 4" →|

1 Place crosswise grain of knit fabric below the PICK-A-KNIT Rule™, away from the cut edge of fabric, as shown.

2 Hold fabric with thumbs at each end of the 4″ area.

3 Keeping left thumb anchored firmly, stretch fabric gently with right hand to end of rule.

4 If fabric stretches to at least the end of the rule, your knit is suitable for the pattern. Your knit may stretch slightly beyond the rule and still be suitable.

fabrics. The need to purchase extra fabric so as to allow for matching may also be indicated.

12. *Finished Garment Measurements.* These measurements provide lower-garment-edge circumferences and finished lengths. They are useful in comparing fullness of pattern styles as well as in determining possible length adjustments.

13. *With/Without Nap* (Also W/WON, */**). These symbols indicate whether the yardage computed may be used with a one-way (nap) or two-way (without nap) pattern layout.

    Pattern pieces should be placed in one direction when cutting out garments from many checked, striped, plaid, pile, or one-way printed fabrics. This ensures that some garment sections will not be cut out with the design reversed.

14. *Required Fabric Quantity.* The yardage block indicates the amount of fabric, interfacings, linings, and/or trims to be purchased. Yardages are precomputed for pattern view, size, fabric width, and sometimes for one-way (nap) pattern layouts.

Study the metric yardage block on the sample pattern to see how the yardage was computed:

a. Circle the view or garment type: Dress. View B.

b. Circle the size: Misses 10.

c. Circle the fabric width: 150 cm (60 in)**.

d. Find the yardage at the intersection of the vertical size column and the horizontal fabric width column: 1.85 m (2 yd).

If no fabric quantity is specified for the fabric width you purchase, refer to the Fabric Conversion Chart below. It will let you convert fabric quantities from one fabric width to another.

15. *Notions.* Required or optional notions and

Fabric Conversion Chart (Metric–English)

Fabric Width	90 cm 35–36"		100 cm 39"		103 cm 41"		115 cm 44–45"		127 cm 50"		135 cm 52–54"		150 cm 58–60"		168 cm 66"	
	m	yd	m	yd	m	yd	m	yd	m	yd	m	yd	m	yd	m	yd
	1.60	1¾	1.40	1½	1.40	1½	1.30	1⅜	1.15	1¼	1.05	1⅛	.95	1	0.80	⅞
	1.85	2	1.60	1¾	1.60	1¾	1.50	1⅝	1.40	1½	1.30	1⅜	1.15	1¼	1.05	1⅛
	2.10	2¼	1.85	2	1.85	2	1.60	1¾	1.50	1⅝	1.40	1½	1.30	1⅜	1.15	1¼
	2.30	2½	2.10	2¼	2.10	2¼	1.95	2⅛	1.60	1¾	1.60	1¾	1.50	1⅝	1.40	1½
	2.65	2⅞	2.30	2½	2.30	2½	2.10	2¼	1.85	2	1.75	1⅞	1.60	1¾	1.50	1⅝
	2.90	3⅛	2.55	2¾	2.55	2¾	2.30	2½	2.10	2¼	1.85	2	1.75	1⅞	1.60	1¾
	3.10	3⅜	2.75	3	2.65	2⅞	2.55	2¾	2.20	2⅜	2.10	2¼	1.85	2	1.75	1⅞
	3.45	3¾	3.00	3¼	2.90	3⅛	2.65	2⅞	2.40	2⅝	2.20	2⅜	2.10	2¼	1.95	2⅛
	3.90	4¼	3.20	3½	3.10	3⅜	2.90	3⅛	2.55	2¾	2.40	2⅝	2.20	2⅜	2.10	2¼
	4.15	4½	3.45	3¾	3.35	3⅝	3.10	3⅜	2.75	3	2.55	2¾	2.40	2⅝	2.30	2½
	4.35	4¾	3.70	4	3.55	3⅞	3.35	3⅝	3.00	3¼	2.65	2⅞	2.55	2¾	2.40	2⅝
	4.60	5	3.90	4¼	3.80	4⅛	3.55	3⅞	3.10	3⅜	2.90	3⅛	2.65	2⅞	2.55	2¾

(Left axis label: Fabric Quantity)

Purchase an additional 0.25 m (¼ yard) when:
• the fabric width conversion is great
• one-way nap or directional fabric is used
• sleeves are cut-in-one with the garment

recommended sizes are listed for each view. The sizes suggested are scaled to complement the garment style lines. Purchase notions at the same time fabric is purchased to ensure a close color match.

16. *Standard Body Measurements.* Patterns are sized to fit standard body measurements. These measurements may be compared with personal measurements to predict the need for two-dimensional pattern adjustments.

17. *Pattern Company Name and Address.*

Pattern Instruction Sheet

The pattern instruction sheet provides all information essential to constructing the garment, including:

Garment design illustrations; pattern pieces diagramed, named, and number-coded.

Definitions of basic construction terms and techniques.

Brief step-by-step sewing instructions with corresponding diagrams.

PATTERN PIECES DIAGRAMED

Line drawings of the pattern pieces are organized for each garment type. The pattern pieces are named and number-coded to ensure that the correct pieces are used.

PATTERN LAYOUT GUIDES

Layout guides provide recommended pattern placement for fabric width, pattern size, and view. "With nap" or "without nap" layouts are also specified.

BASIC CONSTRUCTION TERMS AND TECHNIQUES

Each pattern company briefly describes some of the terms or techniques used in the sewing directions. Background information and suggested procedures are also included.

STEP-BY-STEP SEWING INSTRUCTIONS

Brief step-by-step sewing instructions describe the construction sequence. This sequence follows the *unit method* of organization. To save time, the *process* organization method can be substituted (see Chapter 12).

Pattern

The pattern pieces provide a paper guide for cutting out the fabric sections needed to construct the garment. Each pattern is cut to fit a standard figure type and size. Wearing and style ease are also incorporated in the pattern dimensions. The pattern should be checked and, if necessary, adjusted for fit before the fabric sections are cut out (see Chapter 8).

Each pattern piece is printed with coded symbols that are useful in laying out the pattern pieces and constructing the garment. An understanding of this code simplifies pattern adjustment, layout, and construction.

Each pattern symbol is decoded below:

Grain Line. The grain line of the pattern must be parallel to the fabric grain or yarn direction. Most often it runs parallel to the fabric selvage for the *lengthwise* grain. For border prints, scallop-edged laces, or other similarly designed fabrics, the grain line may be positioned parallel to the *crosswise* fabric yarns. Note whether the pattern indicates the grain direction next to the grain line.

Place on Fold. A bracketed grain line means that the indicated pattern edge is to be placed even with the folded fabric edge during layout.

Cutting Line. The cutting line forms the outer perimeter of each pattern piece. After the pattern is pinned to the fabric, the fabric sections are cut out along this line.

Seam Line. Long, unbroken lines, usually parallel to the cutting line, designate the stitching lines. Fabric layers are joined by stitching them together along the seam lines. A small arrow or picture of a presser foot located on this line indicates the stitching direction.

Seam Allowance. The area between the cutting line and seam line is the seam allowance. Most seam allowances are 1.5 cm (⅝ in) wide, although other common widths include 1.0 cm (⅜ in) and 6 mm (¼ in). The seam allowance creates a buffer between the raw fabric edge and the seam line to provide strength and prevent seam fraying.

Notches and Numbers. Solid diamonds on the cutting line are used to match corresponding seams accurately before stitching. The number adjacent to each notch matches that along the seam line of the pattern piece to be joined. The numbers also indicate the construction order.

Matching Points. These symbols include dots, squares, or triangles printed on the tissue pattern to ensure accurate joining of intricately cut garment sections. They are particularly useful in distributing gathers or ease evenly or in laying out the pattern to match plaids or stripes.

Alteration Lines. Horizontal double lines are printed to indicate areas where lengthening or shortening may be done to adjust the pattern for variations in body length. Adjust the pattern before fabric cutting.

Darts. Broken lines forming a *V*-shape within the pattern symbolize the dart location and stitching lines. The solid black line between the broken lines indicates the fold line used to fold the dart for stitching. The dart helps to contour flat fabric so that it will fit over body bulges.

Easing Line. A single row of short, broken lines between two dots indicates the portion of the seam to be eased (drawn) in to fit a slightly shorter seam line on the piece to be joined.

Gathering Lines. A double row of short, broken lines located between two dots indicates that the longer seam is to be gathered in to fit a shorter corresponding seam. Two rows of stitching are needed to control the longer fabric length.

Location Lines. These indicate where pockets, welts, and decorative trimming are to be positioned for permanent stitching. If the pattern piece length has been adjusted slightly to ensure design balance on the body, the location markings must be respaced.

Other Pattern Lines. These indicate garment center front or center back positions or fold line locations used during construction.

Button and Buttonhole Markings. These provide size and position markings for both buttons and buttonholes. If the pattern has been adjusted for length, the location markings must be respaced.

Zipper Placement. This symbol indicates the placement of the zipper along the seam line. The terms *pull tab* at top and *stop* at the bottom indicate the exact length of zipper to be used.

Hem Fold Line. The hemline indicates the level at which the lower garment edge is to be folded up. This line may have to be adjusted for various body postures or if the fabric stretches unevenly.

Pattern Information. A pattern name and number identify each pattern piece. Pattern styling number, pattern company, name of pattern piece, and pattern size are grouped together to simplify the identification of each pattern piece.

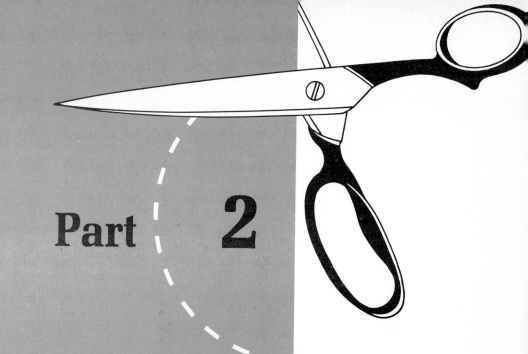

Part 2

Handling Major Sewing Equipment

Although having a *sewing machine* at your disposal is a prerequisite to sewing, it is no less important to have a selection of small-scale *tools* available. Tools (i.e. tape measure, seam ripper, shears, and so forth) are more minute, but their small size does not reduce their importance. With only a sewing machine, you could not perform the many sewing tasks that these tools will help you to perform, including measuring, fitting, cutting, marking, sewing and trueing.

You will need some tools immediately—others can be purchased later as they are needed. Generally it is wise to wait until you decide which fitting and construction methods will be used so you can avoid purchasing items you may never use. For example, if you plan to mark your fabric using the pencil and pin method, it will not be necessary to purchase a tracing wheel and carbon paper.

The basic parts and functions of the sewing machine are discussed in Chapter 6, "The Sewing Machine." Sewing machine mechanisms may vary slightly among models, so it is a good idea to study the manual supplied with your particular machine. Review the parts and accessories and their functions before attempting to use your machine.

Basic stitching operations are also discussed. If you have never sewn before, or if you are using a new or unfamiliar machine, you should practice using the machine until you can easily perform the following operations:

- Thread the machine and bobbin.
- Adjust the machine control dials for your fabric and purpose.
- Start and stop a seam.
- Patch a seam.
- Stitch seams of even width.
- Stitch square corners.
- Stitch evenly rounded corners.

It is important to note that each time you begin a sewing project (particularly if your machine is also used by others), you will need to pre-test the tension and stitch appearance on scraps of your garment fabric. Some deluxe machine models require no tension adjustment, but most other models still do. It is also wise to pre-test more complex construction techniques (i.e. inset corner, buttonhole) on fabric scraps before performing them on your garment. As a result you will not be surprised by your fabric's manipulative characteristics.

Your construction may be superior, but it will not be evident unless your garment is also well-pressed. Good *pressing* can often hide a multitude of minor construction errors as well as poor fabric handling. Pre-test your fabric's response to heat, pressure, and moisture on fabric scraps to avoid surprise shrinkage, melting, or stretching. Be aware that previously shrunk fabrics may shrink further under a hot iron. With good pressing techniques, fabric surface characteristics should remain unaltered.

Following is a list of tools and equipment needed to begin a sewing project. This list does not include all the supplies you may need for your sewing project—because some items are dependent upon your choice of construction technique. Each of these items is described in this unit.

Sewing Machine:
General Purpose and Zipper Feet
Buttonholer, if not built-in
Machine needles in size suitable for your fabric

Sewing Tools:
Tape Measure
Metal Gauge
Meterstick (yardstick) and/or Ruler
Dressmaker Shears
Embroidery Scissors
Seam Ripper
Box of "dressmaker" or "silk" pins (for woven fabrics)
Box of "ball point" pins (for knitted fabrics)
Hand sewing needles in assorted sizes and types
Beeswax
Thimble/Band-Aid
Spline for fitting pants
Pencils with different colors of lead

Pressing Equipment:
Iron
Ironing Board
Press Cloths
Tailor's Ham

After you have reviewed this unit, the chart on page 48 can be used to help predict any additional supplies you will need for a specific project. Complete the chart as you work through the organizational planning and selection of construction techniques discussed in Chapter 12, "Organization and Fitting Strategies."

Chosen Technique	Tools and Other Needed Supplies
FITTING	
FABRIC PREPARATION	
PATTERN LAYOUT	
CUTTING	
MARKING	
HAND STITCHES	
CONTOURING (Interfacing, Padding)	
CONSTRUCTION Seams	
Edge Treatments	
Closures	

5 Sewing Tools

To select and coordinate basic tools with specified individual sewing requirements.

Although an abundance of sewing tools and aids are available on the market, only a few basic items are really essential. Consider the amount and type of sewing you plan to do *before* purchasing many pieces of equipment.

The absolute essentials include a selection of measuring, cutting, marking, fitting, and hand-sewing tools. Sewing machine and pressing equipment are discussed in succeeding chapters. Purchase additional equipment as the need arises.

MEASURING TOOLS

A firm, nonstretchy plastic *tape measure* 150 cm (60 in) long is necessary for taking measurements to determine pattern size, adjust the pattern for better fit, and measure lengths of fabric. The tape measure will be easier to use if it is marked on both sides and if each opposite end begins with the digit 1. Metal-tipped ends prevent cloth tapes from fraying.

A 15.0-cm (6-in) adjustable *metal gauge* is used to measure areas where a constant measurement is desired. It is ideal for marking hems, tucks, pleats, buttonhole spacing, and pattern adjustments. In addition, it can be used as a stitching gauge for measuring distances not marked on the sewing machine. It should be clearly marked, and the adjustable tab

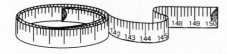

MEASURING TOOLS

Tape measure (150 cm)

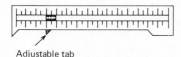

Meterstick (100 cm)

Metal gauge
(15.0 cm)

Adjustable tab

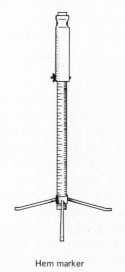

Hem marker

should slide easily but remain set at the desired point.

Other useful measuring tools include a *meter stick* (yardstick) for ruling long straight lines, measuring hemlines and for checking grain lines. A *hem marker* is used to measure skirt hem lengths evenly from the floor. The pin-marker model is the most exact, but it requires the help of another person. You can mark your own hem length with the chalk-marker model, but the chalk cannot be removed from all fabrics. Any marker model should be adjustable to all possible hem lengths.

FITTING TOOLS

To improve the fit of your garment, your pattern may have to be altered or adjusted before you begin to sew. The measuring tools described above as well as the fitting tools described below are used to fit the garment.

A *plumb line* is used during fitting to check grain and seam alignment. Make your own plumb line by tying a weight to one end of a long cord.

Clear plastic *rulers* with marked grid lines simplify pattern adjustment computation. A *French curve* or a *combination curve* (French

Fitting Tools

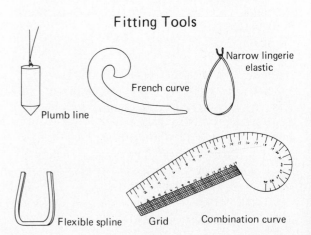

Plumb line

French curve

Narrow lingerie elastic

Flexible spline   Grid   Combination curve

curve + hip curve + straight edge + grid) is used to true (smooth) curved seams after the garment has been fitted. The combination curve can also be used to rule straight and curved lines, compute and mark buttonhole spacing, and make pattern adjustments.

Use the *flexible spline* to compare the wearer's front and back waist-to-crotch contours and lengths with those of the pattern. Crotch depth can be determined, as well as front and back crotch length measurements.

Narrow lingerie *elastic* (3-mm or ⅛-in) can be tied around the shoulder joint to help mark the armhole location when body measurements are taken. To mark bust or chest, waist, and hip levels before taking body measurements, tie 1.3-cm (½-in) *twill tape* around the body at these levels.

CUTTING TOOLS

Dressmaker shears, on which one handle is larger than the other, are more satisfactory than scissors for cutting fabric. The handles are either bent or straight. Bent-handled shears permit more accurate cutting because the blades operate parallel to the table, thus lifting the fabric very little. The blades vary from 12.5 to 30.5 cm (5 to 12 in) in length and are not identical in shape. Shears with 18.0- or 20.5-cm (7- or 8-in) blades are satisfactory for most apparel fabrics and are designed for both left- and right-handed persons.

Shears made of high-quality steel hold a sharp cutting edge and are a good investment. The blades should move easily and cut smoothly along their entire length; the points should come together. Blades joined by a screw rather than a rivet can be adjusted when necessary. They will retain their sharp edges longer if you do not cut paper with them.

A small pair of *trimming scissors* 10.0 to 15.0 cm (4 to 6 in) long, is convenient for clipping

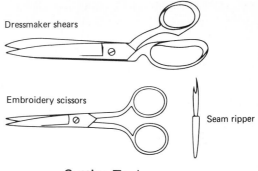

Cutting Tools

thread ends, trimming, and clipping curved seams. Scissors have sharp points, identical blades, and are more lightly constructed than shears. *Embroidery scissors* with 7.5- to 10.0-cm (3- to 4-in) blades are used for hand-sewing, ripping, clipping, and slashing buttonholes.

The *seam ripper* is used to remove unwanted hand or machine stitches. The point can be used to pick out stitches; the blade cuts seams open and can be used with care to slash buttonholes open.

MARKING TOOLS

Purchase of marking tools is dependent upon the marking method you will use for your particular fabric. Refer to Chapter 11, "Marking Techniques," before selecting marking tools.

The *tracing wheel* is used with or without dressmaker's carbon paper to transfer pattern markings to the fabric. The points must be smooth and sharp so they will not snag the fabric. Tracing wheels feature a variety of edges: a needle-point wheel makes a faint line that is desirable on fine, thin fabrics. A serrated edge produces a prominent line that is good for marking many fabrics. The smooth wheel marks a solid line on loosely woven or other hard-to-mark fabrics and protects delicates, velvets and knits from snagging. *Dressmaker's carbon pa-*

Marking Tools

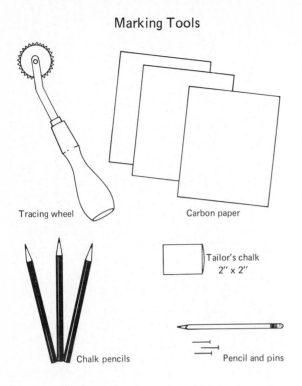

Tracing wheel

Carbon paper

Tailor's chalk
2" x 2"

Chalk pencils

Pencil and pins

weight fabrics. Longer 3.2-cm (1¼-in) pins are best used with heavier fabrics. "Ball-point" pins are designed for use on knits, since the rounded point slips between the fabric yarns. Select only stainless steel or brass pins, since these will not rust or leave a discoloration on the fabric. Pins are used throughout the construction process; they hold the pattern to the fabric during cutting, hold the fabric together while sewing, hold the pattern or fabric together during fitting, and are useful for making alterations. Wearing a small *wrist pincushion* with an elastic or plastic wristband will keep a supply of pins close to your work. Wool, hair, or cork filling in the pincushion will protect the pins from rust.

The needles most commonly used for hand-sewing are "sharps," "crewels," and "betweens" in sizes 5 through 10. The greater the number, the finer the needle. Sharps are of medium length and are the most commonly used type. Crewel (or embroidery) needles have longer eyes, making them easier to thread. They can be used for most hand-sewing as well as for embroidery. Betweens are short for taking short stitches. Ball-point needles are similar to sharps but they have rounded points and are used to penetrate between the yarns of knit fabrics. Needles of fine-quality steel are tempered so they will not bend easily and also not be brittle. They should have sharp, smooth points so they will slide easily and will not snag the fabric. When choosing a needle, consider the fabric structure, thread thickness, and type of stitch to be used. Generally, use a fine needle with fine fabrics and fine threads, a longer needle for longer stitches, a shorter needle for shorter stitches, and a ball-point needle for knitted fabrics.

The *thimble* protects the middle finger as it pushes the needle through the fabric during hand-sewing. It should be made of hard, lightweight metal (brass or nickel silver) with a closed top in a size to snugly fit the middle

per is available in white and several colors. Be sure to purchase carbon paper that is removable by laundering.

Tailor's chalk is a clay chalk that comes in 5-cm (2-in) squares. Avoid the wax type, since it may stain some fabrics. Some chalk marks remain visible until they are exposed to the heat of the iron. *Chalk pencils* can be sharpened, thus leaving a fine, accurate line. Chalk is available in white and pastels. It may be used to mark placement lines and alterations.

SEWING TOOLS

Straight pins are classified by diameter and length. Generally, as pins increase in length, they also increase in diameter. "Dressmaker" or "silk" pins are suitable for light- to medium-

Sewing Tools

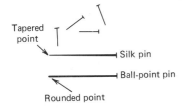

Tapered point — Silk pin

Ball-point pin

Rounded point

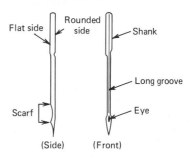

Flat side | Rounded side — Shank

Scarf

Long groove

Eye

(Side) (Front)

Machine Needle

Thimble

Beeswax in holders

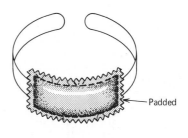

Padded

Wrist pincushion

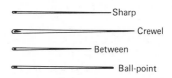

Sharp

Crewel

Between

Ball-point

Hand Needles

finger of the right or left hand. The best thimbles are those in which the depressions (knurlings) are put in by hand. Mass-produced thimbles are stamped out, so the knurlings are generally not deep enough to hold the needle securely. When a thimble is not available, a band-aid can be wrapped around the middle finger with the padded portion placed over the finger base.

Run your thread through *beeswax* before hand-sewing. The beeswax strengthens the thread and helps reduce its tendency to tangle and knot.

Sewing machine needles are designed for specific machine models. Purchase needles for your machine model number. Purchase the needle size for your fabric and thread. Medium-weight fabrics require a Singer size 14 needle. Use a small needle (Singer size 9) with thin fabrics and fine threads and a large needle (Singer size 16) for heavy fabrics and threads.

TURNING TOOLS

To simplify the turning of collar, cuff, and waist-band corners, use a *point turner* to push out the corners from the inside.

Use a *bodkin* to thread elastic or cording through a casing or to turn bias tubing right side out. A *loop turner* or a large *safety pin* can also be used to turn bias tubing and belts.

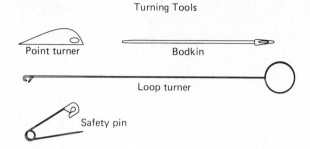

Turning Tools

Point turner

Bodkin

Loop turner

Safety pin

6 Sewing Machine

OBJECTIVES

1. To become familiar with your machine's parts and functions and its regulating dials (tension, pressure, stitch length, stitch width, reverse lever).

2. To perform basic stitching functions (straight and curved stitching, reverse stitching, various seam widths).

3. To pinpoint common causes of machine breakdown.

Your *sewing machine* is the major tool you will use to construct your garments. Machine stitching combined with hand stitching holds the garment fabric sections together.

To achieve your intended design, *you* must be in *control* of the machine. You must know its parts, how they function individually and as part of a system, and how to use the machine creatively. Perhaps you can use an accessory intended for one function to perform another function that otherwise could not have been executed as successfully. For example, the wired over-edge foot, designed to stitch and finish a seam simultaneously, can be used to top-stitch close to garment edges. With it, the stitching can easily be kept equidistant from the garment edges since the wire acts as a visual stitching guide. Other presser feet do not work as well for this function.

The sewing machine is the most expensive long-term sewing investment you will make. Before purchasing your first machine, take a sewing class and try out several of the models available. Read consumer evaluations of recent products. Visit several retail shops and try out those machines in which you are most interested. Take one home on a trial basis.

How much sewing do you plan to do in the future? Consider the types of garments, complexity of construction, and fabric hand and thickness you plan to work with.

The machine should perform basic functions well, so that the quality level of your construction is maintained. Your machine-handling skills can be improved but the machine's performance cannot. The machine should perform the following basic functions with a minimum amount of tension or pressure adjustments and hand manipulation: straight and zigzag stitching, reverse stitching, buttonholes. Additional attachments should enable you to insert zippers and to topstitch evenly. If you plan to do decorative embroidery, choose a machine that can do a variety of stitches. Some machine models also feature stretch and extra-long basting stitches. Test *all* machine functions on a variety of fabrics to ensure quality performance on many fibers, thicknesses, and degrees of stretch. Tension, pressure, and stitch length and width should be easily regulated.

Sewing Machine Parts and Functions

Become familiar with the basic parts and functions of the sewing machine by studying the illustration and part descriptions provided below. Once you are familiar with them, refer to the operation manual supplied with your particular machine model for specific part variations.

Balance Wheel and *Stop-Motion Knob*. The balance wheel controls the up-and-down movement of the thread takeup lever and needle. Always turn the wheel counterclockwise toward you when you begin to sew. The stop-motion knob, located in the

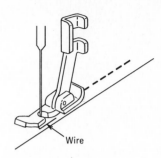

Topstitch near garment edge, using overedge foot wire as a guide

center of the balance wheel, engages the balance wheel with the stitching mechanism. It must be loosened when you are filling the bobbin.

Spool Pin. The spool pin holds variably sized spools of thread during stitching. The spools may be vertically or horizontally positioned on the top of the machine body.

Bobbin-Winding Mechanism. The bobbin-winding mechanism used to fill your bobbin with thread varies somewhat from model to model. Refer to your operation manual for a specific description.

Thread Takeup Lever. The thread takeup lever draws the thread from the spool as it moves up and down. It also controls the flow of thread as the machine's stitching speed is varied.

Face Plate and Threading Diagram. The face plate swings open for access to a threading chart and pressure dial.

Thread Guides. Thread guides help to direct the thread in a proper working sequence through the machine stitching mechanism.

Presser-Foot Lever. The presser-foot lever enables you to raise and lower the presser foot or any other attachments fastened to the presser bar.

Presser Foot. The presser foot holds the fabric against the feed dog during the stitching process.

Needle Bar. The needle bar holds the needle in its stitching position. As it moves up and down, it carries the needle in and out of the fabric.

Needle. The needle is positioned in the needle bar so that the long grooved side faces in the same direction as the last thread guide. This position

THE SEWING MACHINE AND ITS PARTS

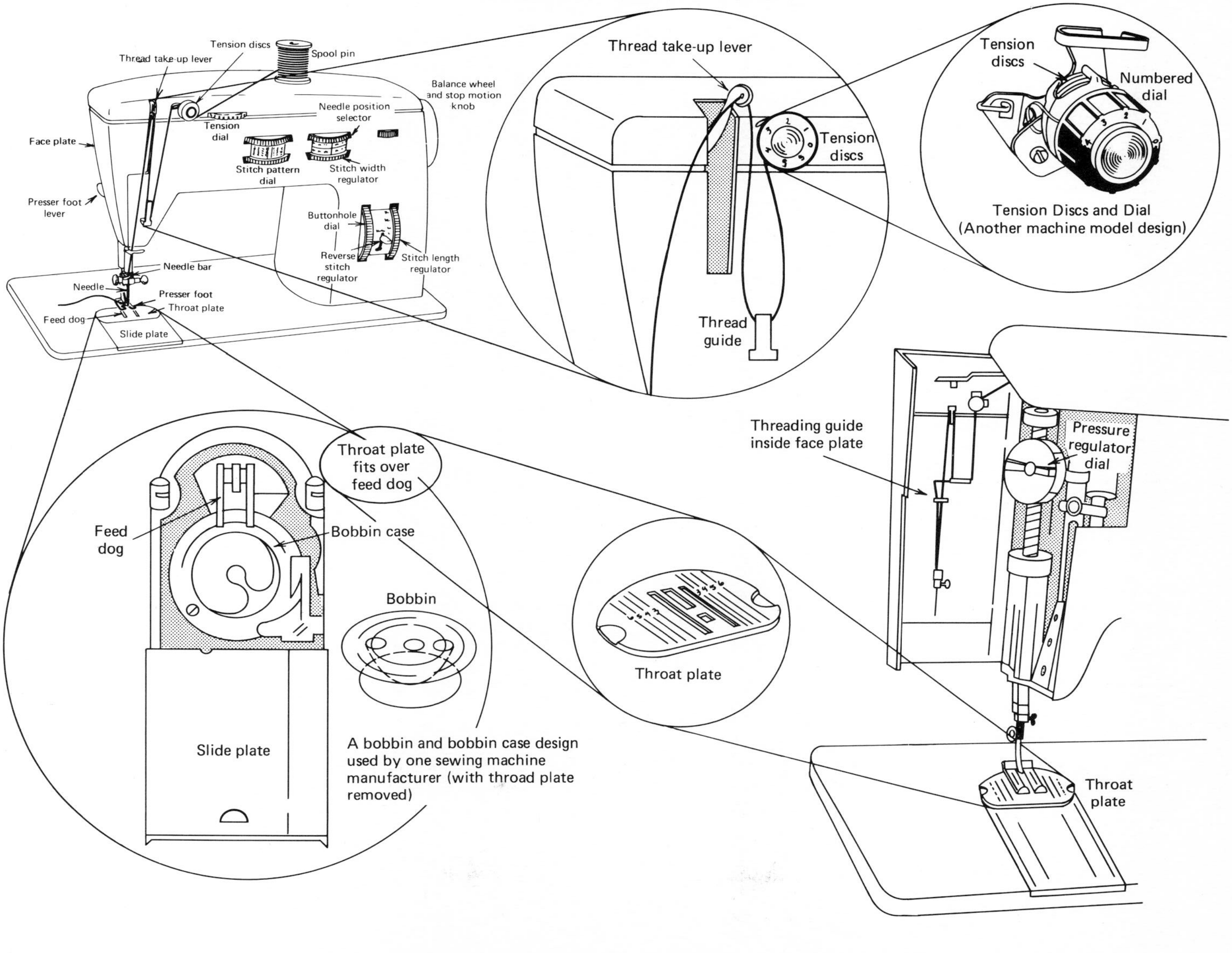

Tension Discs and Dial
(Another machine model design)

Numbered dial

Tension discs

Tension discs

Thread take-up lever

Thread guide

Pressure regulator dial

Throat plate

Threading guide inside face plate

Throat plate

Throat plate fits over feed dog

Bobbin case

Bobbin

A bobbin and bobbin case design used by one sewing machine manufacturer (with throat plate removed)

Spool pin

Balance wheel and stop motion knob

Needle position selector

Stitch width regulator

Stitch length regulator

Buttonhole dial

Reverse stitch regulator

Stitch pattern dial

Tension discs

Tension dial

Thread take-up lever

Face plate

Presser foot lever

Needle

Needle bar

Presser foot

Throat plate

Slide plate

Feed dog

Feed dog

Slide plate

reduces any friction imposed on the thread and thus keeps it from fraying or cutting.

Feed Dog. The feed dog draws the fabric under the presser foot a specified amount for each stitch, thus controlling stitch length.

Throat Plate. The throat plate fits over the feed dog and covers the lower stitching (bobbin) mechanism. Lines located on the right and left sides of the plate act as guidelines for stitching even seams of consistent width. Cross lines are guides for pivoting corners.

Slide Plate. The slide plate moves outward for access to the bobbin and bobbin case.

Bobbin and *Bobbin Case.* The bobbin, which holds the lower thread supply, is stored in the bobbin case during all stitching. The notch located in the bobbin case controls the lower thread tension (tightness or looseness).

STITCHING CONTROL DIALS

Tension Discs. The tension disks regulate the tightness or looseness of the upper thread. The tension dial permits manual adjustment of the tension to make it coordinate with your fabric, thread, and stitch.

Pressure Regulator. The pressure dial regulates the pressure that the presser foot exerts on the fabric. It features an all-purpose setting plus a light setting for thin fabrics, a heavy-pressure setting for thick fabrics, and an extra-light setting for darning.

Needle-Position Selector. The needle-position selector moves the needle to a left, center, or right stitching position.

Stitch-Width Regulator. The stitch-width regulator controls the width of the zigzag stitch.

Stitch-Length Regulator. The stitch-length selector controls the length of straight and zigzag stitches. The numbers refer to the number of stitches per centimeter (or per inch).

Reverse-Stitch Regulator. The reverse-stitch lever instantly reverses the stitching direction for reinforcement back stitching. When the lever is released, the machine automatically returns to forward stitching

Sewing Machine Accessories

A number of extra attachments are included with your machine. They lend greater versatility to the types of stitching operations that you can perform and are easily removed or fastened to the machine when needed. These accessories include a wide variety of presser feet, several throat plates, and stitching guide attachments. The types of accessories may vary from model to model and with the types of apparel currently in vogue. A number of these accessories and their functions are described below.

PRESSER FEET

The most commonly used presser foot is the *general-purpose foot,* which is ideal for all sewing. It can be used for either straight or zigzag stitching because of the wide opening for the needle.

The *straight-stitch foot,* designed for straight stitching, provides close control when needed. This foot is especially useful for precision stitching of curved edges, decorative topstitching, and edge stitching.

The *zipper foot* enables you to stitch close to a raised edge. It is designed for zipper insertion as well as for covering cording or piping. The foot also adjusts to both the right and left sides of the needle.

The *invisible-zipper foot* is designed for the insertion of invisible zippers only. It has special grooves that fit over the zipper teeth, so you can stitch very close to them. There are separate invisible-zipper feet for metal and for synthetic zippers.

The *buttonhole foot* includes guidelines to help stitch balanced machine-worked buttonholes. It may be clear plastic or metal.

The *over-edge foot* enables finishing stitches to enclose the fabric edges. It can also be used for topstitching close to the edge of the fabric. This foot has a wire along one side that prevents the fabric from bunching as you machine overcast.

The *even-feed foot,* with its own presser foot and feed dogs, works with the machine feed dogs to

PRESSER FEET

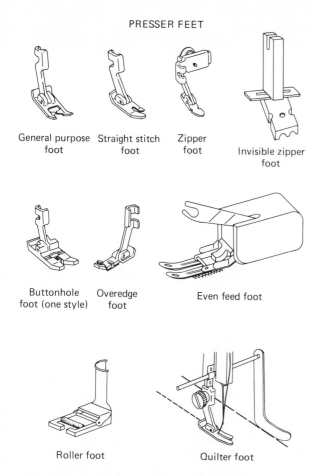

General purpose foot   Straight stitch foot   Zipper foot   Invisible zipper foot

Buttonhole foot (one style)   Overedge foot   Even feed foot

Roller foot   Quilter foot

THROAT PLATES

The *general-purpose throat plate* is used with the general-purpose foot. Always use them together when alternating between straight and zigzag stitching.

The *straight-stitch throat plate* is used with the straight-stitch foot. They are used together when your fabric or sewing procedure requires close control.

The *feed-cover throat plate* actually covers the feed dogs to prevent the fabric from feeding. It is used for button or buttonhole sewing and for free-motion darning.

THROAT PLATES

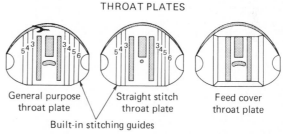

General purpose throat plate   Straight stitch throat plate   Feed cover throat plate

Built-in stitching guides

BUTTONHOLER

The *buttonholer* is a separate attachment used to make straight and keyhole buttonholes. The type and length of buttonhole are varied by inserting a template into the buttonholer; the width of the bight (sides of buttonhole) is regulated for narrow or wide stitching. Buttonholes may also be formed by using a *built-in stitch pattern system*.

Buttonholer

draw the two fabric layers through evenly and smoothly. Use it for bulky, slippery, or stretchy fabrics; for topstitching; and for matching plaids, stripes, or patterns.

The *roller foot* rolls smoothly over the surface of knit fabrics without catching and snagging the fabric. It is used when stitching loopy bouclé knits or bulky, loosely knitted sweater knits.

The *quilter foot* is especially adapted to stitch lightly padded fabrics and for the placement of straight stitching in block, floral, or scroll designs. The adjustable guide bar simplifies topstitching away from a garment edge, since the bar extends away from the presser foot and can follow a guideline on the garment.

STITCH PATTERN CAMS

Stitch pattern cams are inserted in the machine to produce a variety of functional and decorative stitches. Many machines now include *built-in stitch patterns.*

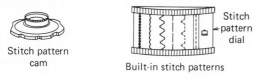

STITCH PATTERN CAMS

Stitch pattern cam

Built-in stitch patterns

Stitch pattern dial

STITCHING GUIDES

The *seam guide* enables you to stitch seams of uniform width. It is attached with a screw in the small hole to the right of the slide plate. The seam guide allows you to guide stitches at any distance between 3 mm (⅛ in) and 3.2 cm (1¼ in) from the fabric edge, so it is useful for very narrow or unusually wide seams, for all curved seams, and for topstitching close to the fabric edge.

Seam guide

Sewing Machine Operation

The ability to operate the sewing machine efficiently is a necessary prerequisite to quality sewing. You should be familiar with the following basics of machine usage:

• How the basic parts operate.
• How to thread the machine.
• How to adjust the machine for your fabric and function.
• How to perform basic operations.

Refer to your machine operation manual to learn how to control speed; interchange presser feet, throat plates, and needles; wind the bobbin thread and thread the bobbin; and thread the machine.

THREADING

Machines usually have an *upper or needle thread* and a *lower or bobbin thread* that interlock to form the stitches. Correct machine threading from both thread sources is essential to secure smooth, evenly spaced stitches. When the machine is incorrectly threaded, tangling and breaking of threads may result.

Most machines share a common threading sequence pattern, although this may vary slightly from one model to another. Generally, the upper thread runs from the spool pin through the thread guides, the tension discs and springs, the thread takeup lever, more thread guides, and finally the needle. The thread usually follows the last thread guide along the needle groove to the eye.

Raising the Bobbin Thread

To raise the bobbin thread through the needle hole in the throat plate, hold the end of the needle thread with your left hand. Turn the hand wheel slowly counter-clockwise one complete turn with your right hand. This enables the needle thread to interloop with the bobbin

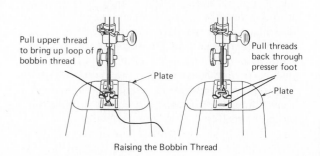

Pull upper thread to bring up loop of bobbin thread

Plate

Pull threads back through presser foot

Plate

Raising the Bobbin Thread

thread. When the needle has risen to its highest point, pull the needle thread until the bobbin thread disappears. Pull both threads until they are 7.5 to 10.0 cm (3 to 4 in) long and then draw them back between the toes of the presser foot.

STITCHING PRELIMINARIES

To enable your machine to form perfect stitches on a variety of fabrics, you must coordinate needle size, stitch length, presser-foot pressure, and thread tension for each fabric you use. *Needle size* is discussed in Chapter 5, "Sewing Tools."

Use the stitch-length regulator to vary the machine *stitch length*. The numbers on the regulator indicate stitch length in millimeters (or number of stitches per inch). Thus the higher the number, the smaller the stitch will be. Select the stitch length for your intended usage by following the guidelines below:

Basting: 2½ to 3 stitches per centimeter (6 to 8 per inch)

Standard Stitching: stitch length varies with fabric texture. Guidelines include the following:

Lightweight fabrics: chiffon, organza, batiste, silks, voiles, etc.—5½ to 7 stitches per centimeter (14 to 18 per inch).

Medium-weight fabrics: gingham, challis, flannel, velveteen, broadcloth, jersey, terry, twill, tweed, etc.—4 to 5½ stitches per centimeter (10 to 14 per inch).

Heavyweight fabrics: sailcloth, corduroy, canvas, duck, etc.—3 to 4 stitches per centimeter (8 to 10 per inch).

Stay stitching: same stitch length as for standard stitching.

Easing, Gathering: dependent upon fabric thickness. Usually the standard stitch length minus 2 stitches per centimeter (minus 3 to 4 stitches per inch).

Curved, Scalloped, Bias-Cut Seams: use stitches slightly shorter than standard for the fabric to provide greater strength and elasticity. Usually the

standard stitch length plus 2 stitches per centimeter (plus 3 to 4 stitches per inch)

Reinforcement Stitching: 6 to 7.0 stitches per centimeter (16 to 18 per inch).

The stitch conversion chart will let you set your stitch length for your machine type.

Stitch Conversion Chart (Metric to English)

Stitch Length	St/Cm	Metric Dial Setting	St/In (English Dial Setting)
Longer	2½	4	6
	3	3	8
	4	2½	10
	5	2	12
	5½	2	14
	6	1½	16
Shorter	7	1½	18

Correct presser-foot *pressure* enables the fabric layers to feed evenly and smoothly without damage to the fabric surface. Generally, thick, heavy fabrics require heavy pressure, medium-weight fabrics require medium pressure, and light-weight fabrics require light pressure. Also consider fabric surface texture: softer fabrics require less pressure than crisp fabrics.

Tension influences the interlocking of the needle thread with the bobbin thread during stitch formation. When the tension on the upper and lower threads is balanced, the stitch will be perfectly formed. Both threads will be drawn to the center of the fabric layers. No loops of thread will be visible on either fabric surface.

Before you begin a sewing project, adjust the tension for your fabric. First, establish the thread type, needle size, stitch length, and pressure you plan to use. Use the same number of fabric layers you will use when constructing your garment. Stitch about 7.5 cm (3 in) on the true bias of your fabric swatch. Remember which side of the fabric has the upper thread and which has the bobbin thread.

A perfectly formed stitch looks the same on each side because both the needle and the bobbin threads are balanced. The stitches will not draw or pucker the fabric. If loops form on the upper side, decrease the upper thread tension; if loops appear on the lower side, increase the upper tension. Retest.

To test further, hold the fabric at both ends of the stitching line and pull sharply until one of the threads breaks. The broken thread indicates the side on which the tension is too tight. If both threads require more force to break and break evenly, the tension is balanced. If the thread breaks on the upper side, decrease the upper thread tension; if the thread breaks on the lower side, increase the upper tension. Retest. The bobbin thread tension seldom needs adjustment.

BASIC STITCHING OPERATIONS

Learn to *control* machine speed and stitching direction by practicing on an unthreaded machine. Develop a smooth, steady pressure on the knee or foot pedal to get even, straight stitching. Practice starting and stopping, avoiding quick, jerky feeding of the fabric.

Practice using the *reverse stitching* direction until you can reach for the lever and backstitch without looking away from the stitching action.

Hold fabric layers in place during stitching by pin- or hand-basting. Pin-baste by inserting the pins at right angles to the cut fabric edges so that they just nip into the fabric at the stitching line. Never place pins on the underside of the fabric in contact with the feed dog, as they will catch. Vary pin spacing according to the complexity of the construction details. Place pins every 10 to 15 cm (4 to 6 in) apart on long, straight seams. Space pins closer together (up

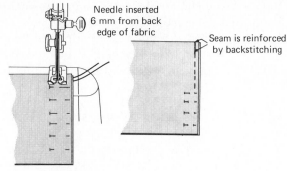

Needle inserted 6 mm from back edge of fabric

Seam is reinforced by backstitching

Starting a Seam

to 1.3 cm or ½ in apart) when seams are curved or when construction details are intricate.

To *start a seam,* raise the presser foot, place the needle thread under it, and draw both the bobbin and needle threads to the back. Place the fabric edge under the presser foot so that the edge is 6 mm (¼ in) behind the needle. Keep the bulk of the garment fabric to the left of the presser foot so it will be out of the way. Turn the hand wheel toward you to position the needle in the fabric about 6 mm (¼ in) from the starting edge and on the seam line. Lower the presser foot. Turn the hand wheel slowly toward you as you slowly increase the speed. Press the reverse-stitch lever and hold in place. Backstitch to the end of the fabric for reinforcement.

Release the reverse-stitch lever and *stitch the seam* in a forward direction as you guide the fabric. These reinforcement stitches should be directly on top of one another. Gradually increase the machine speed if the seam is a long, straight one. Maintain a slower, steadier speed for curved or short seams.

To *keep the seam straight,* align the fabric edge with one of the numbered guidelines on the throat plate. The numbers represent the distance from the needle. The standard seam allowance for home sewing is 1.5 cm (⅝ in), so line up your fabric with that guideline for most sewing. For additional control in keeping the

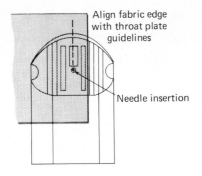

Align fabric edge with throat plate guidelines

Needle insertion

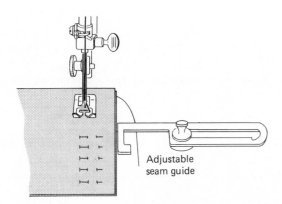

Adjustable seam guide

tion of the seam, thus requiring the seam to be *patched* to correct the irregularity. Carefully remove the uneven stitches with a seam ripper. Restitch, overlapping about five stitches at each end of the patch.

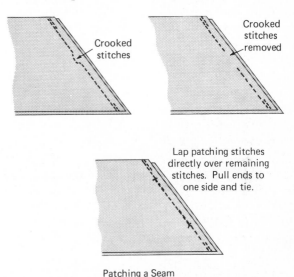

Crooked stitches

Crooked stitches removed

Lap patching stitches directly over remaining stitches. Pull ends to one side and tie.

Patching a Seam

seam straight, you may wish to use the adjustable seam-guide attachment. It is useful for stitching narrow or unusually wide seams. You can also use the width of the presser foot as a guide for stitching 6-mm (¼ in) seams.

To *end a seam*, stitch to the end of the fabric. Press the reverse-stitch lever and hold as you backstitch to reinforce the end of the seam. Release the lever. Stop with the needle at its highest position to avoid unthreading the machine later, when you begin stitching a new seam. Raise the presser foot and remove the fabric by drawing it to the back and left of the needle bar. Keep the needle thread between the toes of the presser foot so the threads will be in a ready position the next time you sew. Clip the threads with your scissors or with the thread cutter at the rear of the needle bar.

Sometimes stitching may be uneven in a por-

To *turn a square corner*, stitch a straight seam until you reach the marked corner point. Stop stitching with the needle inserted in the fabric. Raise the presser foot and pivot the fabric on the needle, bringing the bottom edge of the fabric in line with the seam guide. Lower the presser foot and continue to stitch in the new direction.

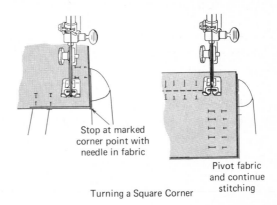

Stop at marked corner point with needle in fabric

Pivot fabric and continue stitching

Turning a Square Corner

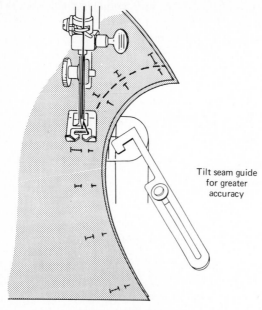

Tilt seam guide
for greater
accuracy

Stitching a Curved Seam

Reduce your stitch length before beginning to stitch a *curved seam*. Since stitching becomes more difficult with increasing curvature, reduce the machine speed as the curve increases in sharpness. Use the adjustable seam guide set with one corner opposite the needle for better control of the seam allowance width. Guide the fabric edge along the corner of the gauge rather than the flattened edge as you stitch. To keep the curve smooth and even, it is sometimes necessary to stop the machine, needle down, and pivot the fabric slightly into a better stitching position. The sharper the curve, the more often it is necessary to stop and pivot.

Common Causes of Machine Trouble

Possible Causes of Upper Thread Breaking:
1. Machine is improperly threaded.

2. Tension is too tight.
3. Needle is bent or has a blunt point.
4. Thread is too coarse or too fine for needle size or fabric.
5. Needle is incorrectly set.
6. Needle is too long for machine.

Possible Causes of Lower Thread Breaking:
1. Lower tension is too tight.
2. Bobbin thread is wound unevenly.
3. Bobbin is wound too full.

To Avoid Breaking Needles:
1. Use proper needle size for thread and fabric.
2. Be sure pressure foot or attachments are securely fastened to the presser bar.
3. Be sure that the needle does not strike the edge of the throat plate, the presser foot, or an attachment.
4. Do not pull the material under the presser foot as it is stitched; this may bend the needle.

Possible Causes of Skipping Stitches:
1. Needle is blunt, bent, or incorrectly set into needle bar.
2. Needle is too small for thread used.
3. Needle is too short for machine.
4. Needle is incorrect type for fabric.

Machine Does Not Feed Properly:
1. Pressure is too light for fabric.
2. The stitch regulator may be set so that the feed is out of action.
3. Heavy amounts of lint have accumulated on top of the feed dog or underneath the throat plate.

Keep your machine clean and oiled to maintain its efficiency over a long period of time.

CRITERIA FOR EVALUATION

SEWING MACHINE: STITCHING

Check to insure quality performance:

___ **1.** Stitching is smooth and even.

___ **2.** Stitches are an even distance from the cut edge.

___ **3.** Upper and lower tensions are adjusted; stitches appear the same on both sides of the fabric.

___ **4.** The pressure is adjusted so that the fabric feeds evenly.

___ **5.** Reverse stitches or patching stitches directly overlap previous stitches.

___ **6.** During stitching, corners and curves are pivoted with the needle inserted in the fabric.

___ **7.** Stitch length is appropriate for the intended usage and fabric thickness; stitch length is uniform.

___ **8.** There are no gaps, puckers, or broken stitches.

7 Pressing

OBJECTIVE

To coordinate pressing variables, including temperature, moisture, and pressure, for a variety of fibers, fabrications, and textures.

Skillful pressing is essential for quality construction. Pressing equipment used correctly aids in achieving flat seams, smooth edges, sharp creases, and smoothly molded contours—in short, a professional tailored appearance. Good pressing can minimize the effects of poorly constructed details; poor pressing can destroy the appearance of a well-constructed garment.

Pressing Equipment and Its Use

In addition to the sewing tools and sewing machine discussed previously, good pressing equipment is also essential.

An *ironing board* is for "flat" pressing, including the pressing of pleats, flat-faced garment sections (e.g., collar, cuffs, yokes, etc.), and pants.

A *steam iron* is more effective for pressing new construction than a dry iron because it allows moisture to be applied directly to the fabric. Use distilled water in the iron to avoid mineral deposit buildup and eventual clogging of the steam vents. Allow a steam iron to heat completely before using it so that water will not sputter out over your fabric.

Use the tip of the iron to press into gathered fullness and to press armscye seam allowances flat from the inside.

Your choice of *press cloth* depends upon the kind of fabric to be pressed. Fabrics used for press cloths should be white or colorfast and washed to free them of sizing and lint. Transparent cloths enable you to see what you are pressing. Firm muslin or several thicknesses of cheesecloth make satisfactory press cloths for smooth cotton and linen fabrics or where moisture is needed for best results. A piece of soft wool fabric may be used to press wool garments.

Pressing hams are cut in various shapes; they are covered with heavy cotton on one side and wool on the other. The firm, rounded surfaces of pressing cushions—not the ironing board—should be used for pressing the contoured areas created by darts, eased seams, and curved seams. The woolen side of the pressing ham holds the steam as woolen fabrics are pressed; the cotton side can be used to press all fabrics.

The *sleeve board* is a small version of the large ironing board. It is used to press details on small or narrow garment sections, including sleeves, shoulders, collars, sleeve caps, and children's clothing.

A *collar board* is a long, narrow wooden board that tapers to a point at one end. This point provides a small, hard pressing surface for reaching the enclosed seams of shaped pieces such as collars, cuffs, and lapels.

The *pounding block* is used after steam-pressing to obtain sharp creases at seams, lapels, pleats, and hems while the fabric is still moist and pliable. It forces excess steam out of the garment while flattening it and also helps the fabric to hold a crease longer after it dries. The pounding block can also be used to flatten seam

lines on leather garments. Grooves cut into its sides make it easier to hold.

A *needle board* is an excellent tool to use with pile fabrics such as velvet, velveteen, and corduroy. It is covered with fine steel wires set vertically to simulate pile fabrics. When the pile is placed face down on the needle board, the wires fit between the pile and prevent it from matting.

A *seam or sleeve roll* is used to press long, narrow seams open. It allows the seams to be pressed open without marring the rest of the fabric, since it raises the seam above the rest of the garment.

General Pressing Procedures

Pressing should not be confused with ironing. *Ironing* is a sliding motion of the iron on the fabric, whereas *pressing* is a process by which the iron is raised and lowered in a series of up-and-down motions. As a result, pressing is less likely to stretch the fabric. Both techniques should be performed directionally with the fabric grain to maintain surface size.

Correct pressing during garment construction is critical to the creation and maintenance of the garment's contours. Pressing may enlarge or shrink the fabric in desired areas. By pressing darts and curved seams over pressing cushions, one can mold and shape the fabric so that the garment will better correspond to the body contours. Poor pressing can alter the desired shape of the garment or destroy the fabric's texture.

Three factors are critical in all pressing situations: heat, moisture, and pressure. To control *heat,* set the iron at the temperature setting recommended for the fiber content of your fabric. Use the care label provided with the yard goods at purchase to indicate temperature. When two or more fibers are included in the fabric, select a temperature setting for the most heat-sensitive fiber. Any time you are unsure about fiber content, begin pressing with a low temperature setting and then work up.

Moisture is as necessary to set a crease as it is to remove creases and wrinkles. The amount of moisture required is dependent upon the fiber content, the fabric thickness, the types of finishes applied, the extent of the wrinkles to be removed, and the sharpness of crease to be obtained. For instance, a crease-resistant fabric usually requires more moisture than the same fabric without a finish. In addition, silks and synthetic fibers may waterspot when moisture is used.

Generally, for thicker and crisper fabrics, greater *pressure* must be exerted on the fabric to set in creases. The pounding block can be used immediately after steaming an area to force it to hold a sharp crease. Many delicate or heat-sensitive fabrics require a light touch to avoid marring their surface with shiny press marks.

Due to the broad range of fibers, fabrications, and finishes on the market, it is impossible to predict how each fabric will react to pressing. For this reason, it is wise to test each fabric before you begin construction.

To *test press,* select a large scrap of your garment fabric. Adjust the iron thermostat for the fiber content. Try pressing first without moisture and with a light pressure. Will the fabric crease? Do wrinkles disappear? If not, gradually increase the amount of moisture and pressure used. Each time you test press, check the fabric for maintenance of texture, sharpness of creases, press marks, glazing or shine, and puckering or shrinking.

Increase moisture by applying water directly to the surface of the press cloth with a sponge, by steaming the fabric with an iron, or by placing cheesecloth (three to four layers dipped in water and wrung), over the fabric surface. Gradually increase the arm pressure on the iron. If this is not enough, use a pounding block with steam. Some hard-to-press fabrics will only crease when the temperature is increased slightly beyond the fiber's maximum dial setting and the fabric is steamed (and sometimes pounded) through several layers of wet cheesecloth.

Additional pressing guidelines include the following:

1. Lightly press the fabric before pattern layout to remove any wrinkles and to improve cutting accuracy.
2. Press all seam lines *before* crossing them with another stitching line.
3. To avoid unnecessary pressing during construction, keep the fabric sections laid out flat.
4. You may use the tip, side, or flat of the iron when pressing.
5. Do not allow the cord to drag over your pressed work.
6. Press cotton, linen, and rayon fabrics until they are dry; stop steam-pressing wool fabric before it is completely dry to avoid damaging the fibers.
7. Press directionally with the grain to avoid stretching.
8. Pressing over pins or bastings may leave permanent impressions. Avoid this when possible.
9. Press all seams flat (as stitched) to embed the stitches in the fabric and eliminate puckers before pressing them open.
10. Press shaped garment areas over the pressing cushion to maintain their contours.
11. Press the backs of faced garment areas first, then press them from the right side over a press cloth.
12. Press all vertical darts toward the garment centers; press all horizontal darts downward.

The final temperature setting, moisture application, and pressure exerted on the fabric should not alter the fabric's surface texture or hand. Some guidelines for preserving fabric surface texture follow:

Pile-surfaced Fabrics. To protect the pile surfaces of velvet, velveteen, and corduroy, press them on a needle board. Place the fabric with the pile surface against the wire surface of the needle board. Hold the iron over the fabric, allowing the steam to penetrate the fabric, and then press lightly. Protect fabrics that waterspot with a dry press cloth.

When a needle board is not available, use a piece of sturdy pile fabric in the same way as the needle board. This method, however, is not as satisfactory as the needle board because the pile tends to flatten over time.

Pile fabrics may also be pressed using an upright iron. Stand the iron on end. Place a damp cloth against the wrong side of the fabric.

With the damp cloth between the garment and the iron, draw the fabric over the iron. Avoid handling the fabric while it is moist because it may retain finger marks.

Shiny-surfaced Fabrics. Glazed chintz and most other shiny fabrics are pressed on the right side. Satin-weave fabrics are an exception because their surface sheen is due to fabric construction and fiber content. The right side of these fabrics may be marred by the iron, so they should be pressed on the wrong side.

Smooth, Dull-surfaced Fabrics. Press dull-surfaced fabrics on the wrong side to avoid overpressing. Any resulting shine will then be on the wrong side, leaving the right side unmarred. In addition, use a seam roll to prevent the seam-allowance edges from press-marking the fabric.

Acetate and other synthetic fibers may be softened by too much heat, creating a shine that will be permanent. Test the temperature of the iron very carefully before pressing heat-sensitive fabrics.

Raised-surface Fabrics. Raised-surface fabrics should be pressed on the wrong side against a soft surface, such as a thick terry cloth towel. When the raised design is pressed into the soft surface, the design will sink into the towel without being flattened. If it is necessary to use the iron on the right side of the fabric, place the terry cloth between the garment and the iron.

Not all fabrics can be pressed with the same pressing techniques. Some require special treatment. Some cannot be pressed at all; heat and moisture may melt them or damage their finishes.

Wool Fabrics. Do not press wool fabrics completely dry. After pressing, hang wool garments to allow them to dry completely. Do not handle woolen fabrics immediately after pressing.

To press wool on the wrong side, set the temperature regulator on the iron to "wool" or "moderately hot."

Place a wool press cloth on the ironing board, place the right side of the garment against the press cloth, and then place a damp cheesecloth over the area to be pressed. Hold the iron so that it barely touches the fabric and allow the steam to penetrate. Raise the iron before the fabric stops steaming. Raise the press cloth occasionally to allow the steam to escape. This is important, because the finished fabric should be neither damp nor dry; it should retain a suggestion of moisture to avoid fiber damage. Finish pressing pleats, hems, or other details on the right side of the garment with a press cloth if necessary.

To press wool from the right side, place the garment right side up on the ironing board or pressing ham. Place a wool press cloth over the garment. Hold the steam iron over the area to be pressed and allow the steam to penetrate the press cloth and garment. Lower the iron, then raise it again while the wool is still slightly moist. When using a dry iron, place a damp press cloth over the wool press cloth. Raise and lower the iron, allowing it to rest momentarily on the damp cloth to create steam.

Remove the press cloth while the garment is still steaming and, if necessary, brush lightly to restore the texture.

Fabrics Made from Synthetic Fibers. Use the iron temperature recommended for the specific fiber in the fabric. Remember that many synthetic fibers melt at low temperatures but that not all of them melt at the same temperature. Press with a dry iron or with steam after testing the fabric for iron temperature, moist or dry heat, and water spotting. Make sure that every seam is stitched correctly before pressing, since creases are difficult to remove when alterations are made after the stitching lines are pressed.

Silk Fabrics. Use the iron temperature recommended for silk and press on the wrong side using a dry iron or steam. Since silk may water-spot, protect it with a press cloth.

Knit and Stretch Fabrics. Press on the wrong side using the recommended temperature for the fiber. Press knit fabrics in the direction of the lengthwise ribs. Press lengthwise stretch fabrics with the crosswise grain; press crosswise stretch with the lengthwise grain to avoid stretching the fabric. Do not allow the garment to hang from the ironing board while pressing because these fabrics tend to stretch more when damp than when dry.

Crepe and Lace Fabrics. Press from the wrong side of the garment over a soft pad of toweling to preserve the surface texture. Follow the pressing techniques for the fibers.

Tissue paper placed between the garment fabric and the iron will prevent the edges of the lace from curling and will retain the surface texture of the crepe.

CRITERIA FOR EVALUATION

PRESSING

To ensure quality performance, check to see that:

__ **1.** The original texture of the fabric is maintained.

__ **2.** No shine or press marks are visible on the right side of the fabric.

__ **3.** No wrinkles or crinkled areas are visible.

__ **4.** The fabric does not fold over the seam line or look bubbled.

__ **5.** No water marks are visible.

__ **6.** Creases are sharp.

__ **7.** Each construction detail is pressed before being crossed by another construction detail (during the construction process).

__ **8.** Seams are pressed open smoothly on the seam line. There are no ridges from seam allowance edges visible on the right side.

__ **9.** Darts, curved seams, and eased seams have smoothly molded contours derived by pressing over a pressing ham.

__ **10.** Gathers appear as soft folds without any creases.

__ **11.** The total garment appears smooth; inner construction details (i.e. seams, darts, interfacings, hems) are not apparent from the right side.

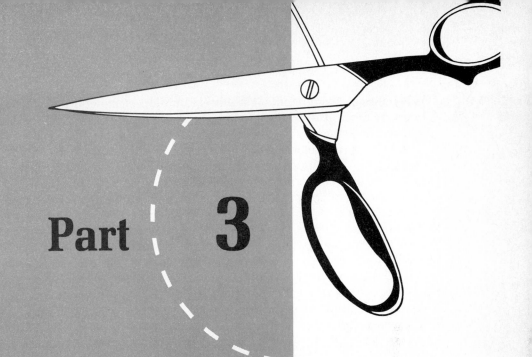

Part 3

Getting Ready to Sew

As with other skilled crafts, careful preparation of materials is essential for formulation of a quality product. In garment construction, it includes adjusting and altering the pattern for improved fit, preshrinking and trueing the fabric for size retention and balanced grain, careful layout of pattern pieces on the fabric to achieve balanced grain and matched pattern design, and accurate cutting and marking. Well-fitted and constructed garments are unattainable goals when these preliminary steps are not performed with precision.

Adjusting or altering the pattern pieces assures that the contours of the constructed garment will correspond more closely with those of the body. When a garment fits very well, one has a sense that the clothing no longer exists. There is no binding of limbs or restriction of movement. The garment follows you. There is unity between body and garment. Yet once the movement is completed, the garment returns to its original position on the body.

You may decide that perfect fit is not essential for the type of garment you are constructing. If so, your choice of fitting method can result in a lower standard of good fit. Although two-dimensional fitting techniques can provide good fit, hard-to-fit figures may find that three-dimensional fitting procedures enable garments to fit the more varied contours much more readily.

Fabric is the fundamental raw material used to compile the garment. It requires careful preparation to ensure that the garment will fit and support the style lines as you projected. Shrinking or dry cleaning the fabric prevents a reduction in garment size after it is constructed. Sometimes a garment shrinks so much that it no longer fits. Balanced grain results in a balanced, evenly hanging garment. Stripes, plaids and other patterned designs can be matched easily.

Once the fabric has been prepared for cutting, the fitted pattern pieces can be laid out on the fabric. Again grain balance is critical. Each pattern grain line must lie parallel to the grain of the fabric (usually lengthwise) to ensure that the garment hangs evenly on the body. Some fabrics, such as those that are napped, patterned, or striped, require special layout procedures. These may 1) reduce fabric wear (nap runs down on corduroy), 2) ensure that the nap runs in the same direction for all pattern pieces—thus avoiding color variation from front to back or side to side, and 3) enable stripes and plaids to be matched or prints to be carefully positioned on the pattern.

The final preparatory steps include cutting and marking. Precision remains essential. An uneven cutting line may force seamlines to be stitched unevenly. Sloppily marked pattern symbols may mean that fabric sections will be joined inaccurately. Permanent markings may show through to the right side of the fabric. Any discrepancy will result in a poor appearance and may also destroy the acquired fit.

Take the time to handle these preliminaries with special consideration. They are essential to your garment's ultimate quality.

8 Components of Fit

OBJECTIVE

To observe, analyze, and solve the various problems of fitting by utilizing the five fit factors: grain, ease, set, line, and balance.

The pattern you have chosen functions as a blueprint for your garment's styling and fit. Before marketing it, the pattern company tested and corrected the design on a "standardized" body form for line, proportion, and fit. This does not mean, however, that the garment will fit you the same way it fit the form. You may recall that some of your body measurements differ from those listed for your "best" pattern size. Perhaps your hips are slightly larger or your back waist length is slightly shorter than the standardized measurements for your size. Such differences may force your skirt to cup under your seat or your bodice to ripple around your midriff.

Just what is fit? *Fit* refers to the relationship of the garment form to the human form. To fit well, the three-dimensional contours of the garment must correspond with those of the body and any undergarments worn beneath the garment.

In addition, the smooth set of a *well-fitted garment* disguises figure variations that would otherwise be emphasized by wrinkling, pulling, or bagging. The design ensures comfort and enhances individual body proportions. Its ease is consistent with current fashion. The garment accommodates human movement, enabling the wearer to walk, climb stairs, reach, or sit easily. After each completed movement, the garment returns to its original position. Most importantly, the wearer can remain unconscious of it.

The garment becomes psychologically comfortable when—because of its design and fit— it conceals undesired proportions and contours or emphasizes desirable ones. It also meets individual preferences for closeness of fit and length. Although pleated trousers will fit pelvic and leg contours smoothly, they will not be comfortable if they dangle loosely about the ankles.

In contrast, when a *garment fits poorly,* there is a lack of harmony with the body structure. Signs of misfit include wrinkles, strain lines, or bagging.

This chapter, entitled "Components of Fit," considers both structural and functional human needs. Because no standardized pattern can economically accommodate the infinite variations in human contour and proportion and provide the degree of desired comfort, the pattern must be altered to fit these variables. *Two- and three-dimensional fitting methods* are examined and compared. Choice of method will vary with experience, degree of structural variation between body and pattern, garment design complexity, time available, and the quality of fit desired.

The Human Form

Some knowledge of body structure and function can help you to understand the mobile, three-dimensional form over which the garment must fit.

STRUCTURE

The human body is three-dimensional, possessing characteristics of length, width, and depth. The chest and pelvis form the upper and lower torso, respectively; the legs, arms, and head-neck segment form the appendages.

The torso and appendage contours are created by muscle and fatty tissue covering the skeleton. Therefore the body appears to be a series of convex and concave curves and planes. The male form appears more angular than the female form because of its greater muscular definition and lower percentage of fat. The finished garment must smoothly accommodate convex curves (bulges) created by the shoulders, chest, bust, shoulder blades, abdomen, hips, buttocks, thighs, elbows, and knees. The fabric usually spans concave curves (hollows) found above and below the bust, between the shoulder blades, between prominent pelvic bones, and below the back waist level. A flat abdomen or back forms a plane over which the fabric lies smoothly.

The human form may deviate from normal through proportional, structural, or postural variations. *Disproportion* is characterized by symmetric differences in torso or appendage lengths, although contours remain standard. Arms, back waist lengths, crotch depths, and thighs may be longer or shorter than standard. The *divergent* figure differs in contour, structure, or postural tilt from the standard figure conceived by the pattern company. Examples of divergence include smaller- or larger-than-standard bulges as well as asymmetry. Subtle variations in hip curve or height, erectness of posture, leg lengths, and the slope of each shoulder influence the garment fit.

Such physical variations will force the garment made from a symmetric, standardized pattern to hang abnormally on the figure. Wrinkles may appear, grain may sag or rise, seams may tilt forward, or the garment may swing to one side.

FUNCTION

A garment is traditionally fitted on a nonmoving body since it is easier to work on an unmoving structure. Humans, however, are rarely stationary. They are in constant motion as they perform their daily activities—walking, sitting, running, reaching, crawling in and out of cars, writing, opening doors, typing, bending, carrying packages, and so on.

The movement of the body unit and its segments is produced by the forced motion of bones at joint articulation points. The direction of body limb movement is dependent upon the joint type involved. The hinge joints of the elbow and knee permit flexion (bending) in only one direction. Flexion also occurs at the neck, shoulder, spine, and hip, but usually in more than one direction. In addition, body segments rotate at the neck, shoulder, trunk (waist), and elbow. The shoulders can be elevated or lowered. Circumduction occurs at the neck, shoulder, waist, hip, wrist, and ankles.

Movement of the limbs creates simultaneous changes in their length and circumference. When you flex your elbow or knee, these joints each lengthen about 35 to 40 percent. Elbow circumference increases an average 15 to 22 percent, whereas knee circumference increases an average 12 to 14 percent. Reaching forward extends the back about 13 to 16 percent while the seat increases about 4 to 6 percent.[1]

Clothing must permit daily activities without excessively restricting range of motion. If you must hike up your pant leg before climbing into a car, pull down your shirtsleeve after raising your arm, pull your pant legs down after rising from a chair, or tug at your sleeve before you can raise your arm, then your clothing is not meeting minimal needs for function.

Enough vertical and horizontal ease should be provided to permit comfortable expansion of the body. Daily activities usually require less comfort ease than do specialized activities such as sports, dance, or some industrial jobs. Garments designed for these special functions should not inhibit the more extreme and speedier movements required. Additional ease and expandable design features can facilitate these activities. Measuring flexed and extended appendage positions—such as the back leg elongation of the runner or the waist, hip, and back-crotch length of the seated clerical worker—can help to establish specific ease needs. Compare these specific ease requirements with the minimums listed under "Measurements for Pattern Size and Fit" in Chapter 3. How much more ease is required for the specialized activity?

Additionally, the garment should be balanced on the body so as not to inhibit movement of body appendages. Junctions of garment appendages (i.e., sleeve, pant leg, elbow darts) should fall at the torso-appendage junctions of the body (i.e., armscye, waist, neck, hip). For example, if the crotch or armscye is too low, the wearer will find it difficult to raise his or her arms or legs.

The Pattern-Fabric-Garment Structure

Both pattern and fabric are two-dimensional structures possessing length and width. The shaped pattern pieces serve as dies for cutting out duplicate fabric sections. When stitched to-

[1] "Stretch Clicks in Many Markets," *American Fabrics,* No. 95, p. 22, fall 1972.

gether according to plan, the shaped fabric sections create a three-dimensional garment form with contours replicating those of the body.

PATTERN

Pattern perimeter shape and dimension, incorporated with internal fitting devices (i.e., darts, seam angles, tucking, pleats, gathers, or ease), control the derived garment's styling and size. To ensure quality fit of the finished garment, the pattern (or a test garment made from the pattern) must first be fitted to correspond with the wearer's body structure. Only then can it be used to cut out the fabric sections.

Two fitting approaches are generally followed: (1) *two-dimensional pattern adjustments* based upon comparisons of body and pattern dimensions or (2) *three-dimensional fitting* of the pinned pattern or a muslin test garment directly on the wearer.

FABRIC

Fabric contributes two components that influence the ultimate garment form: grain and hand. *Grain* simply refers to the predominant direction of a fabric's threads—the warp and filling in the case of a woven fabric. Garments are generally cut with the lengthwise grain (warp) plumb and the crosswise grain (filling) parallel to the floor surface. Cut traditionally, fabric tends to fall directly downward, following the heavier lengthwise yarns; fabrics with heavier crosswise yarns, like poplin or shantung, tend to fall farther away from the body. When cut on the bias, the same style will fall closer to the body, stretching over convex curves and clinging to concave curves. Stretch wovens and knits will follow body contours in varying degrees of closeness, depending upon the elasticity and drapability exhibited by individual fab-

rics. They vary from a low stretch range of 12 to 17 percent up to high performance range exhibiting 25 to 35 percent or more stretch.[2]

Fabric *hand* is dependent upon the fabric's flexibility, thickness, and weight. If one were to construct two shirts with the same previously fitted pattern, following the same grain direction but utilizing two different fabric hands, the shirts would not fit in the same way. A shirt made from corduroy will fall away from body contours, creating a more rigid silhouette, whereas a silk crepe de chine shirt will fall closer to the body, producing a softer, more body-revealing silhouette. To ensure good fit despite variations in fabric hand or grain, all garments should be fitted as they are constructed. Refer to "Organization and Fitting Strategies" in Chapter 12 for fit-as-you-sew approaches.

GARMENT

The three-dimensional form of the garment is obtained through the manipulation of internal and perimeter fitting devices. Internal fitting devices, including gathers and pleats, are constructed first; then the shaped seam lines (perimeters) are joined. Additional structural contouring is derived from internal support systems, such as interfacings, padding, and boning. Most garments, however, are incapable of maintaining the derived form without support from the body.

Garment type influences the complexity of the fitting job required. Generally, the order of difficulty of fitting garments seems to be as follows:

[2] de Llosa "Stretch For All Seasons," *American Fabrics and Fashions*, No. 120, (fall 1980) pp 32–33.

Less complex

More complex

Skirt
Sleeveless shirt, top
Sleeved blouse, shirt
Loose dress, jacket,
  coat
Jumper
Fitted dress, pants,
  shorts
Fitted jacket, coat

In most cases, loose silhouettes tend to simplify the fitting manipulations needed, as these garments skim over body contours.

Standards of Fit

Standards of fit vary individually. A man may spend many hours with his tailor in order to achieve an excellent customized fit; another may purchase a ready-to-wear suit that can be quickly altered by the shop; a third may purchase a suit and wear it as it is. Each suit will provide a different level of fit quality. Because few ready-to-wear consumers are aware of the aesthetic and physical comfort of a custom-fitted garment, their standards of fit may be less exacting than those of the wearer of custom apparel.

A *well-fitted garment* enhances individual contours and proportions. There is a correspondence of contour between the garment form and the body form, which helps to eliminate wrinkles, snugness or looseness, pulling, imbalance, or other evidences of misfit. Divergent body structures appear symmetrically normal and personal preferences for ease and balance are respected. Garment segments easily follow corresponding body segments during movement. (The sleeve moves with the arm.) Once a total movement is completed, the garment returns to its original position without adjustment. The designer's intended style is also retained and de-

sign details harmonize in scale and placement with the wearer's proportions.

In this text, primary emphasis for analyzing fit is upon the criteria that harmonize the garment with the body. Five interrelating factors are present in every fitting problem: set, ease, line, balance, and grain.[3] Each factor varies in degree of visible misfit for every case evaluated, so that some factors may be more predominantly misaligned than others.

Set indicates that garment surfaces are smooth and without wrinkles or tautness. When the garment is neither too loose nor too tight and allows for comfortable movement, *ease* requirements are correct. *Line* shows that the structural seams of the garment follow corresponding body silhouette lines and fall at body joint locations. The garment is *balanced* when the body is centrally located within it. *Grain* is correctly aligned when vertical grain lines are plumb at center front and center back and horizontal grain lines are perpendicular to the centerlines at the bust, waist, hip, and scye levels.

SEQUENTIAL ANALYSIS OF FIT

Rather than randomly analyzing the fit of each garment and making haphazard decisions regarding solutions to any perceived problems, a systematic plan can be followed that will simplify the entire fitting process. *Sequential analysis* can be used to evaluate problems and to diagnose solutions for both two-dimensional and three-dimensional fitting approaches. The sequence for analysis is described starting on page 78, followed by detailed charts illustrating the analysis process for each fit factor. Read across the charts.

[3] Mabel Erwin, *Practical Dress Design*, p. 8.

1. *Know the standards for each fit factor.* Although the standards describe the fit of basic fitted garments, they can be applied with some modification to virtually all garment styles.
2. *Survey the pattern or garment for symptoms of misfit. Two-dimensionally:* Compare pattern dimensions with corresponding body-plus-ease measures. Discrepancies greater than 6 mm (¼ in) indicate potential fit problems.

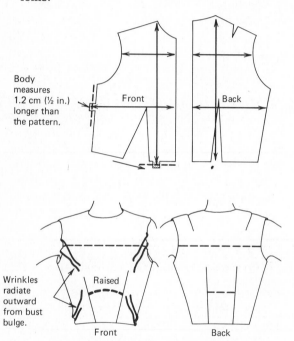

Body measures 1.2 cm (½ in.) longer than the pattern.

Front   Back

Wrinkles radiate outward from bust bulge.   Raised

Front   Back

Three dimensionally: Examine one garment unit at a time, checking first for problems in set and ease, then for line and balance, and finally for grain misalignment. Are wrinkles present? Is the garment too tight? Do vertical seams fall perpendicular to the floor? Is the body centrally located in the garment? Are the horizontal grain lines balanced from side to side at center front and center back?

3. *Make a diagnosis by specifying the probable cause of the symptom(s). Two dimensionally:* Note any differences in pattern and body lengths, widths, or circumferences. Do they indicate variations in proportion, girth, or body-contour size? Might they indicate asymmetry of contour?

Three-dimensionally: Begin by examining each unit and working from the upper units to the lower units. Since the garment hangs suspended from the body, the cause of the misfit is often directly above the symptom. A divergent contour may pull the grain line directly below it out of alignment. A larger-than-average contour or an asymmetrically positioned contour may create diagonal wrinkles, whereas a too-snug or too-long garment unit may create horizontal wrinkles. In the case of diagonal wrinkling, the grain and structural seam lines may be pulled out of position, forcing the garment off balance on the body. As you can see by this example, the visible symptoms are often interrelated and may be caused by just one divergent contour.

4. *Propose a solution for correcting the misfit. Two-dimensionally:* Generally, patterns are enlarged by slashing and spreading; they are reduced by tucking. Minor changes can be made by extending or bringing in the seam lines. Length is adjusted first, followed by circumference and contour adjustments.

Three-dimensionally: When the *primary* causes of the misfit are solved first; other fit discrepancies are often solved simultaneously, thus minimizing additional fitting manipulations. Several probable solutions can be tested before a final choice is made. Test check by first pinching out a tuck over any location of probable cause. If the tuck makes the problem worse, an opposite adjustment is indicated. Release the pattern or garment section by slashing and spreading over the divergent contour until the garment falls into position.

5. *Correct the misfit by adjusting the pattern or by altering the test garment directly on the body and transferring the changes to the pattern.* Two approaches for fitting a larger-than-average body curve are illustrated. Refer to the adjustment and alteration charts beginning on page 93 for the method of correction.

6. *Draw conclusions defining the basic causal relationships present.* How can these relationships be used to analyze future fit problems? Consider that other larger-than-average body contours might be fitted following an approach similar to the two illustrated in the sample problem.

CORRECTION:

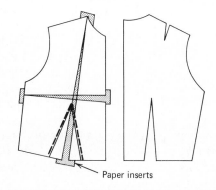

Paper inserts

CORRECTION:

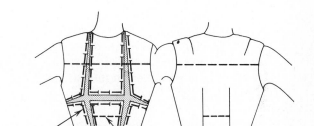

Muslin inserts

Grain leveled

Sequential Analysis of Grain

Appearance Standard

Vertical grain is plumb at the center front, center back, and from the sleeve-cap dot to the elbow line.

Horizontal grain is parallel to the floor at the bust or chest, scye, and hip levels. The grain is balanced from the right to left sides of the body unless the design is asymmetric.

Symptoms: Two-Dimensional	Symptoms: Three-Dimensional
Symptoms of grain misfit are not visible when a two-dimensional comparison of measurements is made. Misfit is caused by divergent contours or structural imbalance; it is difficult to assess accurately by a measurement comparison.	*Vertical Grain* The vertical grain is not plumb when: a. Center front or center back grain swings to one side. b. Sleeve grain swings forward or backward. *Horizontal Grain* The horizontal grain is not parallel at one or more of the body levels when: a. The grain rises at the bust or chest, scye, or hip levels. b. The grain drops at the bust or chest, scye, or hip levels.

Diagnosis	Solution
Vertical Grain	*Vertical Grain* Correction of the vertical grain may also correct the horizontal grain when the physical cause is asymmetric.
Possible causes: a. A divergent, asymmetric body bulge pulls the grain in the direction of the bulge (e.g., left bulge pulls grain line to the left). b. A divergent, asymmetric hollow drops the grain toward the other side of the body. c. Structural imbalance of the body may force the grain to one side (e.g., leg length variation).	To return grain to position: a. Increase garment length at location of prominent contour. b. Decrease garment length at location of hollow. c. Increase or decrease length as needed for structural imbalance.
Horizontal Grain *Raised grain:* prominent convex curve present directly above the misalignment.	*Horizontal Grain* To raise the grain: a. Decrease garment length over the hollow. b. Take in the seam allowance above the hollow.
Dropped grain: smaller-than-standard convex curve or concave curve present directly above the misalignment.	To drop the grain: a. Increase garment length over the prominent contour. b. Let out the seam allowance above the bulge.

Sequential Analysis of Ease

Appearance Standard

The garment is comfortable and is not too *snug* nor too *loose*. Allowance for body expansion and movement will vary with body build, fabric, fashion (e.g., smaller bodies need less ease; wovens require more ease than stretch wovens or stretchy knits; style trends vary). Horizontal reference lines (bust or chest, scye, hip levels) fall at corresponding body reference lines.

Symptoms: Two-Dimensional	Symptoms: Three-Dimensional
Too Snug The pattern dimension is *less* than the corresponding body-plus-ease measurement for length, width, or circumference.	*Too Snug* a. The fabric draws or pulls across the body. b. The garment is too short. c. Horizontal reference lines are too high. d. The garment is snug across a convex curve.

Too Loose
The pattern dimension is *greater* than the corresponding body-plus-ease measurement for length, width, or circumference.

Too Loose

 a. The fabric droops or bags.
 b. The garment is too long.
 c. The horizontal reference lines are too low.
 d. The garment is loose across a convex curve.

Diagnosis	Solution

Too Snug
The garment lacks ease:

 a. Body circumference is greater than standard.
 b. Body length is greater than standard.
 c. Convex curves are larger than standard.

Too Snug
To increase garment ease:

 a. Increase the circumference.
 b. Let out the side seams.
 c. Enlarge for a larger-than-standard bulge (symmetric/asymmetric).

Too Loose
The garment has excess ease:

 a. Body circumference is less than standard.
 b. Body length is less than standard.
 c. Convex curves are smaller than standard.

Too Loose
To decrease garment ease:

 a. Decrease the circumference.
 b. Take in the side seams.
 c. Reduce for a smaller-than-standard bulge (symmetric/asymmetric).

Sequential Analysis of Set

Appearance Standard

Garment surfaces are smooth and free from horizontal and diagonal wrinkles or areas of tautness. The garment surfaces form convex curves or planes; no concave curves are present unless it is a special style. Ease is evenly and smoothly distributed.

Symptoms: Two-Dimensional	Symptoms: Three-Dimensional

Horizontal Wrinkles

 a. The pattern dimension is less than the corresponding body-plus-ease measurement for circumference.
 b. The pattern dimension is greater than the corresponding body-plus-ease measurement for length, width, or circumference.

Horizontal Wrinkles

 a. The garment draws around the body, creating wrinkles.

 b. The garment is loose around the body; bagging is present. The garment droops over convex curves.

Diagonal Wrinkles
The pattern dimension is less than the corresponding body-plus-ease measurement for length and/or width over a prominent body bulge.

Tautness
Tautness is difficult to assess two-dimensionally; it may be apparent when the pattern dimension is less than the body dimension.

Diagonal Wrinkles
Diagonal wrinkles radiate outward from a prominent bulge.

Tautness
Areas of tautness are visible:

a. Over convex curves.
b. Spanning a concave curve.

Diagnosis	Solution
Horizontal Wrinkles The garment lacks ease: body circumference or width is greater than standard.	*Horizontal Wrinkles* To enlarge the garment: a. Increase the circumference or width. b. Let out the side seams.
The garment has excess ease: a. Body circumference is less than standard. b. Body width is less than standard. c. Body length is less than standard. d. Convex curves are smaller than standard.	To reduce garment size: a. Decrease the circumference. b. Take in the side seams. c. Decrease the garment width. d. Decrease the garment length. e. Reduce for a smaller-than-standard bulge.
Diagonal Wrinkles The garment lacks ease: convex curves are larger than standard.	*Diagonal Wrinkles* Enlarge the garment for a larger-than-standard bulge.
Tautness Possible causes: a. Divergent body contours are present (symmetric/asymmetric). b. Body circumference is greater than standard.	*Tautness* To enlarge the garment: a. Alter to increase the vertical and/or horizontal ease over a specific convex curve. b. Increase the garment circumference or width.

Sequential Analysis of Line

Appearance Standard

The garment's structural seams follow corresponding body contour lines and joint locations.

Silhouette seams:

Vertical seams are plumb; the shoulder-underarm-side seam line divides the body in half from front to back.

Circumference seams:

Seams are even, smooth, and comfortable, perpendicular to the silhouette seams, and correspond with body joint locations. The neckline seam follows the base of the neck; the armscye seam is oval and falls at the shoulder joint; the waistline seam appears parallel to the floor (but back dips) at the waist indentation; the wrist seam falls at the base of the wristbone; the crotch seam follows the body crotch curve.

Symptoms: Two-Dimensional	Symptoms: Three-Dimensional

Line misfit is difficult to assess two-dimensionally by comparing body-plus-ease dimensions with pattern dimensions because it is caused by divergent contours or variations in physical structure. The wearer's past fit experiences may be used to predict line misfit.	*Silhouette Seams*
	Seams are not perpendicular to the floor; they are located too far forward or backward.
	
	Circumference Seams
	  a. Seams are wavy; they rise and fall.
	  b. Seams fall short of or extend over a joint location.

Diagnosis	Solution
	Line misfit is usually corrected when grain, ease, and set are restored. If it has not been corrected, the following solution(s) may be necessary.

Silhouette Seams
Possible causes:
 	
  a. A divergent body contour is present.
  b. Some portion of the front or back of the body is larger (more prominent)-than-standard.
  c. Body is asymmetric.
	Silhouette Seams
	To shift seam forward, increase back width and reduce front width.
	To shift seam backward, increase front width and reduce back width.

Circumference Seams	*Circumference Seams* After silhouette seams are corrected, circumference seams can be fitted.

a. Divergent body contours are present.

b. Portions of the torso unit are longer or shorter than standard.

One segment of the body (e.g., shoulder, upper arm, back waist length) is longer or shorter than standard.

To drop seams:

a. Alter for a larger-than-standard contour (symmetric/asymmetric).

b. Increase length.

To raise seams:

a. Alter for a smaller-than-standard contour (symmetric/asymmetric).

b. Decrease length.

To enlarge garment area:

a. Increase garment width (e.g., shoulder seam).

b. Increase garment length (e.g., sleeve length).

To reduce garment area:

a. Decrease garment width.

b. Decrease garment length.

Sequential Analysis of Balance

Appearance Standard

The body form appears *centrally* located within the garment form from:

Front to back.
Side to side.
Armscye front to back and top to bottom.
Crotch front to back.

Seams rest smoothly on the body. The armscye forms a smooth oval. The crotch curve corresponds with the body curve. Sleeve cap ease is balanced from front to back.

Symptoms: Two-Dimensional	Symptoms: Three-Dimensional
Balance misfit, usually caused by divergent contours or structural asymmetry, is difficult to assess two-dimensionally. The wearer's past fit experiences may help to predict imbalance.	One portion of the garment hugs the body while its counterpart swings away from the body. The garment may swing forward, backward, or to either side.
	Some segment of a seam may hug the body closer or fall farther away from the body than it should for good balance.

Diagnosis	Solution

Possible causes:
 	
  a. A divergent, asymmetric body bulge is present.
  b. The body's contours may vary subtly from the standard contours of the garment.
  c. The body may be structurally imbalanced (asymmetric).
	Balance misfit is often corrected or improved after grain, ease, set, and line are restored.
	
	To alter garment contour:
	
	  a. Enlarge the garment area by increasing the vertical and/or horizontal ease over the divergent contour.
	  b. Reduce the garment area by decreasing the vertical and/or horizontal ease over the divergent contour.
	
	To correct the garment for structural imbalance, reduce the garment size for the smaller or shorter side of the body.

Choice of Fitting Method

Garment fit can be improved by manipulating patterns *two-dimensionally* or by fitting them *three-dimensionally* on the body. Garments are fitted two-dimensionally when all pattern changes are done in the "flat" on the basis of a comparison of body and pattern dimensions. Body measurements may be compared with *standard size measurements* or with *pattern dimensions.* Garments are fitted three-dimensionally by fitting a pinned *pattern* or a stitched *fabric test garment* on the wearer. Fitting changes are made directly on the body, enabling the fitter to take in or let out the garment as required by individual body contours.

Two-dimensional pattern manipulations, called *pattern adjustments,* involve changes in length, width, circumference, body bulge size, and dart length or angle. *Pattern alterations* include tucking, slashing and spreading, and reshaping or relocation of seam lines performed directly on the body. The resulting changes include those of length, width, circumference, symmetric and asymmetric body bulges and

hollows, dart changes, reshaping or relocation of seam lines. Different levels of fit are provided by each method. Body measurement comparison fits the nearly standard and disproportionate figure well but does not take asymmetric contour variation into account unless measures are taken for both the right and left side. By comparing many body and pattern measurements, one can fit the divergent figure fairly well. Balance, line, and grain cannot be controlled as readily in two-dimensional fitting as they can when fitting is done directly on the body. Comparison of the pinned pattern form or the stitched garment form to the body form provides excellent fit in all criterion areas. Disproportion and divergent contours can be readily fitted. The stitched fabric test garment will provide the closest approximation to the fit of the final garment since it has a grain direction; unlike the "tissue" pattern. When well executed, three-dimensional fitting will provide the highest level of fit.

Choice of fitting method is dependent upon

the body to be fitted, garment function, and the quality of fit desired. Is the body nearly standard or disproportionate, and therefore relatively easy to fit? Or is the body structure asymmetric or divergent in contour, requiring more complex fitting procedures for a good fit? Is the garment a closely fitted style to be fabricated in a tightly woven, nonstretch fabric? Or will abundant style ease skim over nonstandard body contours?

Approaches to Fit

Two-Dimensional Approach: Dimensional Comparison

Body measurements to standard size measurements.
Body measurements to pattern measurements.

Three-Dimensional Approach: Form Comparison

Pattern garment form to body form.
Fabric garment form to body form.
Final cut-garment form to body form during construction.*

* See Chapter 12, "Organization and Fitting Strategies," for method.

DIMENSIONAL COMPARISON: BODY MEASUREMENTS TO STANDARD-SIZE MEASUREMENTS

This simplest of the two-dimensional fitting methods compares the measurements of your bust, waist, hip, and back waist length and your skirt- and pant-length measures with the standard measurements for the size you selected. This comparison permits adjustment of only basic circumference and length measurements.

Procedures: To determine whether the pattern must be adjusted, fill in the chart below with your body measurements and the standard measurements for your selected size. Compare the two sets of measurements by subtracting

your body measurements from the standard measurements. A positive difference indicates that the pattern must be reduced; a negative difference indicates that the pattern must be enlarged.

Dimensional Comparison for Women

Measurement	Standard − Body = Difference
Bust	
Waist	
Hips	
Back waist length	
Garment length	

Dimensional Comparison for Men

Measurement	Standard − Body = Difference
Chest	
Waist	
Hip	
Neckband	
Shirt sleeve	
Garment length	

Study the sequential fitting analysis charts for ease and set. Compare any measurement differences you find with the two-dimensional symptoms described in the chart. Read across the chart to find the diagnosis, solution, and recommended pattern adjustment for your symptom. Pattern adjustment procedures are found beginning on page 93.

DIMENSIONAL COMPARISON: BODY MEASUREMENTS TO PATTERN MEASUREMENTS

When using this two-dimensional fitting method, compare "body measurements plus ease" with corresponding pattern measurements to determine whether the pattern will require adjustment. All the measurements recorded in Chapter 3, "Measurements for Pattern Size and Fit," will be used unless they are not included in the garment style (i.e., sleeveless garment, pants). This method works best for adjusting *fitted* garment styles, since minimum ease requirements are known. However, when the garment design features style fullness, it is impossible to estimate the amount of ease the designer has incorporated. When this is the case, compare the "body measurements without ease" to the standard measurements listed for the pattern size. This ensures that larger body dimensions will not use up style ease, thus reducing intended style fullness. If the garment (e.g., jacket, overshirt) will be worn over other garments, even more ease is needed to enable the outer garment to hang smoothly without clinging or drawing.

Procedures: Complete the adjustment chart on pages 88–89 (same as chart in Chapter 3). Add the ease indicated to each corresponding body measurement, using the minimum amounts if the body is slender and the maximum amounts if the body is fleshier and expands more during movement or if you are quite active.

Prepare the pattern for measurement by marking it with horizontal and vertical reference lines corresponding to key body locations. Draw horizontal lines perpendicular to center front and center back at the bust or chest, hip, and scye levels. Pattern bust-level position is found at (1) the intersection of a waistline and underarm or armscye dart, (2) about 2.5 cm (1 in) beyond the tip of a single bust dart, or (3) at the point of maximum width on the side pattern section of a princess-style garment. Pattern chest-level position is located below the armscye and perpendicular to the center front and back. Since individual hip levels vary, hip level is found at the fullest area of the hip. See the individual waist-to-hip measure and measure along side seam of pattern from waist seam to determine. Rule a line across the pattern perpendicular to the grain line. The sleeve scye

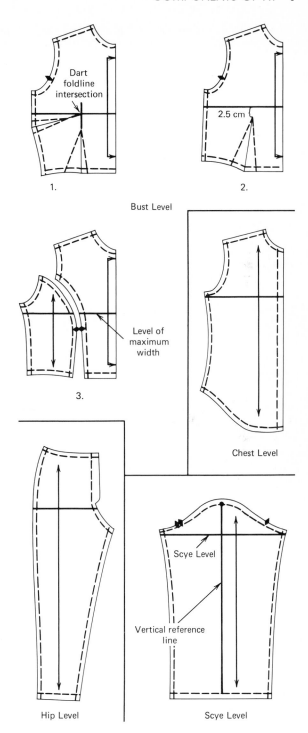

Sizing and Adjustment Chart: Women

Determine	Body Measurements	For Size:[1]	For Pattern Adjustments:			
		1 Body Measurements	2 Minimum Ease	3 Body + Ease	4 Pattern	5 Change Needed
Figure Type	1. Height		—	—	—	—
	2. Back Waist Length		0.0–0.6 cm			
Size	3. High Bust		3.8–7.5 cm			
	4. Bust		5.0–10.0 cm			
	5. Waist		1.3–2.5 cm			
	6. Full Hip		5.0–7.5 cm			
Additional Pattern Adjustments	7. Shoulder-to-Bust Point		—			
	8. Shoulder		0.0–1.0 cm			
	9. Front Waist Length Over Bust		0.0–0.6 cm			
	10. Front Waist Length		0.0–0.6 cm			
	11. Arm Length: Total		—			
	11a. Arm Length: Shoulder-to-Elbow		—			
	11b. Arm Length: Elbow-to-Wrist		—			
	12. Biceps		5.0–7.5 cm			
	13. Waist-to-Hip		—			
	14. Hip High		2.5 cm			
	15. Crotch Level		1.3–2.0 cm			
	16a. Crotch Length: Front		—			
	16b. Crotch Length: Back		—			
	17. Back Width		1.3–2.0 cm			
	18. Skirt Length		—			
	19. Pants Length		—			

Figure type:

Pattern size:

Record measurements in centimeters.

[1] Instructions for determining pattern size begin on page 33.

level is found by connecting the armscye-underarm seam intersections across the sleeve width. The vertical reference line of the sleeve is found parallel to the grain line and intersecting the large dot at the high point of the sleeve cap.

Using the reference lines as guides, measure the pattern at all points corresponding to the body measurements taken. Exclude any darts and seam allowances in your totals. Add front and back circumference measurements together and double them so they can be compared accurately to total body circumferences. Note any differences between each "body plus ease"

Sizing and Adjustment Chart: Men

Determine	Body Measurements	For Size:[2]	For Pattern Adjustments:			
		1 Body Measurements	2 Minimum Ease	3 Body + Ease	4 Pattern	5 Change Needed
Figure Type and Size	1. Height		—	—	—	—
	2. Neckband (includes 1.3 cm ease)		—			
	3. Chest		5.0–2.5 cm			
	4. Waist		2.5 cm			
	5. Hip/seat		5.0–7.5 cm			
	6. Shirt sleeve length		—			
Additional Pattern Adjustments	7. Shoulder		0.0–1.0 cm			
	8. Back width		1.3–2.0 cm			
	9. Arm length: total		—			
	9a. Arm length: shoulder to elbow		—			
	9b. Arm length: elbow to wrist		—			
	10. Biceps		5.0–7.5 cm			
	11. Crotch level		1.3–2.0 cm			
	12a. Crotch length: front		—			
	12b. Crotch length: back		—			
	13. Outseam		—			
	14. Inseam		—			

Figure type:

Pattern size:

Record measurements in centimeters.

* © 1977 Simplicity Pattern Company, Inc., 200 Madison Avenue, New York, N.Y. 10016.
[2] Instructions for determining pattern size begin on page 33.

measurement and its corresponding pattern (or standard size) measurement. A positive difference indicates that the pattern is too large and must be reduced in that dimension; a negative difference indicates that the pattern is too small and must be increased to fit the body dimension adequately.

Review the sequential fitting analysis charts for ease and set (pages 79–85) by comparing your findings with the two-dimensional symptoms described. What is the diagnosis, solution, and recommended pattern adjustment for your symptom? Once you have determined which

pattern adjustments are needed, refer to pattern adjustment procedures on pages 93–95 for the technique.

FORM COMPARISON: GARMENT[4] FORM TO BODY FORM

Garment fit may be previewed and corrected three-dimensionally by fitting either the pinned

[4] In this text *Garment* refers to both the three-dimensional "pinned" pattern form and to the three-dimensional "stitched" fabric form.

pattern or a stitched fabric (muslin) test garment directly on the body. Although preparation of the pattern garment for fitting differs from fabric garment preparation, the visual fit analysis and alteration procedures for the two garment forms are quite similar.

Alterations are made directly on the body by tucking or slashing or by manipulating the darts or seam lines to accommodate body contour variations. Changes are usually made within the body of the garment rather than at seam lines, although this depends upon the alteration required and the size of the change. To secure the best fit with a minimal number of alterations, it is crucial that the primary cause of the misfit be diagnosed and corrected first. Familiarity with pattern adjustment proce-

dures can aid in suggesting placement and type of alteration to be made. For assistance refer to adjustment and alteration procedures on pages 93–95. Once the garment has been altered to meet the fitting standards, the alterations must be *refined* before the pattern can be used. Refining is necessary because the alterations often force the pattern to bubble and ripple when it is laid out two-dimensionally. Refining returns the pattern to flatness while also incorporating the fitting changes needed for the wearer's contours.

Procedures: Because of the similarity of the analysis and alteration procedures followed for each method, they are discussed jointly. Any differences between the two are highlighted.

Form Comparison

Pattern Garment Form	Fabric Garment Form
Select the pattern pieces required for your garment (e.g., pants, shirt, dress, jacket) or the view of the garment you plan to make. Isolate the major pattern pieces from any facing, interfacing, or lining pieces.	
The major pieces will be fitted first, the minor pieces later.	
Trim any excess tissue away from the *cutting lines* of each pattern piece.	Preshrink, straighten, and true the test fabric.
Mark vertical and horizontal reference lines on the pattern tissue. *Vertical reference lines* include the center front, center back, and center lines of pants legs and sleeves. For pants, rule a line along the pants crease line parallel to the printed grain line. For the sleeve, rule a line parallel to the grain line intersecting the large sleeve cap dot.	
Horizontal reference lines are perpendicular to vertical reference lines and include the bust or chest levels, the hip level, and the scye level. The scye level is found at the base of the armscye seam intersections on the sleeve and perpendicular to the vertical reference line.	
	Transfer the vertical and horizontal reference lines and all stitching lines to the right side of the test fabric.
Join the pattern or fabric pieces into garment units (e.g., upper and lower torso units, appendages) by pinning or stitching. Refer to the pattern instruction sheet to determine the order of joining. Generally, darts,	

| **Pattern Garment Form** | **Fabric Garment Form** |

tucks, gathers, and pleats are constructed first, followed by internal style seams and vertical seams. Major circumference seams (which join garment units) are joined after each unit has been individually fitted and after any additional alterations are made.

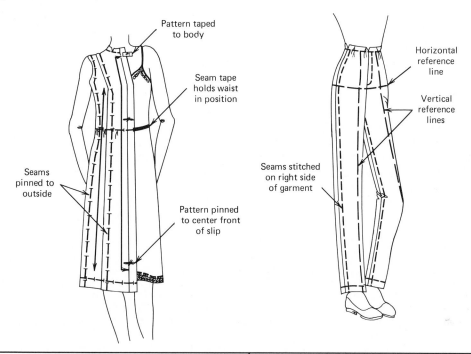

Pinning Procedures: Join the pattern by pinning to fit the larger side of body with seams and darts to the outside for easier altering. Place pins on seam lines with pin heads toward the wearer's head so they will not fall out. Pin ease or gathers as small tucks when attaching to the control seam.

Stitching Procedures: Stay stitch the neck, waist, and armscye seams directly on the stitching lines. Construct each unit by machine basting darts and seams to outside. The reference lines should be visible on the right side of the garment. Cut a piece of nonstretchy tape.

Turn any self-facings to the inside along the fold line. Turn hemlines to inside as designated by pattern. Cut a piece of nonstretchy waistline tape equal to twice the pattern waist measure plus 10 cm (4 in) for overlap. Pin the tape to the waist of each torso unit as it is fitted to maintain its position on the body.

With the help of your instructor or a fellow student, position garment units on body directly over undergarments or any other clothing the garment will be worn over often (e.g., shirts, sweaters). Darts and seams should be visible and away from body. Fit over shoulder pads of the correct thickness if they are to be used in construction. Posture should represent typical body alignment. Begin with the upper unit and work downward. Clip neck, between notches of underarm and crotch, and other curved seams as needed for garment to lie smoothly.

Align the center-front and center-back lines with the central vertical lines of the body (sternum to navel to crotch in front; cervical neck bone along spine to crotch in back). Pin the waist tape in place; tape the pattern tissue to the body with short strips at the neck and hip levels. Place a paper handkerchief or dress shield at the underarm to keep pattern dry.

To attach sleeve appendage to upper torso unit for fitting, turn under the sleeve-cap seam allowance. Draw in ease slightly until cap begins to take on a curved shape. Begin by pinning the underarm into position from inside; then working from the outside at the notches, adjust the ease and pin the cap into position with the pins perpendicular to the seam line and markings matched.

With seam lines matched, overlap and pin any openings. Pin the waistline tape in place. If the test garment is too snug and cannot be pinned closed, refer to step 1, page 93 of the alteration procedures, to determine how to add adequate ease.

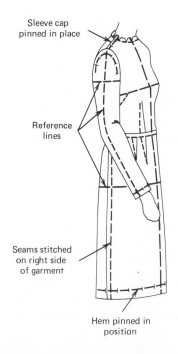

Sleeve cap pinned in place

Reference lines

Seams stitched on right side of garment

Hem pinned in position

Make a general assessment of the overall fit, noting any inconsistencies between pattern or garment form and the body form. Beginning at the top of each unit, work downward and outward, since the lower garment portions and the garment perimeters take their positions from upper-central portions.

Utilize the sequential analysis fitting chart on pages 79–85 to assess the symptoms of fit and misfit, to make a diagnosis, and to determine how to alter the pattern or garment. Alteration procedures are found beginning on page 93. Alterations are complete when the garment appearance meets the five standards for fit.

Since the altered pattern does not always lie flat, it must be refined before it can be used to construct the garment. Refer to the pattern refinement procedures beginning on page 104. If the required refinements were complex—that is, if a high quality of fit is desired and time permits—the garment fit should be retested by constructing another test garment.

Adjustment and Alteration Procedures

Although pattern adjustments are performed two-dimensionally and alterations are performed three-dimensionally, the fitting changes made often parallel one another. Garment dimensions are enlarged by slashing and spreading; they are reduced by tucking. Variation in contour size or bulge location can be fitted by both methods; however, subtle contour variations are best fitted three-dimensionally. A spline can be used as an aid to determining seam-line shape when fitting two-dimensionally, although it is generally easier to relate pattern perimeter shape to body form when fitting directly on the body. Misfits created by asymmetrically located contours or structural imbalance are readily corrected three-dimensionally.

Before making that first fearful slash into the fabric, it can be very useful to know how a similar misfit problem was approached two-dimensionally. A series of drawings on pages 93–100 illustrates the basic fitting procedures necessary to correct the diagnosed misfit through pattern adjustment and garment alteration.

Common adjustment and alteration manipulations include slashing and spreading, tucking, releasing or taking in seams, and reshaping pattern perimeters. Techniques are described below:

1. *Slash and spread* makes it possible to enlarge a garment through changes that increase length, width, or circumference. First the pattern or garment is slashed and spread the desired amount. Then tissue paper or muslin strip inserts are taped or pinned in place to maintain the change. When increasing length, keep center front and back or grain lines aligned so the pattern maintains its character.

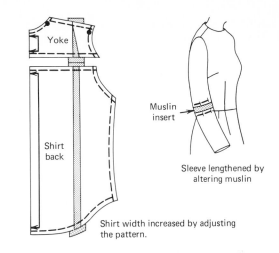

Shirt width increased by adjusting the pattern.

Sleeve lengthened by altering muslin

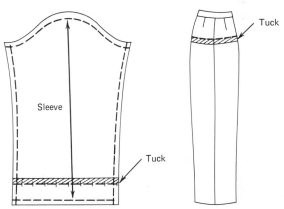

Join the broken seam lines, tapering shaped seam lines.

2. *Tucking* permits reduction of the garment through changes that decrease length, width, or circumference. Pleat the pattern the desired amount. Note that the depth of the tuck

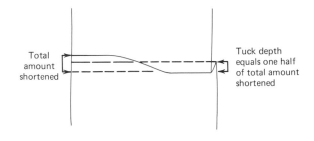

Total amount shortened

Tuck depth equals one half of total amount shortened

is always equal to one-half of the total change. Tape or pin. Join the broken seam lines, tapering shaped seam lines.

3. *Letting out or taking in the seams* changes the garment size at the perimeters of the pattern pieces. Seam-line fitting changes are less desirable than internal fitting changes, since they alter the seam line and pattern perimeter and may easily destroy their character. In addition, the seams should not be let out or taken in more than 6 mm (¼ in). To adjust, the seams are redrawn as needed; to alter, the seams are released and pinned as needed.

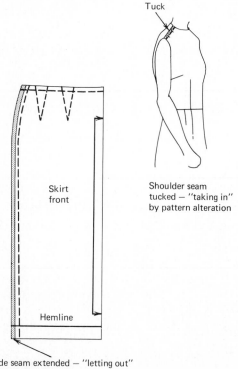

Shoulder seam tucked — "taking in" by pattern alteration

Side seam extended — "letting out" by pattern adjustment

This method can be used in combination with slashing and spreading or tucking when variable amounts of change are needed to fit the body. For example, the waist may require a 6-mm (¼-in) change while the hips require a 1.3-cm (½-in) change. A 6-mm (¼-in) internal change can be made along the length of the garment. The garment can also be let out at the side seams, with the allowance tapering from the waist to the hip and downward to the hem.

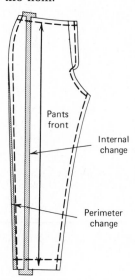

4. *Reshape pattern perimeters* to improve seam angle or curve correspondence with body angles and contours. The spline can be used

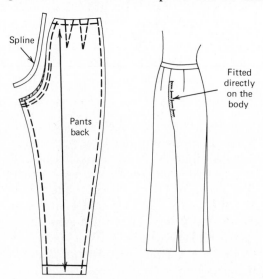

to reshape the seams of the two-dimensional pattern (e.g., crotch, hip curve). These seams, however, are more easily reshaped when fitting directly on the body.

FITTING MANIPULATIONS

Alteration techniques also include the following fitting manipulations:

1. *Regular and irregular ellipse-shaped* changes are usually made in concave body areas or between convex body curves. The alteration is located completely within the pattern body; it does not change the pattern perimeter dimensions. This will cause the perimeter to change subtly in shape and result in the needed fit change.

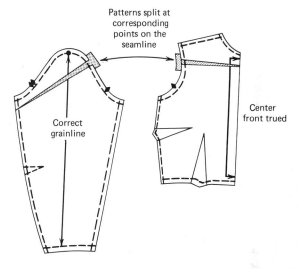

Alteration transferred to the pattern

Patterns split at corresponding points on the seamline

Correct grainline

Center front trued

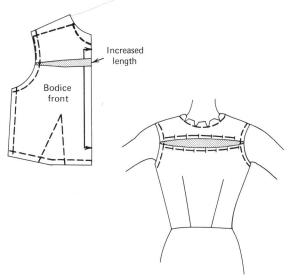

Increased length

Bodice front

Both these alterations must be *refined* to flatness in the pattern before the pattern can be used to cut out the garment. (See page 104 for refinement instructions.)

PRINCIPLES OF PATTERN ADJUSTMENT

Follow these guidelines when adjusting your pattern:

2. *Wedges or ellipse-shaped* changes may intersect a seam or dart as they extend from one quadrant of the body to another. In this way the pattern area, perimeter length, and perimeter shape are changed. For example, an ellipse-shaped spread from sleeve cap to bodice front fits a fleshy upper arm.

1. Retain the character of the pattern pieces so that the designer's intended style is maintained. Making pattern adjustments internally reduces the chances of distorting the pattern edges.

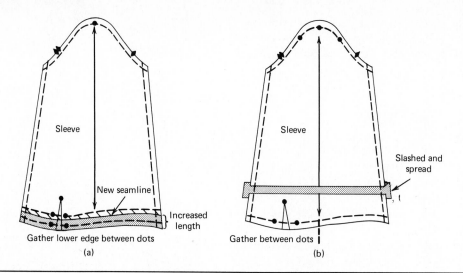

(a)

New seamline

Increased length

Gather lower edge between dots

Sleeve

(b)

Sleeve

Slashed and spread

Gather between dots

2. When a fitting change intersects a seam line, adjust the adjoining pattern piece(s). When the bodice front is lengthened, the front facing and the bodice back must also be length-ened. Lay the minor pattern piece over the corresponding major pattern piece and make the same adjustment.

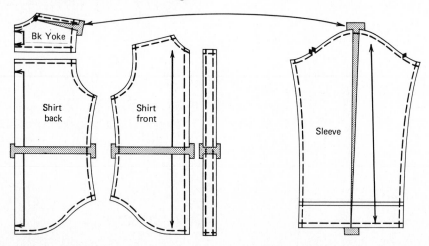

Bk Yoke

Shirt back

Shirt front

Sleeve

3. To enlarge a pattern piece, slash and spread it the desired amount. Insert paper strips and tape in place using frosted transparent tape. True in the lines over the tape. To reduce a pattern piece, tuck it one-half the desired amount and tape closed.

4. The final adjusted pattern must lie perfectly *flat*. Make adjustments on a penetrable sur-face (e.g., cork, Celotex, etc.) so that the changes can be pinned flat before they are taped in position.

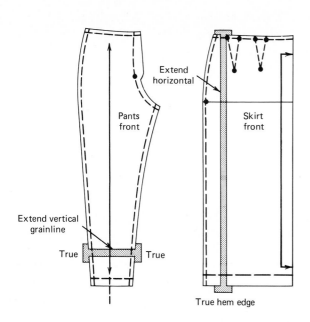

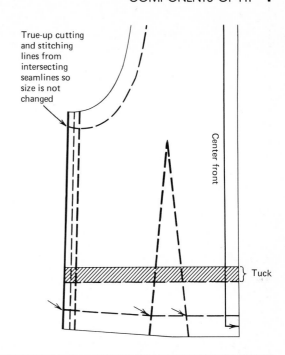

5. When pattern perimeter seam lines are relocated, be sure to add regulation seam allowances beyond the stitching line.

6. Dart legs and corresponding seams should be equal in length and similar in character. Style seams are exceptions.

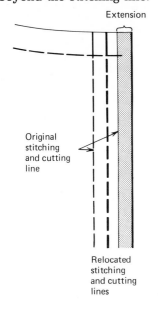

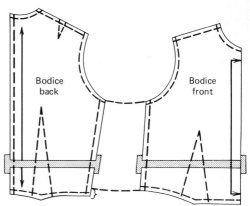

ERROR: The back side seam is longer than the front side seam. The pattern must be remeasured and readjusted to ensure equal seam length.

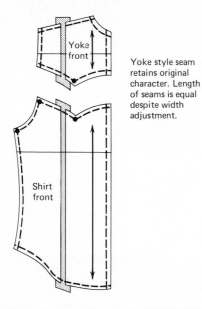

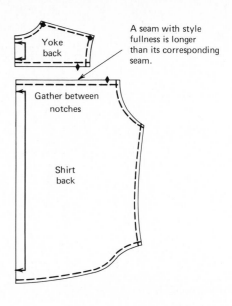

Yoke style seam retains original character. Length of seams is equal despite width adjustment.

A seam with style fullness is longer than its corresponding seam.

Gather between notches

7. The grain line in the less fitted portion of the pattern is extended for the pattern's length and used as a guide for pattern layout.

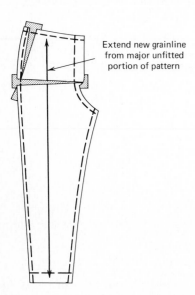

Extend new grainline from major unfitted portion of pattern

8. Avoid making changes through a set of notches or darts. Make the change above or below these pattern markings. This is critical in the armscye seam, where dot and notch location control ease distribution over the upper arm.

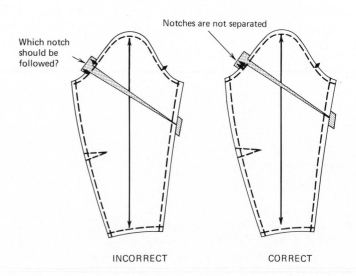

Notches are not separated

Which notch should be followed?

INCORRECT   CORRECT

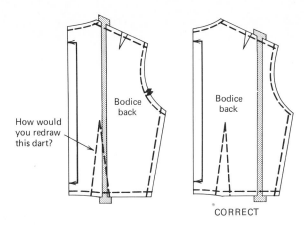

Bodice width can be increased
without intersecting a dart

9. A full pattern, including right and left sides, should be made when the changes are asymmetric from side to side.

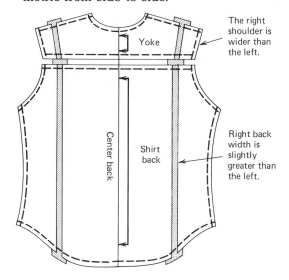

PRINCIPLES OF PATTERN ALTERATION

1. Fit each unit individually, working from the top downward. Join the units and recheck fit. If the test garment is so snug that it cannot be pinned closed, release it at the side seams until the closure can be pinned shut on the seamline.

2. First determine the primary cause of the misfit, then make the necessary alteration.

3. To determine the best location for making an alteration, consider how the same problem would be corrected two-dimensionally. There are many similarities between the two methods.

4. To determine the type of fitting change (tuck or slash) to be made, first take a tuck. If the garment lies smooth, this is the correct alteration to make. If the misfit becomes worse, the garment should be slashed and allowed to spread until the problem has been corrected.

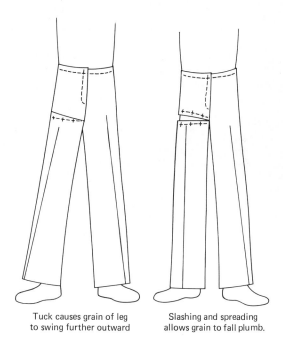

Tuck causes grain of leg
to swing further outward

Slashing and spreading
allows grain to fall plumb.

5. Avoid overfitting. Keep the depth of the tuck or spread to the minimal amount needed to correct the misfit. This also makes it easier to refine the pattern later.

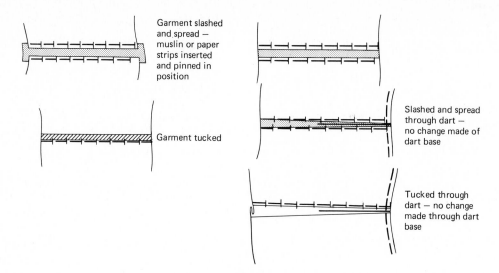

Garment slashed and spread — muslin or paper strips inserted and pinned in position

Garment tucked

Slashed and spread through dart — no change made of dart base

Tucked through dart — no change made through dart base

Length

Parallel Changes

↑ Length

↓ Length

↑ and ↓ Length

↑ Length

↓ Length

↑ and ↓ Length

Alterations

Adjustments

Wedge Changes

Alterations

Adjustments

Width/Circumference

Parallel Changes

↑ Circumference

↓ Circumference

↑ Circumference

↓ Circumference

Alterations

Adjustments

Wedge Changes

Alterations

Adjustments

Ellipse Changes (Bulge-Size Variation)

Alterations

Adjustments

Contour Variation

Dart Direction and Length

Direction:

Length:

Alterations

Adjustments

Divergent Contours (Often Asymmetric)

Alterations

Adjustments

Pattern Perimeter Shape

Shoulder Slope

Alterations

Adjustments

Waist/Hip Curves

Alterations

Adjustments

Crotch Curve

Alterations

Adjustments

6. Several small changes often provide better fit and are also easier to refine than a few large-scale alterations.

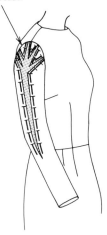

Several narrow spreads are easier to refine than one or two large spreads.

7. When fitting the pattern garment, do not let the center front or center back of the pattern pull in to fit the hollows between the breasts or shoulder blades. Place a pencil across any hollows to check.

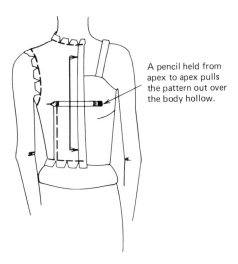

A pencil held from apex to apex pulls the pattern out over the body hollow.

8. Although ellipse-shaped changes are more difficult to refine to flatness, they provide a higher level of fit.
9. Retain the character of the pattern pieces so that the designer's stylistic intention is maintained.

PATTERN REFINEMENT

Altered patterns must be refined to flatness before they can be used to cut out the fabric sections. *Pattern refinement* refers to the methods used to flatten a pattern altered directly on the body. The ellipse-shaped tucks are most difficult to refine because they involve pointed and curved shapes. Refinement also connects and trues any stitching lines broken or bent by altering.

Procedures

Before removing the altered garment from the body, check it to be sure all changes are well marked, including depth of change and termination points. Leave in all pins or basting stitches used to maintain the alterations. If the alterations are simple parallel changes (tucks or spreads), carefully measure their location and depth and transfer them to the tissue pattern. Do remove any pins or basting used to hold the garment structure together, including darts, tucks, pleats, and seams.

Rule a straight line on fresh tissue paper. Position the altered pattern over the line with the center-front line, center-back line, or the grain line (sleeves, pant legs) following it. If the pattern lines are bent inward, connect the end points to form a straight line.

Carefully begin to smooth the pattern outward from the ruled line. Working from this line, attempt to extend the pattern perimeter to its maximum. Pin in place. To do this, you may first need to:

1. *Work through nearby darts* by:
   a. Partially folding out the dart wedge (reducing dart angle) or eliminating the dart.

   OR

   b. Slashing and spreading through the dart wedge (increasing dart angle) or adding a new dart.
   Distribute the change through several darts if possible. True up dart stitching lines.

   OR

2. *Work through fitted areas* by:
   a. Slightly increasing the width of a slash without changing its maximum width.

   OR

   b. Slightly increasing the length of a slash.

   OR

   c. Slightly decreasing the width or length of a tuck.

Continue to settle and flatten the pattern.

3. *Flatten ellipse-shaped alterations* by:

1. Slightly decreasing the width or length of a tuck.
2. Working through dart wedges, as discussed above.
3. Making several slashes perpendicular to and through the alteration. This retains the fitting change while adding a small amount of extra length or width to the pattern.
4. Introduce a seam or dart along a fitting change location (e.g., french dart, yoke).

Once the pattern has been flattened and pinned securely, tape down the changes. True the pattern by connecting the broken stitching lines of darts and seams. Retain their original linearity or circularity when possible. Draw in any changes in perimeter seam shape. Straight lines should be ruler straight; curved seams should curve smoothly. Extend grain lines from an unaltered portion of the pattern into the altered portion. Corresponding seams should be equal in length.

Refine any appending pattern pieces (e.g., collar, cuffs, facings, waistbands, etc.) to correspond with the major unit alterations. Changes should equal the amount and location of the primary alteration. Changes in the torso armscye require an equivalent change in the sleeve armscye. Alter the sleeve at the same location but perpendicular to the armscye seam.

Test-check the refined pattern fit by tracing it, pinning together, and trying it on. The pattern form should correspond smoothly with the body form. Make any necessary changes and transfer them to the pattern.

CRITERIA FOR EVALUATION

FIT

To insure quality performance, check to see that:

__ **1.** *Grain* is balanced horizontally and vertically at garment reference points.

__ **2.** Garment *ease* provides for easy movement, but garment is neither too snug nor too lose.

__ **3.** Garment *sets* smoothly without horizontal or diagonal wrinkles or taut areas. Ease is evenly distributed.

__ **4.** Garment structural *lines* follow corresponding body contour lines and joint locations.

__ **5.** *Balance* is achieved through central location of body within the garment.

9 Fabric Preparation

OBJECTIVE

To prepare your fabric for pattern layout by preshrinking, straightening, and trueing it as determined by its fiber content, weave, and washability.

Once fabric and pattern are purchased, the desire to proceed quickly to cutting out the fabric and constructing the garment is understandable. It is exhilarating to be caught up in the excitement of creating a new garment. Unfortunately, one must slow down a bit and take several preliminary steps to ensure that the completed garment will perform satisfactorily. A garment that shrinks or hangs unevenly after laundering is an unpleasant surprise.

To prevent any unwanted surprises, three procedures must be followed in preparing the fabric for cutting. They include:

Preshrinking
Straightening
Trueing

Preshrinking eliminates possible fabric shrinkage and reduction of garment size after construction. Laundering or steaming the fabric allows the fabric yarns to relax into their natural positions and removes any sizing applied to the fabric for body.

Straightening and *trueing* are two procedures used to even fabric ends and to correct the grain alignment of woven and knitted fabrics. Before the pattern sections can be cut out, the lengthwise and crosswise yarns must form right angles with one another. This ensures that the completed garment will retain its balance in hanging on the body.

Preshrinking

Woven and knitted fabrics are capable of shrinking the first time they are cleaned. Natural fibers are particularly susceptible, but synthetics can also shrink.

Generally, it is good practice to preshrink all fabrics before cutting out the fabric sections. The process used commonly follows the procedures for laundering or dry cleaning recommended on the care label.

SHRINKAGE TEST-CHECK

The preshrinking process can be eliminated if the fabric can pass a test check. To *test-check* for possible shrinkage, follow these procedures:

1. Thread baste a 15-cm (6-in) square several centimeters away from fabric edges, following grain lines.
2. Place a damp press cloth over the square and press several times with a hot iron. Be careful not to melt heat-sensitive fabrics. Allow the square to dry undisturbed.
3. Remeasure the square. If it has decreased by 3 mm (⅛ in) in either direction, the fabric must be preshrunk.

If the fabric will be preshrunk, follow the preshrinking procedures applicable for washable or nonwashable fabrics.

PRESHRINKING WASHABLE FABRICS

Wash and dry the fabric following the care instructions provided. Use the same water and drying temperature to be used later to launder the completed garment.

PRESHRINKING NONWASHABLE FABRICS

Two methods can be used to preshrink nonwashable fabrics. Before using either process, straighten and true the fabric following the procedures beginning on page 108. Fold the fabric in half lengthwise with straightened ends together. Hand- or machine-baste the ends together about 2.5 cm (1 in) from the cut edge.

1. *London Method*
   a. Baste the selvages together, if desired, to keep them even.
   b. Fold a wet sheet so that it is slightly wider and about 30.5 to 46 cm (12 to 18 in) longer than the fabric. Spread it out on a flat surface.
   c. Center the fabric over the sheet.
      Fold one extended sheet end over the fabric. Continue folding the two layers together so that the damp sheet touches each layer of wool.
   d. Wrap the rolled fabrics in plastic and allow them to rest until the inner fabric is damp. This may take from about six hours to overnight.
   e. Remove the fabric from the sheet. Spread it out on a flat surface, trueing it so that it will dry in a grain-perfect position. Do *not* hang the fabric to dry, as it may stretch out of shape.
2. *Dry-Clean Method*
   This method may be used for all nonwashable fabrics.

a. Take the prepared fabric to a reputable dry cleaner.
b. Provide the dry cleaner with these instructions:
   (1) Dry clean the fabric.
   (2) Have the presser true (square up) the fabric grain alignment when it is steam-pressed. *Indicate that the folded edge must not be pressed.*

Yarn Alignment: Straightening and Trueing

As indicated earlier, perfect fabric grain alignment is crucial to the balance of the garment on the body. To determine whether the fabric yarns are in alignment, certain general fabric characteristics must be understood. If necessary, review the discussion of fabric selection in Chapter 2. A fabric is considered *on grain* when the lengthwise and crosswise yarns lie perpendicular to one another throughout the fabric length. If the pattern is cut from off-grain fabric, it may be difficult to fit the garment so that it hangs symmetrically on the body.

Fabric ends must be straightened *before* the fabric can be trued. Fabrics treated with a resin finish *cannot* be trued; therefore it is also not necessary to straighten them. They should, however, be preshrunk.

STRAIGHTENING

All fabrics must be straightened prior to trueing to:

1. Determine whether the fabric is already grain-perfect.
2. Determine whether steps must be taken to perfect (true) the grain alignment.

Fabric ends are *straight* with the grain when a crosswise yarn can be pulled freely across the fabric width.

Begin by examining the fabric ends. The fabrics may have been cut or torn when purchased. Fabric that has been torn should already be straight with the crosswise grain. Check by pulling a crosswise thread. If it pulls away freely, the fabric end is straightened. Both ends must be straightened.

If the fabric end is not straight with the grain, select one of the following three methods to straighten *woven* fabrics. A technique for straightening *knits* is given on page 109.

Tearing

Only firmly woven fabrics should be torn. Snip into the selvage of the edge that is least off grain. Pull the fabric firmly on both sides of the clip until it tears; continue tearing until the sections separate at the opposite selvage. If they separate midway, clip again and repeat tearing process.

Cutting Along a Prominent Filling Yarn

When a filling yarn is readily visible, the fabric may simply be cut from selvage to selvage following a crosswise yarn. Distinctive crosswise yarns are easily found where there are woven horizontal stripes or variations in yarn diameter.

Pulling a Filling Yarn

Examine the fabric end. Begin by gently pulling a filling yarn from the side that is least off grain.

Pull the filling yarn carefully (it breaks easily) until the fabric puckers. Cut along the puckered line to the pulled yarn but without cutting it. Repeat the pulling and cutting process until the opposite selvage is reached.

After completion of any of the above three

methods, one filling yarn should pull across the fabric end from selvage to selvage; this indicates that the fabric is straightened.

Knitted Fabrics

Examine the fabric ends. Since knits do not fray, a yarn cannot be pulled across the end to establish straightness. Instead, the fabric must be examined visually to determine the location of the course, or crosswise row of loops. Run a row of even basting stitches along a course yarn on both fabric ends.

TRUEING

Trueing refers to perfecting the grain alignment of the yarns. When the yarns are *true*, they will be at right angles to one another along the entire length of the fabric.

Some fabrics, however, cannot be trued. These include fabrics with a resin finish and synthetics that have been heat-set.

To determine whether the fabric is true, lay it on a flat table with a corner of the fabric next to the square corner of the table. Place the selvage along the table edge. If the cross-wise edge does not lie even with the end of the table, the fabric is *off grain;* if the ends match exactly, the fabric is *on grain* and true.

To true off-grain fabric, pull the fabric on the *true bias.* Firmly pull the opposite short corners. If the fabric is very long, two people may be needed to pull the fabric.

Recheck the fabric angle on the table. If it is still not square with the table, repeat the pulling process. Pull the fabric diagonally along its length until the corners are square.

CRITERIA FOR EVALUATION

FABRIC PREPARATION

Check to ensure quality performance:

__ **1.** Fabrics tested for potential shrinkage and preshrunk if necessary, using a method corresponding with the fiber content and accompanying care instructions.

__ **2.** Fabric (without finish) straightened: crosswise ends are even with a filling yarn.

__ **3.** Fabric (without finish) trued: crosswise and lengthwise yarns are perpendicular to one another.

10 Pattern Layout and Cutting

OBJECTIVES

1. To select the most appropriate pattern layout for your fabric's surface texture or pattern.
2. To accurately position the pattern pieces on the fabric for grain alignment and pattern match.
3. To cut out each fabric section with cut fabric edges smooth and with fabric sections the same size as the pattern piece.

Pattern layout refers to placement of the pattern pieces on the fabric before cutting. It is usually a simple process in which the pattern layout specified on the pattern instruction sheet is followed. The process becomes more complex, however, when the chosen fabric is plaid, striped, printed one way, or border printed. In these cases, the layout must be planned carefully to ensure that the fabric design will match at the seams and that the design will look pleasing within the garment style lines and upon the figure. Special layout procedures for fabrics requiring matching are included. The fabric sections are *cut* once the pattern pieces have been positioned accurately on the fabric.

Pattern Layout Procedures

General pattern layout procedures can be followed for most fabrics, including those without nap. These steps include the following:

1. *Select Pattern Pieces.*
   Refer to the section of the pattern instruction

sheet that illustrates the pattern pieces. The pattern pieces are named, coded, and often grouped by garment type or view. Pull out only the pattern pieces needed; return the remaining pieces to the envelope.

2. *Examine Pattern Pieces.*
Notice that the pattern pieces are made only for the *right* half of the body. Coverage for both sides of the body is provided by cutting out the garment sections on a *double* fabric layer.

Smaller pattern pieces such as facings, pockets, and cuffs are often grouped on a single piece of pattern tissue so that they will not be lost. Cut these apart.

3. *Note Number of Fabric Sections to Be Cut.*
Make a mental note of the *number of fabric sections to be cut* from each pattern piece. Two fabric sections are commonly cut from each pattern piece in order to cover both sides of the body or to face a garment appendage, such as a collar. One fabric section may be cut for a piece such as an unlined pocket or for part of an asymmetric garment. At other times four sections may be needed, as in the cases of self-faced cuffs or two lined pockets.

4. *Prepare the Pattern.*
It is not *necessary to trim* the extra tissue from around the pattern. However, it can be trimmed away if there is a great deal of it.

Smooth out the pattern pieces by hand. Press *only* if the pieces are extremely wrinkled; use a warm *dry* iron to avoid shrinking the pattern.

Extend the pattern grain lines the length of the pattern.

5. *Adjust the Pattern.*
If it has not yet been done, fit the pattern by following the procedures described in Chapter 8, "Components of Fit." Check to be sure that all corresponding pattern pieces, such as facings, have been adjusted.

6. *Lay Out the Pattern Pieces.*
a. Select the pattern layout for the garment or view, pattern size, fabric width, and fabric type (with or without nap).
b. *Fold the fabric* by following the diagramed pattern layout for the garment to be constructed. Fold the fabric with either right or wrong sides together, depending upon the type or marking technique to be used or the fabric type. Velveteen pile may adhere to itself; therefore it should be folded with wrong sides together. Place the fabric on a flat surface without letting it hang over the edges.
c. Before pinning the pattern pieces, do a *trial layout* to be sure that there is enough fabric and double-check all the pattern pieces. *Have all corresponding* pattern pieces been adjusted? Remember, if one fabric section is cut the wrong size, there may not be enough fabric to recut it later. Make any necessary changes.

7. *Pin Pattern to Fabric.*
After placing the pattern pieces on the fabric in the desired arrangement, permanently pin the pattern pieces. Follow these steps:
a. To economize fabric yardage, place the pattern pieces close together, without overlapping cutting lines.
b. Position and pin the grain lines first. Align bracketed fold lines with fabric fold. Place long grain lines parallel to fabric selvages by measuring from each end of the grain line to the selvage.
c. Smooth out each pattern piece and insert a pin diagonally in each corner to hold. Fill in with pins inserted parallel (or perpendicular) to cutting lines and about 10 cm (4 in) apart. Place the pins in the seam allowances to avoid marring the fabric. Place the pins closer together if the fabric is slippery; use extra long pins for bulky fabrics.

8. *To interpret* the instruction-sheet layouts, study the following sample layouts, noting any reference to special pattern-sheet instructions such as those shown below.

SAMPLE PATTERN LAYOUTS

Lengthwise Fold

Fold the fabric in half parallel to the lengthwise grain and with selvages even.

Partial Lengthwise Fold

Fold one edge of the fabric parallel to the lengthwise grain. The depth of the fold should be even throughout and is based upon the width of the pattern piece to be cut from the folded area.

Double Lengthwise Fold

Fold both edges along the lengthwise grain parallel to the selvage. The depth of the fold is based upon the width of the pattern piece to be cut from the folded area.

Crosswise Fold or Cut

Notice that this pattern layout includes "special instructions." The fabric must be *cut* in half crosswise. The two sections are then positioned wrong sides together (or right sides together), with the nap or design running in the same direction.

When using a *crosswise fold* layout, only a "without nap" layout can be used.

Various Combinations of Lengthwise and/or Crosswise Folds

Both full and partial lengthwise folds can be used in one layout. The fabric must be cut in two crosswise before the pattern can be laid out using both layouts.

No-Fold Layout

To minimize fabric waste, the fabric is left open. Note that the pattern pieces must be reversed and cut again. To simplify layout, make duplicates of each pattern piece and lay out both at one time.

When Pattern Piece Extends Beyond Fabric

Lay out and pin the pattern pieces to the fabric as shown, leaving space for the extended pattern. Pin the extended pattern on grain, catching only the upper fabric layer. Cut out all but the extended pattern pieces. Open out the fabric; finish by pinning and cutting out the remaining piece(s).

Special Layout Considerations

To ensure that napped and directionally patterned fabrics enhance the garment style lines, special layout procedures must be considered. Those covered include procedures for napped, plaid, striped, printed, knitted fabrics.

NAPPED FABRICS

Loosely defined, *napped* refers to all fabrics that must be cut with the pattern lying in one direction, using the "with nap" layout. They include brushed and shaded fabrics, piles, and small one-way prints. Brushed, shaded, and pile fabrics reflect the light differently depending on the angle at which they are held, thus creating directional shading differences. One-way prints must be cut following the print direction.

Cut napped and pile fabrics with *wrong* sides together, so that the fabrics will not cling to each other. If a crosswise *fold* layout is suggested, change to a crosswise *cut* layout with the fabric layers arranged directionally.

Short naps and piles include brushed denim, flannel, wool, corduroy, velour, and velvet. Cut these fabrics with the nap running *upward* for richer color, downward for a lighter effect. To determine the nap direction, rub your palm up and down over the fabric lengthwise. You will feel resistance in the upward direction and smoothness in the downward direction.

Shaded fabrics, such as satins and iridescents, may also reflect light differently. Therefore these fabrics should be cut in one direction following a "with nap" layout.

One-way printed fabrics must be cut with the design following the same (usually upright) direction.

FABRICS THAT MUST BE MATCHED

Fabrics such as plaids, stripes, large prints, and one-way designs pose several problems in both layout and construction that are not encountered with solids or small prints. The placement of the design both on the figure and within the seam lines of the garment is crucial. If a large floral design is placed over a body bulge or if it is cut up by too many seam lines in the design, neither the fabric, the design, nor the individual proportions are being aesthetically considered.

Placement of the design pattern must be considered fully *before* the fabric is purchased, since *extra fabric* is usually needed to achieve a balanced and matched design. The computed fabric yardages on the pattern envelope do *not* include enough fabric to match plaids or other special fabric designs. Fabric quantities are indicated only for fabric layouts with or without nap. Because there is so much variability between fabric pattern sizes, the pattern company cannot estimate the additional fabric needed for each fabric design that might be matched. Generally, the additional fabric quantity is based upon the size of the match or repeat and the number of pattern lengths to be cut.

Pattern *repeat* refers to the distance from a given point on one design unit to the same point on the next identical design unit, whether in a crosswise or lengthwise direction.

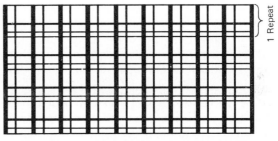

Plaid Fabric

Plaids

Plaid designs add an additional dimension to the construction of many garments. Their design consists of bars of similar or varying width that intersect at 90-degree angles. Variations in bar color, size, and contrast produce both subtle and bold patterns.

When selecting a plaid, avoid garment designs with many seam lines that may break up the lines of the design. Keep the size of the plaid in *scale* with both the garment silhouette and the individual wearing it. A large plaid on a small figure can be overwhelming.

For best results, plaid fabrics should be used only in styles recommended by the pattern company for plaids. Generally, if the pattern envelope features an illustration of the design in plaid, the pattern is suitable. If the pattern envelope states "not suitable for plaids," the plaid will not match properly at the seam lines. If the plaid is *printed* onto the fabric (in which case the dyes will be lighter and less even on the wrong side) rather than woven, check carefully to see that the lines of the plaid follow the fabric grain lines. It is not wise to purchase fabric that is printed off grain: the fabric will not match if cut on grain, not will it hang evenly if the design is matched, as it will then be cut off grain.

Determining Yardage for Plaid Fabrics

1. *Consider Plaid Type: Even or Uneven*
   An *even plaid* is one in which each quarter of the unit is identical with every other quarter. Examine the plaid sketched here. The lengthwise and crosswise lines are identical in size and spacing for each quarter of the plaid.
   If a plaid is even, it will not necessarily have square units. An even plaid may have rectangular units if the corners are identical. When the plaid is even, the pattern pieces may be arranged with the upper edge of the pattern pieces running in either direction, a "without nap" layout. This is because the upper and lower halves of the units are identical.
   Uneven plaids are unusual because they are composed of a greater variety of stripes in both the lengthwise and crosswise directions. Each quarter of the design unit in an uneven plaid may be different, or the plaid may be uneven in only the lengthwise or the crosswise direction. Study the examples of uneven plaids. A plaid is *uneven lengthwise* when the vertical bars are spaced unevenly. The plaid cannot be balanced from the center of the body: *uneven crosswise* plaids have unevenly spaced crosswise bars. Uneven plaids are cut following a one-way or "with nap" layout.
   The type of plaid and the direction of unevenness, if any, can be identified by diagonally folding the fabric through the center of the plaid unit. The bars of an even plaid will match in both directions. The bars of

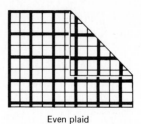

Even plaid

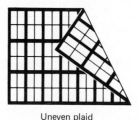

Uneven plaid

Uneven plaid

Plaid Types

an uneven plaid will not match in one or both directions.

2. *Consider Plaid Repeat Size*
   The type of plaid influences the amount of fabric needed, but the *size of the plaid repeat* is also a factor. Large plaid units require more yardage for matching and balancing than do smaller units.

3. *Consider Pattern Lengths*
   A third factor to consider is the number of *lengths* of major pattern pieces required by the cutting guide. By studying the layout that will be used, one can estimate that one additional repeat will be needed for each major pattern piece. Multiply the length of the re-

peat by the number of lengths (minus one length) needed to determine the additional quantity of fabric required.

Even plaids may be cut on the true bias to create a *chevron* (bars meeting at 45-degree angle at seams). To determine yardage for matching bias-cut plaids, lay out the pattern pieces on the fabric prior to purchase.

Preparation for Matching Plaids. Even plaids are relatively easy to match if some general rules are followed. They can also be cut on the true bias to create a chevron.

To prepare the pattern for matching plaids rule in one or two vertical lines parallel to the lengthwise grain line and extending the length of the pattern. Rule a line down the center of the sleeve beginning at the shoulder dot. Rule in two or three horizontal lines perpendicular to the grain line. They should intersect crosswise match points such as the front armscye dot and side seam notches or dots. Include minor pattern pieces such as facings, collars, and waistbands. Use these ruled guidelines to align

the pattern perfectly with the plaid. The ruled lines on the pattern should be parallel with the plaid bars on the fabric.

Prepare the fabric for one of two layout types:

Single thickness layout. For perfection in matching plaids, cut out each pattern piece from the right side of a single fabric layer. Cut out one lengthwise sector of the fabric at a time and mark the fabric sections (see Chapter 11); then remove the pattern tissue. Flip over the cut fabric sections and use them to cut out the other half of the garment. Align them over the plaid, matching vertical and horizontal bars precisely; pin. Cut out carefully without cutting off any of the previously cut piece.

Lengthwise fold layout. Fold the fabric along the lengthwise bar or space that will follow the center of the body. The selvages may or may not meet but will be parallel. To reduce mismatching, intersperse pins throughout the fabric layers to hold identical bars together.

A "without nap" layout can be used, but the "with nap" layout will eliminate the risk of shading variations.

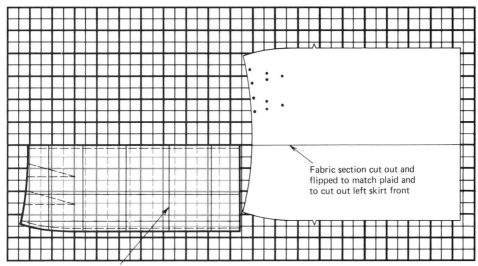

Fabric section cut out and
flipped to match plaid and
to cut out left skirt front

Ruled guidelines are used to
align pattern on the fabric

Matching Guidelines for Even Plaid Layouts.
Once the fabric has been prepared for layout, carefully consider the following procedures for matching:

1. Place a *dominant vertical bar* down the center of the garment *or* space two dominant vertical bars on either side of the garment

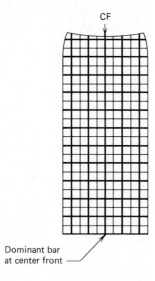

Dominant bar at center front ——

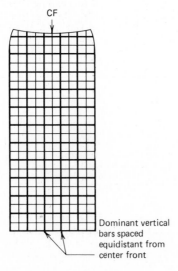

Dominant vertical bars spaced equidistant from center front

Vertical Plaid Bar Placement

center lines. Consider how the dominant lines of the plaid units will meet at side and shoulder seams before you decide which bar or space location to use.

Layout Procedure: Position the pattern pieces with the centers (fold or seam lines) of tops, shirts, dresses, skirts, pants, jackets, and sleeves following the *center* of a dominant bar or space. Do not pin in place yet.

2. Place the *dominant horizontal* bar so it ends at each *hemline* (not cut edge) and is completely visible.

Layout Procedure: Reposition pattern pieces so that the lower edge of a dominant horizontal bar falls even with the hemline.

3. For visual continuity, the *crosswise bars* of the plaid must match at vertical seams. Always match crosswise bars at *seam lines*—not cutting lines.

Layout Procedure: To aid in matching *crosswise seams*, place the pattern pieces so that corresponding notches and symbols lie at the *same point* on the same *crosswise lines*. Use the ruled-in horizontal guidelines to align the pattern with the bars. Consider the following match points:

For *shirts, jackets, and bodices,* match the plaid at the side seam beginning at the hemline or waistline. If there is an underarm dart, the plaid will not match above it. Consider how the plaid will fall over the hip or chest area. De-emphasize these areas by placing the subtle horizontal bars over them. If this garment unit is to be worn with a plaid skirt or plaid pants, the spacing between dominant crosswise lines must be maintained for a smooth transition from the upper to the lower unit.

For *waistline seams,* match the plaids of the bodice and skirt from center front to the first dart or tuck.

Match the side and center seams of *pants* and *skirts* for the entire seam length.

Match *sleeves* to the torso armscye notch

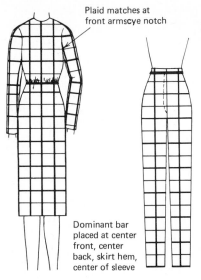

Plaid matches at front armscye notch

Dominant bar placed at center front, center back, skirt hem, center of sleeve

Bars match at center front waistline, side seams, front armscye notch, hem, crotch seam, inseam

Skirt side seam

at the *front seam line*. Sleeves match only in the front.

For a *collar*, match the center back of the collar with center back of the bodice. Plan the horizontal bars at the *finished* lower edge of the collar to match the bars they touch on the bodice. The collar may also be aligned so the center of the design unit is at the center of each collar point.

Match Points

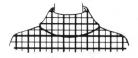

Collar points may match in front.
Center back of collar must match garment

---

4. For *chevron* layouts, even plaids can be cut on the true bias so the bars of the plaid meet at identical 45-degree angles at a seam.

    To adapt a pattern, redraw the grain lines at 45-degree angles to the lengthwise grain lines. Layout on a single fabric thickness is simplified if *reverse* duplicates of each front and back pattern are made. All pattern pieces can then be laid out on the fabric at once. In positioning pattern pieces, consider

Bias-cut skirt with chevron at center front seam

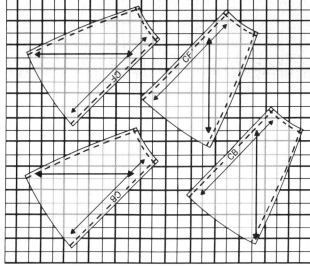

Chevron Layout

location of dominant plaid lines on the body and matching units at the seam lines. The dominant lines usually point upward at the center and downward at the sides.

Matching Guidelines for Uneven Plaid Layouts. Uneven plaids are matched using essentially the same method as with even plaids, although they are somewhat more difficult because the outlines of each unit are not as easily recognized. Uneven plaids present these additional problems:

1. As with even plaids, all crosswise bars can be matched. With uneven plaids, however, it is important to place the heavier or darker, more prominent half of the unit near the lower garment edges.
2. Uneven lengthwise plaids are visually balanced across the body by spacing the most dominant vertical bars to each side of the body centerline. Less dominant vertical bars are not equally spaced.
3. Uneven plaids are cut out following the "with nap" layout. They may be cut using a length-

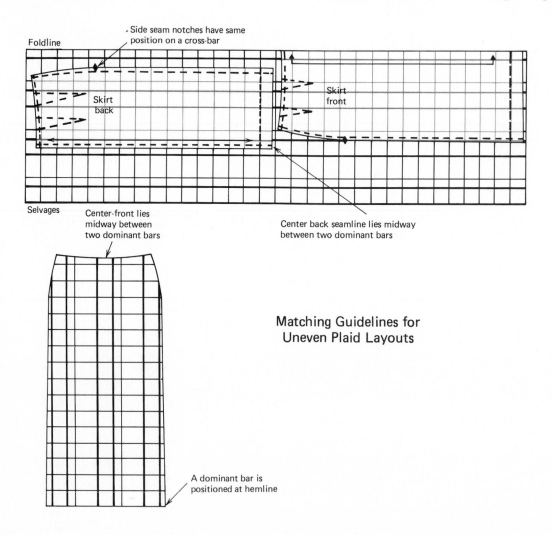

Matching Guidelines for
Uneven Plaid Layouts

wise fold or a single-thickness layout. Fold the cloth lengthwise midway between two dominant vertical bars.

When using a single thickness, follow the procedures used for even plaid layout, page 116. Use the dominant vertical lines to space the plaid on the pattern pieces.

A balanced appearance can be achieved when the fabric is uneven lengthwise, the plaid is woven and reversible, and the design has center seams. To accomplish this, cut out two right sides; then reverse one set to use for the left side.

Checks

Checked fabrics, such as gingham or houndstooth, feature a series of contrasting squares.

The size of the check determines whether checked fabrics should be matched. Checks 6 mm (¼ in) square or larger are usually matched following the procedures listed under even plaids. Smaller checks do not need to be matched because they are less conspicuous in the finished garment.

Stripes

Striped fabrics consist of parallel horizontal or vertical bars. They may vary in width, spacing, and color. The principles for working with stripes also apply to wide-wale corduroy and other obviously wide-ribbed fabrics. Stripes work up best in simple garment styles with few seams to distort the fabric design. If the pattern is marked "not suitable for stripes," it will not allow stripes to be matched properly or its design lines will be spoiled by stripes.

Stripes may be evenly or unevenly spaced. *Even stripes* are equal in width and spacing throughout the fabric. Only two colors are used.

Uneven stripes may vary in width, spacing, and color. If several stripes are grouped together to form a dominant part of the design, they should be treated like one stripe during layout.

Although the method of layout for stripes is basically the same as for plaids, stripes are easier to match because the design runs in only one direction. Guidelines follow:

1. The amount of extra fabric required to match horizontal or uneven vertical stripes depends

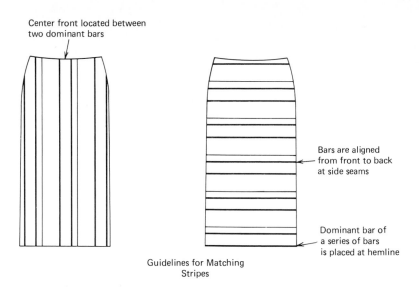

Center front located between two dominant bars

Bars are aligned from front to back at side seams

Dominant bar of a series of bars is placed at hemline

Guidelines for Matching Stripes

upon the size of the stripe repeat and the number of pattern lengths given in the pattern's cutting guide. Refer to the discussion entitled "Determining Yardage for Plaid Fabrics," steps 2 and 3, page 114.

2. Utilize the *dominant vertical stripe* at the centerline or space two dominant vertical stripes on each side of the centerline. Place the *dominant horizontal stripe* near garment hemlines. Avoid placing the dominant stripes over the chest or hip areas.
3. Match *horizontal stripes* at vertical seams; match set-in sleeves at the front-armscye seamline notch.
4. Stripes should generally run in the same direction throughout the garment. However, stripes look best if they follow the shape of smaller garment sections such as cuffs, yokes, bands, collars, and waistbands. For example, a vertically striped shirt should feature a horizontally striped collar, yoke, and cuffs.
5. Whenever possible stripes on a notched collar should match those on the lapel.
6. Buttonholes should follow the direction of the stripes (vertical with vertical). If the stripes are very large, the buttonhole stitches should match the color of the stripe.

Prints

For pattern layout procedures of one-way prints, refer to the discussion of one-way printed fabrics under "Napped Fabrics" on pages 112–113.

Large-Scale Prints. Fabrics with large patterns must be cut in such a way that the two halves of the costume are visually balanced. The same quantity of any one dominant color or the same number of design units must be balanced on each half of the figure, both front and back. The design cannot be mathematically spaced on the figure with the same precision possible with plaid, checked, or striped fabrics, but it must appear visually logical and systematic.

1. Before cutting, hold the length of fabric up to the figure and view the effect from a distance. This will provide a general idea of how the units may be spaced.
2. There will often be several alternatives. Pin the pattern together and test it on the figure to determine the desired hem length. Mark this on the pattern. To simplify design balance and layout, make complete tissue pattern pieces for both sides of the body. Lay out the pattern on a single fabric layer so that you can see the entire expanse of the fabric and ensure better balance of the design on the figure.
3. Begin by laying the pattern front sections in position; then balance all the other sections with the front sections. It is important to balance the design with attention to the effect created by a composite of all the units. Consider how the design flows from one garment section to the next through use of color and pattern scale.
4. There will be losses in width and length on all layouts. *Remember that large-scale designs require extra fabric to compensate for the loss in the lengthwise direction and possibly for losses in width.*

Border Prints. The border print usually runs parallel to one lengthwise edge of the uncut cloth. If a one-way pattern is used, it may limit the position of the border to lower garment edges. If it is not directional, the border might be used at the top of the garment or as a vertical band down the garment length, providing both visual balance on the figure and garment design complexity. Border prints cannot be used if the garment is flared.

CRITERIA FOR EVALUATION

PATTERN LAYOUT

Check to ensure quality performance:

__ **1.** Pattern fitted before layout on fabric.

__ **2.** Pattern pieces arranged with grain lines parallel to warp yarns (lengthwise grain) of wovens and parallel to the wale (lengthwise rib) of knits.

__ **3.** Pattern pieces pinned securely to the fabric to prevent the fabric from shifting, thus ensuring an even cutting line; ballpoint pins used with knits.

__ **4.** Correct number of fabric sections to be cut out are planned for.

__ **5.** For *napped* and *one-way printed* or *shaded fabrics:* Pattern pieces lie in one direction.

__ **6.** For *plaids, stripes,* or *large prints,* pattern pieces are positioned to ensure perfect design match.

Cutting Techniques

Cutting accuracy is necessary in order to construct a garment that precisely duplicates the pattern size and design. The location of almost all seams is based upon the cut fabric edge: unevenly cut edges inevitably result in uneven seam lines and less than perfect fit.
The following are general guidelines to consider when cutting out any pattern:

1. To ensure greater accuracy and to optimize time, cut out all parts of the garment (i.e., garment, interfacing, lining) at the same time.
2. The fabric should lie flat on a large, smooth cutting surface. Avoid shifting the fabric or letting part of it hang over the table edge, as it may then stretch or the grain may shift. Walk around the table rather than moving the fabric.
3. Use *bent-handled shears* rather than scissors because they lift the fabric only slightly above the table, distorting it less. Do not use pinking shears; they make it difficult to determine the exact stitching line during construction. As a result, the seam line may be out of line and the garment may not fit as intended.
4. To *cut* the fabric:
   a. Allow the fabric to lie as close as possible to the table. Do not pick it up with the scissors as it is cut.
   b. Control the fabric next to the edge being cut with one hand. If it creeps, anchor it down or pull it taut parallel to the cutting line. Additional pins may also help control the fabric.
   c. Using even, steady slashes, cut *exactly* on the pattern cutting line. Some patterns will feature an arrow or a pair of shears on the cutting line or seam line, indicating the direction to cut, staystitch, and sew each seam.
   d. Cut *with* the fabric grain to help fabric yarns remain smooth and stretch less.
   e. *Cut notches outward,* not inward, by using the tips of the scissors. To cut a group of notches (two or more notches next to each other), cut around them as a block rather than singly.
   f. Check to be sure each pattern piece has been cut the correct number of times. Pockets, cuffs, and welts often require more than the usual two pieces.
5. Additional cutting tips:
   a. For greater accuracy, cut out very bulky fabrics one layer at a time.
   b. To stabilize thin or slippery fabrics, pin them to sheets of tissue paper before laying out the pattern. Cut, using serrated shears.

CUTTING TECHNIQUES

Check to ensure quality performance:

___ **1.** Fabric sections are cut *exactly* on the cutting line.

___ **2.** Cut edges are smooth and even.

___ **3.** Notches are cut outward; multiple notches are cut together.

___ **4.** Correct number of fabric sections are cut for each pattern piece.

___ **5.** Thin or slippery fabrics are stabilized with tissue paper or by some other means.

54" (140 cm) fabric with or without nap for sizes 12-14-16

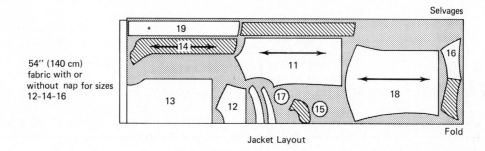

Jacket Layout

11 Marking Techniques

Before the pattern is removed from each cut garment section, construction match points must be marked. *Marking* includes a variety of techniques used to temporarily code pattern symbols onto the cut fabric sections. Marking of the construction match points ensures accurate alignment of fabric sections before the seams are stitched. Garment sections can then be joined as the patternmaker intended.

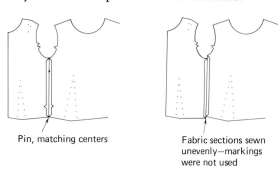

Pin, matching centers   Fabric sections sewn unevenly—markings were not used

Notches are examples of match points marked by cutting out fabric wedge extensions along the cutting line. Because they are located on the cutting line, notches are less accurate than pattern symbols located on the seam line. Therefore they are used primarily to mark straighter, more easily constructed seams. Pattern construction symbols located on seam lines include large and small dots and sometimes squares. Other construction symbols to be marked are location lines. Examples of each type of pattern symbol to be marked include

Dots such as those marking sleeve shoulder ease, gather distribution, darts, tucks, pleats, stitching lines, collar shoulder and center, and center front neckline.

Location lines such as those marking, center front and back lines, fold lines (facing, pleats), pockets, welts, buttons and buttonholes.

Criteria for Selection of Technique

A variety of techniques can be used to mark construction dots and location lines. Several techniques are described in this chapter. Base the choice of marking technique upon these criteria:

- *Accuracy.* The imprint made is small, precise, and remains visible throughout construction.
- *Fabric Type.* Delicate fabrics can be damaged easily, whereas some markings may leave a colored imprint visible through sheer or translucent fabrics. It is often difficult to leave a clear imprint on thick, spongy fabrics or loosely woven fabrics.
- *Fabric Color.* For sheer or translucent fabrics use a marking technique which leaves no color that is similar in color value and can be easily removed after construction. When fabrics are opaque, contrast the marking color with the fabric color for greater visibility.
- *Speed.* Usually, the simpler the technique,

the quicker it can be performed. When time is short, both speed and accuracy are essential.

Review the table entitled "Marking Technique Selection" on page 125 before selecting a marking method.

Marking Techniques

PENCIL-DOT

The pencil-dot method is quick, easy, and extremely accurate. The small dot remains visible throughout construction and can be used to mark a variety of fabrics. The dot is usually not visible on grayed or dark colors, but the sheen of the lead may still show up on the fabric. This method should be avoided on sheer fabrics since the dot may show through to the right side and may be difficult to remove.

Procedures

Cut out the garment sections with the *wrong* sides of the fabric together. Insert straight pins through each dot or square on the pattern. Location lines can be designated by inserting pins several centimeters apart along the line. Remove a few of the pins holding the pattern to the fabric so that the layers can be separated and marked.

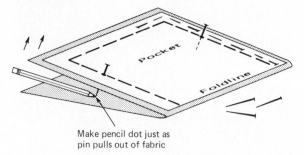

Make pencil dot just as pin pulls out of fabric

Marking Technique Selection

Selection Criteria	Pencil- Dot	Pin and Chalk	Tailor's Tacks	Carbon Tracing	Pins	Clipping
			Marking Techniques			
Accuracy	+	0	0	+	0	−
Fabric type:						
Delicate	0	+	+	−	−	+
Sheer	−	+	+	−	−	+
Spongy	+	0	+	−	+	+
Loosely woven	−	−	0	0	−	−
Fabric color:						
Translucent, similar value	+	+	+	−	+	+
Opaque, contrasting	+	+	+	+	+	+
Multicolor	0	0	+	−	+	+
Speed	+	+	−	0	+	+

Key: + = good choice   0 = neutral choice (dependent upon circumstances)   − = poor choice

Carefully separate the fabric layers, allowing the inserted marking pins to slip out slowly one at a time. Before each pin slips out, have a pencil ready to mark the pin hole. Hold the pencil point directly on the pin insertion point: as the pin slips out, drop the pencil onto the pin hole and pivot lightly. The dot should be light but visible. Repeat the process for the remaining markings, being careful not to let any marking pins slip out.

PIN AND CHALK

White or colored chalk can be used, with the aid of a pin, to make a relatively accurate imprint on the fabric. Avoid wax chalks as they may be difficult to remove from some fabrics. Test colored chalks on translucent fabrics before using them to be sure that they do not show through to the right side. The chalk method is quick and—if removable white chalk is used—can serve to mark a variety of flat-surfaced fabrics including sheers.

Procedures

Insert pins through the centers of pattern dots or squares and at 4- to 5-cm (1- to 1½-in) intervals along location lines to be marked. Remove a few of the pins holding the pattern to the fabric so that the fabric layers can be separated. Remove more pins as needed.

With the pattern side up, slowly separate the fabric layers. As each marking pin begins to slip out of the lower fabric layer, insert another straight pin in its place until all match points are pinned. To mark with chalk, pivot the pin in four directions to form an X. At each pivot point, chalk the fabric over the pin, using the pin ridge to create a fine chalk line. Repeat the chalking process until a chalked X is formed.

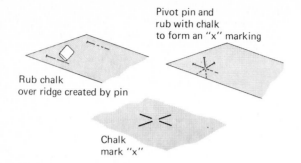

Pivot pin and rub with chalk to form an "x" marking

Rub chalk over ridge created by pin

Chalk mark "x"

two fingers, hold each thread loop in place between the pattern and the fabric; gently pull away the pattern. Small tears will appear in the pattern as the thread loops are pulled through. Separate the fabric layers about 1.3 cm (½ in) at each tailor's tack and cut the thread between the layers.

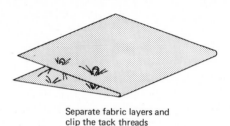

Separate fabric layers and clip the tack threads

TAILOR'S TACKS

Although somewhat less precise and more time-consuming, tailor's tacks can be used on a variety of fabrics when other methods are not suitable. No visible or permanent marks remain on the fabric except when the fabric is one that can be permanently punctured. All marking threads must be carefully inserted and then removed after stitching without cutting the fabric.

Procedures

Use an unknotted double thread in a color contrasting with the fabric. Take a short stitch (6 mm or ¼ in) through the pattern and both fabric layers, centering the stitch over the match point. Draw the thread through, leaving a 3.8-cm (1½-in) thread tail at the beginning. Take a second stitch in the same location, leaving a 2.5 cm. (1-in) loop. Repeat as needed along the line of the dart or other construction details.

DRESSMAKER'S CARBON TRACING

Dressmaker's carbon can be used to quickly trace a colored line on the fabric, designating location or stitching lines or match points. Use the carbon tracing method on flat, firm fabrics and lightweight fabrics if the carbon line will not be visible through to the right side. Delicate, sheer, and spongy fabrics cannot be marked using this method. The colored line may not be easily followed on multicolored fabrics unless enough color contrast can be achieved. If the carbon shows through to the right side or is inadvertently applied to the right side of the fabric, it may leave a permanent line. Purchase dressmaker's carbon, which can be removed by laundering or dry cleaning.

Procedures

Pretest the dressmaker's carbon tracing on a scrap of the fabric, following the same procedures which will be used to mark the garment. Choose a carbon color that contrasts little with the fabric color yet is still visible and test using a tracing wheel to imprint the fabric. In addi-

Make tailor's tacks directly through pattern markings

2.5 cm loop

3.8 cm tails

Tailor's tack

Before removing the pattern from the fabric, cut the thread between each tailor's tack without cutting the loop. Unpin the pattern. Using

tion, press the fabric to determine the effects of heat and steam on the carbon line.

To prepare the fabric for a carbon tracing, remove a few pins from the pattern so the carbon paper can be placed inside. Fold the paper with the carbon sides out if the garment has been cut with wrong sides together; insert the carbon paper around the fabric layers with the pattern on top. The carbon must be placed against the *wrong* side of the fabric. Both of the wrong sides of the fabric are marked at the same time.

To use the tracing wheel, place a straight edge along the pattern stitching or location lines to be marked. Position the tracing wheel next to the straight edge and roll it along the line being marked, using light to medium pressure. Excess pressure can puncture the fabric or leave a carbon imprint on the right side.

Use the tracing wheel to mark stitching lines within the fabric section for such elements as darts, tucks, or pleats and location lines for pockets or flaps. Mark dots or squares by intersecting two short lines across the center to form an X. Before removing the carbon, check to be sure that both fabric layers have been marked.

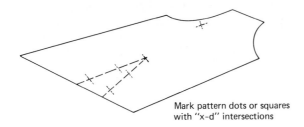

Mark pattern dots or squares with "x-d" intersections

PINS

Pins temporarily inserted at match points provide a quick, easy method for marking all fabrics except those that can be permanently punctured or are slippery. Unfortunately, if the pin falls out, the marking location is lost.

Insert pin through pattern marking

Flip over pattern and fabric; insert pin through same marking

Procedures

Insert pins into the centers of pattern dots or squares and through both fabric layers. To mark location lines, insert the pins at intervals along the line. Flip the pattern-fabric layers over so that the pattern is lying on the table and the pins are pointing upward. Insert a second pin through the fabric and pattern at the exact location of the previously inserted pin.

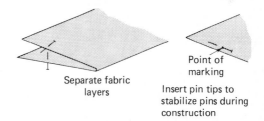

Separate fabric layers

Point of marking

Insert pin tips to stabilize pins during construction

Turn the pattern-fabric layers back to their initial position with the pattern on top. Unpin the pattern and carefully remove it without removing the marking pins. Small holes are made in the pattern as the pinheads are pulled through it. Separate the fabric layers gently and insert the pins fully into the fabric to avoid losing them. Handle the fabric sections carefully to avoid losing the pins before the marking is needed during construction.

CLIPPING

Match points can be marked simply by clipping into the seam allowance a short distance. The clipping method cannot be used in areas of intricate construction because it is less accurate than other techniques. It cannot be used to mark loosely woven or easily frayed fabrics as such clips could easily be lost. Other marking techniques must be used for curved location lines and match points located within the pattern section.

Procedures

Clip into the seam allowance at a point perpendicular to the match point. Avoid cutting into the seam line by taking short 3-mm (⅛-in) cuts using the tips of the shears.

Clipping can be successfully used at the sleeve-cap shoulder dot, at center-front and center-back location lines, at fold lines, and at the beginning of a dart, tuck, or pleat on the cutting line.

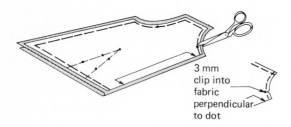

3 mm
clip into
fabric
perpendicular
to dot

CRITERIA FOR EVALUATION
MARKING TECHNIQUES

Check to ensure quality performance:

__ **1.** Method selected is appropriate for the fabric weave, transparency or opaqueness, and color(s).

__ **2.** All match points needed to construct the garment are transferred to the fabric (i.e., dots and placement lines).

__ **3.** Construction match points are transferred precisely to the fabric section from the pattern location.

__ **4.** All markings except thread tacks do not show on the right side of the fabric.

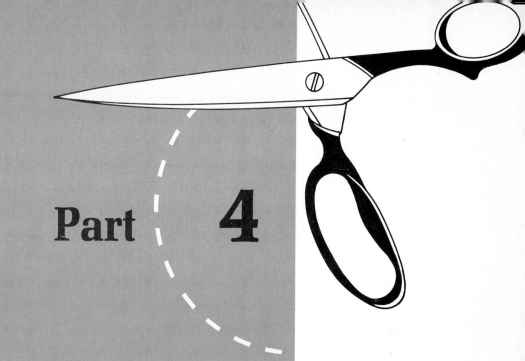

Part 4

Strategies for Construction

What are your tactics for constructing your garment? Do you have a reasonable plan outlined? Have you thought ahead so that unanticipated problems can be solved before they happen? Is your plan efficient? Will it minimize time and maximize quality workmanship? Chapter 12, "Organization and Fitting Strategies" provides two construction plans to enable you to organize your construction and fitting procedures. Both plans produce well-constructed garments. The Unit Construction Plan is easier for a beginning sewer to understand while the Process Construction Plan requires some sewing background. Fitting procedures are incorporated into the construction process so that fabric and construction variables can be taken into account.

Once you have established the construction steps you will follow, stitching and contouring strategies can be developed. Specified instructions have been provided for many commonly used stitches. Although these stitches will usually meet your needs, you may find it necessary to modify a stitch for your fabric or construction problem. Because the variables will change with each project (or portion of a garment), your stitching techniques must also change to deal with them. There is no one correct stitch choice. However, the final choice and its implementation should correspond with and meet your project goals.

Garment contouring can be confronted in the same manner. Survey the inner fabrics and other potential support fabrics available in the fabric shops. Consider their weight, crispness or softness, and their color. Which interfacing type should be used to shape the collar, support the pockets, or create a shoulder shape? The choices may create many different garment contours.

12 Organization and Fitting Strategies

OBJECTIVES

1. To organize construction, fitting and pressing procedures following the organizational strategy that best matches your skill level and maximizes your time.
2. To incorporate three fitting checks in the construction sequence to accommodate fabric hand and fabric handling variations.

Finally, all the preparation is complete! You can now begin to construct your garment. A plan for organizing fitting and construction procedures can help you to make the best use of the total amount of time you will spend completing the garment. It can also ensure a higher level of fit and construction quality.

Organization Strategies

Two organizational strategies—the *unit construction plan* and the *process construction plan*—are presented. Each has advantages and disadvantages. After reviewing each plan, consider which will best meet the needs of your skill level, time allowance, and quality requirements.

Both methods include steps for fitting the garment as it is constructed so that fabric variations are accommodated. Each method can also be varied two ways to meet individual fitting requirements: (1) all stitching lines can be basted and checked for fit *or* (2) only side seams and circumference seams can be basted and checked for fit. The choice between these is dependent upon how confident you are with any previous pattern fitting changes and with the hand of your fabric. If you fitted by comparing your measurements to standard size measurements, you may now wish to correct for any physical variations not accommodated by that method. If you carefully fitted the pattern three-dimensionally and your fabric is relatively stable, you may choose to fit only the side and circumference seams. Fitting changes are examined at the end of this chapter.

UNIT CONSTRUCTION PLAN

The *unit construction plan,* as its name implies, requires the sewer to complete the construction of each individual garment unit before all the completed units are joined together. A garment *unit* comprises a portion of the garment, such as the bodice, skirt, pants, sleeve, or collar. Each of these units may be divided into *subunits,* which are individually constructed before the total unit is joined. Since each unit is constructed separately, garment handling, stretching, wear, and soiling are reduced. This organizational plan makes it easier for the beginning sewer to understand how the fabric sections are joined to form each unit.

Procedures:

1. Separate all fabric and interfacing sections into piles by unit. If necessary, divide each unit into subunits. For a man-tailored shirt, fabric sections are divided as follows:

Unit	Subunit	Fabric Sections
Shirt body	Shirt front	Shirt front, front band and facing, band interfacing
	Shirt back	Shirt back, back yoke, back yoke facing
Collar		Collar, collar facing, interfacing
Sleeve	Sleeve	Sleeve, placket
	Cuff	Cuff, cuff facing, interfacing

2. To prepare each *unit,* complete all construction of each subunit before joining it with another subunit. Follow this sequence for each subunit:
   a. *Staystitch.*
   b. *Apply* any interfacing (or underlining) pieces. Make bound buttonholes now if your garment includes them.
   c. Baste *or* stitch[1] any darts, tucks, pleats, ease, or gathers.
   d. Baste *or* stitch[1] any style seams: center front, center back, princess, yoke, front bands, etc.
3. After each subunit is completed, prepare for the first fitting:
   a. *Baste* shoulder and lengthwise seams.
   b. *Pin baste* circumference seams together to join units (i.e., sleeve to bodice, pants to waistband, collar to neckline); match closure lines and pin.
4. *First Fitting.* Check grain, set, ease, line, and balance.
5. After the first fitting:
   a. *Stitch* and press all seams as approved.
   b. Construct any closures that do not cross into another unit (e.g., pants or skirt zipper, neckline placket).
   c. *Baste* all circumference seams together.
6. *Second Fitting.* Check circumference seam locations.
7. After the second fitting:
   a. *Stitch* and press all seams as approved.
   b. Construct any vertical closures intersecting a circumference seam (e.g., zipper or

---

[1] Whether you baste or stitch these seam lines is dependent upon the fitting method you chose.

button closure crossing the waistline seam of a dress).

8. Prepare for the final fitting by letting the garment hang for 24 hours.
9. *Final Fitting.* Mark the garment hem.
10. After the final fitting:
    a. Stitch in the hem as marked.
    b. Complete all remaining details: buttonholes, buttons, fasteners, trims, etc.
    c. Press the completed garment.

PROCESS CONSTRUCTION PLAN

Construction techniques may also be organized by the construction procedure to be completed. The *process construction plan* enables the sewer to stitch *all* darts or apply *all* interfacings or stitch *all* seams at one machine sitting. Thus each process is performed consistently and quickly. This plan, however, may be more confusing for beginning sewers, because the fabric sections comprising each unit are easily separated and the organization differs from that shown on the pattern instruction sheet. When using this plan, it is a good idea to preview the pattern instruction sheet to catch any variations in the construction order resulting from unusual detailing.

Procedures:

1. *Stay stitch* all fabric sections for all units.
2. *Apply* all interfacing (or underlining) pieces. Make bound buttonholes now if your garment includes them.

3. Prepare for the first fitting:
   a. Baste *or* stitch[2] all darts, then all tucks, then all pleats, etc.
   b. Baste *or* stitch[2] all style seams: center front, center back, princess, yoke, front bands, etc.
   c. *Baste* shoulder and lengthwise seams.
   d. *Pin-baste* circumference seams to join units (e.g., collar to neckline, sleeve to armscye, skirt to bodice, waistband to pants or skirt, etc.).
4. *First Fitting.* Check grain, set, ease, line, and balance.
5. After the first fitting:
   a. Permanently stitch and press (following process method) as approved: all darts, tucks, pleats, etc., all seams.
   b. Construct any closures that do not cross into another unit (e.g., pants or skirt zipper, neckline placket, etc.).
6. *Second Fitting.* Check circumference seam locations.
7. After the second fitting:
   a. *Stitch* and press all seams as approved.
   b. Construct any vertical closures intersecting a circumference seam (e.g., zipper or button closure crossing the waistline seam of a dress).
8. Prepare for the final fitting by letting the garment hang for 24 hours.
9. *Final Fitting.* Mark the garment hem.
10. After the final fitting:
    a. Stitch in the hem as marked.
    b. Complete all remaining details: buttonholes, buttons, fasteners, trims, etc.
    c. Press the completed garment.

[2] Whether you baste or stitch these seam lines is dependent upon the fitting method you choose.

CONSTRUCTING A SHIRT BY THE . . .

Unit Construction Plan:

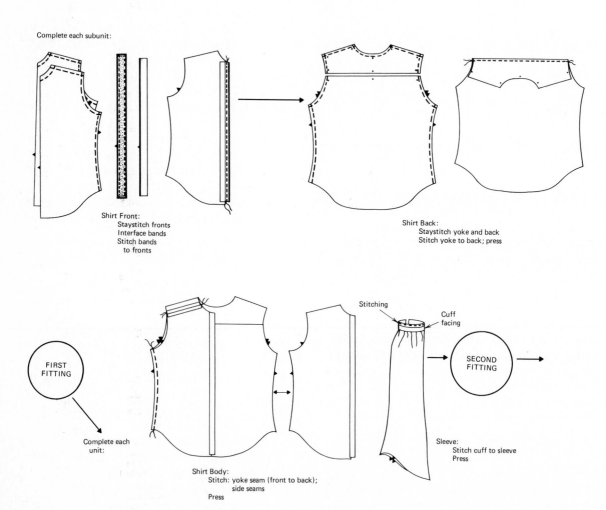

Complete each subunit:

Shirt Front:
  Staystitch fronts
  Interface bands
  Stitch bands
    to fronts

Shirt Back:
  Staystitch yoke and back
  Stitch yoke to back; press

FIRST FITTING

Complete each unit:

Shirt Body:
  Stitch: yoke seam (front to back);
    side seams
  Press

Stitching

Cuff facing

SECOND FITTING

Sleeve:
  Stitch cuff to sleeve
  Press

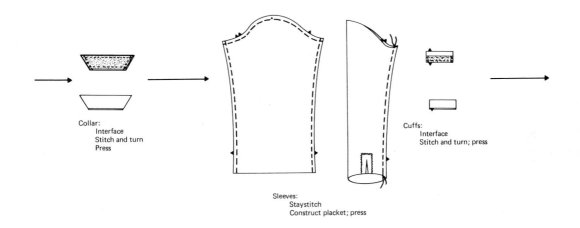

Collar:
    Interface
    Stitch and turn
    Press

Sleeves:
    Staystitch
    Construct placket; press

Cuffs:
    Interface
    Stitch and turn; press

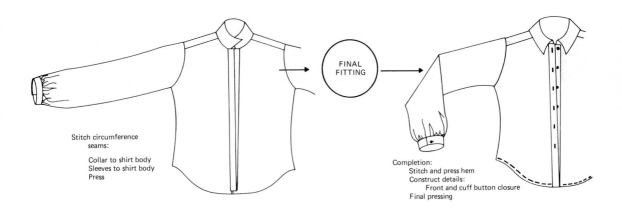

Stitch circumference
   seams:

   Collar to shirt body
   Sleeves to shirt body
   Press

FINAL FITTING

Completion:
   Stitch and press hem
   Construct details:
      Front and cuff button closure
   Final pressing

Process Construction Plan:

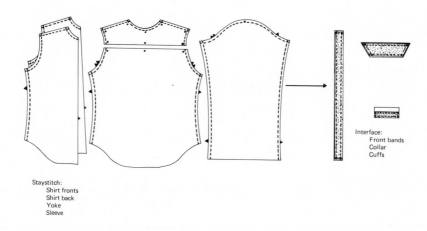

Staystitch:
    Shirt fronts
    Shirt back
    Yoke
    Sleeve

Interface:
    Front bands
    Collar
    Cuffs

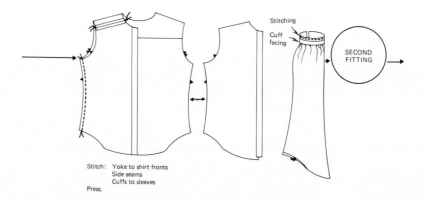

Stitching

Cuff
facing

SECOND
FITTING

Stitch: Yoke to shirt fronts
          Side seams
          Cuffs to sleeves
Press.

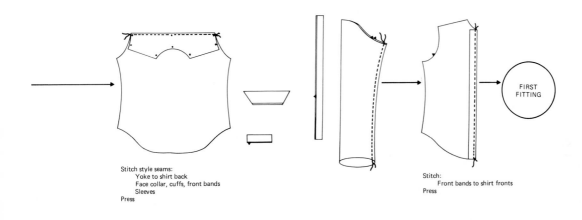

Stitch style seams:
    Yoke to shirt back
    Face collar, cuffs, front bands
    Sleeves
Press

Stitch:
    Front bands to shirt fronts
Press

FIRST FITTING

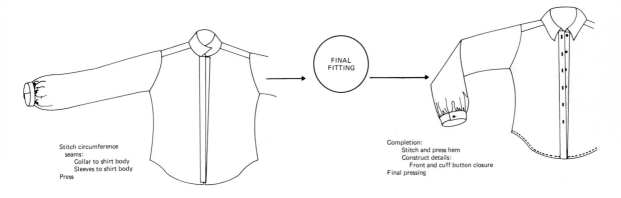

Stitch circumference
  seams:
    Collar to shirt body
    Sleeves to shirt body
Press

FINAL FITTING

Completion:
    Stitch and press hem
Construct details:
    Front and cuff button closure
Final pressing

CONSTRUCTING PANTS BY THE . . . .

Unit Construction Plan:

Complete each subunit:

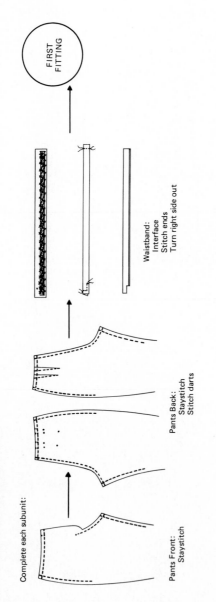

Pants Front:
Staystitch

Pants Back:
Staystitch
Stitch darts

Waistband:
Interface
Stitch ends
Turn right side out

FIRST
FITTING

Complete each leg unit:

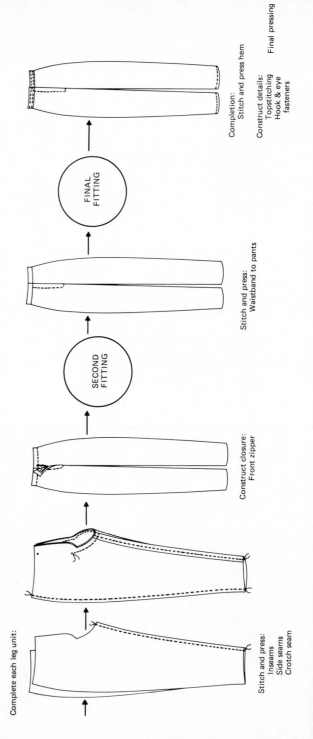

Stitch and press:
Inseams
Side seams
Crotch seam

SECOND
FITTING

Construct closure:
Front zipper

Stitch and press:
Waistband to pants

FINAL
FITTING

Completion:
Stitch and press hem

Construct details:
Topstitching
Hook & eye
fasteners

Final pressing

Process Construction Plan:

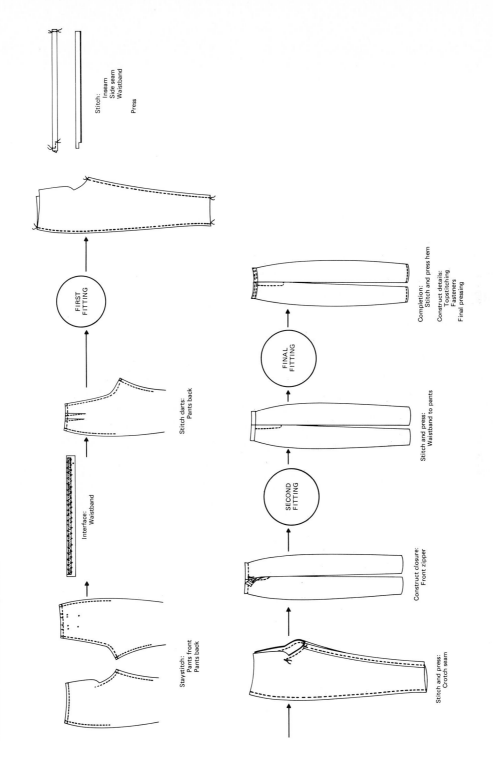

Stitch:
Inseam
Side seam
Waistband

Press

FIRST
FITTING

Stitch darts:
Pants back

Interface:
Waistband

Staystitch:
Pants front
Pants back

FINAL
FITTING

Completion:
Stitch and press hem

Construct details:
Topstitching
Fasteners
Final pressing

Stitch and press:
Waistband to pants

SECOND
FITTING

Construct closure:
Front zipper

Stitch and press:
Crotch seam

CRITERIA FOR EVALUATION

ORGANIZATION STRATEGIES

Check to insure quality performance:
The Construction Plan chosen:

__ 1. Matches your skill level

__ 2. Maximizes your allotted time.

If the *Unit Construction Plan* is followed:

__ 3. The garment fabric sections are properly organized into groups by sub-unit and unit.

__ 4. Construction is organized so that the:
  __ a. Sub-units are constructed and fitted.
  __ b. Units are joined and fitted.
  __ c. Hem is measured and constructed.

If the *Process Construction Plan* is followed:

__ 5. Fitting, stitching, and pressing of like constructions are performed at one sitting.

__ 6. Three fittings are incorporated in the plan.

Fitting Strategies

By fitting the basted garment to the body periodically throughout the construction process, you can preview the appearance of your garment. Since the fabric may drape differently than the paper or muslin pattern you fitted previously, minor fitting changes can be made by altering seam-line locations. Alterations to enlarge are limited by the width of the seam allowance. Changes only up to 6 mm (¼ in) per seam allowance can be made, leaving a minimum seam allowance of 1.0 cm (⅜ in).

Fitting during construction includes three separate surveys: a *first fitting* to check dart locations, vertical seam locations, shoulder angles, and garment circumferences; a *second fitting* to check circumference seam locations; and a *final fitting* to mark hemline locations.

Remember to use the same fit factors discussed in Chapter 8, "Components of Fit," when analyzing your garment's fit. These included grain, ease, set, line, and balance. When making each fitting survey, refer to the following chart for examples of fitting points to check:

Fitting Check Points

Fit Factor	First Fitting	Second Fitting	Third Fitting
Grain	Adjust at shoulder and waist.	Adjust at cap (armscye).	—
Set	Change dart size; Check circumference and vertical ease.	Check sleeve cap and collar.	—
Ease	Check circumference ease.	Check vertical ease.	—
Line	Center front and center back; darts; shoulder, neck, underarms, side, and style seams.	Armscye, wrist, waistline, collar, other circumference seams.	Hems
Balance	Correct with ease and line.	Correct with ease and line.	—

FIRST FITTING

Prepare the garment as directed for the organizational plan you are using. Try the garment on over the same undergarments and shoes you plan to wear with it later. Ask a friend to pin the garment closed, matching closure lines. Working from the top downward, survey the fit. Remember that correcting higher fitting problems first often corrects any fitting discrepancies located below. Your friend should make all the alterations by removing the basting stitches and repinning or basting along the new seam lines. These alterations should be made directly on the body.

First check the *neckline position.* If necessary, clip the seam allowance to the stay stitching to allow the garment to settle into position. If the stay-stitched neckline is still too high or snug, redraw with chalk and clip to just short of this line. If the stay-stitched neckline is too low, redraw the neckline at the higher location, remove old stay stitching, and re-stay-stitch along new line.

Check *dart locations.* They should end 1.3 to 2.5 cm (½ to 1 in) away from the tip of the body bulge. Darts will pucker if they go past the bulge prominence. Lengthen or shorten if necessary. Adjust dart size if it is incorrect for body bulge size.

Check *vertical grain and seam-line* locations, including center front and back, side seams, and style seams. They should hang perpendicular to the floor. Side seams should divide the body visually in half from front to back. If necessary, increase one seam allowance and decrease the other until the seams are balanced.

Check *shoulder seam positions.* Are they straight across the high point of the shoulder? Do they follow the shoulder slope?

Check garment *circumference size.* Is ease adequate across the chest and back and around the waist, hips, thighs, biceps, elbows, and wrists? Is the body centrally located within the

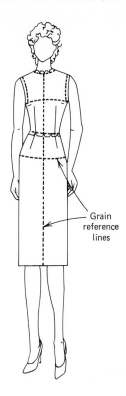

Grain reference lines

First Fitting

garment? Alter the side or underarm seams as needed. Do not make changes in the closure areas or center front and back seams.

Check *circumference seam openings.* Does the neckline comfortably encircle the base of the neck? Does the armscye curve smoothly around the shoulder? The lowest point of the armscye should be about 2.5 cm (1 in) below the armpit.

SECOND FITTING

After the alterations you made for the first fitting have been stitched in, the garment units will be completely constructed. Before they are permanently joined, the circumference seams are checked to ensure that they correspond with body joint locations.

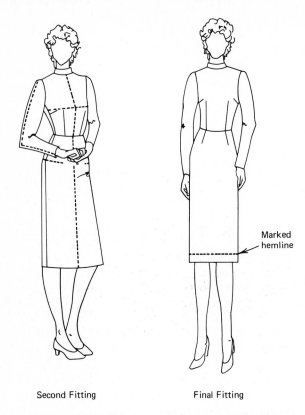

Second Fitting   Final Fitting

Check the armscye seam by examining the *sleeve cap height and ease distribution.* Does the armscye encircle the arm so that arm can move freely?

Check the *collar* stand and roll. Does the collar roll smoothly around the neckline? The collar should hug the back of the neck without gaping. Does the collar apear symmetrical?

Check the *waistline position.* Does it fall at the natural waistline without dipping or rising? Any horizontal wrinkles above the waistline may indicate that the vertical ease is too long for the body.

FINAL FITTING

Nearly all construction has been completed by this point. Allow the garment to hang for 24

hours before you mark the hem length. To determine the hem length, measure from the floor up to the desired level.

When construction is completed re-evaluate the garment's fit using the five Fit Factors of grain, ease, line, set and balance.

CRITERIA FOR EVALUATION

FITTING STRATEGIES

Check to insure quality performance:
FIRST FITTING checks:

__ **1.** Neckline position.

__ **2.** Dart length and position.

__ **3.** Center front and center back markings (or seams) and vertical seams are perpendicular to the floor.

__ **4.** Shoulder seam position.

__ **5.** Circumference size includes adequate ease.

__ **6.** Circumference seam openings: size and position.

SECOND FITTING checks:

__ **7.** Sleeve cap height and ease distribution.

__ **8.** Collar stand and roll.

__ **9.** Waistline position.

FINAL FITTING checks:

__ **10.** Hemline is parallel to the floor.

__ **11.** Recheck the completed garment to ensure that the grain, ease, line, set, and balance are correct.

13 Stitching Strategies

OBJECTIVE

To analyze the requirements of each stitching situation and select the stitch that will best meet the garment area's need for flexibility, strength, and invisibility.

Fine, skillfully made *hand stitches* are symbols of quality in both hand-sewn and ready-to-wear apparel. Temporary basting stitches as well as permanent finishing stitches can set a professionally finished garment apart from an amateur project.

When time is limited or if the garment must meet strict performance standards, as in functional sportswear or work apparel, a *machine stitch* may be a better choice than a hand stitch. Many machine stitches are facsimiles of hand stitches. Although generally very sturdy, machine stitching does not permit the same degree of control when fabric layers are joined that hand stitching does.

Stitches hold two or more fabric layers in a desired position with thread. They may fall into one of four classifications:

Securing stitches hold thread ends in position so that stitches do not pull out.
Temporary stitches hold fabric layers in position during permanent stitching and then they are removed.
Permanent stitches hold fabric layers in position invisibly for the garment's life.

Stitch Classification

Security		Temporary		Permanent		Decorative	
Hand	**Machine**	**Hand**	**Machine**	**Hand**	**Machine**	**Hand**	**Machine**
Fastening	Backstitching	Even basting	Machine basting	Exposed catch stitch	Regulation machine stitches[1]	Saddle stitch	Machine topstitching
Knotting	Knotting	Uneven basting		Unexposed catch stitch	Zigzag[1] Machine padding	Pick stitch	
		Diagonal basting		Tailor's hemming stitch	Machine buttonhole[2]		
		Slip basting		Blind/slip stitch			
				Felling stitch			
				Whip stitch			
				Back stitch			
				Prick stitch			
				Padding stitch			
				Buttonhole stitch			

[1] Refer to Chapter 6 and individual sewing-machine instructions.
[2] Refer to instructions for button and buttonhole closures, Chapter 24, as well as individual sewing-machine instructions.

Decorative stitches permanently and visibly accent seaming or other garment details; they may or may not hold fabric layers in position.

Commonly used examples of these stitches are categorized in the stitch classification table.

STITCH SELECTION GUIDELINES

After reading Part Four, use the following guidelines to determine which of the stitches will best solve each construction need.

1. *Determine the function of the garment.*
   Under what circumstances will the garment be worn? How much stress will it receive? Will different portions of the garment receive more stress than other areas? Is the fabric stable or stretchy? What are the garment's needs for *strength, flexibility, visibility,* and *permanency?*
2. *Determine the stitch classification: Temporary, permanent, or decorative.*
   Will the fabric layers to be joined require *temporary* stitches to hold them in position while the garment is fitted? Are *permanent* stitches required to join the sleeve to the shirt body? Will the collar be *decoratively* stitched?
3. *Determine the stitch type: hand or machine.*
   Hand stitches can be controlled and adapted to varied construction situations—for example, hemming a stretchy knit or back-stitching a seam that is hard to reach by machine. Machine stitches will join most seams quickly and easily, while providing strength. Machine stitching, however, is not as easily modified as hand stitching.
4. *Select the stitch.*
   Will a specific stitch fulfill the requirements of the area to be joined? If not, many stitches can be modified to meet specific needs. Re-

view the Stitch Classification Table prior to selecting a stitch from those in the chapter.

For example, after reviewing the uses of each stitch in the temporary hand-stitch category, the diagonal basting stitch was selected to turn and favor the collar perimeter. It will also hold the fabric layers in position when the collar is pressed and will prevent the layers from shifting as the collar is topstitched. A blind/slip stitch (permanent hand stitch) will invisibly secure the upper collar neck edge to the neckline. This stitch can be modified slightly to improve security along the neckline by spacing the stitches closer together and pulling them snug. To provide decorative topstitching for the outer collar edge, a machine stitch will be used.

5. *Select the thread.*
   Can the same thread used to construct the garment be used for this stitch? Which thread type will be most compatible with the stitch and the fabric fiber content? Generally, the fiber content of the thread will correspond with the fabric fiber content, although this may not be true for temporary or decorative stitches. (Refer to the table on page 146.)

   For example, silk thread in a contrasting color is used to diagonal-baste the collar perimeter because it leaves no imprint on the fabric when pressed and is also easy to remove. For permanent hand stitches, the same thread used to construct the garment is generally appropriate. To topstitch a broadcloth blouse, a single thread will be used, since a double thread or buttonhole twist would be too thick for the lightweight fabric.

6. *Select the needle.*
   Which needle type and size (refer to Chapter 5) will be compatible with both the fabric and the stitch?

   The correct needle can make hand-sewing less frustrating. Often the needle used is so large that it is difficult to insert into the fab-

Thread Selection

Stitch Classification	Temporary Stitches	Permanent Stitches			Decorative Stitches	
Fabric Fiber Content	Any Fiber Content	Cellulose Fibers	Protein Fibers	Synthetic Fibers	Natural Fibers	Synthetic Fibers
Thread fiber content	Silk ——— Cotton	Cotton ——— Cotton-covered polyester	Silk	Polyester ——— Polyester-covered cotton ——— Nylon	Silk buttonhole twist ——— Silk, single or double thread ——— Cotton, single or double thread	Polyester buttonhole twist ——— Polyester, single or double thread ——— Polyester-cotton, single or double thread

ric. Furthermore, it is nearly impossible to pick up only one or two threads from the fabric with a needle that is too large. As a result, large stitches are visible on the right side of the garment and the fabric is sometimes punctured with large needle holes. Generally, a fine, slender needle is easiest to control. For example, a size 8 or 9 sharp or embroidery needle can be used to diagonal-baste and blind-slipstitch the collar.

7. *Select a securing stitch.* Selection of a securing stitch is based upon the stitch classification and type. For example, basting threads may be knotted, since they are temporary and will be removed later.

PRINCIPLES OF HAND-STITCHING[1]

Hand-sewing requires very different manipulative skills from machine sewing. Following are basic principles for performing quality hand stitches.

1. To reduce tangling and ease handling, thread *length* should be no more than about 46 cm (18 in).
2. Use a *single strand* of thread for nearly all hand-sewing. Use a *double thread* to in-

[1] The basic techniques of machine-sewing were covered in Chapter 6, in the discussion of the sewing machine.

Single thread

Double thread

crease strength when visibility is not a factor and to attach buttons and other fasteners to the garment.

3. A *fine, slender needle* (size 8 or 9) slips readily into the fabric, making it easier to control than a large needle. Long needles (sharps, embroidery) work best with multiple stitches and fine fabrics; short needles (betweens) handle short, single stitches (e.g. diagonal basting stitch).

4. Synthetic threads tend to *tangle* and knot more readily than natural-fiber threads. Two steps can be taken to reduce this:
   a. Run the thread through *beeswax* before sewing; this will also strengthen it slightly.
   b. Sew loosely. Pulling the thread taut may stretch it, causing it to curl as it relaxes. It may also be necessary to drop the needle and thread periodically to let them unwind.

5. *Pin- or thread-baste* the fabric layers into the desired position before stitching to minimize fabric shifting and improve accuracy.

6. Hand-stitch from *right to left* unless the directions state otherwise (e.g.) to catch stitch).

7. *Left-handed* individuals should reverse all directions for hand stitches.

Practice to develop an individual technique that ensures uniformity of stitch style and length. Approach each area to be stitched creatively: modify stitches or develop effective new ones when necessary.

STITCH MODIFICATION

Although instructions for hand stitches are often presented in exacting detail, this does not mean that they cannot be modified to meet individual requirements for security, flexibility, or invisibility.

To maximize *security* (as on waistbands or pants hems), shorten each stitch and increase thread tautness as necessary for the specific problem. At the same time avoid creating puckers on the right side of the garment.

Flexibility becomes important when hand-hemming a stretchy knit or bias cut garment. A loose stitch provides the give needed to prevent puckering and drawn or broken stitches. To *reduce visibility*, lengthen and loosen the stitches slightly. Make the stitches as long (2 cm or ¾ in) and as loose as possible while still retaining enough security to hold the fabric layers together.

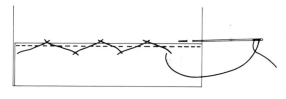

The catch stitch is loose and flexible . . . a good choice for knits

Securing Stitches

To prevent thread ends from slipping out of the fabric during and after construction, they must be secured at both ends.

SECURING HAND STITCHES

To anchor the thread ends with hand sewing, use the fastening stitch or knot the thread. The fastening stitch produces smoother results, since it, unlike a knot, will not make a lump that might show on the right side of the garment.

Fastening Stitch

To Begin a Row of Stitches. Draw the needle up through the fabric from the wrong side, leaving a 10.0-cm (4 in) loose end. Insert the needle back 3 mm (⅛ in) and bring it out again at the point where it first emerged; pull the thread through. Repeat over the first stitch and proceed with the desired hand stitch.

For extra strength, repeat the stitch a third time over the first two stitches. Cut off the free thread end.

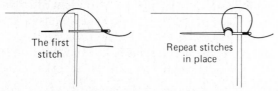

The first stitch   Repeat stitches in place

Fastening Stitch—Beginning a Seam

To End a Row of Stitches. Insert the needle back 3 mm (⅛ in) from the end of the last stitch and bring it out at the point where the last stitch ended. Repeat the stitch a second and third time (for additional security) directly over the first stitch.

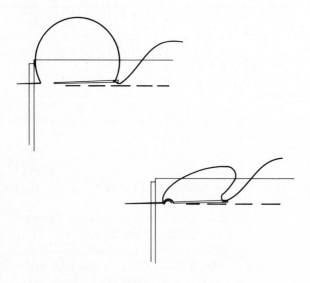

Fastening Stitch—Ending a Seam

Knotting

To Begin a Row of Stitches. Using the left hand, loop one end of the thread around the index finger crossing the ends; hold this intersection in place with the thumb.

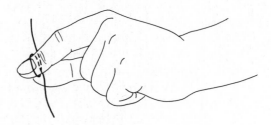

Roll the thread off the fingertip by pushing with the thumb and keeping the long thread taut.

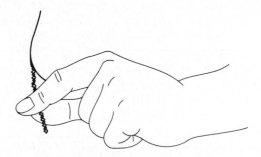

Pinch the loop of thread between the thumb and second finger. Pull it into a small, fine knot.

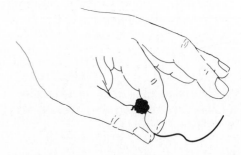

To End a Row of Stitches. Loop the thread clockwise around the last stitch; insert the needle underneath the thread and up through the loop.

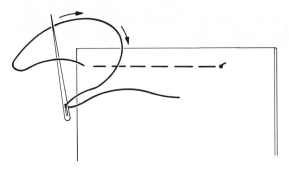

Pull the needle up through the loop. Using the three outer fingers of the left hand, hold the loop open and to the left.

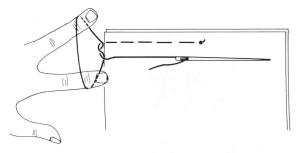

Use the left index finger to hold the thread intersection above the last stitch as the needle is pulled to the right. Pull the needle, removing the three fingers from the loop as it becomes smaller; pull into a small knot.

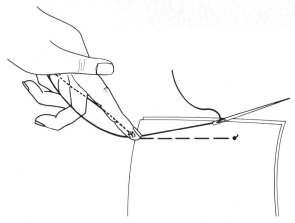

One or two more knots may be formed directly over the first for additional strength.

SECURING MACHINE-STITCHES

Although machine stitches are generally tighter than hand stitches, they may also pull out at seam ends if they are not reinforced.

Backstitching

When beginning or ending a seam, the machine stitches may be reversed over themselves by depressing the reverse stitch lever for about 1.3 cm (½ in) at both ends of the seam. The stitches should lie directly on top of one another to ensure that an exact seam allowance is taken.

Tying Knots

Often it is necessary to stop in the middle of a seam or a row of topstitching because the machine has run out of thread. The seam must be continued with no visible gap or overlap of stitches. On other occasions a seam may end in the middle of the fabric and not at the cut edge. The stitches can be secured by tying a knot or backstitching (refer to Chapter 6). An unevenly stitched seam can be patched by removing the uneven stitches and rejoining the broken seam. The break in the stitches should not be visible.

Knotting the Thread to Secure It in Midseam. Leave 5 to 7.5 cm (2 to 3 in) thread ends at the end of the seam or where the stitching ends. If the thread has run out, rip out a few stitches until the thread ends are long enough to tie.

Pull one of the thread ends, usually the one on the wrong side of the garment, until a loop

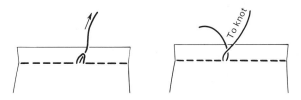

is formed by the other thread end as it is pulled through the fabric layers.

Insert a pin or the point of a seam ripper through the loop and pull the loop until the thread end comes through to that side. Tie the thread ends with a double or triple knot.

If the garment has been topstitched, the thread ends—which have been left 7.5 to 10.0 cm or 3 to 4 in long—can be threaded onto a needle and drawn to the inside of the garment after knotting. The knot can also be tied from the inside of faced portions if the garment is still open. Both techniques reduce friction and prevent the thread ends from raveling.

To Patch a Broken Row of Stitching. Place the fabric under the presser foot with the end of the stitches near the needle. Carefully insert the needle in the fabric at the point where the last stitch was taken. Lower the presser foot and continue stitching.

Pull the thread ends through, as directed above, and knot.

Temporary Stitches

All *basting* stitches are *temporary stitches,* as they are not used to hold the garment together for wearing purposes. Basting holds the fabric layers in position only during the construction processes. Temporary stitches can be used to:

Hold the garment together during fitting.
Hold two or more fabric layers together during permanent or decorative stitching to ensure greater accuracy.
Guide topstitching.
Mark center-front and center-back lines.
Hold enclosed seams (e.g., outer seamed collar edges) in position during pressing and topstitching.

Use a single strand of thread about 61 cm (24 in) long; choose a contrasting color to simplify removal later. Cotton thread from previous sewing projects may be used; however, silk thread has several advantages over it. Silk thread slips out easily during removal and can be pressed over without leaving thread imprints on the fabric. Other threads should be removed before the final pressing. Silk thread is also less likely to damage delicate fabrics.

Once the seams are permanently stitched and lightly pressed, basting threads can be removed carefully with a seam ripper or needle.

HAND-BASTING

Even Basting (Running Stitch)

Even basting is a firm basting used on seams that are subject to strain.

Uses
To hold garment together in areas that receive strain during fitting.
To provide guideline for topstitching.
To hold difficult-to-control fabric layers (such as slippery fabrics) in position during stitching.

Procedures. Space even stitches about 6 mm (¼ in) long by weaving the needle in and out through all the fabric layers. For added firmness, backstitch every few stitches. Gear the

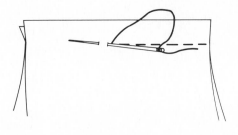

Even Basting

length of the stitches to the fabric and degree of security desired.

Uneven Basting

Uneven basting is a looser, less secure basting used on areas subject to little strain.

Uses

To hold the garment together in areas that receive little strain during fitting (e.g., those seams that fall away from the body).

To mark position lines (e.g., center-front and center-back lines; hemlines).

To hold easily controlled fabric layers together during stitching (e.g., firm, flat fabrics).

Procedures.   Take long stitches (2.0 to 2.5 cm or ¾ to 1 in) on top of the fabric layers and short stitches (6 mm or ¼ in) underneath.

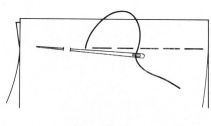

Uneven Basting

Diagonal Basting

Diagonal basting, a stitch similar to the padding stitch, has several unique functions.

Uses

To hold the edges of enclosed seams in a favored position after turning, during pressing, and while topstitching.

To hold the underlining next to the outer fabric, forcing the two layers to act as one during construction.

Diagonal basting stitch holding underlining next to outer fabric during construction

Procedures.   Take short, horizontal stitches at right angles to the edge. This will result in diagonal stitches on the upper side and horizontal stitches on the lower side. Work may proceed in an upward or downward direction. Spaces between stitches should be much longer when the underlining is being attached to the outer fabric.

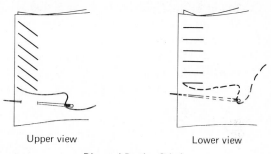

Upper view   Lower view

Diagonal Basting Stitch

Slip-Basting

Slip-basting, a variation of the slip stitch, is used to position and match intricate details from the right side of the garment.

Uses

To match stripes, plaids, and prints precisely and to prevent these matched fabric layers from shifting during machine-stitching.

To make fitting adjustments from the right side.

Procedures.   Press under the seam allowance of one seam edge. Run a basting stitch

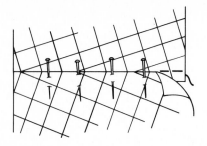

along the stitching line of the corresponding seam. With right sides up, position the folded edge on the basted seam line. Match the design and pin in place.

Bring the needle up from the back into the folded seam allowance just below the fold. Insert the needle directly above this first point into the single fabric layer just above the fold. Bring the needle out 6 mm (¼ in) to 2.5 cm (1 in) to the left of the first stitches and again just below the fold. The length of this stitch is always dependent upon the size of the design. The design will match better if each stitch is taken at a dominant design line. Repeat this process until the seam is completely matched.

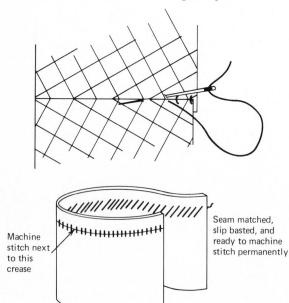

Machine stitch next to this crease

Seam matched, slip basted, and ready to machine stitch permanently

When finished, open out the folded seam allowance. There will be long, slanted stitches on one side and short, horizontal stitches on the other side. Machine-stitch directly over the short stitches, using the fold line as a guide for the stitching line. After stitching, check to be sure the design is perfectly matched before removing the basting. Correct it if necessary.

Machine-Basting

Although machine-basting is quicker to do than hand-basting, it is also less accurate in some cases and more difficult to remove.

Uses

To hold fabric layers together when construction is not intricate.

To apply interfacing to the corresponding fabric section.

To quickly baste those fabrics not marred by needle punctures.

Procedures. Thread the machine with contrasting thread and use your machine's longest stitch length. Use matching thread to apply interfacings. Carefully match and pin the fabric layers together before stitching. After permanent stitches are satisfactorily executed, the basting stitches may be removed carefully.

Permanent Stitches

Permanent hand stitches provide a nearly invisible method for holding fabric layers in position while also providing that aspect of quality attainable only through hand craftsmanship. Machine-stitching may be used to replace some of these stitches (1) as a function of current styles (as in machine topstitching), (2) as a time-saving tactic, or (3) to make a functional garment sturdier.

Both hand and machine sewing can serve a variety of functions:

Hemming
Joining hard-to-reach seams
Inserting zippers
Finishing raw edges
Attaching linings and interfacings
Creating shape and support in the application of interfacings
Making buttonholes
Understitching

A single strand of matching thread about 46 to 50 cm (18 to 20 in) long having a fiber content compatible with the fabric should be run through beeswax before beginning. Use the same thread used to construct the garment.

Although general guidelines are presented for each stitch, it is still advisable to adapt the stitches to fabric and purpose each time they are used. To securely join fabric edges, shorten and tighten the hand stitches as much as possible without creating unwanted puckers. Hemming stitches will generally be somewhat loose, with stitches taken into the garment (catching only one to three yarns) being farther apart.

Important. Some hemming stitches are made so that the edge of the hem facing lies *between* the stitch and the outer garment fabric

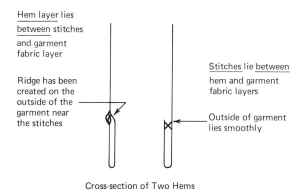

Hem layer lies between stitches and garment fabric layer

Ridge has been created on the outside of the garment near the stitches

Stitches lie between hem and garment fabric layers

Outside of garment lies smoothly

Cross-section of Two Hems

layer. In this case there is a greater chance that the stitches may force the hem edge forward, creating an undesirable ridge on the right side of the garment.

Realize also that pattern companies commonly use the terms *slip stitch* and *blind stitch* for a variety of stitches. Therefore you will have to select a stitch from the following that will *best* meet individual needs.

CATCH STITCH

Both the exposed and unexposed variations of the catch stitch provide elasticity and flexibility. They are quite inconspicuous from the right side of the garment and allow for some shifting or play of the fabric layers. The exposed catch stitch is not suitable for garments that will be subjected to harsh wear, since the exposed thread may snag easily.

Uses

Securing the raw edges of interfacing flat to the wrong side of the garment; stitches exposed.

Hemming (especially stretchy or heavy fabrics); stitches exposed or unexposed.

Sewing pleats and tucks in linings; stitches exposed.

Procedures. The catch stitch is the only stitch that progresses from left to right. Note, however, that the needle still points to the left. The stitches may vary in length from 6 to 20 mm (¼ to ¾ in) apart. If the fabric ravels, finish the raw edge before you begin hemming.

Exposed Catch Stitch

Take a small horizontal stitch about 6 mm (¼ in) down from the hem edge, catching only the upper fabric layer. Move along the desired distance 6 to 20 mm (¼ to ¾ in) to the right and take a small stitch (catching only one or two

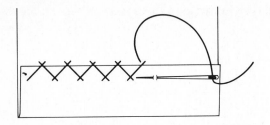

Exposed Catch Stitch

threads) in the garment just above the edge of the upper fabric layer.

Continue to alternate the stitches, keeping them the same distance apart and relatively loose.

When used *to hold a pleat or tuck* in position, as in a lining, the exposed catch stitch does not overlap the fold used to create the pleat. Using buttonhole twist or a double thread, take the stitches through all three fabric layers.

Unexposed Catch Stitch

Machine-stitch 6 mm (¼ in) from the hem edge. Turn up the hem and baste it in place about 1.3 cm (½ in) from the upper edge. Fold the hem back against the garment, letting the hem edge extend outward about 6 mm (¼ in); use the machine stitching as a guideline. Loosely catch-stitch the hem to the skirt or pant leg and press the edge flat over the stitches.

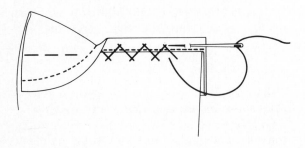

Unexposed Catch Stitch

Advantages

The inside hemming stitch prevents the creation of an impression on the right side of garment.

The stitches are less likely to be snagged because they are hidden.

Tailor's Hemming Stitch

The tailor's hemming stitch, although not quite as elastic as the catch stitch, is a highly inconspicuous hemming stitch with unexposed stitches that cannot be easily snagged.

Use. Hemming

Procedures. Finish the raw edge and/or machine-stitch 6 mm (¼ in) from the raw edge. Turn up the hem and baste in position 1.3 cm (½ in) from the hem edge. Fold the hem back against the garment with the hem edge extending out about 6 mm (¼ in). Begin by taking a small horizontal stitch in the hem 6 mm (¼ in) down from the edge. Move to the left the desired stitch length and pick up one or two threads in the garment. The average stitch length is 1.3 cm (½ in), but stitches may be shorter or longer. Continue alternating stitches; do not pull taut.

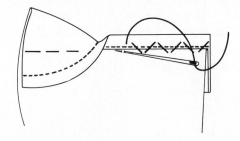

Tailor's Hemming Stitch

BLIND OR SLIP STITCH

Many texts use the terms *blind* or *slip stitch* to designate the same or similar stitches. The stitch is often used to hem folded edges, but it can also be used with straight edges if the technique is varied slightly. There may be a tendency for a ridge to show on the right side of the garment because the stitches encase the hem edge and force it against the garment. It is an excellent stitch, however, for hemming faced sections because it can be varied in a number of ways.

Uses

Hemming the facing edges of bands, bindings, collars, cuffs, waistbands, etc.
Hemming utilitarian or functional garments.
Attaching linings.
Procedures.   The stitch length may vary from 3 to 13 mm (⅛ to ½ in) depending upon the security desired.

Folded-Edge Finish

Finish the hem edge by turning under and stitching, binding, or using another folded-edge finish. Anchor the thread inside the fold of the hem finish and slide the needle out through the folded edge. Directly above this point, catch one or two yarns of the garment and, with the same motion, insert the needle into the folded edge of the hem just to the left of the previous stitch.

Slide the needle through the fold for the stitch length desired, 3 to 13 mm (⅛ to ½ in). Repeat until finished. Secure thread ends.

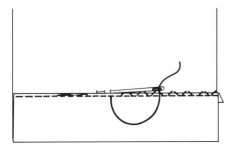

Blind/slip stitch with folded edge

Straight-Edge Finish

Finish the hem edge by machine-stitching 6 mm (¼ in) from the edge, zigzagging, or attaching seam binding. The stitching procedures remain the same as for the folded-edge finish with one exception: after the stitch is made in the garment, the needle is slanted *behind* the straight edge for the long stitch.

Felling Stitch

This variation of the blind/slipstitch is used to securely insert linings or to attach facings.

Uses

Attaching linings
Hemming the free facing edges of collars, cuffs, waistbands, or other bands

Procedures.   Stitches are usually about 6 mm (¼ in) apart, but may vary from 3 mm to 13 mm (⅛ in–½ in) in length.

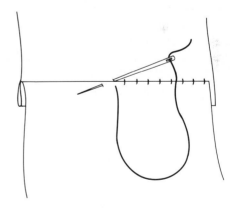

Felling Stitch

Turn under the raw lining or facing edge and position over the adjoining garment section. Bring the needle out close to the folded edge of the lining or facing. Take a stitch in the facing (if you are attaching a lining) or garment seam allowances (if you are securing a facing), run-

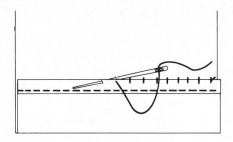

Blind/slip stitch with straightedge finish

ning the needle under this fabric layer for about 6 mm (¼ in). Bring the needle up close to the folded edge of the lining or facing as before. Repeat until finished. No stitches should go through to the right side.

Whipstitch

The whipstitch is used to invisibly join two abutting edges.

Uses
Joining two finished edges
Joining lace or ribbon to a garment edge
Holding a raw edge against a flat surface
Hemming

Procedures. Hold the finished edges even with one another. Insert the needle close to and perpendicular to the finished edges, catching

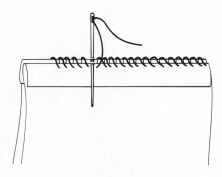

Whipstitch

only a few threads. The floating threads between each stitch will appear angled. The distance between each stitch may vary from short to long.

BACKSTITCHES

The various versions of the backstitch make *very strong* hand stitches. Each type (backstitch, pick stitch, prick stitch) will be discussed individually; the pick stitch will be discussed under Decorative Stitches, page 158.

Backstitch
Use. Stitching strong seams in areas which the sewing machine cannot easily reach.

Procedures. Bring the needle up through the fabric about 6 mm (¼ in) from the edge on the seam line. Insert the needle back 3 mm (⅛ in) to the right of the first stitch. Continue by inserting the needle at the end of the last full stitch and bringing it out one stitch (6 mm or ¼ in) ahead. From the top, the backstitch looks like a machine stitch, but underneath the stitches overlap.

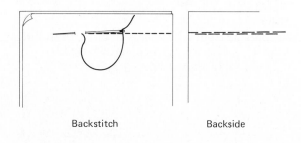

Backstitch   Backside

Prick Stitch
Use
Inserting zippers.
Understitching a facing to prevent the edge from rolling to the right side.

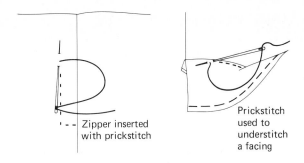

Zipper inserted
with prickstitch

Prickstitch
used to
understitch
a facing

Procedures. Use a double thread or, for decorative purposes, buttonhole twist. Bring the needle up through the fabric close to the edge and on the desired stitching line. Insert the needle back two or three yarns and bring it out about 6 to 10 mm (¼ to ⅜ in) to the left of the first stitch. There will be tiny stitches on the fabric surface, while the stitches will be slightly overlapped underneath.

PADDING STITCH

Padding stitches help to build permanent shape or support between interfacing and facing layers by holding the layers together.

Hand Method

Hand-shaping and stitching provide more control over the shaping of the fabric layers than machine padding because the hand method permits more control. The garment section can be rolled the desired amount as the stitches are taken to help build in the shape.

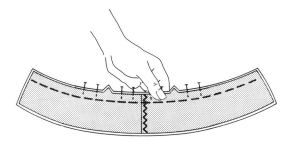

Use. Shaping collars and lapels of tailored garments.

Procedures. Roll the interfacing-facing section into the shape desired and pin outer edges into position. Hold the two layers in position with the left hand.

Working with the interfacing on top, hold the needle so it points left and insert it through the two fabric layers. Take a tiny stitch, barely catching the facing fabric.

Drop down about 1 cm (⅜ in) and take another tiny stitch. Do not pull the thread taut. Repeat until the row is completed, then work upward. These stitches are similar to diagonal basting stitches. Shorter distances between stitches give greater control over shaping, whereas longer stitches serve primarily to hold fabric layers together.

The stitches will create a herringbone or chevron effect on the interfacing side. No stitches should be visible on the right side.

Short padding stitches
provide greater stiffness
and shaping

Longer padding stitches
provide minimal shaping

Machine Padding

The interfacing-facing layers are machine-stitched directionally following the grain lines of the interfacing. Less shaping can be obtained by sewing flat on the machine; however, by varying stitching directions and closeness of rows of stitching, some shaping control can be provided.

Use. To provide support for interfacing-facing layers in garment sections such as collars or waistbands.

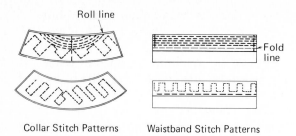

Collar Stitch Patterns   Waistband Stitch Patterns

Procedures. (1) Cut the undercollar and interfacing pieces on the bias for better roll. (2) Set up a symmetric stitch pattern on the interfacing by following interfacing grain lines. Several stitch patterns are illustrated.

Stitch along the marked stitch pattern lines. Begin stitching at the center front or back if the stitching pattern is symmetric or, if there are several rows, alternate stitching direction for each row.

Buttonhole Stitch

Use. To make hand-worked buttonholes.

Procedures. Thread the needle with buttonhole twist or with a *double* thread. Insert the needle from the wrong side 3 mm (⅛ in) from the edge. Loop the thread by swinging it around in a counterclockwise circle.

Insert the needle from the wrong side just to the left of the first stitch, keeping the loop under the needle eye. Draw the thread through the loop, pulling it toward the edge to form a "purl" (knot) at the edge. Repeat, keeping stitches right next to one another and of even length. Form an even ridge along the edge with the purls.

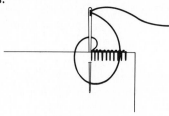

Buttonhole Stitch

Decorative Stitches

Seams and garment edges may be structurally decorated with topstitching done by hand or machine. *Topstitching* refers to stitching that appears on the right side of the garment. Hand topstitching is less likely to harm delicate fabrics than machine topstitching and also provides high-quality hand detailing. Various colors, threads, and stitch patterns may be used to obtain varying effects. Use regular thread for topstitching lightweight fabrics. For other fabric weights, use buttonhole twist or, as an alternative choice use a double strand of regular thread.

Saddle Stitch

This is a simple hand-topstitching which is done after the garment is completed.

Use. Topstitching.

Procedures. Thread a long slender needle with buttonhole twist, embroidery floss, yarn, or double thread. The thread color may be slightly lighter or darker than the fabric or it may contrast.

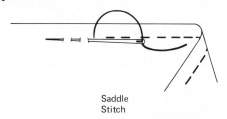

Saddle
Stitch

Bring the needle up from underneath about 3 mm (⅛ in) in from the edge and along the desired stitching line. Weave the needle in and out of the fabric in evenly spaced 6 mm (¼ in) stitches.

Pick Stitch

The pick stitch is an elegant and subtle hand stitch done after the garment is constructed. It leaves tiny beads of thread lying on the fabric surface.

Use. Topstitching.

Procedures. Use buttonhole twist or a double thread of matching or contrasting color. This stitch is formed like the prick stitch except that the bottom fabric layer is *not* caught when backstitching. Only the upper fabric layers are caught in the stitch. Do not pull the thread taut but allow it to lie beadlike on the fabric surface.

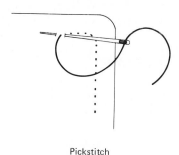

Pickstitch

Machine-Topstitching

Besides adding structural detailing, machine topstitching also helps keep garment edges flat and crisp. To look professional, topstitching must be *perfectly straight.* Machine-topstitching, unlike hand-topstitching, is partially done during construction. Be sure the garment fits *before* topstitching, so the stitches will not have to be ripped out and restitched.

Uses
Structural detailing.
Construction of pockets, pleats, and man-tailored shirts.
Procedures.   consider each of the following factors:
Thread. If you use a double thread, thread the machine in the usual manner with *two* regular-weight threads; wind the bobbin with the same two threads. If you use buttonhole twist,

it may be necessary to use a size 14 or 16 needle. The thread color may match or contrast with the fabric.
Machine Adjustment. Adjust the stitch length to one stitch per centimeter, although stitches may be shorter. Check tension and stitch length on similar layers of fabric and interfacing scraps; make any necessary machine adjustments.

Straight Topstitching

To make sure that your topstitching is very straight, experiment using different types of guidelines: seam guide, tape, basting line, quilting foot, or the widths of various presser feet.

To make *double rows of topstitching,* use an over-edge foot (with wire running down one side) to stitch close to the edge and the general-purpose foot to stitch 6 mm (¼ in) from the edge. Line up the edge of the presser foot with the garment edge.

Always stitch on the top side of the garment. To prevent upper fabric layers from shifting forward, use the diagonal basting stitch along all topstitched areas to hold them in position. If the fabric is thick, the stitches may be lost in the fabric loft. If so, stitch two rows next to one another. Leave the thread ends long enough to thread a needle; draw the threads to the inside and tie them.

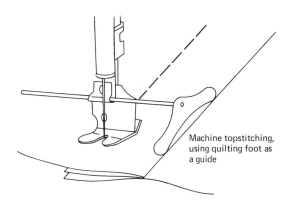

Machine topstitching, using quilting foot as a guide

CRITERIA FOR EVALUATION

HAND AND MACHINE STITCHES

Check to ensure quality performance:

Securing Stitches

___ **1.** Thread ends are secured without creating puckers, lumps, or changes in seam widths.

___ **2.** Thread ends are drawn to the inside and tied when topstitching or other visible stitching is done.

Temporary Stitches

___ **1.** The stitch holds and controls fabric layers in the desired position until permanent stitching, pressing, or fitting is completed.

___ **2.** If used as a stitching guide, basting stitches are placed precisely where intended.

___ **3.** Silk thread is used when pressing is to be done.

Permanent Stitches

___ **1.** Hemming stitches, as well as the fabric hem edge, are invisible from the right side of the garment.

___ **2.** Stitch length and tautness are modified to provide the desired degree of strength, flexibility, security, and invisibility.

___ **3.** The selected stitch fulfills the needs of the area in which it is used.

___ **4.** Visible stitches are evenly spaced and sized and also neatly executed.

Decorative stitches

___ **1.** Topstitching is perfectly even from garment edge or seam line; stitches are equal in size.

___ **2.** Thread chosen provides contrast either in thickness, color, or texture.

___ **3.** Thread ends are drawn to the inside and secured invisibly.

14 Contouring Strategies

OBJECTIVES

1) To determine whether contour retention, support, or creation is needed in the garment area to be contoured.
2) To provide smooth even contouring to meet the needs of your design.

Flat, malleable fabric layers can be manipulated and molded into structures relating to the three-dimensional contours of the human form by stitching shaped fabric sections to one another. Contouring techniques such as layered support, taping, shrinking, or padding may also be used. These support fabric layers aid in the *retention*, *support*, or *creation* of desired garment contours.

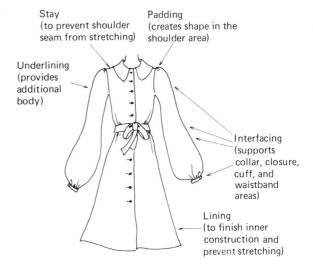

Stay
(to prevent shoulder
seam from stretching)

Padding
(creates shape in the
shoulder area)

Underlining
(provides
additional
body)

Interfacing
(supports
collar, closure,
cuff, and
waistband
areas)

Lining
(to finish inner
construction and
prevent stretching)

As can be seen in the sketch on page 161, various types of fabric support layers may perform several functions within one garment.

More than one type of contouring layer is commonly used in each garment, but the types used will vary with the garment structure desired. *Structure* refers to the degree of stability of the garment's contours. An item such as a suit jacket, which can partially maintain the form of the body through extensive use of inner supporting fabric layers, is considered a highly *structured* garment. A very limp garment, with no apparent shape of its own when off the body, is *unstructured*, with minimal or no inner shaping layers. Most apparel, however, will not fit into either extreme category. These garments will primarily use interfacings to give support to styling details such as collars, waistbands, or closures.

Normal   Soft, clingy Soft, exaggerated Stiff, exaggerated

The structures of the *styling details* (collar, cuffs, pockets, etc.) take their cues from the silhouette. Details on a stiff, exaggerated garment silhouette will be more highly supported, whereas a soft, gathered garment will have less structured support.

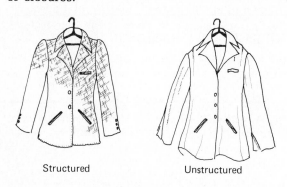

Structured   Unstructured

DECISION-MAKING PROCESSES

Each time a garment is constructed, several preliminary decisions must be made on the basis of the final structure desired. The body-design-fabric interrelationship must be analyzed.

Garment Design. Consider both the silhouette and styling details, particularly as they influence the fall of the fabric upon body contours. The *silhouette* may vary from soft and figure-conforming to normal to stiff.

Fabric. How will the hand of the fabric maintain the shape of the silhouette and style details? Examine the softness or crispness of the fabric. Is it light and airy, fluid and draped, thick and heavy, or stiff and rustling? Is the fabric stretchy and clinging or stretchy and full-bodied? Consider the quantity of fabric used in the garment. Extensive gathering, tucking, or pleating requires different inner shaping than a dart-filled garment. Each fabric type, garment design, and planned structure requires different inner shaping.

Fit. The relationship between the fabric hand, the design silhouette, and the body contour is another factor useful in planning the final garment structure. Will the garment merely follow the body contours or will it attempt to camouflage unwanted bulges, hollows, or proportions? Crisper fabrics fall away from the body, hiding contours, whereas soft, stretchy jerseys cling to the body. Stiffer inner support layers will help to hold the outer fabric away from the body. Lightweight underlinings provide generalized body and shaping. Inner fabric shaping may hamper the clinging of a jersey. Undesired hollows may be padded out to create a smooth plane.

CONTOURING CLASSIFICATION

The internal techniques used to shape and mold the garment to body contours may be classified as contour retainers, supporters, or creators, depending on their function.

Contour Retention

Techniques used to reduce strain and stretch and to maintain length or size within a garment unit.

Seam Length. The length of weight-supporting seams must be stabilized. Seam length is maintained by stay stitching and stay taping. Stay taping controls fullness in eased, gathered, or pleated seams or curved and bias seams.

Major Garment Portions. Full or partial underlinings prevent stretch or bagging and reduce strain on stress areas (e.g., seat, knees) to preserve the original garment shape.

Contour Support

Techniques for lending body to a specific part or generalized area of a garment by using one or more fabric layers varying in crispness and body.

Edges and Appendages. Interfacings and underlinings shape and support faced edges and style details such as collars, cuffs, pockets, or button closures.

Major Garment Portions. Underlining and interfacing lend additional body and shaping

to limp or lightweight fabrics in order to achieve a desired silhouette.

Contour Creation

Techniques designed to mold garment contours and to create extreme structural contours by means of padding, stiff interfacings, stays, and so on.

Improved Body Appearance. Padding, stiff interfacings, or fabric layering can camouflage body distortions and create a more symmetric physical appearance.

Special Effects. The designer's imagination—as well as padding, soft to stiff interfacings, stays, or quilting—can create unique garment designs displaying unusual, exaggerated contours.

TECHNIQUE SELECTION

To plan your construction procedures, first predetermine the silhouette and contouring of the final garment structure. Familiarity with the contouring techniques in this chapter as well as review of the chart below will help you to select suitable techniques.

Matching Technique to Desired Final Garment Structure

Construction Technique	Contour		
	Retention	Support	Creation
Stay stitching	X		
Interfacing		X	X
Underlining	X	X	
Partial underlining	X		
Stay	X		
Padding			X

Stay Stitching

OBJECTIVE

To directionally stay stitch slightly bias and curved fabric edges to prevent seam stretch and loss of fabric shape during construction.

Stay stitching refers to a row of stitching placed close to the seam line of cut fabric sections that stabilizes them during construction. It ensures retention of the exact shape and seam dimensions of the original pattern piece. Garments cut from the same pattern but different fabric types may still fit differently.

Procedures. To avoid stretching, stay-stitch each cut fabric section *immediately* after marking and removing the pattern tissue. To stay-stitch:

1. Thread the machine with matching thread.
2. Set the stitch length at 4 to 5 stitches per centimeter (set machine dial at 2½ to 2 or 10 to 12 stitches per inch).
3. Stitch through *one* fabric layer only.
4. Stitch from cut edge to cut edge; do not pivot at corners.
5. Stitch 1.3 cm (½ in) from the cut edge.
6. Do not backstitch.

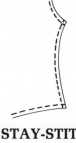

EDGES TO BE STAY-STITCHED

Edges to be stay-stitched will generally be cut on a curve or at a slight bias with the grain line. As a result, they tend to stretch during fitting and construction. Examples of edges that should be stay-stitched include:

Curved Edges	Slightly Bias Edges
Neckline	Shoulder
Armhole	Side
Waistline	Zipper
Hipline	Pant inseam
Crotch	
Yokes	

EDGES THAT DO NOT REQUIRE STAY STITCHING

It is not necessary to stay-stitch true bias edges, free edges, controlled edges, or those cut with the grain. Examples of these edges include:

True Bias Edges	Free Edges	Controlled Edges	Straight Edges
Side seams	Hems	Eased	Cut with crosswise grain
	Facing outer edges	Gathered	
		Pleated	Cut with lengthwise grain
		Tucked	

True-bias edges should *not* be stay-stitched because the natural give of the bias cut would be destroyed. Because the fabric is cut on the true bias to obtain special stretching and draping characteristics, stay stitching would force the seams to draw up and hang unevenly.

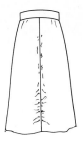

Directional Stitching. Stay-stitch with the direction of the grain to prevent distortion of the cut fabric sections. Stay stitching against the grain may stretch fabric edges and change the perimeter size of the fabric piece.

With the grain: yarns smoothed

Against the grain: yarns roughed

To determine the stitching direction, run your finger along the cut edge. If the yarns remain smooth and flat, you are stroking *with* the grain; if they rough up, you are stroking *against* the grain. Always stitch directionally *with* the grain to preserve the fabric shape.

These common garment pieces are usually stay-stitched directionally:

After stay-stitching, check each piece for accuracy by placing the stay-stitched garment sections on top of their corresponding tissue pattern pieces. If an edge is too long, draw up the bobbin thread until the edge matches the pattern exactly. Loosen the stitches to release an edge if it is too short. This ensures that all garment pieces will match in size when they are stitched together.

CRITERIA FOR EVALUATION
STAY STITCHING

Check to ensure quality performance:

__ **1.** Only slightly bias and curved edges are stay-stitched.

__ **2.** Only a single fabric layer is stitched.

__ **3.** A regular-length stitch is used.

__ **4.** No corners are pivoted; stitching runs from cut edge to cut edge.

__ **5.** Pieces are stay-stitched directionally.

__ **6.** Stay-stitched garment sections are the same size as corresponding pattern sections.

Interfacing

OBJECTIVE

To select an interfacing fabric (weight, stiffness, grain direction) and construction technique to achieve the desired, predetermined garment shaping (silhouette, style details).

Interfacing lends support and shaping to various sections of a garment. Generally, these sections are faced areas or appendages featuring enclosed seams that require body or special

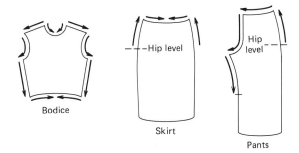

Bodice

Hip level — Skirt

Hip level — Pants

shape support. Interfacing fabrics tend to have more body than underlining fabrics, although softer fabrics such as broadcloths and underlinings may be used.

Collars, pockets, waistbands, button closures, and other details require varying degrees of interfacing support. Within a single garment, interfacings of varying *weight, stiffness,* and *grain direction* may be used so as to achieve differing degrees of support and structure. A stiff, heavy interfacing is necessary to prevent a waistband from buckling during wear, whereas only minimal lightweight support is needed to retain the shape of patch pockets. Rolling capabilities of collars, cuffs and other garment sections may be enhanced by cutting their interfacings on the bias.

Interfacings may be applied by hand, machine, or heat fusion. The first two methods generally provide the most compatible fabric layer combinations with the greatest flexibility. *Hand* applications create less additional bulk within the enclosed seams than machine methods because interfacing seam allowances are eliminated. The *machine* application, although flexible, does not eliminate seam allowance bulk, nor does it decrease the size of the interfacing so that it will fit smoothly inside the smaller enclosure between the outer fabric layers. *Fusible* interfacings tend to stiffen and change the general character of the outer fabric. As a result, they are commonly used for structural effects rather than for soft, unstructured silhouettes.

Sheer-weight nonwoven and knit fusibles can be used with light- to medium-weight fabrics. To avoid a stiff appearance yet still provide needed body, apply the fusible interfacing to the facing rather than to the main garment section.

Before beginning the actual construction, it is a good idea to test the fabric layers to be joined by arranging them in the position they will hold during wear. This check may lead to adjustments in grain, crispness, or weight that can eliminate later shaping problems. If you anticipate needed support in areas other than those designated by the pattern, interfacing or another support fabric can be cut out using the main pattern piece for that garment section. Sometimes entire garment sections are interfaced to create special silhouette effects.

When added support is provided, the bulk created in the enclosed seam must be minimized. This bulk can be reduced either before or after application, depending upon the method chosen. Only the hand method eliminates interfacing seam allowances completely.

Preparation—Eliminating Excess Bulk Before Application

1. Trim corners of interfacing diagonally 3 mm (⅛ in) inside corner seam intersections.

2. Trim 1.3 cm (½ in) from all interfacing edges *without* seam allowances.
3. Overlap and match stitching lines of interfacing darts (slash to point first) and seams.

   Trim seam to 6 mm (¼ in) on each side of seam line. Stitch 3 mm (⅛ in) from each side of the seam line to reinforce before trimming.

Cross-section of Enclosed Seam Layers
for All Interfacing Applications

Hand

Machine

Fused

——————— Garment layer
– – – – – – – Interfacing
— - — - — - Garment facing

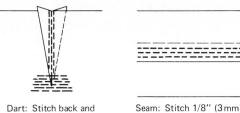

Dart: Stitch back and
forth across point

Seam: Stitch 1/8" (3 mm)
on each side of seam

INTERFACING APPLICATION PROCEDURES

Hand Applications

1. *Trim- and Catch-Stitch Method*

Although this application method may be used with all fabric and interfacing weights, it is particularly useful with heavier, bulkier fabrics to eliminate excess bulk. This application may not be as secure in functional or machine-laundered garments unless a "gentle" machine laundering setting is used.

Procedures:

a. Trim 1.5 to 1.7 cm ($\frac{5}{8}$ to $\frac{11}{16}$ in) away from seam allowance edges of interfacing.

b. Place interfacing against wrong side of corresponding fabric section and within the seam allowances.

c. Catch-stitch interfacing to fabric along seam line.

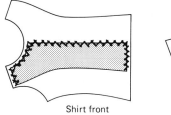

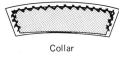

Collar

Shirt front

2. *Trim and Hand-Baste Method*

If the outer edges of the interfaced garment sections will be topstitched, the interfaced edges may be quickly basted into position rather than catch-stitched.

Procedures:

a. Trim 1.5 to 1.7 cm ($\frac{5}{8}$ to $\frac{11}{16}$ in) away from interfacing seam allowance edges.

b. Place interfacing against wrong side of corresponding fabric section and within the seam allowances.

c. Even-baste interfacing to fabric about 4 mm ($\frac{3}{16}$ in) inside the cut edge.

Attach interfacing to shirt body, not facing.

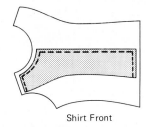

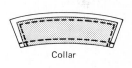

Collar

Shirt Front

3. *Hand-Pad-stitching Method* (Tailored Garments)

Pad stitching lends support and control to the shape and roll of collar and lapels by holding facing and interfacing layers in the final desired position. Permanent shaping is built in because the two fabric layers are held in this position as the pad stitches are made.

Procedures:

a. Trim away 1.5 to 1.7 cm ($\frac{5}{8}$ to $\frac{11}{16}$ in) from seam allowance edges of interfacing.

b. Place the trimmed interfacing against the wrong side of the corresponding fabric section and within seam allowances.

c. Fold the fabric layers along the roll line until they lie in the desired wearing position; pin and baste along the roll line. Note: The roll line usually starts 3.2 cm (1¼ in) in front of the shoulder seam and arches about 3.8 cm (1½ in) at the center back.

d. Pad-stitch, placing stitches closer together where more support is needed (e.g., collar stand, points). *To set in shape, hold fabric layers in wearing position as stitches are made.*

Machine Applications

1. *Machine-Baste and Trim Method*
   This method suits light- to medium-weight fabrics best, since the interfacing seam allowance is caught in the seam, creating additional bulk. It creates excess bulk when used with heavier fabrics.

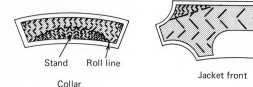

Stand   Roll line

Collar

Jacket front

Procedures:
   a. Pin the interfacing to the wrong side of corresponding garment section, matching seam lines and markings.
   b. Machine-baste (using longest stitch) 1.3 cm (½ in) from all edges.
   c. Trim interfacing close to basting.

2. *Machine-Padding Method*
   Pad stitching by machine provides support and shaping to faced and interfaced garment sections (e.g., collar, waistband, cuffs) by holding the two layers together; the stitching is done directionally with the grain and provides additional stiffening.

Procedures:
   a. Cut undercollar and collar interfacing on the true bias for a smoother roll.
   b. Machine-baste interfacing to wrong side of facing 1.3 cm (½ in) from edge; trim interfacing close to stitching.

c. For tailored collars only, determine the roll line by placing collar on a dress form in the wearing position.

   The roll line usually begins about 3.2 cm (1¼ in) in front of the shoulder seam and arches about 3.8 cm (1½ in) at the center back. Mark the roll line. Machine-stitch along roll line, easing slightly; stitch three additional rows 6 mm (¼ in) apart and toward the neckline.

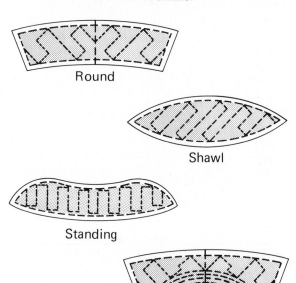

Round

Shawl

Standing

Tailored

Foldline

Foldline

d. Mark the stitching pattern following the grain lines on the interfacing.

   The rectangular stitching lines on the collars are about 2.5 cm (1 in) apart.

e. On waistbands, begin sewing at the center back and work outward in 2.5-cm (1-in) segments to stitch the two layers together directionally.

Fused Applications

Fused interfacings provide more support and firmness than might usually be anticipated by testing (*holding* the fabric layers together to check their compatibility). The resin used to adhere the two layers is responsible for this additional stiffness and change in the character of the outer fabric. As a result, test-fusing the two fabrics as well as laundering or dry-cleaning the sample to check for bubbling and good adhesion, becomes doubly important. If the two fabrics are not compatible, either a different fusible or a nonfusible interfacing should be used.

The following application method is one commonly used. However, always read the individual instructions provided with the interfacing before fusing.

1. *General Fusing Procedures*
   a. The outer fabric must be preshrunk before fusing. Preshrinking of woven fusible interfacing may prevent bubbling of the outer fabric after laundering. To preshrink fusible interfacings, soak in hot water, wring gently by hand, and line-dry. *Do not* machine-dry, as the resin may be dislodged.
   b. Trim interfacing corners diagonally 3 mm (⅛ in) inside the corner seam intersections.
   c. Trim 1.3 cm (½ in) from all seam allowances to reduce bulk. This leaves 3 mm (⅛ in) to be caught in the seam for security.
   d. Position the interfacing with the resin against the wrong side of the corresponding garment section, matching seamlines

and markings. The layers should be smooth and flat, without wrinkles.
   e. To fuse:
      With the interfacing on top, cover both layers with a damp press cloth.
      Set the iron on for steam and wool; apply steam and pressure for 10 seconds to each portion of the fabric layers, overlapping with the previously fused area. *Do not* slide the iron across the fabric.
      Flip fabric layers over and repeat the process. Check to be sure that the two layers have fused and repeat the pressing procedure if they have not.
   f. If an error has been made and the layers are misaligned, remove the fused interfacing by steam-pressing the area for 10 seconds. Gently pull the layers apart while they are still hot.
2. *Speed Padding Method*
   Spot-stabilization with an extra layer of fusible interfacing can provide additional support and reinforcement without the usual hand work. It can be used with machine padding if desired.

Procedures:
   a. Prepare the fabrics as for the general fusible application: trim interfacing, fuse undercollar and jacket front interfacings to corresponding garment sections.
   b. To spot-stabilize:
      (1) Cut the interfacing piece 3 mm (⅛ in) inside the collar roll line and neckline seam to support the collar stand. If

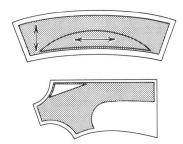

the interfacing has one-way stretch, cut it so the lengthwise (stable) direction goes around the neckline. Fuse to the stand area of the collar.

c. For added body in the lapels, cut a wedge-shaped piece of interfacing 3 mm (⅛ in) inside the roll line and the outer seam lines. Fuse to the lapel area of the previously fused front section.

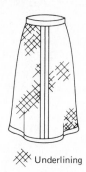

✕ Underlining

CRITERIA FOR EVALUATION

INTERFACING

Check to ensure quality performance:

___ **1.** Excess bulk has been eliminated by trimming.

___ **2.** Interfacing darts and seams are overlapped and stitched.

___ **3.** Interfacing and outer fabric layers lie together smoothly without buckling.

___ **4.** Interfacing and outer fabric layers are compatible in weight, stiffness, and grain direction.

___ **5.** Desired degree of support and shaping is provided for faced areas or appendages.

Underlining

OBJECTIVE

To determine whether and where partial or full underlining may be needed to perform the necessary underlining application techniques.

Underlinings are lightweight fabrics used to back major garment portions fully or partially. Fabric and underlining are cut from the same main pattern pieces. The two layers are basted together; they are then treated as one layer during construction.

This additional fabric layer has numerous functions. It can support and shape the garment silhouette, add body to limp fabrics and, retain the size of loosely woven fabrics. Wrinkling is reduced, shape is retained, and construction details remain hidden.

When a garment is entirely underlined, it is usually not necessary to interface it unless extra support is needed to shape special details. Interfacing fabrics may be used instead of the underlining fabric to shape areas that are usually interfaced, such as collars, cuffs, or waistbands.

Underlining may also back only portions of a garment. Possibly only the bodice section of a blouse or the skirt of a dress may need support or shape retention. Specific sections that stretch or bag, such as the seat of a skirt or the knee area of pants, can be underlined.

APPLICATION PROCEDURES

1. Cut the underlining from the same major pattern pieces used to cut your garment. Collars, facings, cuffs, and waistbands are usually not cut from underlining; interfacing is used to support these areas. Mark the underlining only.
2. Stitch the darts of the outer fabric and those of the underlining separately. Press the gar-

ment darts toward the center or downward; press underlining darts in the opposite direction to minimize bulk.

3. Working on a flat surface and with the wrong sides together, position the underlining over the corresponding garment section, pin, and press fabric layers together to smooth them. The fabric edges may not match exactly because of variations in fabric "give" so it may be necessary to trim off any excess underlining.

4. Mark center lines and fold lines with hand basting. Machine-baste the outer perimeter 1.3 cm (½ in) from the edge, stitching directionally and leaving the hem edge free. Using large stitches, diagonally baste the garment sections together to prevent slippage of the layers during construction.

5. Handle the remaining construction of the garment as though the two layers were one.

6. To hem: Mark the desired hem length; trim underlining even with the hem fold line. Take hemming stitches into the underlining layer only.

Partial Underlining

To underline only partially, determine which part of the garment must be supported to retain its shape and prevent distortion. For example, the back or seat section of a skirt may be underlined to prevent the seat from bagging during wear. In some fabrics, pants knees may also be partially underlined.

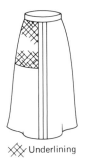

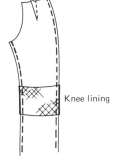

Knee lining

XXX Underlining

Procedures:

1. To underline a *skirt* partially, cut out only the back fabric section from underlining. To underline only the seat, cut the underlining so it will end just below the seat when sitting.

2. Pants knees: Cut two sections from underlining or lining fabric 25 cm (10 in) long and the width of the front pants knee area. Baste the underlining to the knee area of each front pants leg; construct the pants as usual.

   If desired, loosely catch stitch the underlining to each pants leg to hold in position.

CRITERIA FOR EVALUATION

UNDERLININGS

Check to ensure quality performance:

__1. Underlining and outer fabric layers mold smoothly together without wrinkling.

__2. Darts are stitched separately.

__3. Underlining is trimmed evenly with hemline.

__4. Hand stitches catch only the underlining.

__5. The underlining provides the desired degree of body and shape retention.

Stays

OBJECTIVE

To determine when and where a stay is needed to retain seam length and perform the necessary construction technique.

A *stay* is a narrow strip of tightly woven fabric used to prevent stretching, reinforce seams receiving strain, and secure eased, gathered, or pleated garment seams. Shoulder, crotch, underarm (tailored garments, kimono sleeves), and dress waistline seams are commonly stayed because they are curved or cut on the bias and stretch easily when strained.

Narrow (6-mm or ¼-in) cotton or linen twill tape, seam binding, or a selvage strip from self-fabric or underlining-weight fabric may be stitched to the seam to be stayed.

APPLICATION PROCEDURES

1. Cut the stay the length of the section to be stayed by placing it over the *seam line* of the corresponding area of the pattern. Mark the position of any darts or notches on the stay to ensure accurate distribution of the fabric in the seam.

    Position the stay over the seam line with 3-mm (⅛ in) of it extending over the stitching line toward the garment; pin. Machine baste 1.3 cm (½ in) from the garment edge; stitch seams as usual.

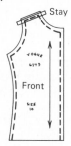

CRITERIA FOR EVALUATION

STAYS

Check to ensure quality performance:

__ **1.** Length of area stayed matches length of corresponding area on pattern tissue.

__ **2.** Stay is positioned 3 mm (⅛ in) over seam line.

__ **3.** Stay prevents seamed area from stretching.

Padding

OBJECTIVE

1. To determine, based upon desired garment styling and symmetry of figure, whether padding is necessary and what type of padding to use.

2. To customize size, shaping, and thickness of padding used and insert the pad or padding layers smoothly and securely in the garment.

Padding—made of lofty or crisp fabrics such as lamb's wool, polyester fleece, felt, or canvas—provides built-in shaping or layering. The creation of special effects (e.g., quilting) or the camouflage of undesirable body contours are prime functions of padding. Many bodies are *not* symmetric in size or shape as a result of physical accidents, the aging process, or disease. Symmetry may be improved by molding and reshaping the garment below the outer fabric surface. Bulges and hollows may be filled, leveled, and camouflaged by securing padding to underlining or interfacing. The chest area of men's tailored jackets is subtly padded to smooth and fill out the chest area as well as to provide stability.

Consider what is to be accomplished. Is one layer sufficient or will many beveled layers be needed? Decisions must be made about thickness, pliability, stability, care, and the final appearance. To ensure a smooth and well-fitting garment, the layers must be tested over muslin or by securing them to inner support fabrics before final fitting or construction can be completed. Often it will be necessary to add or subtract padding layers by refitting them until the desired appearance is obtained.

Several types of padding procedures are presented to provide technical background. These procedures should be adapted to meet special body or design needs when it is necessary to build in contours.

Shoulder Pads

Shoulder pads provide a smooth shoulder foundation from which the garment hangs. They may be inserted in tailored suits (men's and women's) or in dresses and blouses, depending upon current styles. Thickness and location also vary with fashion.

Triangular in shape, shoulder pads consist of beveled layers of padding (hair canvas or fleece) individually fitted to create the desired physical appearance. They may be used to camouflage uneven, narrow, sloping, or rounded shoulders merely by varying the number and location of layers composing the pad. The pads may also be squared in front to smooth out the hollow between the bust and shoulder.

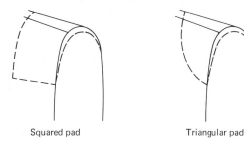

Squared pad   Triangular pad

MAKING SHOULDER PADS

1. To determine the shoulder-pad shape, match shoulder seam lines of pattern pieces. Sketch in the pad shape by beginning at the armscye notches and curving out to within 2.5 cm (1 in) of the neck seam.

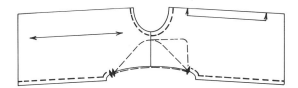

2. Choose polyester fleece or lamb's wool. Cut the layers in decreasing size to reach the de-

sired thickness. Loosely pad-stitch the layers together. The size and placement of layers for each of the pads may vary to create a symmetric appearance. If one shoulder is higher than the other, its pad will need to be thinner; therefore fewer layers will be used.

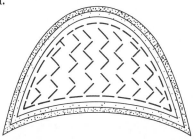

APPLICATION PROCEDURES

1. To locate the position in which the shoulder pad will be placed, try on the garment and manipulate the pad until the desired silhouette is found. Note: You will secure a smoother shoulder line if the shoulder pad extends beyond the armscye seam about 1.0 cm (⅜ in). During fashion extremes or if the individual has narrow shoulders, the pad may extend farther outward. Any adjustments in size or thickness to hide unwanted body contours should be made at this time by adding or subtracting layers. Smooth the garment over the pad and pin in position, catching only the top layers of the shoulder pad. Remove the garment from the wearer.
2. Hold the garment and shoulder pad in the wearing position so they will hang smoothly

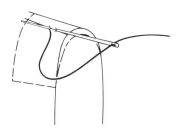

as they are sewn together. Lift the neck facing out of the way. Back-stitch from the outside by taking stitches through any seam line or dart next to the shoulder pad. Catch only the upper layers of the pad and take tiny stitches about 1.3 cm (½ in) apart directly in the ditch of the seam.

Bring the neck facing back into position and loosely baste it to the shoulder pad.

Sleeve Heads

A sleeve head is a strip of lofty fabric used to support and round out the sleeve cap of a tailored garment. It is inserted after the shoulder pads have been inserted.

APPLICATION PROCEDURES

1. Cut a strip of lamb's wool or polyester fleece 15 by 6.5 cm (6 by 2½ in). Round off the corners. Fold under 2.5 cm (1 in) along one long edge.
2. Center the strip in the armscye with the wide side next to the sleeve. Place the folded edge next to the armhole seam line and between the sleeve and the seam allowance. Slipstitch the folded edge to the seam line.

Quilting

Quilting indicates that a soft, lofty fabric is joined by stitching to an outer fabric layer to produce raised and often patterned effects. The padding layer may also be sandwiched between two fabric layers. Major portions of a garment can be quilted or only sections of it, such as yokes or panels.

Cross-sections of Quilted Fabric Layers

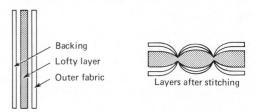

Backing
Lofty layer
Outer fabric

Layers after stitching

Stitching patterns may vary from curved to linear and may be designed to suit the garment, individual areas, or the fabric used. Lamb's wool, polyester fleece, flannel, or cotton wadding may form the lofty layer; muslin may be used as an optional inner layer. One or more filling layers may be used, depending on the degree of loft desired.

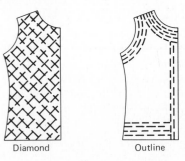

Diamond   Outline

Two stitching patterns

When an all-over stitching pattern is used or if the outline of the outer fabric print is followed, the fabric layers may be quilted before the garment pieces are completely cut out. If the quilting pattern will conform to the shapes of fabric sections, cut out the pattern pieces with 2.5-cm (1-in) seams to allow for shrinkage during quilting; recut to pattern size after quilting.

APPLICATION PROCEDURES

1. Mark the backing fabric with the desired quilting pattern. Pin; baste the outer edges together. Baste close to but not directly on the quilting lines to prevent layers from shifting during stitching.

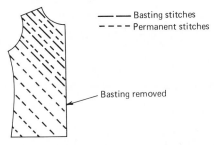

— — Basting stitches
- - - - Permanent stitches

Basting removed

2. Quilting may be performed by machine or by hand.
   a. *Machine-Quilting*. Thread the machine with mercerized cotton or cotton-core thread and set the stitch length at three to four stitches per centimeter (set metric dial at 3 to 2½; eight to ten stitches per inch). Adjust the machine tension and stitch along the guidelines. If the quilting lines are straight, a long, thin, straight edge (e.g., medium-weight cardboard,

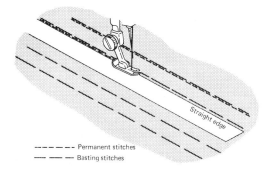

- - - - - Permanent stitches
— — Basting stitches
Straight edge

flexible plastic ruler) may be placed next to the stitching line to help prevent shifting of the fabric layers and to act as a stitching guide. Alternate the stitching direction for each row if the lines are on the bias to prevent stretching. Remove inner basting; leave basting around the outer edges.
   b. *Hand-Quilting*. Thread the needle with quilting or mercerized cotton thread run through beeswax. Use an adjustable embroidery hoop to hold fabric layers taut and smooth. Take two or three 3-mm (⅛-in) running stitches through all fabric layers along the quilting lines by holding the layers in front of the needle flat with the thumb and index finger. Secure at each end with a fastening stitch. After constructing the garment, pull the padding away from the seams and darts to reduce bulk. Binding may be used to finish the outer edges because it creates less bulk than do facings.

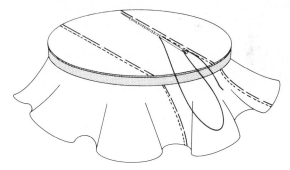

Trapunto

Trapunto is a form of quilting in which smaller, more intricately designed areas are padded to stand out in relief against the rest of the garment. The outer fabric layer is stitched by hand or machine to a backing fabric in the desired design. The motif is then hand-stuffed through slits in the backing. The outer fabric (e.g., satin, wool, crepe) may have some give, but the backing (e.g., muslin, organdy) should be firm and strong to push the padding outward. Fabrics reflecting light emphasize the stuffed motif better than textured fabrics. Trapunto is usually done before garment construction.

Plan the design to fit the garment section to be padded, avoiding dart lines. Consider special design lines within the outline of the motif which may create three-dimensional effects. Remember, however, that if spaces are too small, they will be difficult to stuff.

APPLICATION PROCEDURES

1. Mark the backing fabric with the trapunto pattern. Baste the outer edges of the fabric layers with wrong sides together. To prevent slippage during stitching, cross the basting lines over the motif.

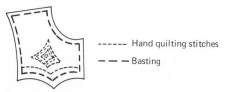

------ Hand quilting stitches

— — — Basting

2. Carefully hand- or machine-stitch along the design lines. Machine-stitch using four to five stitches per centimeter (eight to ten stitches per inch). To stitch by hand, take small 3-mm (⅛-in) running stitches, leaving a small loop underneath every third stitch to provide give and to prevent puckering after stuffing. Remove the basting crossing the design motif.
3. To stuff: Pad long, narrow areas with a bodkin threaded with several strands of wool yarn. Pure virgin lamb's wool or Dacron may be used to stuff larger areas. Make a *small* slit in the *backing* with a seam ripper. Using a bodkin or crochet hook, stuff the area with small portions of corded stuffing. Smooth out

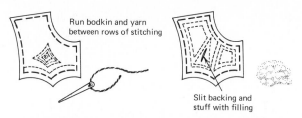

Run bodkin and yarn between rows of stitching

Slit backing and stuff with filling

the stuffing so it does not look lumpy. The slits may be resewn unless this causes puckering. Finish the inside of the garment with an underlining.
4. To press, place right side down over a Turkish towel.

Padded/Soft Hem

Hemlines of couture garments are rarely pressed sharp. To soften a hem and prevent the breaks that sometimes appear in the hem curve, interface or interface and pad the hem.

APPLICATION PROCEDURES

1. Mark the hemline with a basting stitch.
2. Interface the hem with a bias strip of interfacing, lamb's wool, or fleece cut 2.5 cm (1 in) wider than the hem depth. Position this strip over the hem, with 1.3 cm (½ in) extending below the hem fold line. Catch the upper and lower interfacing edges to the garment.
3. Hem using the unexposed catch stitch or the tailor's hemming stitch.
4. The hem can be further softened by first interfacing as described above and then inserting lamb's wool or soft cording in the hem fold.

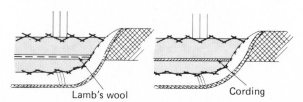

Lamb's wool

Cording

CRITERIA FOR EVALUATION

PADDING

Check to ensure quality performance:

__ **1.** Fiber content of padding and remainder of garment are compatible (e.g., with regard to care and flexibility).

__ **2.** Quality and location of padding create the desired effect.

__ **3.** Padding is secured so it will not slip out of position.

__ **4.** Padded areas conform smoothly with body contours and do not create unwanted lumps or bulges.

__ **5.** Quilted areas are evenly stitched and smoothly padded.

__ **6.** Excess bulk is minimized or eliminated where possible.

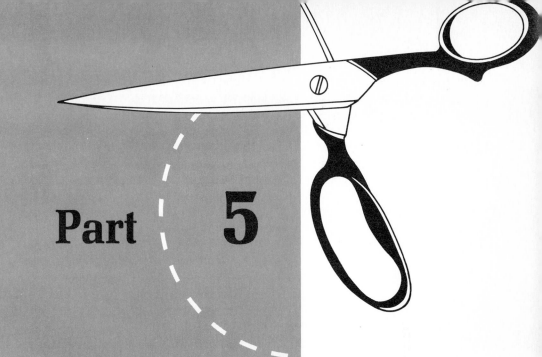

Part 5

Garment Contouring and Styling: Seams

A garment structure is produced by seaming shaped fabric sections together. As these sections are joined, the garment comes into being. Silhouette and design lines become apparent and the flat fabric sections begin to relate to body contours as well as to fulfill the designer's styling concept.

Seaming is a process joining two or more fabric layers by stitching along a predetermined seam line. The seam line may be located near the cut fabric edge or it may lie within the body of the pattern section.

The seaming process also includes treatment of the raw seam edges after they have been stitched. The shape of the seam line as well as seam function must be considered.

Two major types of seams are encountered in garment construction: structural and enclosed seams.

1. *Structural seams* join major garment sections together. Examples are shoulder and side seams. These seams are visible inside the garment.
2. *Enclosed seams* finish the perimeters of collars, cuffs, and other faced sections. Their seam allowances are sandwiched between two fabric sections and are completely hidden from view.

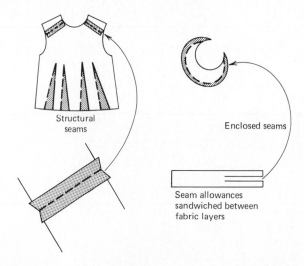

Structural seams

Enclosed seams

Seam allowances sandwiched between fabric layers

Because these two seam types have different functions, they are treated differently after they are stitched. This part deals with *structural seaming techniques* utilized to:

- Create contours within fabric sections (darts, dart tucks, tucks).
- Join fabric sections with seam lines of equal length, including straight, curved, bias, and corner seams.
- Join fabric sections with seam lines of unequal length, including eased, stretched, gathered, and pleated seams.

• Join seams that encircle junctures of appendages with the torso, including armscye, crotch, and waistline seams.

Part Seven, "Enclosed Seams: Concealing and Finishing Outer Perimeters," discusses the construction of enclosed seams. It should be noted that many of the seaming techniques discussed in Part Six, "Structural Seams: Protective and Decorative Functions," may, if concealed, become enclosed seams.

Structural Seams

Accurate stitching of structural seams is crucial to the development of the garment. Once the cut garment sections are stitched together, the perimeter shapes and size of the pattern sections determine how the garment relates to body contours (fit), the silhouette, and the location of design seams. If the pieces are stitched together inaccurately, the fit or styling of the garment may be impaired.

Fullness is often incorporated into the garment design as both a styling feature and a fitting technique. Accurate location and control of excess fabric requires both technical construction precision and knowledge of fabric control.

Structural seams, the building foundation of the garment, are visible from within an unlined garment. Because these seams are visible, they are subject to friction as the seam allowances rub against the body. Fraying may result if the seams are left unfinished. To protect these seams, the seam allowances should remain untrimmed and a raw-edge or enclosed-seam finish applied. A curved seam, however, must be clipped to enable it to lie flat when the seam is pressed open after stitching.

Structural seams directly control the fit, silhouette, and styling of the garment. The construction techniques needed to join seam lines of equal or unequal length along fabric perimeters or within fabric sections are discussed in this part.

15 Creating Contour Within Fabric Sections

OBJECTIVE

To stitch darts, dart-tucks and tucks that are symmetrically spaced and sized, that do not pucker at the point, and that point toward the body bulge.

Fabric may be shaped to relate to body contours by folding and stitching out an area of excess fabric within a fabric section. These stitched-out areas, called *darts* or *tucks,* are common techniques utilized to fit the garment over body bulges. The stitching lines are located *within* the fabric section rather than parallel to the perimeter edges.

Darts are formed by stitching out a wedge-shaped area within a garment section. To fit well, the wedge must point to and correspond with the body bulge.

Tucks are constructed by stitching out rectangular-shaped areas with released fullness at the ends. If the tucks are very narrow—3 mm (⅛ in) or less—they are called *pin-tucks.*

Dart-tucks are created by partially stitching out a dart area, thus releasing fullness, as with a tuck.

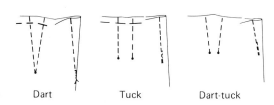

Dart   Tuck   Dart-tuck

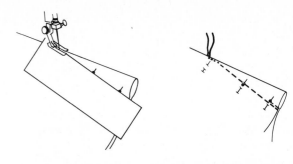

Darts or tucks may lie inside the garment or to the outside if they are decorative. Contrasting or topstitching thread may also be used to stitch decorative seams.

GENERAL CONSTRUCTION PROCEDURES: DARTS AND TUCKS

All darts and tucks require precision marking to ensure that the location is accurate.

1. Fold the dart on the center fold line with right sides of the fabric together (unless decorative). Match the dots by inserting a pin perpendicular to the stitching line through each set of corresponding dots.

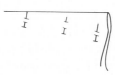

2. To ensure stitching accuracy, a lightweight cardboard template repeating the shape of the dart seam line may be used as a *stitching guide*. It will also prevent the fabric layers from shifting as they are stitched.

   Begin by inserting the needle into the fabric fold at the dart tip. Place the cardboard next to the needle, aligning its edge with the dart seam line. Lower the presser foot and take three stitches directly along the fabric fold to prevent dart-point pucker. Continue stitching the dart with the stitches next to the cardboard edge; backstitch.

3. To secure the thread ends at the dart point, tie them securely. *Do not* backstitch at the point, as this may cause a pucker if the first stitching line was not duplicated exactly.
4. Pressing techniques are described on page 186.

Construction Procedures for Dart Variations

Straight Darts. Commonly found on commercial patterns, these darts have straight seam lines. To stitch the straight dart, use a straight-edged cardboard template as a guide.

Curved Darts. These can follow body curves closely, enabling them to provide a smooth, close fit.

Curved darts may form either slight *concave* or *convex* curves. The stitching lines of concave darts curve outward so the garment may fit closely to concave body curves (below the

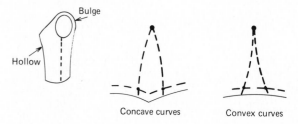

Concave curves   Convex curves

bust). Convex darts fit over convex body curves such as the stomach, large bust curves, or the back shoulder. In this case the dart stitching lines curve toward the dart fold, providing the additional ease needed to fit over these rounded body bulges.

Trim the edge of the cardboard template to match the curve of the dart seam line. Mark starting and stopping points on the guide. Use the template as previously described.

Double-pointed Darts. These are used to fit garments without waistline seams. The fabric is brought in to fit the waist hollow between the bust and hip bulges.

Begin by stitching from each point toward the center of the darts, slightly overlapping stitches in the middle. Clip the dart fold several times to within 3 mm (⅛ in) of the stitching line so it will lie flat when pressed.

Darts in Heavy Fabrics or with Wide Angles. Additional fabric bulk created by thick fabrics or wide-angled darts must be minimized before constructing the rest of the garment.

After stitching the dart, slash it open along the fold to within 1.3 cm (½ in) of the point. Trim the excess fabric to 1.3 cm (½ in) from the seam line if it is very wide. Press the dart open with the point flat.

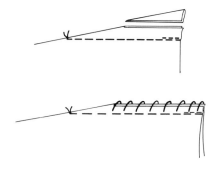

Darts in Sheer Fabrics. These may be constructed like a standard dart or they may be trimmed to reduce their visibility.

To construct a trimmed dart, stitch the dart as usual and then again 3 mm (⅛ in) from the first row of stitching. Trim the excess fabric away close to the second row of stitching. Overcast the raw edges together.

GENERAL CONSTRUCTION PROCEDURES: TUCKS AND DART-TUCKS

Tucks. Fold the fabric along the fold line with right sides together, matching any markings. If the tucks are decorative, fold with wrong sides together. Pin and press the fabric lightly along fold.

Stitch along the stitching line *parallel* to the fold for tucks and pin tucks. Use a cardboard template with a straight edge as a stitching guide.

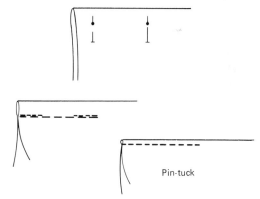

Pin-tuck

Pin-tucks. Fold along the fold line with wrong sides of the fabric together. Pin and press lightly along the fold. Baste to mark the stitching line and prevent the fabric from shifting as it is stitched. Use an over-edge foot to carefully stitch 3 mm (⅛ in) from the fold or along the basting line.

GENERAL PRESSING PROCEDURES: DARTS AND TUCKS

To improve construction accuracy, always press darts and tucks *before* they are intersected by a seam.

Press darts and tucks flat as they were stitched without creasing the fabric beyond the end of the stitches.

Spread open the garment section. Press straight darts and tucks over a flat surface with them turned in the desired pressing direction. Vertical darts are pressed toward the center of the garment; horizontal darts are pressed downward. Tucks may be pressed like darts or following pattern instructions.

Press curved darts over the curved surface of a tailor's ham. Turn the dart in the direction indicated.

To prevent ridges from appearing on the right side of the garment, place heavy kraft paper between the dart and the garment. Press and then carefully remove the paper.

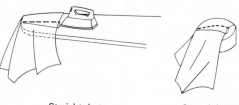

Straight darts   Curved darts

CRITERIA FOR EVALUATION

CREATING CONTOUR WITHIN FABRIC SECTIONS: DARTS AND TUCKS

Check to ensure quality performance:

__ **1.** Corresponding darts or tucks are equal in length, size, and location.

__ **2.** Stitching follows stitching lines precisely:
   a. Stitches at dart point are directly on the fold.
   b. Tuck stitches are parallel to the fold.

__ **3.** Stitches are secured.
   a. Dart points, pin-tuck ends: thread ends are tied.
   b. Tucks and wide dart ends are backstitched.

__ **4.** Pressed smoothly.
   a. Vertical darts are pressed toward center; horizontal darts are pressed downward.
   b. Tucks are pressed as pattern instructs.

In addition, for DART variations:

__ **5.** Dart points are smooth and tapered without an end pucker.

__ **6.** *Double-pointed darts* are clipped two or three times along the fold.

__ **7.** Darts in *heavy fabrics* or with *wide angles* are slashed open and, if needed, trimmed and pressed open.

__ **8.** Darts in *sheer fabrics* are double-stitched, trimmed, and overcast.

16 Joining Seam Lines of Equal Length

OBJECTIVE

To smoothly stitch seamlines of equal length following procedures for joining straight seams, bias-cut seams, and corner seams.

When seam lines of equal length are joined, garment contours are derived from the perimeter shaping of the fabric sections. Curved and angled seam lines help to fit the two-dimensional fabric smoothly over body contours and appendages by taking out wedge- or ellipse-shaped segments similar to those taken out by darts.

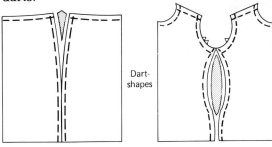

Dart-shapes

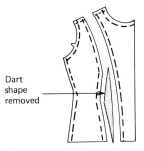

Dart shape removed

In addition, seaming is incorporated into the garment design to vary styling.

General Construction Procedures: Seams

To ensure accurate seam-line location, garment fit should be checked and corrected prior to stitching. Other stitching problems can be avoided by *test*-checking needle size, thread type, stitch length, and machine tension using swatches of the fabric and any inner fabrics planned for the garment. The tests also provide an opportunity to discover potential stitching problems as well as to develop seaming control for the particular fabric *before* the garment is constructed.

Seam allowances on commercial patterns are usually 1.5 cm (⅝ in) wide. In some cases, they may be 1.0 cm (⅜ in) or 6 mm (¼ in). For medium-weight fabrics, the most common stitch length is 5 stitches per cm (dial set at 2; 12 stitches per inch). However, as the fabric becomes thicker, the stitch is lengthened and as the fabric becomes thinner, the stitch is shortened.

Because these are structural seams, their edges are free to rub against the body and they are apt to ravel. The edges may be finished or special seams, such as a flat fell, may be used to enclose the raw fabric edges to eliminate friction.

General Pressing Procedures: Seams

These procedures may be adapted to various seam types.

1. Press the seam flat (as stitched) to blend the stitches and to reduce thread tautness, making it easier to press the seam open.
2. With the fabric sections spread apart and the seam allowances on top, use the tip of the iron to separate and press them open.

STRAIGHT SEAMS

Plain Seams

Plain seams are basic straight seams used to hold the garment together in areas such as the center front or back, at the shoulder, or at the sides. They relate the garment to body contours by their angle to the lengthwise grain of the fabric.

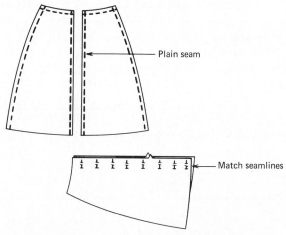

Plain seam

Match seamlines

1. With right sides together and cut edges even, pin fabric layers together. To align, match *stitching lines* at seam ends, match corresponding notches, and insert pins through any corresponding dots. Insert the pins at right angles to the seam line about 7.5 to 10.0 cm (3 to 4 in) apart.
2. Using the machine seam guide, permanently stitch along the seam line through all fabric layers. To prevent flat-finished fabrics (e.g., poplin) from puckering, hold the fabric layers

taut as they are stitched but avoid stretching them. Backstitch both ends of the seam for reinforcement.

Intersecting Seams

Often two seams from different garment units are joined by a third seam. For example, the shirt side seam and sleeve underarm seam are joined by the armscye seam. Special techniques must be used to align the seams precisely at the point of intersection.

1. Insert a pin through the seam–seam-line intersections of each garment section. Match, pin, and stitch the seam.
2. To reduce the bulk created by the seam allowances at the intersection, trim the four corners of the seam allowances diagonally.

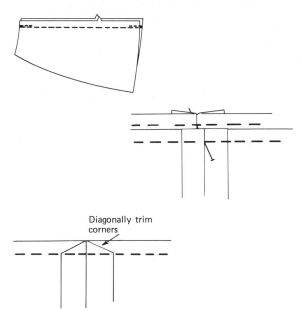

Diagonally trim corners

CURVED SEAMS

Curved seam lines require special construction techniques to simplify stitching and to enable them to lie flat when stitched and pressed.

Like-curved Seams

These have seam lines matching in both degree of curve and curve direction when they are stitched together. The curves may be either concave or convex.

1. Pin the fabric sections with right sides together and edges even. To stitch the curves smoothly:
   a. The cut seam edges must follow the *seam guide only at the point where it is perpendicular to the needle.*
   b. It is often necessary to stop the machine, lift the presser foot, and shift the fabric into position. The sharper the curve, the more frequently the fabric must be repositioned.

Concave Curves

Concave and convex curved seams must be treated with special techniques before they will lie smoothly for pressing.

1. If the seam is to be pressed open, clip the seam allowance just to the stitches at intervals along the curve. Generally, the sharper the curve, the more closely the clips must be spaced. Press seam open using the tip of the iron.

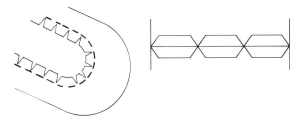

2. If the seam will not be pressed open (e.g., underarm seam of sleeve or crotch seam of pants), the seam may be stitched again 1.0

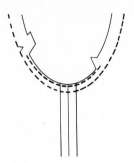

cm (⅜ in) from the edge and trimmed. The seam is left standing as it was stitched.

Convex Curves

To enable the seam allowance to lie flat without rippling, convex curved seams must be notched. To *notch,* cut out wedges from the seam allowance using the tips of the shears. Press open using the tip of the iron.

JOINING UNLIKE CURVED SEAMS OR A CURVED EDGE TO A STRAIGHT EDGE

When seam line shapes differ, the shortest seamline edge must be clipped to release the seam allowance so it will lie flat during stitching.

Concave Curve Joined to Straight or Convex-Curved Edge

Stay-stitch the concave curve 1.3 cm (½ in) from the cut edge. Clip to the stay stitching to allow the seam allowance to spread open to fit the

corresponding seam. Match, pin, and stitch. Notch the convex seam, if necessary, to enable it to lie flat when pressed open.

Convex Curve to Straight Edge

Stay-stitch the straight edge at 1.3 cm (½ in); clip. Pin the fabric sections together, spreading the clipped straight edge to fit the convex curve; stitch. To press the seam open flat, notch the convex seam.

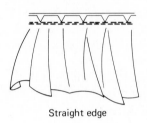

Straight edge

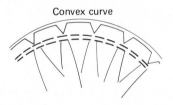

Convex curve

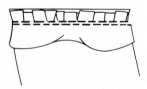

BIAS SEAMS

Garment sections cut on the true bias exhibit some degree of stretch and, as a result, cling more closely to the body than those cut following the lengthwise grain. The give is a desirable characteristic of the bias cut which can be destroyed by incorrect seaming.

If the seam is free-falling, as in a skirt, stitch only the upper 7.5 cm (3 in). Allow the garment to hang until the fabric sections have stretched, about 24 hours. Pin the seams as they hang; stitch, stretching them slightly.

Stitch shorter structural seams, stretching them slightly as they are stitched.

CORNER SEAMS

As with curved seams, the preliminary steps are important to mastery of cornering techniques. Inset corners may be square, acute, or obtuse (e.g., godet, gusset).

Inset Corner

An inset corner is formed by stitching an "inside" corner into an "outside" corner.

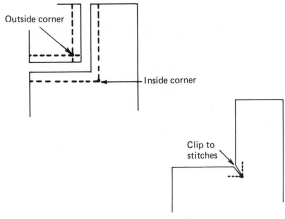

1. Mark each corner seam-line intersection with a dot. Reinforce the *inside* corner by stay-stitching a *scant* 1.5 cm (⅝ in) from the edge for about 2.5 cm (1 in) on either side of the dot. Use very short reinforcement stitches of about 6.5 to 8 stitches per cm (set metric dial at 1½ to 1; 17 to 20 stitches per inch). Clip to the point of the inside corner without cutting the reinforcement stitches.

2. Securely baste the corner sections together, matching the corresponding corner dots precisely. Machine-stitch the seam with the clipped section on top, using short reinforcement stitches for about 2.5 cm (1 in) on each side of the corner point. To pivot at the corner, stop with the needle in the fabric, raise the presser foot, change the fabric direction, and pull the fabric to the back.

3. The corner seam may be pressed in any one of three ways. When the seam is pressed open or in the direction of the outside corner, excess fabric must be trimmed diagonally from the outside corner to eliminate bulk. The corner is then catch-stitched.

   No trimming is necessary when the seam allowances are pressed toward the inside corner.

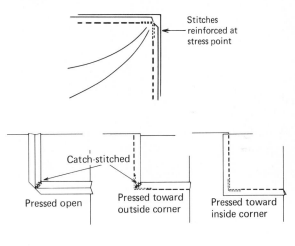

Inset Wedges

Although *godets* and *gussets* are constructed similarly, they differ in function. Both involve setting a wedge-shaped section of bias fabric into a slash or seam.

Godets are triangular insets designed to add flare and fullness to a free-hanging portion of the garment.

Gussets provide freedom of arm movement in garments where the sleeve is cut in one with the bodice—for example, a kimono sleeve. A diamond-shaped fabric section is inserted in the underarm area to permit a close, smooth underarm fit as well as easy arm movement.

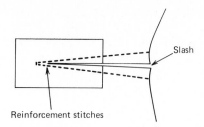

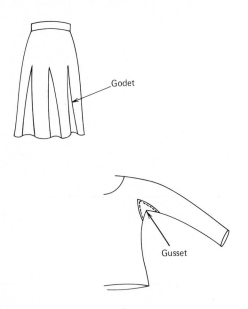

Godet

Gusset

Preparation of Slashed Points

1. Carefully mark all points and stitching lines. Reinforce the points to be slashed:

   a. Cut a 5- to 7.5-cm (2- to 3-in) bias square of organza, underlining, or lining fabric for each point. Position one patch over the right side of each point and pin.

   b. Machine-stitch along stitching lines, using 6½ to 8 stitches per cm (set metric dial at 1½–1; 12 stitches per inch) at the point. *Take one stitch across the point to ensure that the stitches at the point are not so close together that the fabric cannot be slashed to the point.* Slash *to* the point without cutting the reinforcement stitches.

Slash

Reinforcement stitches

2. Press the edges of the patch toward the slashed edge. The edges of the patch will act as *seam allowances* when the godet or gusset sections are being inserted.

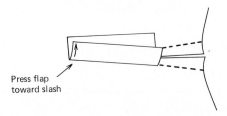

Press flap toward slash

3. *For gusset insertion only:* stitch the bodice side seams and the underarm sleeve seams beyond the underarm markings; press open.

Insertion of Wedge-Shaped Fabric Section (Godet, Gusset)

1. Pin the godet or gusset section to the garment, matching markings precisely and with right sides together. Begin by pinning at the point. Match *stitching lines, not* cut edges. Securely baste the stitching lines together,

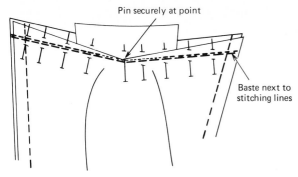

Pin securely at point

Baste next to stitching lines

using a short running stitch; leave pins inserted at points. The patch edges act as seam allowances and should be treated as such when the godet or gusset is being inserted. The remaining two gusset points should be basted into the underarm seam openings, keeping seam allowances free.

2. With the garment section on top, machine-stitch just inside the reinforcement stitching lines. To secure the points, use short stitches—6½ to 8 stitches per cm (set metric dial to 1½ to 1; 17–20 stitches per inch) for 2.5 cm (1 in) on either side of the point. Pivot at the points by leaving the needle inserted in the fabric, raising the presser foot, pivoting the fabric, and pulling the excess fabric back behind the needle. Lower the presser foot and continue stitching.

For godet insertion only: Stitch for 7.5 cm (3 in) on either side of the point. Hang the garment to set the bias, adjust the seam, and stitch.

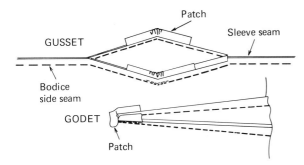

Patch

GUSSET

Sleeve seam

Bodice side seam

GODET

Patch

3. Remove the basting and trim all seam allowances to 1.3 cm (½ in). Finish the raw edges of the gusset or godet by hand- or machine-overcasting. Press the seam toward the garment.

For gusset insertion only: To strengthen the gusset in functional garments, machine-stitch 2 mm (about ⅛ in) outside the seam line and through all layers.

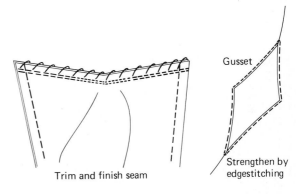

Gusset

Trim and finish seam

Strengthen by edgestitching

CRITERIA FOR EVALUATION

JOINING SEAM LINES OF EQUAL LENGTH

Check to ensure quality performance:

___ **1.** Tension, stitch length, thread type, and needle size have been adapted for the fabric.

___ **2.** Seams are stitched directly on seam lines; seam allowances are even in width.

___ **3.** Fabric layers are smooth, without puckers or tucks.

___ **4.** When necessary, seam allowances have been reinforced or released (by clipping) where needed.

___ **5.** Bulk has been minimized (by notching and trimming) to enable seams to lie flat and smooth when pressed.

17 Joining Seams of Unequal Length

OBJECTIVE

To join seam lines of unequal length by controlling fabric by easing, stretching, gathering, and pleating.

Variations in garment design lines and style ease are seen when corresponding seam lines of differing lengths are joined. Fullness is created by compressing the longer seam line to fit the shorter one. Compression through gathering, pleating, or tucking introduces style fullness into the design. The additional fullness aids in fitting the fabric over body bulges. The amount of added fullness and its location are controlled by the distribution of the longer seam line within the shorter seam or stay.

The technique used to control the excess fabric determines whether the fullness will be directed primarily toward a body bulge or whether it will be generalized over a broader area. Gathering can be used to direct fullness both specifically and generally as it is incorporated into the garment design.

THE EASED SEAM

Easing joins two seams of slightly different lengths without the appearance of added fullness. The slight amount of excess fabric allows the garment to fit over smaller body bulges

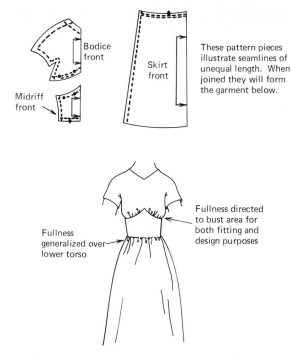

Bodice front

Midriff front

Skirt front

These pattern pieces illustrate seamlines of unequal length. When joined they will form the garment below.

Fullness directed to bust area for both fitting and design purposes

Fullness generalized over lower torso

when a dart is not used. For example, the back shoulder dart or the elbow dart may be eased out to provide a smooth fit over the shoulder blades or the elbow. The cap of a set-in sleeve is eased into the armscye so that the sleeve will fit over the upper arm at the shoulder.

Procedures:

1. Use a *short* machine basting stitch of about 3 to 4 stitches per centimeter (set dial at 2½ to 3 or 8 to 10 stitches per inch) to stitch the area to be eased. *Test* the stitch length on a fabric swatch. Use the shortest stitch possible that will still enable the fabric to be drawn in. Test-pull one thread end. The fabric should compress without large puckers; the thread should not break. Generally, the thinner the fabric, the shorter the ease stitch can be.

 Ease-stitch a *scant* 1.5 cm (⅝ in) from the fabric edge. For curved seam lines, such as

the sleeve cap, ease-stitch again 1.0 cm (⅜ in) from edge. Two rows of stitching provide greater control. Leave thread ends.

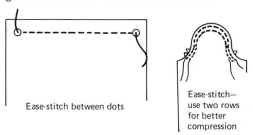

Ease-stitch between dots

Ease-stitch— use two rows for better compression

2. Pin the corresponding seams together, matching markings; pin. Working from one side, pull an easing thread to draw up the longer seam line to fit the shorter one. If two rows of stitching were used, pull the threads from both rows simultaneously. Anchor the pulled thread ends by wrapping them around a pin at each end. Distribute the fullness evenly, smoothing out any puckers; pin. Machine-stitch with eased side up to control fullness and prevent puckering.

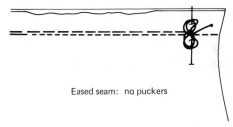

Eased seam: no puckers

3. Press the seam flat to blend the stitches into the fabric and shrink out excess fullness. Press the seam open or in one direction, as the pattern directs.

Procedures:

To eliminate dart-lines from a garment design, the dart take-up at its base (small darts only) can be eased out.

 The dart is not stitched. The excess fabric must be eased out where the dart was located so that the fullness is correctly located for the

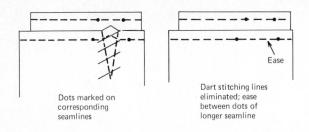

Dots marked on corresponding seamlines

Ease

Dart stitching lines eliminated; ease between dots of longer seamline

body bulge. Mark two points 2.5 cm (1 in) to either side of the dart seam lines. Ease between these markings.

THE STRETCHED SEAM

Sometimes the shorter seam line is stretched to fit a slightly longer seam. Stretching helps the fabric to skim a hollow area of the body, such as the inside of the elbow or below the buttocks.

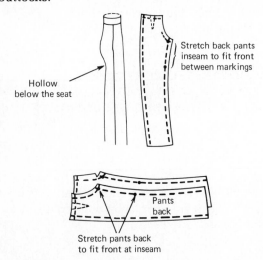

Hollow below the seat

Stretch back pants inseam to fit front between markings

Pants back

Stretch pants back to fit front at inseam

Procedures:

Pin the corresponding fabric sections together, matching markings. As the seam is stitched, pull the fabric taut to stretch the shorter seam until it matches the longer one, keeping cut edges even. Press.

THE GATHERED SEAM

Gathering distributes and controls the excess length of the longer seam by compressing the fabric into *tiny*, *unpressed* folds. No tucks or pleats should be present. Light- to medium-weight fabrics gather easily, whereas heavy fabrics may be too bulky.

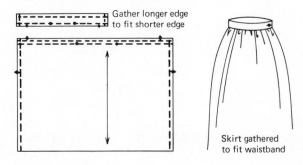

Gather longer edge to fit shorter edge

Skirt gathered to fit waistband

Procedures:

1. Use a machine-basting stitch ranging from 2½ to 5 stitches per centimeter (Set dial at 4 to 2 or 6 to 12 stitches per inch). For *finely distributed fullness*, use the *shortest* stitch length possible that will still allow the fabric to be drawn up. *Test* stitch length on a fabric swatch first and draw in to check size of small folds created. Generally, thinner fabrics require shorter stitches than thicker fabrics.

   Machine-stitch a double row of basting stitches on the longer seam line, following

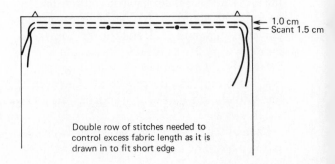

1.0 cm
Scant 1.5 cm

Double row of stitches needed to control excess fabric length as it is drawn in to fit short edge pattern markings. Stitch a *scant* 1.5 cm (⅝ in) and 1.0 cm (⅜ in) from the edge. Leave thread ends for pulling.

2. Pin the corresponding fabric sections together, matching markings. The extra length can be distributed more evenly by pinning the centers of each section together. To evenly distribute fullness:

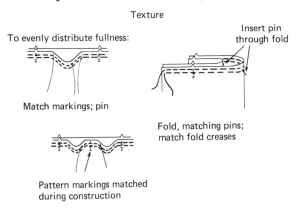

To evenly distribute fullness:

Texture

Match markings; pin

Insert pin through fold

Fold, matching pins; match fold creases

Pattern markings matched during construction

3. To gather the fabric evenly, pull both upper threads from one end *simultaneously*. Work from both ends, drawing up the fabric to the middle. Continue to gather until it is the same length as the shorter seamline. Anchor the thread ends by wrapping them around the end pins.

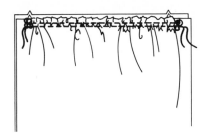

Distribute the fullness evenly and secure; pin or thread-baste in position. If the gathers are loose, draw in the fabric further.

4. Machine-stitch just *inside* and *next to* the line of gathering stitches. Gathering stitches should not be visible from the right side. To control the gathers and avoid creating tucks or pleats, place the fingers on each side of the presser foot and hold the fabric folds perpendicular to the seam line as they are stitched. Stitch again 1.0 cm (⅜ in) from the edge.

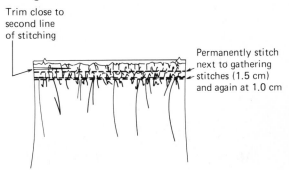

Trim close to second line of stitching

Permanently stitch next to gathering stitches (1.5 cm) and again at 1.0 cm

5. Press the seam allowances flat and then in the direction indicated by the pattern, generally upward. Do not press the gathers.

THE PLEATED SEAM

Pleats may be pressed or unpressed folds. The excess fabric length is controlled by a shorter seam or stay, pressing (optional), and stitching

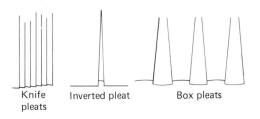

Knife pleats

Inverted pleat

Box pleats

(optional). Pleats may be folded in the same direction, toward each other, or away from each other.

Fit is crucial. Check and correct the garment fit *prior* to cutting the fabric. Note that dart-fit is built into the angle of the pleat lines: they come closer together as the waist narrows above the hips.

Procedures:

1. Working on a large flat surface, mark all fold and placement lines with a running stitch. Use different-color threads to distinguish fold lines from placement lines.
2. For each pleat, fold along the marked fold line and bring the fold to meet the corresponding placement line. To determine fold direction, refer to the pattern arrows. Press (optional); baste the pleats with silk thread to hold in position until garment is completed.

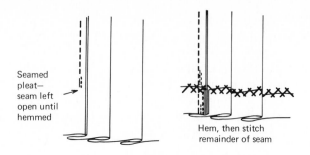

Seamed pleat— seam left open until hemmed

Hem, then stitch remainder of seam

Topstitched knife pleats

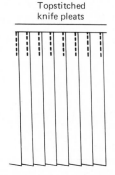

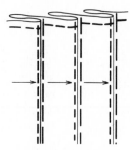

Fold pleat along foldline; bring to meet placement line; baste in position

Some pleats are *partially formed by a seam*. Stitch the seam to within 20 cm (8 in) of the hem. Press the seam flat but not open. Hem the garment *before* stitching the rest of the seam.

3. *Topstitching* is optional. Follow pattern instructions or machine-stitch 3 mm (⅛ in) from the fold line on the right side of the garment. Secure threads by tying them to the inside.
4. If pleats are the pressed type, final-press them after the garment is hemmed. Allow the garment to hang to allow the pleats to set before removing the basting threads.

CRITERIA FOR EVALUATION

JOINING SEAM LINES OF UNEQUAL LENGTH

Check to ensure quality performance:

__ **1.** *Eased seam:* Fullness is distributed evenly without tucks, folds, or puckers.

__ **2.** *Stretched seam:* Seamlines are joined smoothly without easing the longer seam.

__ **3.** *Gathered seam:* Fullness is distributed evenly as tiny, unpressed folds; no tucks or pleats are visible; seam is double-stitched.

__ **4.** *Pleated seam:* Folds are evenly arranged; pressed (optional) along fold lines; topstitching (optional) is even and secured.

18 Joining Circumference Seams

OBJECTIVES

1. To select the construction method—closed, open, semi-closed—that meets individual needs for time and skill level.
2. To smoothly join like or unlike curved seams that encircle body junctures—style fullness accommodated and evenly distributed.

Circumference seams are structural seams that encircle the body, often near a joint where the body flexes. They join major garment units such as a sleeve to the garment body or two pantsleg units to one another. *Full-circumference seams* completely encircle the body. Waistline and armscye seams circuit the body. *Partial-circumference seams* also curve around the body but do not entirely circle it. The pants crotch seam and the raglan armscye seam are examples.

The perimeter shape of a circumference seam may be curved and/or angled. Therefore the seam edges are at least bias and capable of stretching. In addition, these seams often incorporate the extra fullness used to construct darts, tucks, ease, gathers, or pleats. To maintain seam length, a stay can be used.

CONSTRUCTION SELECTION GUIDELINES

Construction procedures are categorized by the direction of the circumference seam and by the construction order. *Horizontal circumference seams* circle the body parallel to the floor. *Verti-*

cal circumference seams (perpendicular to the floor) curve around the body at the point where two appendages meet, such as at the crotch or armscye.

To smoothly join the garment units as well as to simplify fitting, circumference seams are nearly always stitched *after* any intersecting seams are joined. Intersecting seams meet the circumference seam. This is called *closed construction.* In this method, the underarm seam of the sleeve and side seam of the bodice intersect the armscye seam and are stitched before the armscye seam. Pants inseams would also be seamed before the crotch seam. Closed construction enables the intersecting seams to hang smoothly and the circumference seam location to be fitted during construction. The intersecting seams of man-tailored shirts and small children's sleeves are stitched *after* the circumference seam, following *open construction* methods. Sleeve and crotch seams may also be constructed using this quick, easy sequence, but

they do not hang as smoothly unless the seam is clipped drastically. Excessive clipping reduces both seam and fabric strength in these garment stress areas and is not recommended. In addition, bulk is created at the seam intersection.

These two construction methods can also be combined to form the *semi-closed construction* sequence. The advantage of speed is derived from the open construction method, while closed construction enables the garment to hang smoothly. However, because the methods are combined some speed is lost. Beginning sewers who find the closed method difficult may wish to try this method.

The following table illustrates how full (or partial) vertical and horizontal circumference seams may be joined. Note, for example, that set-in sleeves may be joined to the garment unit following closed, open, or semi-closed construction procedures.

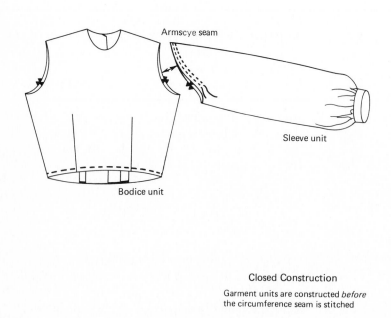

Armscye seam

Sleeve unit

Bodice unit

Closed Construction

Garment units are constructed *before* the circumference seam is stitched

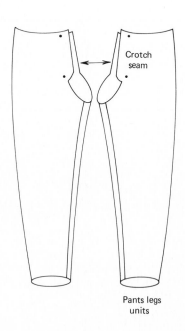

Crotch seam

Pants legs units

Construction Method

		Closed	Open	Semi-Closed

Vertical Circumference Seams		Set-in sleeve
		Crotch
		Raglan sleeve
			Man-tailored
			   sleeve
			Child's sleeve
			Set-in sleeve
			Crotch
			Raglan sleeve
				Set-in sleeve
				Child's
				   sleeve

Horizontal Circumference Seams		Above waistline
		seams:
		   Empire
		   Midriff
		Waistline seam
		Below waist-
		line seams:
		   Hip bone level
		   Hip level
		   Thigh level
			(Horizontal circum-
			   ference seams are
			   rarely constructed
			   using the open
			   method although
			   they may be used
			   for doll clothes or
			   other small items.)	

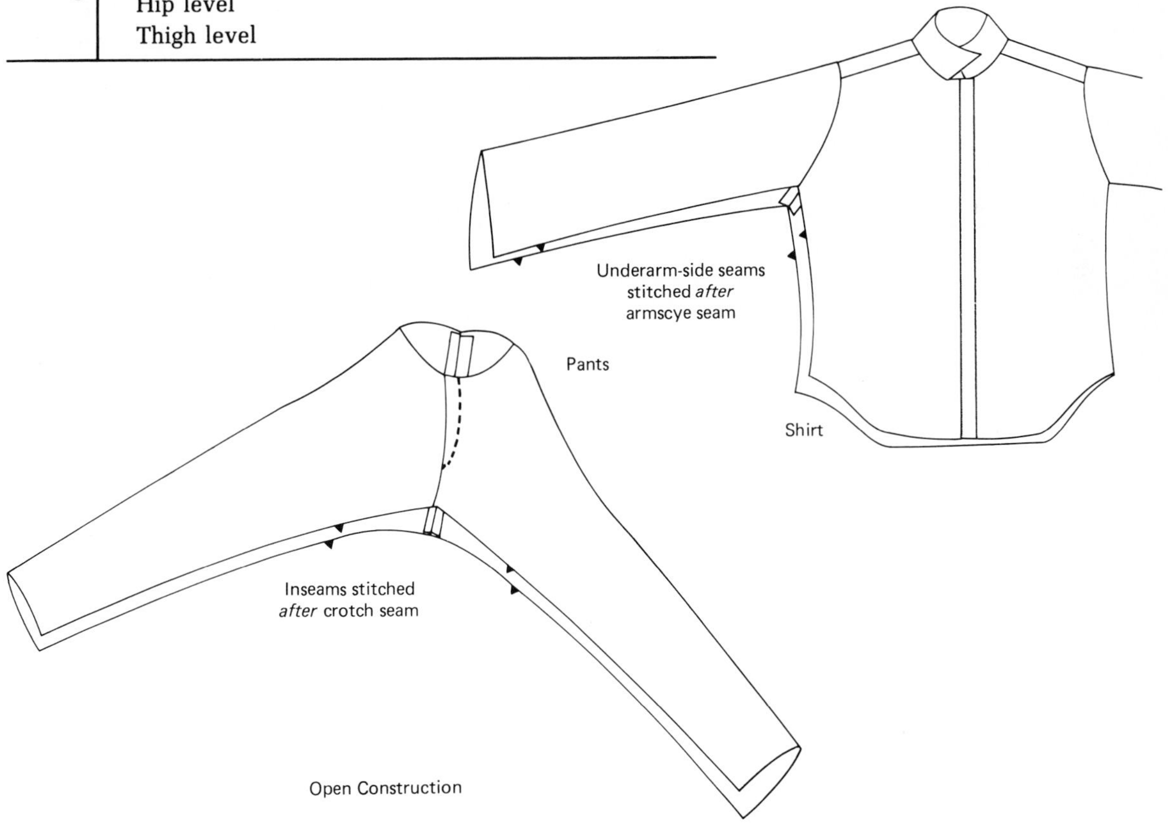

Underarm-side seams
stitched *after*
armscye seam

Pants

Shirt

Inseams stitched
after crotch seam

Open Construction

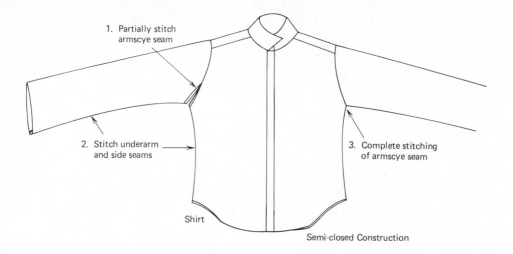

1. Partially stitch armscye seam

2. Stitch underarm and side seams

3. Complete stitching of armscye seam

Shirt

Semi-closed Construction

Once you have determined your seam's direction, and the construction method to be followed, turn to the specific construction procedures in this chapter. They are categorized under Vertical and Horizontal Seams.

GENERAL CONSTRUCTION PROCEDURES: CIRCUMFERENCE SEAMS

Circumference seams are often double-stitched: once at 1.5 cm (⅝ in) and once at 1.0 cm (⅜ in) for improved strength and to flatten any bulk produced by fullness. They are *never* clipped with the exception of partial-circumference seams, which must be clipped twice.

Circumference seams are rarely pressed open due to their curvature and their subjection to body friction.

1. Full-circumference seams are pressed flat and turned in one direction, usually in the direction of least bulk. Commonly, waistline seams are pressed upward and armscye seams are pressed toward the sleeve, although design variations influence choice.

2. Seams curving under the body at the juncture of two appendages, such as the juncture of the legs at the crotch or the arm and upper torso at the underarm, remain in an upright position. They are not pressed in either direction.

Fit is critical. The level of each circumference seam and its location in relation to the body juncture is important, especially when the garment is closely fitted. Waistline, armscye, and crotch seams that are too high or too low may cut into the body or hinder movement. When garments are loosely fitted, body movement is restricted less and there is greater flexibility in locating circumference seams. Visual balance gains importance. Refer to Chapter 8, "Components of Fit," for detailed fitting procedures.

Horizontal Circumference Seams

Horizontal circumference seams, are usually parallel to the floor and they encircle the body at, above, or below the natural waistline. Empire, midriff, waistline, and hip seams are examples. One or more horizontal seams may exist within a garment. Waistline seams are stayed to prevent stretching because they tend to fit the body closely and receive more strain.

CLOSED CONSTRUCTION PROCEDURES

Construction of all horizontal circumference seams is essentially the same. Intersecting vertical seams are stitched to form the upper- and lower-torso units before being joined by the circumference seam. Intersecting closures are constructed after the circumference seam has been completed.

1. Stitch intersecting darts, tucks, or seams, including those at the center front or center back and side as well as style and facing seams. Upper and lower garment units are thus formed. Protect raw seam edges with a finish.
2. If the circumference edge of either unit has style fullness for easing, gathering, or pleating, prepare the edge.
3. Join the circumference seam:

Two rows of stitching

WS

a. *Joining circumference seams with one or no seams to be eased or gathered:* Pin the corresponding circumference seams together, matching markings and intersecting seams. Evenly distribute any eased or gathered fullness. Stitch the seam at 1.5 and 1.3 cm (⅝ and ⅜ in). Trim close to the second row of stitching and edge-finish.

Apply a stay to close-fitting waistline circumference seams. Cut firmly woven grosgrain ribbon, seam binding, twill tape, or self-fabric selvage the length of the waistline seam plus 5.0 cm (2 in). Press under the stay ends at 6 mm (¼ in) and then again at 2.0 cm (¾ in). Machine-hem in position. Attach two sets of small hooks and round eyes to the ends of the stay.

After pressing the seam in the direction of least bulk or fullness, pin the stay to the innermost seam allowance. Align the edge of the stay tape with the seam line and match the center of the length of tape to the center of the garment. Pin the stay to the seam allowances, leaving 5.0 cm (2 in) free on either side of the zipper. Edge-stitch the stay tape near the garment seam line, catching only

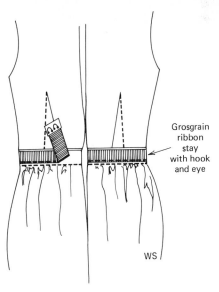

Grosgrain ribbon stay with hook and eye

WS

the seam allowances and stopping 5.0 cm (2 in) from the ends of the tape. The ends are left free so that they can be hooked beneath the zipper to reduce strain on the closure.

b. *Joining circumference seams when both seams have style fullness:* Using the stay pattern provided with the pattern, cut and mark firmly woven grosgrain ribbon, seam binding, twill tape, or self-fabric selvage. Pin the stay to the wrong side of the skirt or pant circumference seam, matching markings and distributing fullness evenly. Machine-baste by stitching next to the gathering stitches but inside the seam allowance.

Pin the two circumference seams together, matching all markings. Adjust fullness evenly. Hand-baste, placing short stitches next to the gathering stitches of both seam lines. Make a fitting check of seam-line location and distribution of fullness.

Machine-stitch next to the gathering stitches outside the seam allowance and with the stay downward. Stitch again at 1.3 cm (⅜ in) to flatten fullness in the seam allowance.

Vertical Circumference Seams

Vertical circumference seams curve around or under body junctures where two body appendages meet: at the shoulder joint where the shoulder meets the arm and at the crotch where the legs come together.

The armscye seam of the set-in sleeve forms a full circle *around* the shoulder joint, whereas the raglan armscye seam and the pants crotch are each partial circumference seams curving *under* the armpit or the crotch.

Construction techniques vary slightly for full-as opposed to partial-circumference seams. The set-in sleeve requires special easing procedures to enable the sleeve cap to fit smoothly over the upper arm. The seams of the raglan sleeve and the crotch are each pressed open above the notches.

Construction may also differ by the sequence in which the intersecting and circumference seams are stitched. Intersecting seams are stitched before circumference seams for most constructions; however, the order is reversed for man-tailored and children's sleeves or for open sleeve construction.

FULL VERTICAL CIRCUMFERENCE SEAMS: SET-IN SLEEVE

The set-in sleeve, the most common sleeve type, is eased, fitted, and stitched into the garment armscye. Sleeves may vary in length, closeness of fit, and design fullness. A variation of the set-in sleeve is the man-tailored sleeve, which is attached to the garment using open sleeve construction methods.

Before construction begins, you should be aware of the sleeve's characteristics. Refer to the sleeve diagram when studying its various parts:

Biceps. The scyeline is an imaginary line perpendicular to the lengthwise grain-line and intersecting the armscye-underarm seam intersection.

Sleeve Cap. The rounded upper portion of the sleeve above the scyeline is the sleeve cap. The cap seam line is eased (between the notches) into the garment armscye to fit over the rounded upper arm. Cap height is measured from the scyeline to the shoulder dot.

Underarm Seams. When these seams are joined, the sleeve is formed.

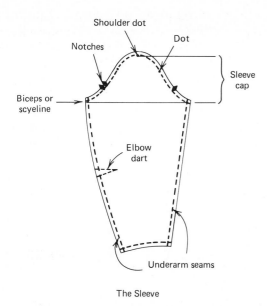

Shoulder dot

Notches

Dot

Sleeve cap

Biceps or scyeline

Elbow dart

Underarm seams

The Sleeve

Construction difficulties may arise when the sleeve cap is being eased into the garment armscye. Fabric pliability, cap height, and cap length between the notches influence how smoothly the sleeve can be eased in. Natural fibers, knits, and spongy fabrics are generally more pliable than synthetics or permanent-press fabrics.

It is important to realize that not all sleeves are cut with the same amount of fabric to be eased in. Location and size of the armscye plus closeness of fit influence cap height and the amount of ease.

The fitted sleeve of a standard women's garment has a high cap with about 3.8 cm (1½ in) ease. Excess ease can be removed by lowering the top of the cap slightly.

When constructed, the upper cap appears slightly rounded. A sleeve head may be inserted to support the rounded cap when a fabric needs support. As the armscye seam drops off the

Elbow Darts.   One or more darts pointing to the elbow bulge of a tight-fitting sleeve allow the arm to bend easily.

Notches.   A single notch indicates the sleeve front.
A double notch indicates the sleeve back.

Dots.   The dot located at the top of the sleeve cap is the *shoulder dot* and is aligned with the garment shoulder line. *Dots midway* between the shoulder dot and each set of notches are used to distribute cap fullness. Two additional dots are sometimes placed on each side of the shoulder dot to indicate that the area between them is not to be eased in.

In order for the sleeve to fit over the rounded upper arm, the sleeve-cap seam must be cut slightly larger than the corresponding garment armscye seam. The sleeve cap is usually eased in to fit the garment armscye, but it may also be gathered or dart-tucked. A loosely fitted armscye style may have no ease in the cap.

Rounded cap

Fitted sleeve has a high, rounded cap

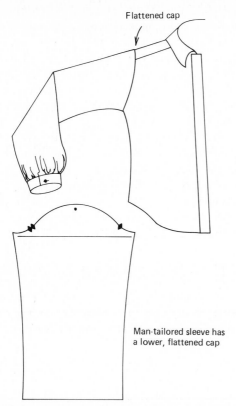

Flattened cap

Man-tailored sleeve has a lower, flattened cap

small children's sleeves with small armscyes are constructed by seaming intersecting seams after the circumference seams using *open* construction procedures. To simplify the joining of the eased or gathered portion of the sleeve to the armscye, the semi-closed method can be used. Base choice of construction technique upon sleeve cap length, size of armscye opening, and ability of the garment to hang smoothly.

Closed Construction Procedures: Set-in Sleeve

The sleeve and garment units are formed before they are joined with a full-circumference seam at the armscye.

1. Ease-stitch the sleeve cap between the notches at 1.5 and 1.3 cm (⅝ and ⅜ in); leave 5.0 cm (2 in) thread ends. The use of a shorter stitch length and a looser bobbin tension makes it possible to draw the cap in smoothly, thus reducing the possibility of puckering.
2. Stitch and finish all intersecting darts and seams, including the sleeve elbow dart and underarm seam and the garment shoulder and side seams.
3. If the sleeve length is accurate, finish the lower sleeve edges by hemming, facing, or banding with a cuff. You will find it easier to finish the sleeve at this point because it is not yet joined to the larger, bulkier garment unit. If the sleeve length may require adjustment, wait to finish the lower edge until after the sleeve is fitted during construction.
4. Measure the garment armscye seamline between the notches. Ease in the sleeve cap by pulling the bobbin thread until the cap is slightly larger than the armscye measure; secure thread ends by wrapping them around a pin in a figure-eight configuration. Notice

shoulder, the sleeve cap also drops. The lowered sleeve cap has less ease between the notches, making it easier to ease in when using less pliable fabrics. This sleeve cap appears less rounded after construction and falls closer to the upper arm. A lowered sleeve cap is flattened, has little or no ease, and often fits into a larger, looser-fitting armscye. The sleeves of man-tailored shirts are cut with a flattened sleeve cap. Therefore they can be constructed from firm fabrics.

Sleeves attached with a full-circumference seam at the armscye may be constructed following one of three construction sequences. Sleeves are *set in* following *closed* construction procedures when intersecting seams are stitched before the circumference seam. Man-tailored sleeves, with little or no cap ease, and

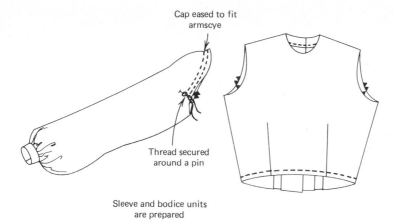

Cap eased to fit
armscye

Thread secured
around a pin

Sleeve and bodice units
are prepared

that the cap eases in most readily in the bias areas on each side of the shoulder. Distribute the ease evenly. There will be no ease for about 1.5 cm (⅝ in) on either side of the shoulder dot. Position most of the ease in the bias areas with less ease near the notches. The upper cap should take on a rounded appearance if there is much length to be eased in.

5. Using the tip of the iron, carefully steam the seam allowances to shrink out excess fullness.

   Note: When the fabric cannot be eased out smoothly, it is necessary to drop the cap seam line slightly. This must be done when using less pliable fabrics such as synthetics or permanent-press materials. To drop the seam line, loosen ease stitches until the sleeve cap lies flat again. Restitch, beginning at the notches and tapering the new stitching line to 3 mm (⅛ in) below the shoulder dot. Ease in the sleeve again following step 4.

6. Turn the garment *wrong* side out and the sleeve *right* side out. Slip the sleeve into the garment armscye with right sides together. Align the underarm and side seams and match the notches and shoulder; pin with the *seam lines* matched. Ease in the remaining sleeve fullness until the sleeve cap fits the armscye. Distribute fullness as in step 4, smoothing out any puckers. Secure thread ends; pin often to hold in place.

7. Hand- or machine-baste, stitching next to the ease stitches and *within* the seam allowance. Begin stitching below the notches and with the sleeve side up, so that the ease can be controlled. Smooth out any fullness with the fingers as you stitch. Try on the garment, pin closed, and check the hang of the sleeve. The cap should be smoothly rounded with no puckers. If necessary, readjust the ease before the final stitching; baste.

8. To permanently join the sleeve to the garment, machine-stitch next to the ease stitching and *outside* the seam allowance. Smooth away any puckers and overlap beginning stitches slightly. Stitch again 6.0 mm (¼ in) from the seam line. Trim close to the second row of stitching; edge-finish.

9. Press the armscye seam flat, as it was stitched, using the tip of the iron to shrink out any remaining fullness. Turn the seam toward the sleeve but do not press it, as this will flatten the cap height.

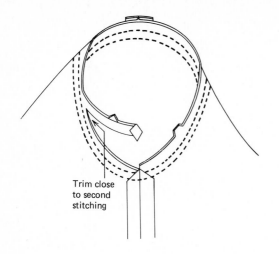

Trim close
to second
stitching

The sleeves of small children's garments are constructed following this same sequence because the armscye openings are often too small to stitch inside with adequate control. Set-in sleeves are easier to construct using the open method, but may not hang as smoothly as when they are inserted using the closed method.

Open Construction Procedures: Man-Tailored Sleeve

1. Stitch and finish garment shoulder seam.
2. With *wrong* sides together and markings matched, pin the corresponding armscye seams together. To check fit, first baste the circumference seam line and then baste the under-arm side seams together. Check fit and adjust if necessary.
3. Permanently stitch the armscye seam, using flat-fell seaming.
4. Pin *wrong* sides of corresponding underarm-side seams together. Stitch using flat-fell seaming.
5. Finish the lower sleeve edge by hemming, facing, or banding.

Open Construction Procedures: Man-Tailored Sleeve, Small Child's Sleeve, Set-in Sleeve

The flattened curve of the man-tailored sleeve, inserted with a flat-fell seam, can be easily constructed when the circumference seam is stitched before the intersecting seams. This sleeve construction is found on classic men's and many women's shirts.

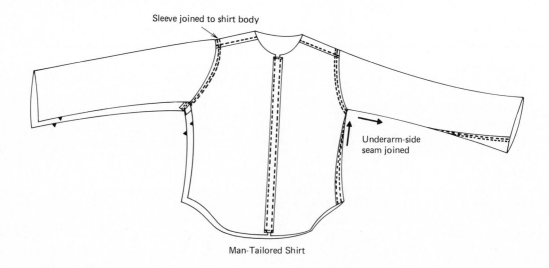

Sleeve joined to shirt body

Underarm-side
seam joined

Man-Tailored Shirt

Open Construction Procedures: Small Child's Sleeve, Set-in Sleeve

1. Stitch and finish the garment shoulder seam.
2. Ease-stitch the sleeve cap between the notches at 1.5 and 1.3 cm (⅝ and ⅜ in); leave 5.0 cm (2 in) thread ends. The use of a shorter stitch length and a looser bobbin tension makes it possible to draw the cap in smoothly, thus reducing the possibility of puckering.
3. Measure the garment armscye seamline between the notches. Ease in the sleeve cap by pulling the bobbin thread until the cap is slightly larger than the armscye measure; secure thread ends by wrapping them around a pin in a figure-eight configuration. Notice that the cap eases in most readily in the bias areas on each side of the shoulder. Distribute the ease evenly. There will be no ease for about 1.5 cm (⅝ in) on either side of the shoulder dot. Position most of the ease in the bias areas with less ease near the notches. The upper cap should take on a rounded appearance if there is much length to be eased in.

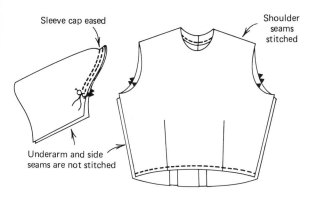

Sleeve cap eased

Shoulder seams stitched

Underarm and side seams are not stitched

4. Using the tip of the iron, carefully steam the seam allowances to shrink out excess fullness.

   Note: When the fabric cannot be eased out smoothly, it is necessary to drop the cap seam line slightly. This must be done when using less pliable fabrics such as synthetics or permanent-press materials. To drop the seam line, loosen ease stitches until the sleeve cap lies flat again. Restitch, beginning at the notches and tapering the new stitching line to 3 mm (⅛ in) below the shoulder dot. Ease in the sleeve again following step 4.

5. With right sides together, match and pin the sleeve and garment armscyes together at the notches and shoulder dot. Draw in any remaining ease, secure, and pin. Hand- or machine-baste by stitching next to the ease stitches and *within* the seam allowance. Baste the underarm-side seams together. Check the fit and adjust if necessary.
6. Permanently stitch the seam at 1.5 and 1.3 cm (⅝ and ⅜ in); trim close to the second row of stitching and edge-finish. Press the seam flat as stitched, shrinking out any remaining fullness. Turn the seam toward the sleeve.

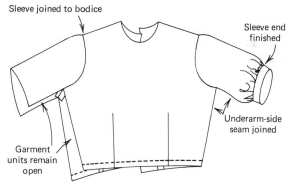

Sleeve joined to bodice

Sleeve end finished

Garment units remain open

Underarm-side seam joined

7. To form the garment and sleeve units, pin and stitch the underarm-side seam. Edge-finish and press open.

Semi-Closed Construction Procedures: Set-in Sleeve

Often it is difficult to insert an eased or gathered sleeve cap smoothly into a seemingly small garment armscye. The process can be simplified by combining the best features of the closed and open sleeve constructions. In this way construction is simplified and the underarm area will hang smoothly and without bulk.

1. Follow the steps for constructing small children's sleeves, but permanently stitch the armscye seam above the notches *only*.
2. Stitch and finish the sleeve underarm seam and the garment side seam; press open.
3. Pin the underarm area of the armscye seam. Stitch the remaining portion of the circumference seam at 1.5 and 1.3 cm (⅝ and ⅜ in). Overlap stitching slightly at notches. Trim the seam close to the second row of stitching and edge-finish.

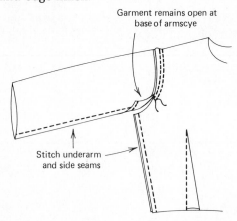

Garment remains open at base of armscye

Stitch underarm and side seams

PARTIAL VERTICAL CIRCUMFERENCE SEAMS

Construction of the raglan sleeve and crotch seams, both partial-circumference seams, is similar, since each seam curves *under* the juncture of two body appendages.

The *raglan sleeve* is attached to the garment unit by a seam extending diagonally from the front neckline, *under* the arm, and diagonally to the back neckline. Therefore this sleeve forms part of the garment shoulder area.

The *crotch seam* joins two leg units to form a pair of pants. The seam begins in the center front, at or near the waist level, curves *under* the crotch, and extends vertically upward toward the center-back waistline.

Construction Procedures: Raglan Sleeve

The raglan sleeve pattern is designed to fit over the shoulder curve by incorporating a dart or a curved seam over the shoulder. The darted sleeve pattern is one piece and the shoulder seamed sleeve is two pieces. Construction procedures for both types follow:

1. Stitch the shoulder dart, tapering and curving the stitching inward near the dart point. Curving it over the shoulder will prevent the finished dart from protruding outward. Slash the dart and press it open.

   Or

   Stitch, finish, and press open the shoulder-sleeve seam.
2. Stitch, finish, and press the sleeve underarm seam and the garment side seam.
3. Pin the sleeve to the garment with right sides together, aligning the underarm seam with the side seam and matching markings. Baste and try on the garment to check both garment and sleeve fit. Make any needed adjustments.
4. Permanently stitch the armscye seam with the sleeve side up. Stitch again between the notches 6 mm (¼ in) from the first row of stitching.
5. Clip to the seam line at each notch and trim the underarm seam close to the second row of stitching. Edge-finish the seam allowances. Press the seam open above each clip; the seam between the notches is left standing.

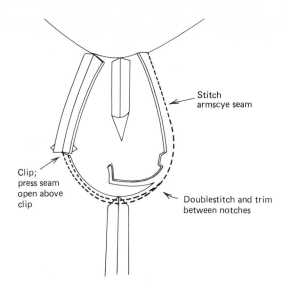

Stitch
armscye seam

Clip;
press seam
open above
clip

Doublestitch and trim
between notches

Construction Procedures: Crotch Seam

The pants legs are joined by the crotch seam. Due to its location, the shape and length of the crotch seam are crucial to pants fit around the buttocks, crotch, and abdomen. Carefully check the fit before trimming the seam.

Some pattern instruction sheets suggest that the intersecting seams (inseams) be stitched *after* the circumference seam (crotch seam). This method is not suggested here because it does not allow the inner pantslegs to hang smoothly and because the construction order suggested here is simpler.

1. Stitch, finish, and press pants inseams. Do not stitch outseams until after the crotch seam and zipper are constructed and the pants can be fitted.

2. Pin crotch seams together, matching markings and inseam intersection; leave an opening for the zipper closure. Stitch; stitch again between the crotch notches 6 mm (¼ in) from the first row of stitching. To prevent the seam from stretching in knits or loosely woven fabrics, stay the seam.

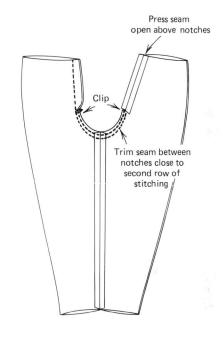

Press seam
open above notches

Clip

Trim seam between
notches close to
second row of
stitching

3. Clip to the seam at the notches and trim the seam between the notches close to the second row of stitching. Edge-finish the seam allowances. Press the seam open above the clips; leave the seam standing between the notches.

CRITERIA FOR EVALUATION

CIRCUMFERENCE SEAMS

Check to ensure quality performance:

__ **1.** *Seam Location:* Circumference seam smoothly encircles the body juncture, allows ease of movement.

__ **2.** Seams are evenly stitched and smoothly curved without puckers and with notches and intersecting seams matched.

__ **3.** Ease and gathers are evenly distributed.

__ **4.** *Construction Order:* Intersecting and circumference seams are stitched in the most appropriate sequence. Consider final appearance as well as ease of construction.

In addition, for *full-circumference seams:*

__ **1.** Seams completely double-stitched at 1.5 and 1.3 cm (⅝ and ⅜ in), trimmed close to second row of stitching, edge-finished.

__ **2.** Seams pressed flat as stitched and turned in direction of least bulk or as pattern directs. Commonly, the waistline seam is turned upward and the armscye seam toward the sleeve.

__ **3.** *Set-in Sleeve:* Ease distributed, forming smoothly rounded cap. More ease located in bias area of upper sleeve; less ease located near shoulder dot and notches.

__ **4.** *Waistline Seams:* Stayed to prevent stretching; stays hook inside garment to reduce strain on the closure system.

In addition, for *Partial-circumference seams:*

__ **1.** Double-stitched and trimmed *only* between the notches.

__ **2.** Seam clipped at each notch to enable the seam above the notches to be pressed open.

__ **3.** *Darted Raglan Sleeve:* Dart curves smoothly over the shoulder; it has been slashed, finished, and pressed open.

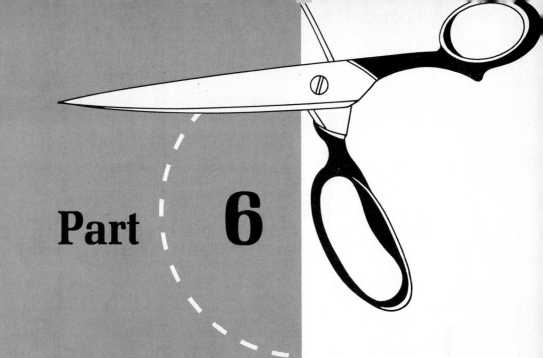

Part 6

Structural Seams: Protective and Decorative Functions

Structural seams were previously discussed relative to their function of joining together major fabric sections of the garment. It was also indicated that structural seam edges receive friction from the body and therefore need to be treated to prevent fraying. Two approaches can be employed to protect raw fabric edges: (1) protective edge finishes and (2) protective decorative enclosed seams.

In addition to being *protective,* structural seams may also be highly *decorative.* Special seaming techniques, color contrasts, and topstitching may be used to accentuate garment design lines.

Protective edge finishes and enclosed seams as well as *decorative* seaming are discussed in this unit.

Construction Selection Guidelines

Because several construction techniques are categorized under each approach, selection of an appropriate technique should be based upon consideration of:

1. *Fabric thickness.*
   Fabric thickness must be considered in relation to the degree of bulk added by some edge treatments. Keeping added *bulk* and *stiffness* to a minimum reduces the chance that the finish will create a visible ridge or that it will detract from the fabric's draping qualities.
2. *Tendency to fray.*
   To determine the degree of security needed, check each fabric's *tendency to fray.* Cut a scrap of the fabric along the bias (not *true* bias) and rough up the edges. If the yarns loosen easily, the fabric will ravel during wear and should be treated. Loosely woven fabrics or those woven of smooth-finished yarns tend to fray more readily. If the fabric frays very little, the treatment may be used to improve garment appearance or to support garment design lines.
2. *Garment end use and life expectancy.*
   How much wear and tear will the garment receive when it is worn? How often will it be worn and over what period of time? Those edge treatments that provide greater strength should be used on work clothing, sportswear, and other functional garments or garments that will be worn over a long period of time. Perhaps the garment is a costume that will be worn only once or twice. In this case, inner finishing is unnecessary unless the fabric frays considerably.
3. *Garment care methods.*
   Some cleaning methods involve greater wear and tear than others. Therefore stronger seaming, hand-sewing, and edge treatments should be used on a garment that will be machine-laundered and dried. Hand-washing, line drying, and dry cleaning are generally not as rough on garment construction or fabric.

19 Protective Raw-Edge Treatments

OBJECTIVE

To protect raw fabric edges by treating them with a finish that (a) prevents fraying and (b) creates minimal bulk and stiffness along seam allowances.

In addition to the prevention of fraying (raveling), protective edge treatments also improve garment durability and the interior appearance of an unlined garment. No protection is necessary when the garment is to be lined, since seam friction is eliminated. Edges cut on the true bias do not ravel. In addition, special edge treatments might destroy the natural give of the bias cut.

To protect the raw edges of basic structural seams, a finish may be used to treat them. Apply the edge finish after the seam has been stitched and checked for fit but before it will be intersected by another seam. For an open seam, finish the edges individually. If the seam allowances are pressed to one side, however, they should be finished together.

PROTECTIVE EDGE FINISHES

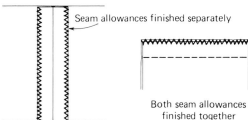

Seam allowances finished separately

Both seam allowances
finished together

EDGE FINISHES ADDING MINIMAL BULK

The following edge treatments add only minimal bulk to the seam edges, because no additional fabric layers are joined to the seam.

Raw Edge

No treatment is necessary if the fabric is firmly woven and will be hand-laundered, if it is a knit, or if it is cut on the true bias.

Procedure. After the seam is stitched, all notches are trimmed so the raw edges will be smooth.

Double-stitch Finish

Curved seams that must be trimmed and left standing are double-stitched to strengthen the seam. Areas of stress commonly treated this way include the underarm and crotch seams.

Procedure. After the seam has been stitched, stitch again 1.0 cm (⅜ in) from the edge. If the seam to be double-stitched is the crotch seam or the underarm seam of a dolman sleeve, the second row of stitches should be placed on the curve between the notches.

Trim the seam allowance close to the second row of stitches. If the seam has been partially double-stitched, clip to the seam line at each end of the finished area.

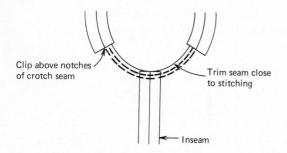

Clip above notches of crotch seam

Trim seam close to stitching

Inseam

For additional protection, zigzag or overcast the edges.

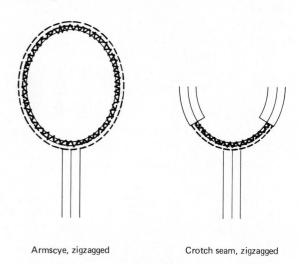

Armscye, zigzagged   Crotch seam, zigzagged

Hand-Overcast Finish

Although time consuming, hand-overcasting does not stiffen or add bulk to seam allowances. Seams remain flexible and delicate fabrics remain unharmed by hand-stitches. Advantages include the following:

1. Draping characteristics of the fabric are retained.
2. The finish is less visible through sheer fabrics.
3. Little bulk is added to heavier fabrics.
4. Delicate fabrics are not damaged.
5. Fraying is prevented.

Procedure. Machine-stitch 6 mm (¼ in) from the raw seam edge and trim to 3 mm (⅛ in). If the fabric is *very* delicate, eliminate this step.

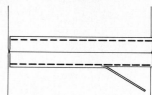

Using a single thread, insert the needle just inside the line of edge stitching and always through the same side of the seam allowance. This forces the thread to encircle the raw edge. Space the stitches 3 to 6 mm (⅛ to ¼ in) apart; do not pull the thread too tight.

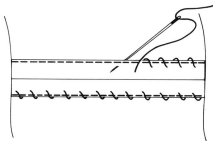

Hand Overcast Finish

To overcast seams in *sheer fabrics,* after stitching the seam, stitch again 1.3 cm (½ in) from the edge. Trim the seam to 3 mm (⅛ in) from the second line of stitching; hand-overcast.

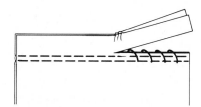

Hand overcast finish: Sheer fabrics

Machine-Zigzag Finish

Because it is simple and quick to do and also prevents fraying, machine-zigzagging is one of the most commonly used edge finishes. Variations of stitch length and width enable the zigzag stitch to be coordinated with the fabric's

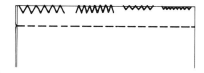

Variations in zigzag width and length

tendency to fray. Long, narrowly spaced stitches provide less control than widely spaced stitches. If the stitches are too short and tightly spaced, they may stiffen the fabric too much causing the seam to be visible from the right side of the garment. Test several variations of the zigzag finish on a fabric swatch before choosing one.

Machine-zigzagging cannot be used to treat all fabrics. The process is often too harsh for delicate fabrics and may stiffen soft fabrics if the stitches are closely spaced. Hand-overcasting may be a better choice in these cases.

Procedure. Readjust the machine tension and test-check the stitch width and length. Zigzag-stitch close to the raw edge of the fabric. If necessary, use an over-edge foot to prevent the fabric edge from tucking.

ZIGZAG FINISH

EDGE FINISHES ADDING SOME BULK

Although the following raw-edge treatments effectively eliminate fraying, they also incorporate more fabric layers along the seam line. If the layers are too thick or stiff, they may be visible from the right side of the garment, or they may influence garment drape.

Before selecting an edge treatment from this group, consider the additional fabric layers and stitching lines to be added to the seam. Each seam allowance of a finish adds bulk; each line of stitching creates some stiffness.

The greatest advantage of these finishes is that they *conceal the raw edges completely.* Used in unlined outerwear, they provide a tech-

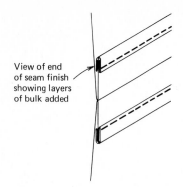

View of end of seam finish showing layers of bulk added

nique for protecting the raw edges from friction as well as concealing them from view.

When pressing these seams, it may be necessary to slip heavy brown paper between the garment and seam allowances to avoid forming a ridge on the right side of the garment.

Turn-and-Stitch Finish (Clean Finish)

The raw edge of the seam allowance is concealed by turning it under and edge-stitching. The hem and facing edges of garments made from light- to medium-weight fabrics are securely protected by this finish. It is also suitable for functional garments such as playclothes, sportswear, or work apparel.

Procedure. Machine-stitch a fold guideline 6 mm (¼ in) from the raw edge. The guideline is helpful in controlling the fabric when it is to be folded along curved or slightly bias edges.

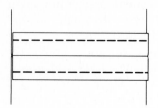

Turn the seam allowance under, following the stitching line and with the stitches turned underneath so that they are not visible. Press; edge-stitch 2 to 3 mm (a scant ⅛ in) from the fold.

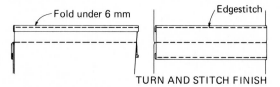

Fold under 6 mm — Edgestitch

TURN AND STITCH FINISH

Self-bound Finish

A seam may be bound by enclosing one trimmed seam allowance within the other. The self-bound seam is a good alternative for sheer fabrics in areas where it is difficult to use a French seam. Seams on garments made from reversible fabrics may also be concealed by self-binding.

Procedure. After stitching the seam, trim one seam allowance to 6 mm (¼ in). *Turn the untrimmed seam allowance under 6 mm (¼ in); press.* To enclose the trimmed seam allowance, bring the folded edge to the seam-line and blind/slipstitch in place. Stitches should not show on the right side of the garment.

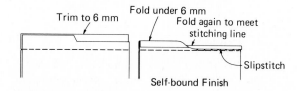

Trim to 6 mm — Fold under 6 mm — Fold again to meet stitching line — Slipstitch

Self-bound Finish

Hong Kong Finish

The Hong Kong finish binds garment edges with lining-weight fabric. It is simple to perform and provides a couture touch to unlined garments. It also works well when used to bind the seam, facing, and hem edges of medium- to heavy-weight fabrics since it adds little bulk or stiffness.

Procedure. Cut true bias strips 2.5 cm (1 in) wide from the lining fabric. With right sides together, pin the bias strip to the edge that will be bound. Machine-stitch 6 mm (¼ in) from the raw edge using short stitches; trim the seam to 3 mm (⅛ in).

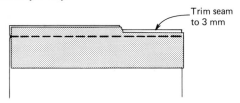

Press the bias strip toward the seam allowances. Fold the strip behind the trimmed seam until only 3 mm (⅛ in) are visible. Press and pin. Stitch in the ditch of the seam line using the hand prick stitch or machine stitching. The stitches will catch the bias strip underneath and hold it in place.

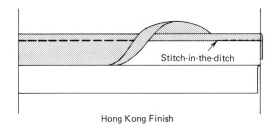

Hong Kong Finish

Bound Finish

Seam edges may be protected and concealed by binding them with purchased seam tape. This treatment adds four fabric layers to the seam allowance, making it much thicker than seams tested with other edge finishes. The bound finish is used primarily to enclose the raw edges of unlined jackets constructed of heavier fabrics.

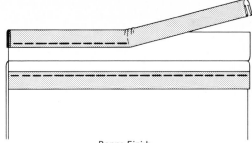

Bonna Finish

Procedure. Encase the raw edge with double-fold bias tape (rayon adds less bulk than cotton). Place the narrower fold on top so that the lower edge can be caught when the binding is stitched to the garment edge. Baste; machine-stitch close to the narrow binding edge, catching all five layers securely.

CRITERIA FOR EVALUATION

PROTECTIVE RAW-EDGE TREATMENTS

Check to ensure quality performance:

Protective Raw-Edge Treatments:

__ **1.** Minimal bulk and stiffness have been added to seam allowances (more bulk can be accommodated to enclose the seams of unlined garments constructed of heavier fabrics).

__ **2.** Seam-edge treatment controls fraying.

__ **3.** Seam-edge treatment can withstand garment wear and care requirements.

__ **4.** Treatment is evenly applied; fabric yarns are trimmed away.

20 Protective/ Decorative Enclosed Seams

OBJECTIVE

To protect raw fabric edges with a finish that may also be decorative by (a) enclosing them within their seam allowances or (b) beneath fabric strips, keeping bulk minimal and topstitching even.

Structural seams may function to enclose raw edges as well as to provide esthetic qualities to a garment design. Check the garment fit carefully before constructing it with one of these seam types. Once the seams are trimmed and constructed, it is difficult to adjust them to accommodate fitting discrepancies.

French Seam

In addition to preventing fraying, the French seam invisibly conceals the raw edges of sheer fabrics by encasing them. French seaming may also be used to finish the seams of delicate blouses, lingerie, and baby clothes.

Procedure. Pin the seam with *wrong* sides together. Stitch a 1.0-cm (⅜-in) seam, trim to 3 mm (⅛ in).

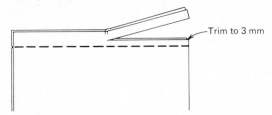

Trim to 3 mm

Press the seam to one side. Bring the *right* sides together, forming a crease along the previous seam line; press. Stitch again 6 mm (¼ in) from the creased edge. Press the seam toward the back of the garment.

By varying the seam widths (e.g., 1.3 cm and 3 mm or ½ and ⅛ in), the final French seam can be made as narrow as 3 mm (⅛ in) to minimize seam visibility on sheer garments.

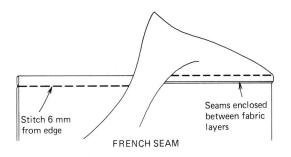

FRENCH SEAM

Stitch 6 mm from edge

Seams enclosed between fabric layers

Flat-Fell Seam

Double rows of topstitching provide both strength and emphasis of structural details. The flat-fell seam is used to construct work and sports clothing, menswear, unlined jackets, and man-tailored garments.

Procedure. Pin the seam with wrong sides together. Stitch a 1.5-cm (⅝-in) seam; trim *one* seam (as pattern designates) to 6 mm (¼ in). Press the seam toward the trimmed seam allowance. Fold under the untrimmed seam allowance 1.0 cm (⅜ in) from the seam line, encasing the trimmed seam allowance. Baste and press.

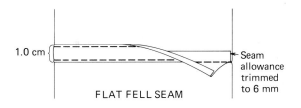

1.0 cm

Seam allowance trimmed to 6 mm

FLAT FELL SEAM

Machine topstitch close to the seam line and again close to the folded edge.

Strapped Seam

The strapped seam decoratively accents structural seams and protects raw edges from friction. It also adds strength to sportswear seams, conceals the seams of unlined garments, and can add color contrast.

Procedure. Stitch a 1.5-cm (⅝-in) seam with *wrong* sides together.

The strap may consist of braid, ribbon, or fabric cut on the bias or straight grain. Bias-cut fabric will curve to match seam contours easily, since it expands and contracts. Cut the strap the width desired plus 1.3 cm (½ in) to provide for seam allowances.

Turn under 6-mm seam (¼-in) allowances on each side of the strap; press. Baste a line down

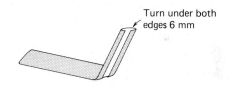

Turn under both edges 6 mm

the center of the strap. Place the strap over the seam allowances, matching the basted center line to the seam line; baste the strap edges to the garment so they will not shift as they are stitched. Topstitch close to each edge.

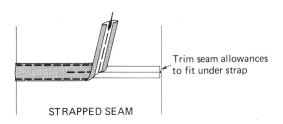

Trim seam allowances to fit under strap

STRAPPED SEAM

CRITERIA FOR EVALUATION

PROTECTIVE/DECORATIVE
ENCLOSED SEAMS

Check to ensure quality performance:

__ **1.** Added bulk and stiffness have been minimized.

__ **2.** Seam-edge treatment controls fraying.

__ **3.** Seam-edge treatment can withstand garment wear and care requirements.

__ **4.** Treatment is evenly applied; fabric yarns are trimmed away.

__ **5.** Decorative detailing coordinates or contrasts (color, texture) esthetically with the total garment design.

__ **6.** Any folds, tucks, seams, and topstitching, are evenly executed.

21 Decorative Seams

OBJECTIVE

To evenly apply decorative accents and/or topstitching parallel to seamlines.

Structural seams may be emphasized by topstitching, padding, or lapping. Cording or piping may also be inserted between seam allowances.

Self-fabric or topstitching may be used for subtle accent; color or textural contrast may provide stronger architectural interest. Consider the influence any contrast will have upon the total garment design and upon physical proportions. Optical illusions can be created by directing eye movement to selected garment areas.

Topstitched Seam

Machine- or hand-topstitching adds subtle detailing to many garment types. Variations in stitch length, thread thickness, and stitch type create many topstitching possibilities. (See the discussion of hand and machine stitches beginning on page 143 for exact stitching techniques.)

Procedure. Stitch from the right side of the garment using seam guides, seam lines, basting lines, or a hem gauge to guide stitching. Adjust

Stitching Guides

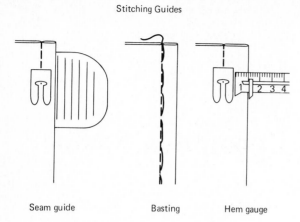

Seam guide   Basting   Hem gauge

tension, stitch length, etc., to the number of fabric layers to be stitched.

Consider the following stitching possibilities:

- Topstitch one or several rows on either side of the seam line.
- Press the seam allowances to one side and topstitch through all layers. To pad further, insert a strip of padding between the garment and seam allowances.
- Use a zigzag or other decorative stitch to topstitch.

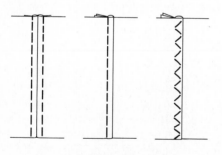

TOPSTITCHED SEAMS

Welt-Seam Variations

The welt seam is topstitched to emphasize structural design and to improve seam strength.

Because one seam allowance is trimmed, it provides a raised effect. The double welt seam looks like the flat-fell seam but encloses only one seam allowance, thereby reducing bulk.

Procedure. Stitch a 1.5-cm (⅝-in) seam with *right* sides together; trim the back seam allowance to 6 mm (¼ in). Finish the raw edge of the untrimmed seam allowance. Press both seam allowances toward the garment back with the trimmed seam underneath.

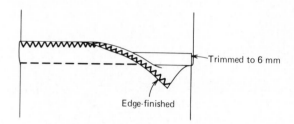

Trimmed to 6 mm

Edge-finished

1. *Welt Seam:* Topstitch from 6 mm to 1.3 cm (¼ to ½ in) from the seam line, catching only the untrimmed seam allowance. The trimmed seam allowance will be encased.

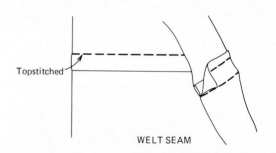

Topstitched

WELT SEAM

2. *Double Welt Seam:* Topstitch close to the seam line and 1.0 cm (⅜ in) from the first row of topstitching.
3. *Padded Welt Seam:* Insert a narrow strip of padding below the trimmed seam allowance. Topstitch 6 mm to 1.3 cm (¼ to ½ in) from the seam line encasing both the padding and the trimmed seam allowance.

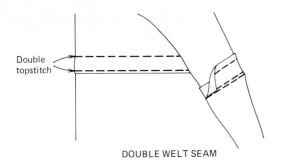

DOUBLE WELT SEAM

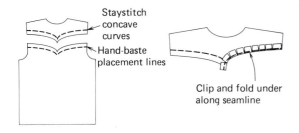

PADDED WELT SEAM

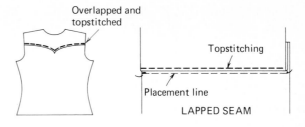

LAPPED SEAM

Lapped Seam

Lapped seam construction is used to simplify the construction of curves, corners, or points. The seam looks like a tuck when completed.

Procedure. Baste placement and fold lines as marked on the pattern. Stay stitch concave curved edges, if they will be folded under, so they can be clipped. Fold under the upper seam allowance; press.

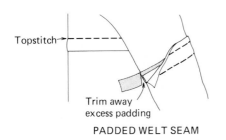

Lap the garment sections, matching seam lines and placement lines; baste in position. Machine-topstitch 3 to 6 mm (⅛ to ¼ in) from the folded edge. Additional topstitching may be added if desired.

Slot Seam

Slot seams are constructed using the lapped seam technique. The seam allowances are turned under and the fabric layers joined by topstitching to a fabric underlay. Variations in fabric color, pattern, and texture are possible.

Procedure. Press under corresponding seam allowances along seam lines. Cut an underlay strip 3.8 cm (1½ in) wide and baste a guideline down the center.

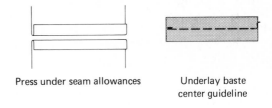

Abut the folded seam edges to one another over the underlay guideline; baste. Machine stitch 6 mm (¼ in) or more from the seam line. Remove basting.

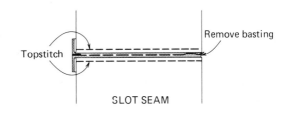

SLOT SEAM

Piped/Corded Seam

Narrow bias- or corded-fabric seam inserts serve to outline both structural and enclosed seams. When made of self-fabric, they finish edges or structural seams very subtly. Width may vary with garment styling and degree of color contrast employed to achieve differing proportions.

CORDED CUFF

Procedure. Cut true-bias strips 3.8 cm (1½ in) in width from self-fabric or another contrasting fabric.

1. For *piped insert:* Fold the bias strip in half; press. Baste along the desired piping width from the fold.
2. For *corded insert:* Fold the bias strip over the cording with right sides out and cut edges meeting. Using a zipper foot, machine-baste close to the cording, enclosing it inside the bias strip.

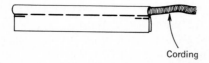

Cording

Covered cording can be purchased, although fabric and color may not necessarily coordinate with the garment being constructed.

Attach the piping or cording insert to one of the seam allowances by matching the

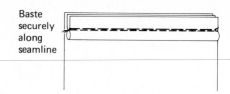

Baste securely along seamline

basted line to the right side of the seam line. The cut edges of the inserts should lie toward the cut edge of the garment seam. Baste securely.

Pin the corresponding seams together, matching markings. Machine-stitch close to the basting line in such a way that these stitches will not show after the seam has been sewn. Use a zipper foot to stitch next to the cording. Press the seam in the desired direction.

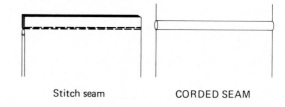

Stitch seam   CORDED SEAM

CRITERIA FOR EVALUATION

DECORATIVE SEAMS

Check to ensure quality performance:

Decorative Seaming:

___ **1.** Decorative detailing coordinates or contrasts (color, texture) esthetically with the total garment design.

___ **2.** Any folds, tucks, seams, and topstitching are evenly executed.

___ **3.** Added bulk and stiffness have been minimized.

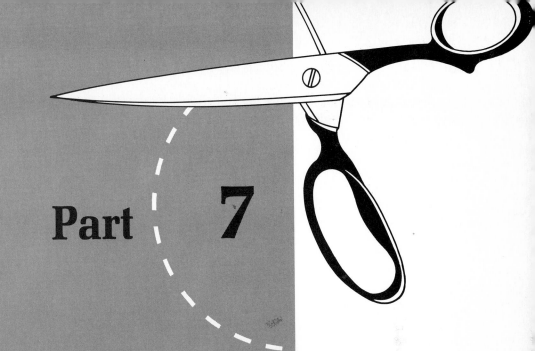

Part 7

Enclosed Seams: Concealing and Finishing Garment Perimeters

Once the garment shell has been formed by joining the major garment sections, the remaining raw boundary edges must be concealed. These raw edges may include the neck, armscye, wrist, waistline, hem, or closure openings of the garment. They are concealed by enclosing them between

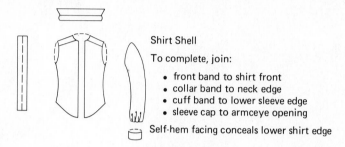

Shirt Shell

To complete, join:

- front band to shirt front
- collar band to neck edge
- cuff band to lower sleeve edge
- sleeve cap to armceye opening

Self-hem facing conceals lower shirt edge

two fabric layers. The methods used to treat these edges may be both functional and decorative. Each method conceals the raw edges and also contributes to the garment's styling. For example, a collar conceals the raw neck edge and lends a styling feature to the total garment design.

Two methods used to finish garment perimeters include:

FACINGS

Facings are fabric sections cut to fit around a garment opening or to back a small garment section. Neck, armscye, and front closure openings, as well as the underside of collars, cuffs, and waistbands are faced. Hems face the outer edges of a garment.

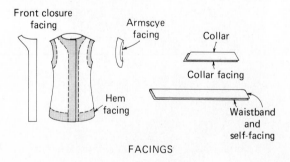

Front closure facing

Armscye facing

Collar

Collar facing

Hem facing

Waistband and self-facing

FACINGS

BINDINGS

Garment edges are also finished by enclosing them inside bindings or bands of fabric which are folded around the raw fabric edges. *Narrow bindings of self-fabric or purchased braid finish the edges of necklines, armscyes, collars, waistlines, and lapped closure edges.*

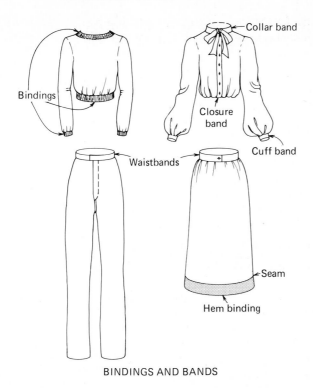

BINDINGS AND BANDS

Wider circumference bands include collars, cuffs, and waistbands. They provide decorative styling, support the garment, control fullness (act as a stay), and are often incorporated with the garment's closure system.

Specific perimeter finishing techniques (e.g. hem facing, shaped and extended facings, shaped cuff, shirt placket) are discussed in detail in Chapter 22. Within each sub-category, related concepts and construction techniques are utilized to finish the perimeter. For example, the basic processes used to construct a shaped facing can be applied to *all* shaped facings, with some minor variations in technique. As with structural seaming, the construction techniques selected must meet the garment's design, function, and durability needs.

BASIC PERIMETER CONCEPTS

Many construction problems encountered when finishing perimeter edges may be treated similarly. Multiple fabric layers, enclosed seams, excess bulk, and favoring of perimeter seams must be dealt with. The concepts necessary to deal with these problems are discussed below. They are followed by general construction procedures which are applicable throughout Part Seven.

Multiple Fabric Layers

To conceal garment perimeters, additional fabric layers are needed to bind and face the raw edges. This is complicated by the fact that neck, collar, cuff, waistline, and closure areas commonly require the support of an additional interfacing or underlining layer.

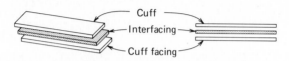

Cross-sections of Multiple Fabric Layers

Enclosed Seam Allowances

When garment perimeters are finished by facing or binding, the edges involved are enclosed between two outer fabric layers. Seam allowances also become enclosed when two structural seams face each other. For example, the shoulder seams of a shirt and its facing are enclosed between the garment and the facing. Construction of faced or bound sections generally requires five to six fabric layers where the enclosed seam allowances

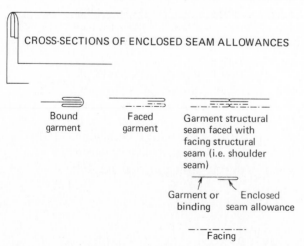

are located. These layers consist of the outer garment fabric and interfacing and facing layers, plus the seam allowances of each layer. Because the seam allowances are enclosed, they receive no friction. Therefore they need no protective edge finish to prevent fraying.

Cross-sections of Fabric Layers Created by Enclosed Seams

Faced and Interfaced

• Interfacing seam allowance trimmed
• 5 layers

Faced and Interfaced

• Interfacing seam allowance untrimmed
• 6 layers

Bound Edge

• 5 layers

———— Garment or binding

– – – – Interfacing

—·—·— Facing

Bulk Reduction Techniques

A visible ridge can be created by the many enclosed seam allowances, especially if the fabric layers are thick. Excess bulk can be minimized by trimming the seam allowances to graded widths (grading) before they are concealed. Just as with structural seams, notching and clipping are needed to enable curved or cornered seams to lie flat without pulling or distorting the garment shape. One seam allowance layer can be eliminated by trimming away interfacing seam allowances before stitching the seam.

Turning and Favoring

To ensure that the garment perimeter seam creates the desired shape, the perimeter seam allowances must be turned to the inside so that they are enclosed between the garment and facing layers. From the right side, the seamed edge must be pulled to the surface of the perimeter edge. *Favor* the perimeter seam by rolling it slightly underneath. Understitching the seam allowances to the facing also prevents the seam from rolling into view. If the fabric can be steam-heat set (i.e., wool), the diagonal basting stitch can be used to smoothly turn and favor the edge seam *before* the garment section is pressed.

GENERAL CONSTRUCTION PROCEDURES: ENCLOSED SEAMS

Enclosed seams are stitched using the same thread, stitch length, seam width, and machine tension used to construct structural seams. Very short reinforcement stitches are often necessary in stress areas. No protective edge finish is needed since the enclosed seam allowances receive no friction. If, however, the fabric frays badly, and if the seam allowances must be closely trimmed, some of the fabric yarns may pull out when the section is turned right side out. For instance, if a collar is very pointed, requiring close trimming of seam allowances, a test sample can be made to determine

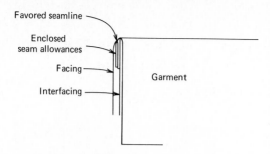

how weak the point may be. If the fabric yarns pull out easily in the test sample, additional measures must be employed to strengthen the area. The stitch length may be shortened further, feather-weight fusible interfacing may be applied to the points, or fabric glue may be applied to the seam allowances.

Graded Seam

Grading is a technique for staggering enclosed seam allowances. As a result, the seam allowances vary in width and are less likely to create a ridge visible on the outside of the garment. Excess bulk created by thicker fabrics is also minimized. All enclosed seam allowances should be graded, unless pattern instructions indicate otherwise.

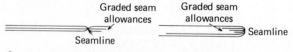

Cross-sections: graded seams before and after turning

To grade, trim the seam allowances to varying widths with the *widest* seam nearest the upper fabric layer. Trim the interfacing to 3 mm (⅛ in), the lower seam allowance to 6 mm (¼ in), and the upper seam allowance to 1.0 cm (⅜ in). If more seam allowances are involved, grade them in increments of 3 mm (⅛ in) with no seam allowance less than 4 mm (³⁄₁₆ in) wide.

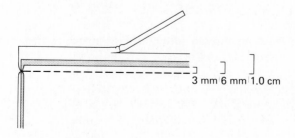

Trimmed Seam

To trim a seam, cut away the excess seam allowance to the desired width. When two structural seam allowances face one another, such as garment and facing shoulder seams, trim one set of seam allowances to stagger the edges. Trim the facing seam allowances to 1.0 cm (⅜ in). Trim corner seams diagonally to within 2 mm (¹⁄₁₆ in) of the stitching.

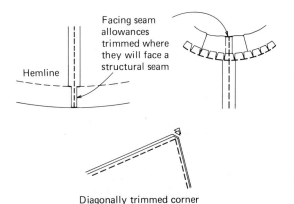

Diagonally trimmed corner

Corner Seams

Corner seams require a more secure stitching technique because the seam allowances are trimmed or clipped close to the seamline. Examples of *outside corner* seams include collar, cuff, and waistband corners. *Inside corners* are found on square necklines.

Construction procedures differ for each type of corner seam:

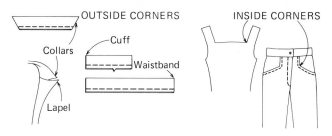

Inside Corner

Inside corner seams are stitched as usual to within 2 to 3 cm (1 in) of the corner dot. Change to short stitches, stitch to the corner, and pivot with the needle in the fabric. Continue stitching with short stitches for 2 or 3 more centimeters before resuming the regulation stitch length. Clip to the corner and grade the seam.

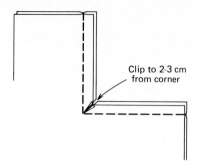

Clip to 2-3 cm
from corner

Outside Corner or Point

Outside corner seams are stitched on each side of the corner point, or, if the garment-facing section is folded in half, only one side of the corner seam is stitched.

1. To stitch the *full corner seam*, use short reinforcement stitches on each side of the corner point for 2 to 3 cm (1 in). *Take one stitch diagonally across the corner point.* By taking up some excess fabric, the diagonal stitch will help to prevent the point from bulging after the corner is turned right side out. Trim diagonally across the corner to within 2 mm ($\frac{1}{16}$ in) of the diagonal stitch. If the corner angle is acute, additional bulk must be eliminated by trimming diagonally along each side of the point for about 3 cm (1¼ in). Grade the remaining seam.

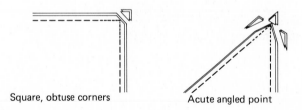

Square, obtuse corners   Acute angled point

2. To stitch the *half-corner seam*, fold the garment-facing section along the foldline with right sides together. Stitch across the end, backstitching at both edges. Trim diagonally across the corner to within 2 mm ($\frac{1}{16}$ in) of the corner point. Grade the remaining seam.

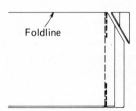

Foldline

Curved Seams

Curved seams may form either inside (concave) or outside (convex) curves. Concave curves exist at the neckline and armscyes; convex curves exist at collar or cuff perimeters. After stitching and grading a curved seam, it must also be notched or clipped to enable the seam to lie flat and curve smoothly.

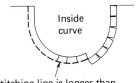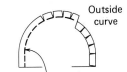

Stitching line is longer than cutting line; therefore, seam must be clipped to spread open

Stitching line is shorter than cutting line; therefore, seam must be notched to fit inside

Inside Curve

After stitching and grading the seam, clip to the stitching. As shown below, clipping enables the shorter cutting edge diameter to spread apart so that the seam allowances can lie flat.

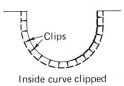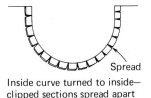

Inside curve clipped

Inside curve turned to inside—clipped sections spread apart

Outside Curve

After stitching and grading the seam, clip out wedge-shaped notches from the seam allowances. In an outside curved seam, the outer cutting edge is longer than the seamline. Notching out the seam allowances permits them to lie smoothly without ripping when turned to the inside. Slight curves require fewer and smaller notches to be taken than do very rounded curves.

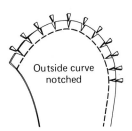

Outside curve notched

Notched-out seam allowance fits inside without overlapping

Unlike Curves

When stitching unlike curves to one another, such as a straight collar edge to an inside curved edge, follow the procedures described in Chapter 16. Grade and clip (or notch) the seam allowances as required by the curve.

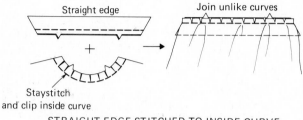

STRAIGHT EDGE STITCHED TO INSIDE CURVE

Turning and Favoring Enclosed Seams

The perimeter seams of faced garment sections—including neck, collar, lapel, cuff, and waistband edges—are very visible parts of the garment. To ensure that their outer edges are smooth and even after these sections are right side out, the seamed edges must be drawn out completely.

The appearance of the garment sections is also improved by turning the perimeter seam line slightly underneath *(favoring)*, thus hiding it from view. Three methods can be used to turn and favor the perimeter edges:

1. *Understitching* helps to favor the seamed edge. By edge-stitching the seam allowances to the facing, one prevents the facing from rolling out into view. This procedure also aids in completely drawing out the seam-line edge.

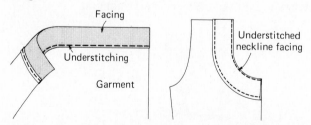

After grading the seam, press the seam allowances toward the facing. Machine-stitch 3 mm (⅛ in) from the seam line, catching only the seam allowances and the facing. In hard-to-reach areas or with delicate fabrics, use the hand prick stitch. Turn the garment section right side out, favoring the upper perimeter edge. Press.

2. *The diagonal basting stitch* favors the perimeter seams of garment sections that will not be understitched (e.g., in tailored garments) or will be topstitched later.

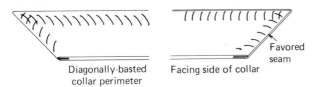

Diagonally-basted
collar perimeter

Facing side of collar

Favored
seam

After grading, turn the faced garment section right side out. Using silk basting thread, slip the needle into the seam line with the needle parallel to the seam. Gently draw out the seam, being careful not to pull out any fabric yarns. At the same time, use the left index finger to roll the seam line underneath about 2 to 3 mm ($\frac{1}{16}$ to $\frac{1}{8}$ in). Take several stitches using the diagonal basting stitch. Repeat this procedure of turning, favoring, and basting until the entire seam has been positioned. If an outside corner must be turned, carefully work out the point with the needle.

3. *Reducing the facing size* before stitching it to the corresponding garment section also helps to favor the seamline. If the facing is not cut smaller in medium to heavier fabrics, favoring will force the now-larger facing side to buckle underneath. Buckling is also apt to happen to the inside fabric layer of a rolled collar or cuff. As a result, the facing sections must be cut smaller to enable the fabric layers to mold together smoothly. When a facing such as a neck facing has a free edge, it is not necessary to reduce the facing size.

To reduce the facing size, one of two methods may be used:

a. When the facing is pinned to its corresponding garment section, drop the garment edge about 2 to 5 mm ($\frac{1}{16}$ to $\frac{3}{16}$ in) below the facing so that a smaller seam allowance is taken. The thicker the fabric the more the seam must be adjusted. As a result, the facing section will be smaller, pulling the perimeter seam underneath.

b. The outer edges of the facing section may be cut smaller by trimming away 2 to 5 mm ($\frac{1}{16}$ to $\frac{3}{16}$ in). Stretch the smaller facing to fit the garment section as they are stitched.

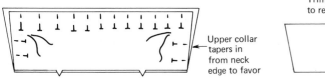

Upper collar
tapers in
from neck
edge to favor

Trim away facing edges
to reduce facing size

CRITERIA FOR EVALUATION

ENCLOSED PERIMETER SEAMS

Check to ensure quality performance:

__ **1.** Stitching lies directly on seam lines.

__ **2.** Excess bulk is minimized without weakening the seamed area by:

    __ a. Grading seam allowances using 3-mm (⅛-in) variations. The seam allowance nearest the right side of the garment is trimmed widest.

    __ b. Trimming enclosed facing seam allowances to 1.0 cm (⅜ in).

__ **3.** Curved seams are notched or clipped as needed to lie flat and curve smoothly.

__ **4.** Outside corners or points are trimmed diagonally; inside corners are clipped.

__ **5.** Stress areas, such as corners or points, are reinforced with short stitches for about 2.5 cm (1 in) on either side of the point.

__ **6.** After the garment unit is turned right side out, the enclosed perimeter seam is drawn out completely.

__ **7.** The visible perimeter layer is favored by:

    __ a. Diagonally basting and pressing; topstitching (optional).

    __ b. Hand- or machine-understitching.

    __ c. Reducing facing size before stitching (used in combination with 7a or 7b).

22 Facings

OBJECTIVE

To apply basic perimeter concepts of bulk reduction, turning, and favoring to the application of facings to finish garment edges.

Facings are fabric sections designed to finish and support the perimeter openings of the garment or to finish, support, and back garment circumference bands (e.g., collars, cuffs, waistbands). They may be (1) pieces that have been cut to fit the shape of the area they will finish, (2) folded extensions, or (3) flexible bias strips. Facing grain direction matches that of the corresponding garment section except when bias strips are used. Neck, armscye, and closure fac-

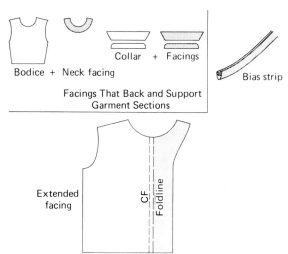

Bodice + Neck facing   Collar + Facings   Bias strip

Facings That Back and Support
Garment Sections

Extended facing   CF   Foldline

ings have a free edge, whereas hem collar, cuff, waistband, and bias facings are each secured along all edges to the section they face.

Although facings are usually concealed by turning them to the inside of a garment, they may also be applied to the right side for decorative purposes. Contrasting or self-fabric may be used.

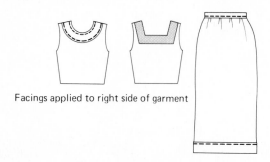

Facings applied to right side of garment

Shaped Facings. These duplicate the shape of the edge they finish. They are about 3.8 to 6.3 cm (1½ to 2½ in) wide, supporting only the garment perimeters, or they back an entire section of the garment, such as a collar or waistband.

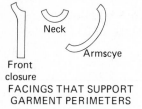

Neck

Armscye

Front closure

FACINGS THAT SUPPORT GARMENT PERIMETERS

Waistband

Collar

Cuff

FACINGS THAT BACK AND SUPPORT GARMENT SECTIONS

Extended Facings. An *extended facing* is cut in one piece with the garment section and then folded to the inside. The garment edge is simply extended. It is used primarily to finish

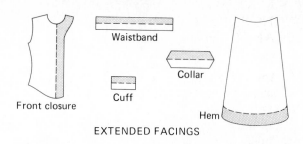

Waistband

Collar

Cuff

Front closure

Hem

EXTENDED FACINGS

straight edges parallel to the grain line. Straight closure, cuff, collar, waistband, and hem edges are commonly extended to form a facing. Excess bulk is eliminated, since the perimeter is folded rather than seamed.

To minimize bulk, two facings are sometimes *combined* by eliminating a common seam line. Closure facings join an extended front facing with a shaped neck facing. Front and back armscye facings are combined at the shoulder seam. When a sleeveless, collarless bodice has a narrow shoulder area, the neck and armscye facings are combined. Combined facings are really variations of shaped or extended facings and should be constructed similarly. Specific procedures are provided.

A layer of interfacing the size of the facing placed between the garment and the facing provides further support to the faced area. Unless additional support is needed for a particular fabric, underlined and unstructured garments are generally not interfaced. When a pattern does not supply a separate interfacing pattern, use the facing pattern. Trim away 1.0 cm (⅜ in) from the free outer edge in order to bevel the interfacing edge with the facing edge.

Bias Facings. Because they are so flexible and easy to mold, bias strips are used to bind garment openings. They can be molded to correspond with the perimeter shape. Self-fabric is commonly used, although light-weight, color-matched fabric strips may be used to minimize bulk. They are not interfaced.

CONSTRUCTION PROCEDURES: SHAPED FACINGS

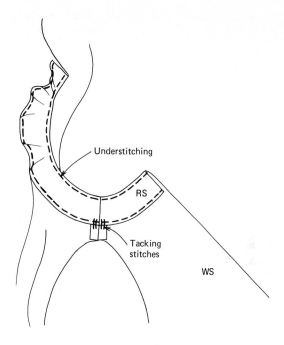

Understitching

RS

Tacking stitches

WS

1. Apply interfacing and stay-stitch any curved garment and facing edges. Stitch corresponding facing seams together; trim to 1.0 cm (⅜ in); press.
2. Finish the free outer edge of the facing using a protective edge finish.
3. Reinforce any stress areas. Pin and stitch

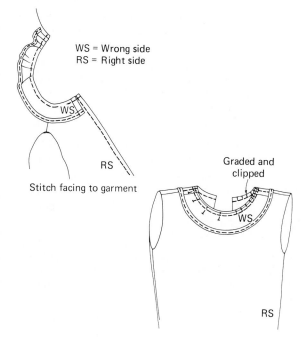

WS = Wrong side
RS = Right side

WS

RS

Stitch facing to garment

Graded and clipped

WS

RS

the facing to the garment section with right sides together. Grade the seam; clip or notch if needed.
4. Press the seam allowances toward the facing. Understitch *or* diagonally baste the enclosed seam, favoring the upper garment edge. Press. To hold the facing in position, tack it loosely to the garment seam allowances. If the garment is underlined, the entire facing edge can be slip-stitched to the underlining layer.

Facing Intersected by a Zipper

Two methods can be used to finish the facing ends:

a. After the facing has been stitched, understitched, and turned to the inside, turn under the facing ends. They should clear the zipper teeth. Use a prick stitch to hold the fabric flat and out of the zipper teeth.

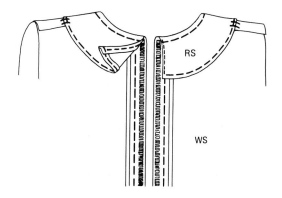

RS

WS

b. As the facing is being pinned to the garment, fold back the facing ends so that they clear the zipper teeth. Trim away excess of 1.0 cm (⅜ in). Pin, stitch, grade, and understitch the seam as usual. Turn the facing to the inside and prick-stitch to the zipper tape. Hand-overcast the visible neck seam.

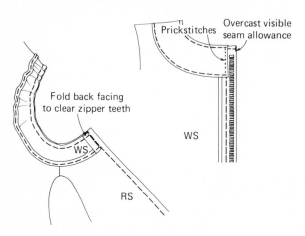

Combined Neck-Armscye Facing

To ensure that the perimeter seams will be favored, cut the facing slightly smaller than the garment. Stitch the underarm seams of the garment and facing; press open. Finish the facing edges. Stitch the garment to the facing at the neck and armscye seams, stopping stitches at the shoulder *seam line.*

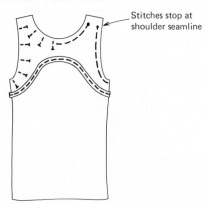

Grade, clip, and turn the facings to the inside. Stitch the garment shoulder without catching the facing in the stitches. Trim the facing shoulder seams to 1 cm (⅜ in) and turn inside. Whipstitch the edges together. If desired, the facing can be hand-understitched.

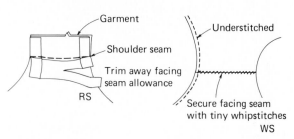

Faced Placket

Both neckline and sleeve plackets can be finished by a rectangular facing. This facing does not match the shape of the area it faces because the opening is located centrally in the garment.

Finish the three outer edges of the facing. Center over the placket opening with right sides together. Machine-stitch, following placket stitching lines. Change to short reinforcement stitches for 2.5 cm (1 in) on each side of the point. Take one stitch across the end.

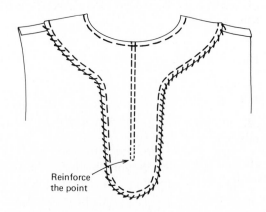

Slash through to point without cutting stitches. Press seam toward the facing. Turn the facing to the inside, favoring the garment;

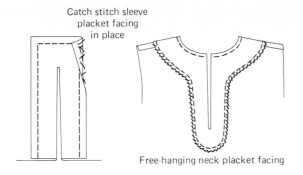

Catch stitch sleeve placket facing in place

Free-hanging neck placket facing

press. Use an invisible catch stitch to loosely hold *sleeve* placket facing in position. It is not necessary to hand-stitch the neckline facing as it hangs in a downward direction and it is likely that the hand stitches will show from the outside.

CRITERIA FOR EVALUATION

SHAPED AND EXTENDED FACINGS

Check to ensure quality performance:

___ **1.** Supports and finishes garment or band perimeters without creating excess bulk.

___ **2.** Faced garment area is supported by interfacing or underlining if needed.

___ **3.** Interfacing is narrower than facing to grade edges.

___ **4.** Free facing edges are finished using a method creating minimal bulk.

___ **5.** Combined facing size is reduced to ensure that the garment is favored.

___ **6.** The facing is turned under and clears the zipper teeth.

___ **7.** Free facing edges are tacked only to seam allowances or to an underlining.

Decorative Facing

This facing is applied to the outside of the garment as a decorative band.

Reinforce the garment shoulder seam where the finished facing will end by stitching just

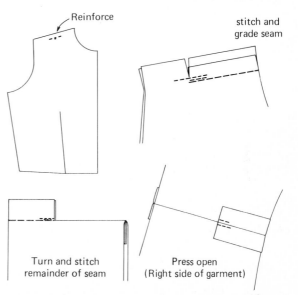

Reinforce

stitch and grade seam

Turn and stitch remainder of seam

Press open (Right side of garment)

outside the seam line. Reverse the garment shoulder seam where it will lie under the facing.

Pin and stitch the right side of the facing to

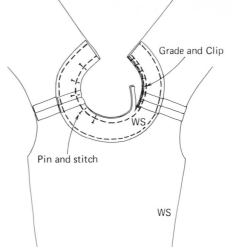

Grade and Clip

WS

Pin and stitch

WS

the wrong side of the garment along perimeters. Grade; press and turn seam toward the garment.

Turn the facing to the right side of the garment. Turn under the facing edges, checking to be sure the facing is even in width. Baste in place. Topstitch near the facing edge.

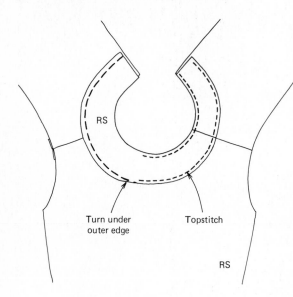

Turn under outer edge

Topstitch

CRITERIA FOR EVALUATION

APPLIED DECORATIVE FACINGS

Check to ensure quality performance:

__ 1. Intersected structural seams are reversed only under the facing to enclose and hide the seam allowances.

__ 2. The facing is turned under evenly and secured smoothly.

CONSTRUCTION PROCEDURES: EXTENDED FACINGS

Construction of four types of extended facings is described:

Extended lapped-closure facings
Extended hem facings
Special hem facings
Extended facings

Extended Lapped-Closure Facings

These facings are found at the lapped openings of shirts, jackets, or coats with straight edges. The facing extends beyond the straight closure edge and is usually combined with a shaped neck facing. Interfacing is used to support the closure.

1. Apply the interfacing to the garment.

   To provide additional support to the folded edge, the interfacing can be extended 1.5 cm (⅝ in) beyond the fold line when it is cut out. If the garment is underlined, interfacing is usually not needed to support the closure.
2. Stay-stitch any curved seam lines. Do not stay-stitch outer facing edges.
3. Extended front facings may or may not be stitched to a back neck facing. If there is a back neck facing, stitch the facings together at the shoulder seams. Trim the seam to 1.0 cm (⅜ in); press open. When there is no back neck facing (garments with collars only), press under the facing shoulder seam.

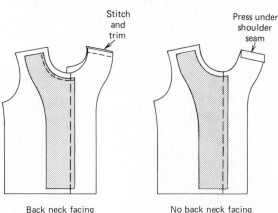

Stitch and trim

Press under shoulder seam

Back neck facing

No back neck facing

4. Finish the free outer edge of the facing, using a protective edge finish.

5. Turn the facing toward the garment along the designated fold line with right sides together. Pin and stitch the neckline seam; grade, clip, turn, and press.

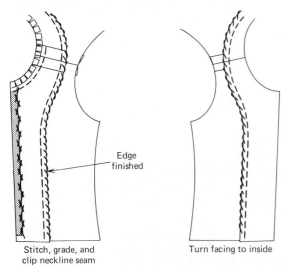

Edge finished

Stitch, grade, and clip neckline seam

Turn facing to inside

CRITERIA FOR EVALUATION

SHAPED AND EXTENDED FACINGS

Check to ensure quality performance:

__ **1.** Supports and finishes garment or band perimeters without creating excess bulk.

__ **2.** Faced garment area is supported by interfacing or underlining if needed.

__ **3.** Interfacing is narrower than facing to grade edges.

__ **4.** Free facing edges are finished using a method creating minimal bulk.

__ **5.** Combined facing size is reduced to ensure that the garment is favored.

__ **6.** The facing is turned under and clears the zipper teeth.

__ **7.** Free facing edges are tacked only to seam allowances or to an underlining.

Extended Hem Facings

Hems are extended facings that finish and often support outer perimeter edges. Additional stiffness or contouring can be created by interfacing or padding the hem. Despite its support function, a hem should be quite inconspicuous. The edge finish and hand stitch selected are crucial to reducing the hem's visibility. To withstand greater wear and tear, a hem may be machine-stitched with matching or contrasting thread.

Edges commonly hemmed with facing extensions include lower garment edges, sleeve edges, straight-cut armscye edges, and shirt hems.

Unless the pattern suggests otherwise, the garment is usually not hemmed until all other construction has been completed. Hang the garment for 24 hours if it is bias or slightly bias to allow the fabric to stretch as it will during wear.

Basic Hemming Steps:
1. Measure hem length.
2. Mark hem depth.
3. Turn up hem; ease in fullness if curved.
4. Press; shrink out any fullness.
5. Trim hem facing seams to 1.0 cm (⅜ in).
6. Edge-finish.
7. Hand- or machine-stitch.

Hemming Guidelines. To determine the *hem length,* consider individual proportions as well as current popular styling. Wear the undergarments and shoes that will be worn with the completed garment.

To ensure evenness, the hem marker used should move around the individual whose hem is being measured so that the garment does not shift. Mark the hem with pins or chalk by measuring from the floor, using a floor hem marker or a yardstick.

Turn the hem to the wrong side of the garment by folding along the hem markings; pin-baste. Check the hem length by trying on the garment.

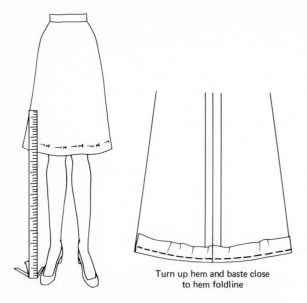

Turn up hem and baste close
to hem foldline

Make any adjustments needed to ensure that the hem is parallel to the floor. Remove the garment and hand-baste 1.3 cm (½ in) from the fold using silk thread. Press close to the folded edge.

The hem facing width depends upon the degree of flare or curve, the garment function, and the location of the edge to be hemmed.

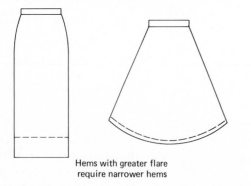

Hems with greater flare
require narrower hems

Generally, the greater the hem curve (garment flare), the narrower the hem must be to accommodate the differential of the perimeters when the hem is turned up.

Sportswear, jersey knits, unstructured garments, and work clothing require a minimum of excess bulk. Therefore these garments may have hems only 1.3 to 2.0 cm (½ to ¾ in) wide. These hems are often machine-stitched to improve durability and washability as well as to follow styling trends.

Hem widths also vary according to the garment area to be hemmed and the fabric stiffness. Shirt hems, sleeves, and very short jackets usually have narrower hems than skirts or pants do. Stiff fabrics will not ease in readily when the hemline is curved, so hem widths may need to be narrowed for these fabrics.

The hem width suggested by the pattern company is usually, but not always suitable for the garment styling, flare, function, and fabric. Guidelines for determining hem-facing widths are provided below.

Once the hem depth has been determined, use a hem gauge to mark the width. Measure from the hem fold line to the gauge indicator; mark the width with pins, pencil, or fine chalk lines. Cut away excess fabric along the guidelines without cutting into the garment.

Selection of the hem facing finish and securing stitch are crucial to *reducing hem visibility* on the right side of the garment.

Finishing the raw hem edge prevents fraying and improves the inner appearance of the garment. Consider the amount of bulk added to the hem edge by each finish, as well as the garment's durability needs, when selecting a finish. Additional layers may result in a ridge on the right side of the garment. The hemmed area may also become stiffer due to the thickness of the finish.

The hem is secured to the garment by means of either machine or hand stitches. Machine stitching improves durability and can create design emphasis when applied in multiple rows or contrasting colors. Hand-stitched hems should be invisible. Hand stitches taken *be-*

Suggested Hem-Facing Widths*

Hem Width	Rolled Hem	1.3–2.0 cm (½–¾ in)	2.5–3.8 cm (1–1½ in)	5.0–6.5 cm 2–2½ in)	7.5 cm (3 in)	12.5–15.0 cm (5–6 in)
GARMENT TYPE	Straight-cut armscyes Blouse hems Sheer and delicate fabrics: chiffons crepe de chine, etc. Scarf edges Lingerie	Shirt, blouse hems Jersey knit tops, skirts Short shorts Sportswear Short-sleeves, work/func-tional gar-ments	Circular hems Flared hems in stiff fab-rics Tapered pants Shorts Jackets Below-elbow-length sleeves	Flared, straight, pleated, and gath-ered skirts Flared pants ¾- to ⅞-length coats Double-knit skirts	Straight-legged pants Floor-length skirts Coats	Sheer fabric in very gathered skirts cut as rectan-gular sec-tions

* If the fabric is firmer or stiffer than average, it may be necessary to select a narrower width.

tween the hem facing and the garment are least likely to show because they do not encase the hem edge.

Although the blind/slip and felling stitches rank low in preventing visibility, they are more secure stitches which are best used to hem collar, cuff, or waistband facings.

Basic Hem-Facing Types

Two basic *hem-facing types* are encountered in finishing perimeter edges:

1. *Straight hem facings* are found only on garment sections that are rectangular in shape, such as straight or gathered skirts and

Hem Facing Finishes and Hand Stitches Ranked By Visibility

Degree of Visibility	Less Visibility		Greater . . . . . . Visibility
Hand stitches	Unexposed catch stitch Tailor's hemming stitch	Exposed catch stitch	Felling stitch Blind/slip stitch
Edge fin-ishes	Hand overcast Machine zigzag	Seam tape Turn and stitch Hong Kong	Self-bound Bound

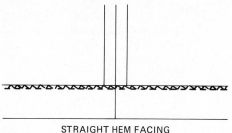

STRAIGHT HEM FACING

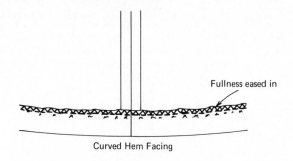

Fullness eased in

Curved Hem Facing

straight-legged pants. The hem is simply turned up parallel to the lengthwise grain.

2. *Curved hem facings* are required when a garment section flares out at the base, as in a flared or circular skirt. When the hem facing is turned up in a flared garment, the circumference of the lower perimeter edge will be larger than the circumference at the stitching level. The greater the flare, the greater the differential between the two circumferences.

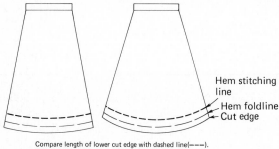

Hem stitching line
Hem foldline
Cut edge

Compare length of lower cut edge with dashed line(———).
Cut edge is much longer. The greater the flare, the greater the differential.

The longer, outer circumference edge is eased in to fit the shorter stitching-level circumference. Ease-stitch 6 mm (¼ in) from the raw edge. If the edge will be overcast, hand-overcast or machine-zigzag it before easing in the hem. For all other edge finishes, ease in the hem edge to fit the garment before applying the tape or binding. Draw in the edge until it is just slightly larger than the garment. Adjust the ease fullness evenly and steam out excess fullness on a pressing ham. If the hem is drawn in too tightly, it will force

the garment to pucker visibly once it is hand-stitched.

Hem Facing Variations:

When straight or curved hem facings are being turned up, special situations requiring specific treatments may arise.

Hem with Pleat Seam. A pleat may be formed by creasing the fabric or by a combination of creased and unpressed seams. Since the pleat seam extends the length of the garment and is not pressed open, special methods are necessary to eliminate excess bulk at the hem and to retain a sharp pleat.

Procedures. Prepare the hem as usual. Before applying the edge finish, clip the pleat seam at the point where the top of the hem meets the seam. Press open the seam below the clip. Trim the hem-facing seam allowance to 1.0 cm (⅜ in).

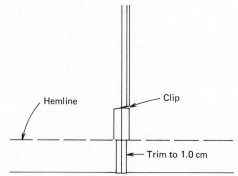

Hemline
Clip
Trim to 1.0 cm

Finish the hem edge. Turn up the hem facing, carefully aligning the pleat seam lines. Hand-stitch the hem to the garment. The seam above the hem remains unpressed to maintain a crisp pleat line. Fold the hemmed portion of the pleat along the seam line and press. Machine- or hand-stitch the hem 3 mm (⅛ in) from the fold to maintain the crease.

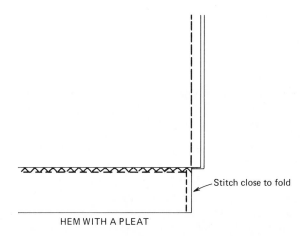

HEM WITH A PLEAT

Corner Hem. A corner hem treatment is needed when a closure facing meets a hem facing. The two facings are joined at the *lower* edge to hide the seam. Bulk must also be minimized.

Procedures. After pressing the closure facing along its fold line and marking the hemline, open out the facing. Turn up the garment hem facing and press. The two creases will intersect.

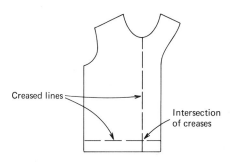

Fold the hem facing; then the closure facing to the inside of the garment. Turn up the closure hem facing until it is slightly shorter than the garment hem, thus favoring the right side of the garment; press.

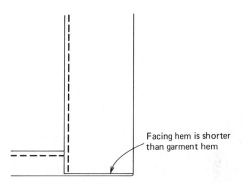

Open out the facing. Trim the closure hem facing and a portion of the garment hem facing (shorter than the facing width) to 1.5 cm (⅝ in) wide.

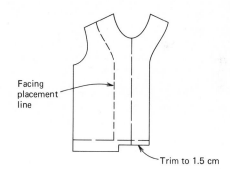

At this point the two facings are joined at the lower edge by hand or machine stitches.

To *hand-stitch*, blind/slip-stitch the lower edges together after hemming the garment. Catch-stitch the closure facing to the garment hem facing.

To *machine-stitch*, match the lower hemline creases with right sides together. Stitch along the crease, grade the seam, and trim the corner. Hem the garment as usual. Catch-stitch the closure facing to the garment hem.

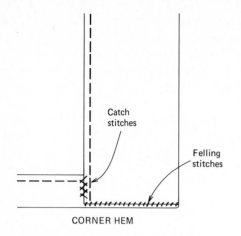

CORNER HEM

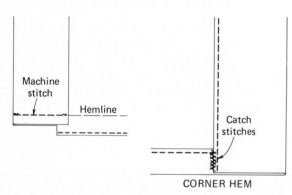

CORNER HEM

Narrow Hem. Blouses, sportswear, jersey knits, and work clothing are commonly hemmed by turning up only 0.6 to 2.0 cm (¼ to ¾ in) of the lower edge.

Procedures. Mark the hem-facing fold line. Trim to the desired hem width, usually 0.6 to 2.0 cm (¼ to ¾ in), plus 6 mm (¼ in) to be turned under. Thicker fabrics require a wider hem to accommodate the thickness smoothly. Press under the hem-facing edge, following a guideline stitched 6 mm (¼ in) from the edge. Turn up the hem, baste, and press. Machine-stitch 3 mm (⅛ in) from the upper hem edge or hand-stitch along the fold line. All functional garments should be machine-stitched for greater durability.

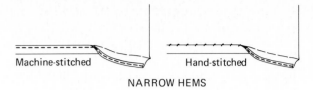

NARROW HEMS

Hand-rolled Hem. Garments made of sheer, delicate fabrics are finished by hand-rolling very narrow hems.

Procedure. Machine-stitch 6 mm (¼ in) from the edge; trim to 3 mm (⅛ in). Using the left thumb and forefinger, roll the fabric into a narrow 3.0- to 4.0-mm (about ⅛-in) hem. Blind/slip-stitch.

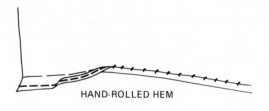

HAND-ROLLED HEM

Double-stitched Hem. Two unexposed rows of hand stitches support the weight of the hem facing in garments constructed from heavy woven or knitted fabrics.

Procedures. Measure and finish the hem as usual. Baste the hem facing to the garment midway along the facing width. Fold back the hem along the basting and loosely catch-stitch it to the garment. Hand-stitch the upper hem edge as usual.

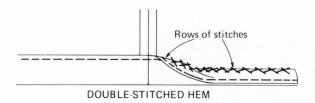

DOUBLE-STITCHED HEM

CRITERIA FOR EVALUATION

EXTENDED HEM FACINGS

Check to ensure quality performance:

__ **1.** Hem length is esthetically pleasing to the individual's proportions as well as those of the garment's style.

__ **2.** Hem is parallel to the floor.

__ **3.** Hem depth is appropriate for fabric stiffness, garment styling, and function.

__ **4.** The edge finish prevents fraying and creates minimal bulk.

__ **5.** The excess fullness created by a flared hem is:

    __ a. Eased in so that the hem is slightly looser than the garment.

    __ b. Steam-shrunk to minimize bulk.

__ **6.** The hem facing is secured to the garment by:

    __ a. Hand-stitching, using a loose, flexible, yet secure stitch; unless they are decorative, the stitches are invisible.

    __ b. Machine-stitching evenly from the garment edge.

__ **7.** *Hemmed pleats:* intersecting structural seams are clipped even with the edge of the hem facing.

__ **8.** *Corner hem:* horizontal hem facing is turned up *before* the vertical facing is turned in.

Extended Facing: Turned-back Cuff

Turned-back cuffs are essentially extra-long hem-faced pants legs or sleeves whose lower edges are rolled up into a cuff.

Procedures:

1. After the pants legs and sleeves have been constructed, determine their finished length before hemming them. Fold up the hem facing and roll up the cuff, following the pattern guidelines. If necessary, adjust the hemline and cuff fold line locations. Mark these lines with a running stitch. Trim the facing extension seam lines to 1.0 cm (⅜ in), stopping at the pants or sleeve hemline.

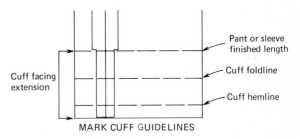

2. Finish the raw edge. Turn the cuff-facing extension to the inside along the cuff fold line; pin and hand- or machine-stitch the hem facing to the garment. This hem can be stitched by machine because the stitches will be covered by the cuff when it is rolled up.

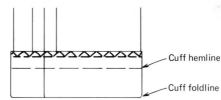

3. To form the cuff, turn the lower folded edge toward the outside of the garment along the cuff and garment hemlines. Both cuffs should be even in width before pressing. If necessary, invisibly tack the cuffs at the seams.

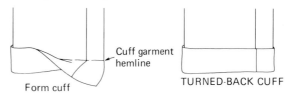

CRITERIA FOR EVALUATION

TURNED-BACK CUFFS

Check to ensure quality performance:

__1. The evaluation criteria for extended hem facings are met.

__2. The cuff is turned back even in depth and tacked at seams if necessary.

Extended Facing: Casings

A casing is formed by threading a machine-stitched hem facing with elastic, cording, or a self-fabric tie to pull in excess garment fullness. It provides a quick, simple method for fitting a variety of sizes. Casings are found at waistlines, necklines, and sleeve or pants openings.

Procedures:

1. When a self-tie or cording is used, make two buttonholes in the garment about 2.0 cm (¾ in) apart and at the point where they will tie outside the garment. Finish the raw edge of the facing extension by machine zigzagging or by turning and stitching if the fabric is lightweight or frays easily.

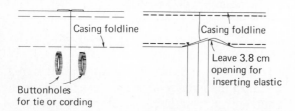

Casing foldline

Buttonholes for tie or cording

Casing foldline

Leave 3.8 cm opening for inserting elastic

2. Fold the casing to the inside of the garment along the designated fold line. Press. Edge-stitch 3 mm (⅛ in) from the folded edge of the casing to better control the gathers. Stitch again along the stitching line through all layers, leaving a 3.8-cm (1½-in) opening to insert

elastic. It is not necessary to leave an opening for cording or ties. The elastic, self-tie, or cording must fit with some ease between the two rows of stitching.

3. Using a safety pin or bodkin, draw the elastic, cording, or self-fabric tie through the casing. Stitch the ends of the elastic together securely and topstitch the remainder of the seam. Distribute the fullness evenly. Pull the cording or ties out through the buttonholes and adjust to fit the body.

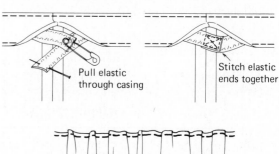

Pull elastic through casing

Stitch elastic ends together

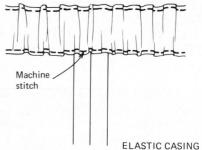

Machine stitch

ELASTIC CASING

CRITERIA FOR EVALUATION

CASINGS

Check to ensure quality performance:

__1. Casing edge is turned under and stitched evenly.

__2. Folded casing perimeter is edge-stitched.

__3. Elastic, ties, or cording draws easily through the casing with slight ease provided.

BIAS FACINGS

Bias facings are true-bias strips of fabric stitched and flexed to conform to the contours of the edge to be finished. They are used when a shaped facing would detract from the design or on garments made of thick fabrics to reduce bulk. Cut the fabric strips on the true bias from self-fabric or other lightweight fabric.

Procedures:

1. Cut strips of fabric on the true bias. To determine the *width,* multiply both the finished width and the seam allowances by two, then add. Bias facings are generally between 1.3 and 2.5 cm (½ and 1 in) wide when finished. For example, the strip width for a 2.0-cm (¾-in) finished bias facing would be determined as follows:

$$2 \times 2.0 \text{ cm } (\text{¾ in}) = 4.0 \text{ cm (about 1½ in) (widths)}$$
$$\underline{2 \times 1.5 \text{ cm } (\text{⅝ in}) = 3.0 \text{ cm (1¼ in) (seam allowances)}}$$
$$7.0 \text{ cm (2¾ in)}$$

To determine *length,* measure the seam line of the edge to be finished and add 5.0 cm (2 in) to turn under the ends.

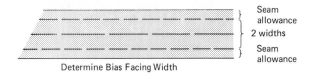

Determine Bias Facing Width

2. Fold the strip in half lengthwise, steam-press flat. Stretch and compress the bias strip, using a steam iron, until it conforms to the shape of the edge to be faced. As the bias strip takes shape, its width may become distorted. To equalize the width, mark the stitching line parallel to the fold and equal to the finished width. Trim away any excess fabric from the seam line.

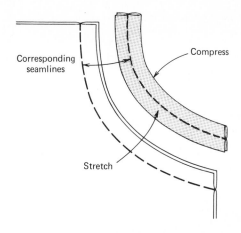

3. When a zipper intersects the edge being faced, insert it before applying the bias facing strip. Pin the folded bias strip to the right side of the garment with seam lines matched. Allow 2.5 cm (1 in) to extend beyond each end of a zipper closure. Abut the ends of a *closed opening* (e.g., armscye), turn back the ends, and trim to 1.0 cm (⅜ in). Stitch, grade, and clip the seam. Trim the bias ends to 6 mm (¼ in). Press the seam toward the bias strip.

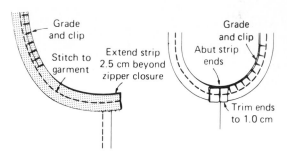

4. Turn the bias strip to the inside of the garment, favoring the garment edge. Fold in the bias ends on a zipper closure; whipstitch the abutted ends of a closed opening. Pin and blind/slip stitch in position, taking tiny stitches into the garment to minimize visibility.

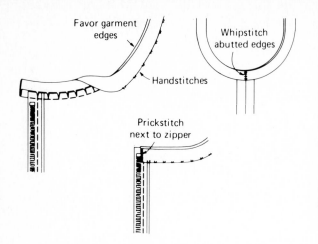

Favor garment edges

Handstitches

Whipstitch abutted edges

Prickstitch next to zipper

CRITERIA FOR EVALUATION

BIAS FACINGS

Check to ensure quality performance:

__ **1.** Enclosed seams are trimmed.

__ **2.** The finished bias facing is even in width.

__ **3.** The facing is invisible from the right side; the garment is favored.

__ **4.** Hand-stitches are as inconspicuous as possible.

23 Bindings and Bands

To apply general enclosed seam theory and methods to the construction of bindings and bands.

Bindings are visible, long, narrow fabric strips that are folded around raw perimeter edges to finish them. They include wider *bands,* such as cuffs, which become extensions of the garment perimeters. Bindings and bands also have an esthetic function. Contrasting bindings may serve as trims that emphasize the structural lines of the garment when applied to collar, lapel, pocket, closure, and hem edges. The width of the bindings must be in scale with the garment and the wearer. The perimeter (curved or pointed) shapes of collars, cuffs, waistbands, and other bands create and support garment design lines. Because they are readily visible, special care must be taken to construct them smoothly and evenly.

Bindings

OBJECTIVES

1. To select bindings complimentary to the garment in color, hand, and scale.

2. To manipulate grain direction and degree of stretch to enable the binding to flex around curves, the corners to be mitered, and the straight garment edges to be evenly bound.

Bindings are made from self- or contrasting fabric cut on the true bias or straight grain line. Purchased prefolded seam tape, knitted bindings, or braids are also available. Bias-cut or knitted bindings are easier to apply to curved edges because of their flexibility.

Edges commonly finished by binding include necklines, collars, sleeve-opening plackets, cuffs, pockets, waistlines, closure edges, and hems. Bindings simplify the hemming and finishing of reversible garments and eliminate the need for facings in garments made from sheer fabrics. Used with strapped seams, they emphasize the structural lines of the garment.

GENERAL CONSTRUCTION PROCEDURES

Basic application techniques for single and double bindings are illustrated, as are special techniques needed to navigate inside and outside corners and curves. The continuous lapped placket, which binds sleeve-placket openings, is included.

Prepare the garment by trimming the seam allowance to be bound to a width equal to the finished binding width. When binding ends must be joined to finish openings such as the armscye or wrist, bring them together at an inconspicuous garment seam.

Single Binding: Regular Application

1. Cut bias strips of fabric four times the finished width. The length should equal to the length of the seam line to be bound plus 5.0 cm (2 in).

2. Fold the strip in half lengthwise and press. Open out the strip and fold the lengthwise edges inward to meet at the center fold; press. If the edge to be bound is shaped, stretch and compress the bias strip to conform.

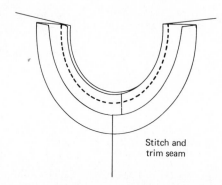

Stitch and trim seam

3. Open out one seam allowance of the binding and pin to the garment edge with seam lines matching and right sides together. Turn back the starting end 1.3 cm (½ in); overlap with the finishing end of the strip and trim it to 1.0 cm (⅜ in). Stitch.

4. Press the seam allowances toward the binding. Techniques used to finish woven and knit bindings differ.

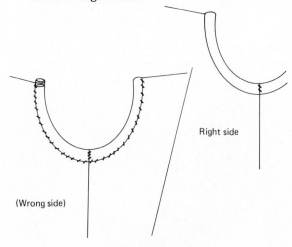

Right side

(Wrong side)

Finishing Woven Bindings

To finish *woven bindings,* turn under the binding along the creased center line, bringing the creased seam line to meet the stitched seam. Pin. Use the felling stitch to secure the binding. Catch the stitches in the seam line and not in the garment. Blind/slip-stitch the binding ends together.

To finish *knit bindings,* open out the remaining binding seam allowance. Turn the binding to the inside of the garment along the center fold line with the seam allowance extending downward. Machine-stitch through all fabric layers in the ditch of the seam. Trim away the excess binding seam allowance, leaving 6 mm (¼ in). Blind/slip-stitch the overlapped binding ends together.

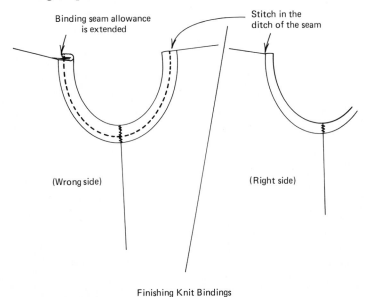

Binding seam allowance is extended

Stitch in the ditch of the seam

(Wrong side)

(Right side)

Finishing Knit Bindings

Single Binding: Topstitched Application

The topstitching method can also be used to apply prefolded braids and bindings.

1. Cut the bias strips four times the finished width and 5.0 cm (2 in) longer than the seam line to be bound. Fold the strip lengthwise

Cut bias strip four times desired finished width

and *nearly in half.* Leave a 3-mm (⅛-in) gap between the two edges; press. Open out the binding and fold the outer raw edges so that they meet at the creased line; press. Press shape the binding to conform to curved edges.

2. Enclose the seam to be bound by folding the binding around the edge, with the *widest* side of the binding to the inside of the garment. The starting end should begin 1.0 cm (⅜ in) beyond an intersecting garment seam. Baste in position to prevent slippage. Machine-stitch close to the edge through all fabric layers, stopping about 7.0 cm (2¾-in) from the

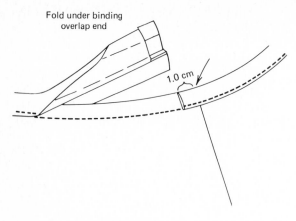

Fold under binding overlap end

1.0 cm

starting point. Leave the machine needle inserted in the garment.

3. Fold under the finishing end even with the intersecting garment seam line and trim to 1.3 cm (½ in). Finish topstitching the binding; blind/slip-stitch the ends together.

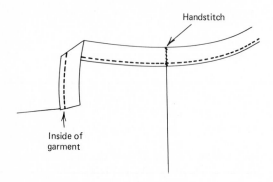

Handstitch

Inside of garment

Topstitched Application

Double Binding Application

Garments constructed of sheer fabrics need the opacity of the double binding to hide seam allowances.

1. Cut the binding strip six times the width of the finished binding and 5.0 cm (2 in) longer than the length of the seam line to be finished.

2. Fold the binding strip in half lengthwise and press. Without opening the strip, fold it in thirds and press again. If necessary, steam-press the binding to conform to the seam line shape.

3. Open up the strip so that it is still folded in half. Pin the doubled strip to the right side of the garment with seamlines matched. Turn back the starting end 1.3 cm (½ in), overlap with the finishing end 1.0 cm (⅜ in). Stitch the seam.

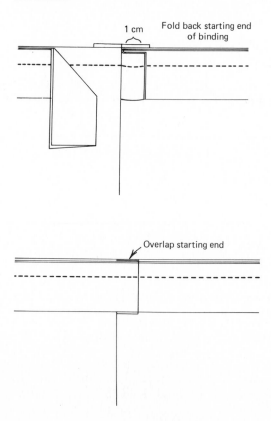

1 cm — Fold back starting end of binding

Overlap starting end

4. Press the seam toward the binding. Fold the binding over the seam allowances until the outer folded edge meets the seam line. Use the felling stitch to secure the binding to the seam line. Blind/slip-stitch the ends together.

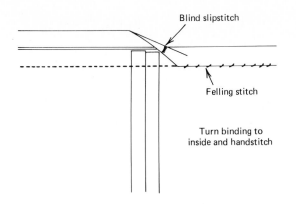

Blind slipstitch

Felling stitch

Turn binding to
inside and handstitch

1. Stitch the binding to the garment, stopping at the corner seam-line point; reinforce by backstitching.
2. Turn the binding to follow the garment edge by forming a diagonal fold at the corner. Stitch, beginning at the raw edge and crossing the diagonal fold.
3. Press the seam allowances toward the binding. Turn the binding to the inside of the garment, mitering excess fabric at the corner. Adjust the miter until it forms a square corner. Pin and hand-stitch into place. Blind/slip-stitch the mitered edges together.

Binding Outside Corners: Mitering

The bound corner is treated by *mitering* the excess fabric, that is, joining it diagonally at the corner.

Binding Inside Corners: Mitering

Inside-corner bindings are also treated by mitering excess fabric to fit the corner smoothly.

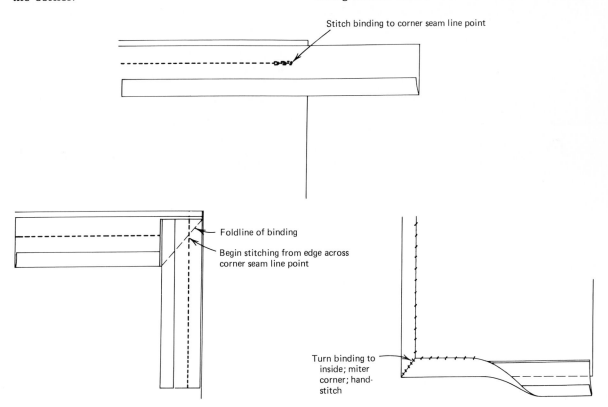

Stitch binding to corner seam line point

Foldline of binding

Begin stitching from edge across corner seam line point

Turn binding to inside; miter corner; hand-stitch

1. Reinforce the inside corner of the garment, using very short stitches placed a scant seam allowance from the edge. Clip to the corner.
2. Pin the garment to the binding by straightening the garment seam line to align with the binding seam line. Stitch with the garment side up.
3. Allow the garment to lie flat with the corner square. Press the seam allowances toward the binding; press the corner miter just to the binding's crease line.

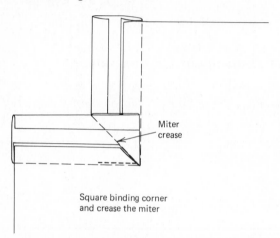

Miter crease

Square binding corner and crease the miter

4. Turn the binding to the inside of the garment, shaping the miter to fit squarely inside the corner. Hand-stitch the binding; blind/slip-stitch the miter.

Binding Outside Curves: Easing

When applied to an outside curve, the outer perimeter edge of the binding must be longer than the inner seam line. To prevent the binding from curling in at the corner, *ease* the binding to the garment to provide the needed length. Only bias-cut or knit bindings will fit smoothly around curves.

Binding Inside Curves: Compressing

Compress the binding yarns to fit the shorter perimeter of an inside curve by shaping the

binding to fit the curve before stitching; steam press. In this way, the outer edge can be stretched slightly to enable the inner edge to compress without rippling. Again, bias-cut or knit fabrics respond best to rounded contours.

Bound Plackets

Bound plackets—such as a sleeve wrist placket or dress side placket—are garment access openings generally found in women's garments. These openings enable close-fitting parts of the garment to open and expand during dressing. Placket edges may be bound with self-fabric or other lightweight woven fabrics cut with the lengthwise grain to prevent the openings from stretching.

Continuous (One-Piece) Bound-Placket Application

One-piece bindings are commonly used to finish the edges of sleeve-wrist plackets found in women's garments. The placket must be long enough to allow the hand to slip through the wrist opening.

1. Cut a lengthwise strip of self-fabric 3.2 cm (1¼ in) wide and twice as long as the placket. Machine-stitch 6-mm (¼-in) guidelines along each lengthwise edge.
2. Machine-stitch just outside the marked placket stitching line. Change to short reinforcement stitches for about 2.5 cm (1 in) on either side of the point; take one stitch *across* the point. Slash to within 1.0 mm (⅟₁₆ in) of the point. Notice that the seam-line width tapers from 6 mm (¼ in) to almost nothing.
3. Baste the binding to the slashed opening with right sides together and stitching lines matched. Spread the slashed opening apart to fit the binding. Carefully stitch along the seam line next to the previous stitching. Pull the excess garment fabric out of the way so that it is not caught in the stitching.

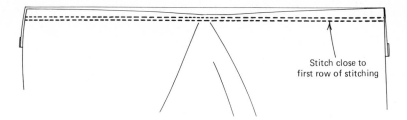

Stitch close to
first row of stitching

4. Press the seam allowances toward the binding strip. Press under the long remaining edge of the strip, using the stitched line as a guide. Fold the strip to the inside, enclosing the seam allowances. Using a felling stitch or machine topstitching, join the binding to the seam line.

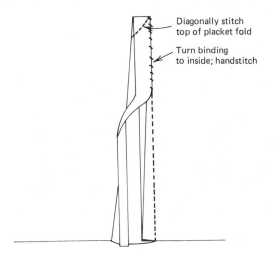

Diagonally stitch
top of placket fold

Turn binding
to inside; handstitch

5. To prevent the placket binding from flipping to the outside of the garment, diagonally stitch across the top of the fold. Press under the side of the placket which will form the overlap.

Two-Piece Bound-Seam-Placket Application

Two-piece bound plackets may be used to finish the side seam plackets of dresses or skirts in place of a zipper. When a garment is made up in a sheer, drapeable, or lightweight fabric, a zipper may be too stiff or may be visible through the fabric. Placket edges are also bound to extend the seam allowances when they are too narrow to insert a zipper securely. Purchased seam binding or self-fabric is used. The garment-back side seam is turned forward to provide the underlap.

1. Stitch the left side seams, leaving an 18-cm (7-in) opening in a skirt and a 23- to 30.5-cm (9- to 12-in) opening in a dress. Reinforce by backstitching.
2. Cut two lengthwise strips of self- or lightweight fabric four times the finished width or about 5.0 cm (2 in). Press the binding in half lengthwise, open, turn in edges to meet at the center, and press.
3. Center the binding over the length of the placket opening with the right sides together and edges even; pin. Turn under binding ends 1.0 cm (⅜ in). Stitch a 1.3-cm (½-in) seam in the garment. Repeat for the other edge.
4. Press the binding toward the seam allowances. Fold the binding to the inside of the garment with the binding edge turned under, enclosing the seam allowances. Use the felling stitch to secure the binding to the seam line of each seam. Turn the side seams out flat as they were stitched. Stitch across the binding ends through all layers without catching the garment. Clip the back seam allowances to enable the bound edge to swing forward, forming the underlap. Press under the bound edge on the front seam. Attach fasteners to the binding.

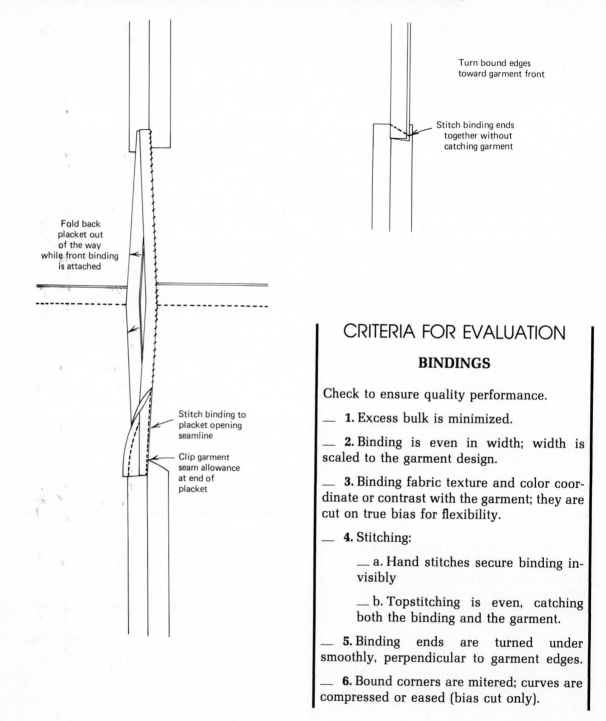

Turn bound edges toward garment front

Stitch binding ends together without catching garment

Fold back placket out of the way while front binding is attached

Stitch binding to placket opening seamline

Clip garment seam allowance at end of placket

CRITERIA FOR EVALUATION

BINDINGS

Check to ensure quality performance.

__ **1.** Excess bulk is minimized.

__ **2.** Binding is even in width; width is scaled to the garment design.

__ **3.** Binding fabric texture and color coordinate or contrast with the garment; they are cut on true bias for flexibility.

__ **4.** Stitching:

    __ a. Hand stitches secure binding invisibly

    __ b. Topstitching is even, catching both the binding and the garment.

__ **5.** Binding ends are turned under smoothly, perpendicular to garment edges.

__ **6.** Bound corners are mitered; curves are compressed or eased (bias cut only).

In addition, for *bound plackets:*

___ 7. Binding is cut on the lengthwise grain (or true bias if plaid).

___ 8. Placket opening is long enough to permit easy access into garment.

___ 9. Ends of garment placket opening are reinforced before binding is applied.

___ 10. Continuous bound placket: bindings are stitched together diagonally at placket point.

___ 11. Placket band overlaps in correct direction for sex of wearer.

___ 12. There is sufficient overlap of bands so underlap is not visible.

Bands

OBJECTIVES

1. **To choose the basic band, man-tailored band, or band variation construction that applies to your project.**

2. **To construct circumference bands, including cuffs, waistbands, and collars, that are supported, symmetric, minimize bulk and smoothly encircle the body.**

Bands consist of rectangular or shaped garment *extensions* that bind perimeter edges and support the total garment design. Bands may be cut from matching or contrasting fabrics. If outer fabrics are thick, the facing may be cut from a lightweight fabric or grosgrain ribbon to reduce bulk. Bands may extend in one direction to the bound edge or, as in the case of collars or cuffs, may be rolled.

Examples of bands include decorative hem and neck bands, shirt-front bands, cuffs, waistbands, collars, and shirt- and sleeve-placket bands.

CHARACTERISTICS OF BANDS

Shape. Symmetry of shape from side to side—as well as evenness of width and smoothness of construction—are crucial to garment appearance.

Circularity. Bands encircle the body, either fitting it closely as do waistbands and cuffs or loosely as at hem edges. As a result of this circularity, the inner facing layer must be cut slightly shorter or smaller to fit inside the shorter circumference smoothly.

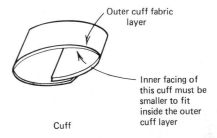

Outer cuff fabric layer

Inner facing of this cuff must be smaller to fit inside the outer cuff layer

Cuff

Grain. To prevent stretching, bands are usually cut with the lengthwise grain. Striped fabrics are cut with the stripe parallel to the band edge; plaids may be cut on the bias for greater emphasis.

Faced. Band perimeters are finished and supported by facings cut of self-fabric. The facings may be extensions of a straight band edge or shaped to correspond to the band shape.

Supported. Band shapes are almost always supported by interfacing or underlining. Interfacings cut on the true bias are generally more flexible, fitting smoothly inside the circular bands.

Enclosed Seams. Enclosed perimeter seams are common. Therefore techniques for controlling bulk and favoring outer fabric layers must be employed. Seaming the band to the garment often involves the joining of seams that are unlike in length or shape. For instance, a skirt may be gathered to a waistband or a straight collar edge may be joined to a curved neckline seam.

Stays. Bands often act as stays to prevent stretching of slightly bias or true bias edges while also controlling gathered, pleated, tucked, or eased fullness.

Closures. Waistbands, cuffs, and plackets are often part of a lapped closure system that permits garment access while also enabling the garment to fit closely. The upper band, forming the overlap, laps over the lower-band underlap.

Direction of Overlap

	Access Location	Overlap Direction
Women's Garment Openings	Center-front placket	Right over left
	Left-side placket	Front over back
	Center-back placket	Left over right
Men's Garment Openings	Center-front placket	Left over right
Men/ Women	Sleeve placket	Front over back

GENERAL CONSTRUCTION PROCEDURES

The following two construction procedures are common to most band applications, including straight and shaped cuffs and waistbands, straight band hems, stand-up or rolled band collars, and shirt-placket bands. They include *basic* and *man-tailored* construction procedures. Variations of the basic procedures follow, describing in detail the straight waistband with stiffener, man-tailored waistbanding application, shirt sleeve and neck plackets, and various collar band applications.

Basic Band Application

1. *Application of Interfacing.* Apply the interfacing to the wrong side of the *outer* fabric section so that it will act as a buffer between the seam allowances and the outer fabric layer. Cuff and collar band interfacings may be cut on the true bias for greater flexibility. Band hems are not usually interfaced but may be doubled or underlined for soft support.
2. *Joining Band to Band Facing.* Shaped band and facing perimeters are joined by seaming. *Extended* band facings are folded to the inside with enclosed seam ends stitched. Favor the upper band. Stitch, grade, clip or notch, and favor all enclosed seams.
3. *Joining Band to Garment.* Prepare the garment seam by stay-stitching, easing, gathering, pleating, or tucking the corresponding seam line. Clip inside curves of garment neckline seams. With right sides together, pin the upper band to the garment edge. If the

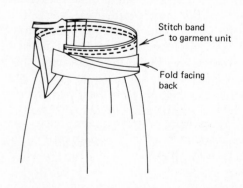

Stitch band to garment unit

Fold facing back

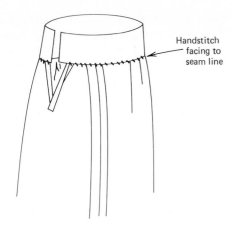

Handstitch facing to seam line

band has an overlap or underlap extension, allow it to extend beyond the garment edge as the pattern directs. Stitch the seam without catching the facing. To hold gathers or outer fullness flat, stitch again 1.0 cm (⅜ in) from the edge. Grade and clip or notch if needed. Press the seam allowances toward the band.

4. *Secure Facing to Garment.* Trim the remaining facing seam allowance inside the band, smoothing the facing to fit. Hand-stitch the facing to the seam line, using the felling stitch. Do not catch the garment with the stitches; catch only the seam line. Press.

Man-Tailored Band Application

Some women's and almost all men's garments are man-tailored. The application is similar to the basic band application. The band is applied entirely by machine-stitching and topstitching. Any of the band variation construction methods may be modified to follow this method.

1. *Application of Interfacing.* After trimming away seam allowances, hand-baste the interfacing to the inside of the upper band. Do not remove basting until the band has been topstitched.

2. *Joining Band to Band Facing.* Shaped band and facing perimeters are joined by seaming. *Extended* band facings are folded to the inside with enclosed seam ends stitched. Favor the upper band taking a smaller seam allowance in the band *or* by cutting the three outer edges of the facing smaller. Stitch, grade, clip or notch, and favor all enclosed seams.

3. *Join band facing* to the garment by pinning the right side of the *band facing* to the wrong side of the garment. Stitch the seam without catching the facing underneath. To hold gathers or outer fullness flat, stitch again 1.0 cm (⅜ in) from the edge. Grade and clip or notch if needed. Press the seam allowances toward the band.

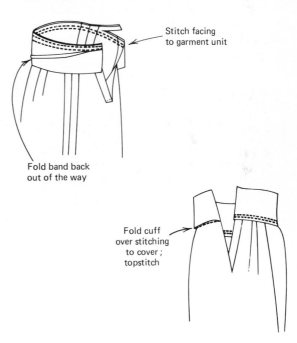

Stitch facing to garment unit

Fold band back out of the way

Fold cuff over stitching to cover; topstitch

4. *Secure band to garment* by first turning under the remaining seam allowance. Be sure the band covers the previous seam line slightly; press. Trim the seam allowance to 1.0 cm (⅜ in). Baste in position. Topstitch from all edges.

CONSTRUCTION PROCEDURES: BAND VARIATIONS

Straight-waistband Application with Stiffener

Purchased waistband stiffener provides greater support, flexibility, and shape retention than most woven interfacings. The stiffener is available in several widths and is used to support both men's and women's *straight* waistbands.

If the stiffener must be trimmed to fit the waistband, place the cut edge at the bottom between the outer band and the seam allowances. This will prevent the cut (and now sharp) crosswise yarns from penetrating the garment fabric and scratching the skin.

Women's Application with Stiffener

1. Stitch a guideline 1.3 cm (½ in) from the long, unnotched waistband edge. Trim to 6 mm (¼ in).
2. Pin the long notched waistband edge to the garment waistline seam with right sides together. Extend the overlap or underlap as indicated by the pattern markings. Double-stitch and trim.

3. Check the pattern to determine the finished waistband width and, if necessary, trim the stiffener to match. If the stiffener is to fit smoothly inside the band, it must be trimmed 2 to 3 mm (scant ⅛ in) narrower than the finished band. The stiffener length is equal to the finished waistband length plus extension.
4. Pin the stiffener to the seam allowances with the band extending 1.5 cm (⅝ in) at each end. Stitch about 6 mm (¼ in) from the seam line through the seam allowances and press both the seam allowances and the stiffener toward the band.

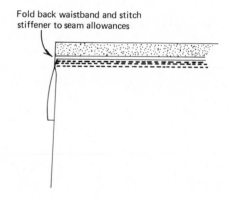

Fold back waistband and stitch stiffener to seam allowances

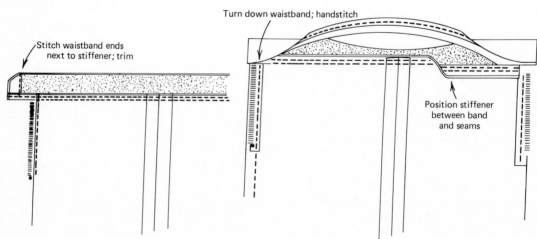

Stitch waistband ends next to stiffener; trim

Turn down waistband; handstitch

Position stiffener between band and seams

5. Fold the waistband lengthwise along the fold line with right sides together; pin. Stitch the end seams without catching the stiffener. Grade the ends. Turn the waistband right side out, folding the facing over the stiffener. Turn the free facing edge inside so that it is even with the waistline seam. Pin. Use the felling stitch to secure the facing to the seam line.

6. The waistband can be topstitched at this point. The waistband can also be applied by topstitching if the man-tailored application method is followed.

Men's Application with Stiffener

Men's waistbands are two-piece, with right and left bands joined by a center-back seam to facilitate any later waistline adjustments. The band is faced by a separate two-piece facing cut from firmly woven fabric such as pocketing. The waistband is applied *before* the crotch seam is stitched.

1. Cut the waistband, facing, and stiffener sections following these guidelines:

Waistband:
Length
(right side) = length from finished edge of fly shield to center-back edge + 1.5 cm (⅝ in).
Length
(left side) = length from front finished edge to center-back edge + 1.5 cm (⅝ in).
Width = finished width + 4.1 cm (1⅝ in).

Facing:
Length of right and left sides are equal to corresponding waistbands.
Width = finished width + 5.0 cm (2 in).

Stiffener:
Length
(right side) = length from finished edge of fly shield to center-back raw edge.
Length
(left side) = length from front finished edge to center-back raw edge.
Width = width purchased according to desired finished width of band, commonly 3.8 cm (1½ in).

2. Stitch the facings to the corresponding waistbands along the upper band edges with right sides together. Grade the seam and press toward the facing. Press under 2.5 cm (1 in) along the remaining facing edge.

3. Baste the upper pocket facings to the garment waistline edge. Stitch waistband sections to pants waistline with right sides together.

4. Pin the stiffener to the seam allowances with the band extending 1.5 cm (⅝ in) from the waistband ends. Stitch about 6 mm (¼ in) from the seam line through the seam allowances and press both the seam allowances and the stiffener toward the band.

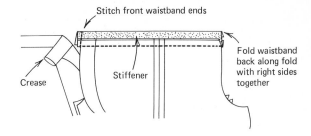

5. Press the waistline seam toward the waistband. Fold the facing to the inside of the garment, favoring the waistband; press a crease into this edge. Fold the facing to the right side of the pants along the crease. Stitch the front waistband ends together and grade.

6. Stitch center-back seam, continuing up through the waistband and the opened out facing. Press seam open and turn facing down along upper crease. Press into position.

7. The facing may be held in position by machine- or hand-stitching.

    a. *Machine Method:* Machine stitch in the ditch of the waistline seam through pants and facing layers.

    b. *Hand Method:* Machine stitch along the free folded facing edge 1.0 cm (⅜ in) from the fold. Use an invisible catch stitch to secure the facing to the pants waistline seam.

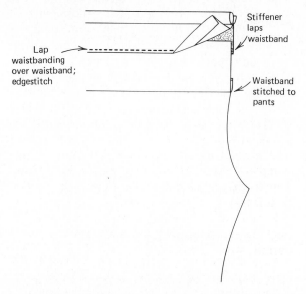

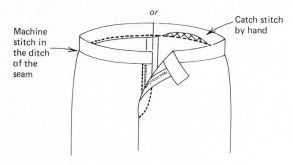

MAN-TAILORED WAISTBANDING APPLICATION

Prepared waistbanding, consisting of a firmly woven facing and stiffener, can be purchased, eliminating several steps from the previous procedures.

1. Cut the waistband to a length equal to each side of the pants plus 1.5 cm (⅝ in). The width should equal the facing width plus 3.0 cm (1¼ in). Cut the waistbanding the same length.

2. Stitch the waistbands to the pants with right sides together 1.5 cm (⅝ in) from the edge. Press the seam toward the waistband.

3. Apply the waistbanding to the waistband by lapping it over the free waistband edge. The stiffener should overlap the waistband by 1.5 cm (⅝ in). Stitch through all three layers close to the facing fold.

4. To finish the front edges, turn the facing to the outside of the waistband and, with right sides together, stitch the ends. Grade and turn the facing to the inside; press a crease along the upper edge.

5. Stitch the crotch–center-back seam by turning out the facing and stitching from the zipper through to the facing edge. Press open the seam.

6. Turn the waistbanding back to the inside of the pants. To finish the waistband, lift up the facing pleat and machine stitch through both the ditch of the waistline seam and the stiffener pleat. Do not stitch the facing pleat. The band may be hand-stitched instead by

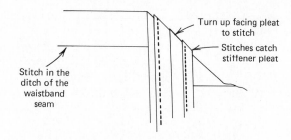

tacking the stiffener pleat to the pocket facings and pants seam allowances.

SLEEVE AND NECK PLACKET BANDS

Shirt bands are inset into the rectangular placket opening of the sleeve or a shirt neckline. The placket consists of an overlap band that completely covers an underlap band. The placket may be closed with a buttonhole closure or left free.

Similar techniques are used to construct a neckline or sleeve placket. One method, with variations, is illustrated.

1. Prepare the placket opening by stay-stitching close to the marked seam line. Reinforce the corners with very short stitches.
2. Apply the interfacing to the wrong side of the *neck* band sections.
3. Prepare the visible overlap end of the band by stitching the end as shown. The ends may be squared or pointed. Stitch the end stopping at the lengthwise seam line; grade and turn right side out. Press.
4. Stitch the underlap band to the placket opening. Machine-stitch the right side of the underlap band to the right side of the corresponding placket edge. Grade and press the seam toward the band. Press under the long

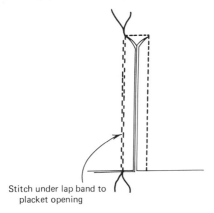

Stitch under lap band to placket opening

edge of the band facing along the seam line; trim to 6 mm (¼ in). Turn the band facing to the inside of the garment, bringing the creased edge to meet the previous seam line. Use the felling stitch to secure to the seam line.

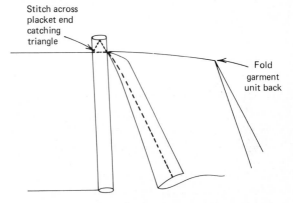

Stitch across placket end catching triangle

Fold garment unit back

5. To stitch the underlap end to the triangle, flip the other side of the garment out of the way. Pin the underlap to the placket triangle, matching seam lines. Stitch, trim, and press seam allowances toward the garment. The triangle is turned to the inside for square corners and to the outside for a pointed placket.
6. Stitch the overlap to the remaining placket opening edge with right side of overlap band facing right side of the remaining placket edge. Grade and press the seam toward the band. Press under the seam allowance on the long free band-facing edge; trim. Turn

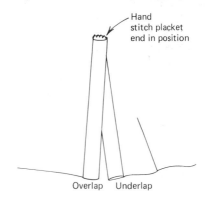

Hand stitch placket end in position

Overlap   Underlap

the band facing to the inside, press. Use a felling stitch to secure the band facing to the seam line. Stitches should not show on the right side of the garment. Press. Apply machine buttonholes, if they will be used, at this time. Blind/slip-stitch lower end of overlap band in place, covering the placket seam line.

COLLAR BAND APPLICATIONS

As a shaped band, the collar provides decorative styling in addition to binding the neckline opening. Collar application varies from the basic band application because more fabric layers are involved. Both the garment neckline and the collar are faced, creating four fabric layers plus their seam allowances. If the collar and the neckline are interfaced, two more layers are added. Trimming of the interfacing seam allowances can eliminate two layers.

Treatment of Neckline Seam. The collar application in *lightweight fabrics* is similar to the basic band method, but with an additional garment facing. Because there is only one neckline seam, all the seam allowances are turned in one direction toward the garment. This method cannot be used with bulkier fabrics.

To construct and apply collars in garments made of *thick fabrics,* two separate neckline seams are stitched: the upper collar to the neckline facing and the collar facing to the garment neckline. These seams are pressed open and placed face to face with two seam allowances turned inside the collar and two turned toward the garment. Since this method is often used in suits or coats, it is called the *notched* method; but it can be used in any garment to control the fabric layer bulk.

Relationship of Collar Neckline Curve to Collar Stand. The degree of curve of the collar neckline seam directly influences:

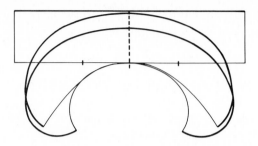

Neckline seam length remains the same, but the perimeter length increases as the neckline curve becomes more rounded

——————— Perimeter edge
——————— Neckline edge

a. Length of the collar perimeter edge.
b. Height of the collar stand.

Generally, the *more curved the collar neckline seam is, the longer the outer collar perimeter will be, enabling the collar to lie close to the body*. Because the collar perimeter circumference nearly equals that of the corresponding body circumference, the circumference is measured out from the neckline seam a distance equal to the finished collar width.

As the collar neckline curve becomes straighter, the collar perimeter circumference becomes shorter than the corresponding body circumference. The collar perimeter pushes up until it finds the matching body circumference, forcing the collar to have a slight stand.

When the collar neckline is straight, the outer perimeter is shortened to match the neckline circumference. Maximum stand is achieved as the collar perimeter pushes up to the matching neckline circumference. The turtleneck and straight shirt collars provide examples of collars with maximum stand.

Collars and Closure Systems

A collar in a close-fitting garment made of woven fabric requires an opening in the neckline to allow the head to slip through. The garment may open by means of a lapped button-hole or a zipper closure. The collar will not overlap, although the band of a shirt collar will lap in a garment with a button closure.

Application of Collar with Full Neck Facing

1. Prepare the garment by stitching the facing shoulder seams together, trimming the seams to 1.0 cm (⅜ in) and pressing them open. Stay-stitch the garment and facing neckline seams.
2. Prepare the collar by applying the interfacing to the upper collar. Stitch the upper collar to the collar facing. Favor the collar by taking a smaller seam allowance in the upper collar. Grade, clip, and turn the collar right side out. Diagonally baste the outer edges and press.
3. Establish the collar roll line by shaping the collar until it rolls like the pattern illustration. Baste through all collar layers, following the roll line where the collar breaks. The neckline edges will not match, but baste them together as they lie 1.3 cm (½ in) from the shortest edge. Trim away excess seam

allowance. The upper collar will be larger than the under collar.

4. Pin the collar to the garment with the collar facing next to the right side of the garment. Clip the garment neck edge as needed. Machine-baste. Turn the garment facing to the outside of the garment and baste it over the collar, clipping the facing neck edge as needed. Stitch the neckline seam. Grade and clip.
5. Press the seam allowances toward the facing. Understitch the back neck facing only. Turn the facing toward the garment with the collar extended. Press. Tack the facing to the garment seam allowances.

Application of Collar with Partial Neck Facing

1. Turn under the facing shoulder seams; press. Stay-stitch the garment and facing neck edges.
2. Stay-stitch the upper collar neckline seam. Clip the neckline seam from the shoulder marking to the shoulder seam of the facing

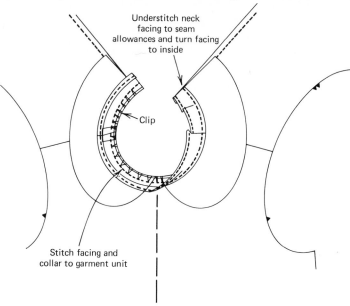

Understitch neck facing to seam allowances and turn facing to inside

Clip

Stitch facing and collar to garment unit

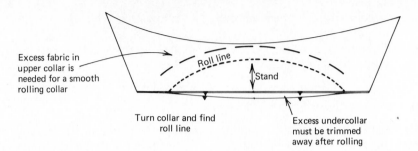

Excess fabric in upper collar is needed for a smooth rolling collar

Roll line

Stand

Turn collar and find roll line

Excess undercollar must be trimmed away after rolling

without cutting the stitches. Trim the back neck seam to 1.0 cm (⅜ in).

3. Prepare the collar by applying the interfacing to the upper collar. Stitch the upper collar to the collar facing. Favor the collar by taking a smaller seam allowance in the upper collar. Grade, clip, and turn the collar right side out. Diagonally baste the outer edges and press.

4. Establish the collar roll line by shaping the collar until it rolls like the pattern illustration. Baste through all collar layers, following the roll line where the collar breaks. The neckline edges will not match, but baste them together as they lie between the center front and the shoulder seam, 1.3 cm (½ in)

from the shortest edge. Trim away excess seam allowance. The upper collar will be larger than the under collar.

5. Pin the collar facing and the basted collar ends to the garment neck edge, clipping the garment neckline as needed. Baste without catching the back upper collar. Turn the front neck facing to the outside of the garment, covering the collar and matching the shoulder seams. Clip the facing neckline if necessary. Machine-stitch the neck edge, pulling the back upper collar out of the seamline where the collar is clipped. Grade the seam. Clip the seam allowances at the shoulder seam.

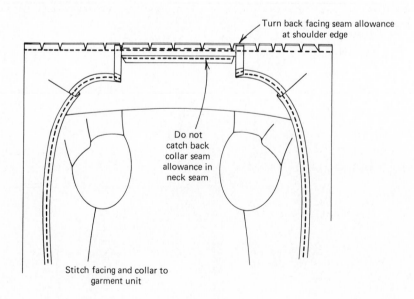

Turn back facing seam allowance at shoulder edge

Do not catch back collar seam allowance in neck seam

Stitch facing and collar to garment unit

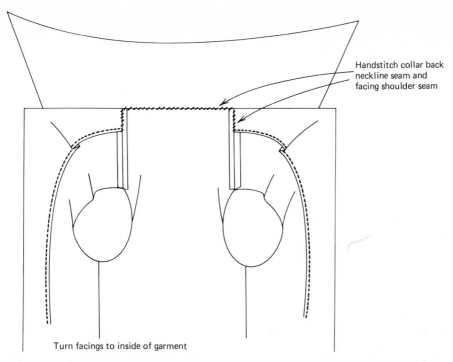

Handstitch collar back
neckline seam and
facing shoulder seam

Turn facings to inside of garment

6. Press the front seam allowances toward the facing; press the back seam allowances toward the collar. Turn under the back upper collar seam and pin it to the neckline seam. Use the felling stitch to secure the collar to the garment and to stitch the facings to the shoulder seams.

Application of Shirt Collar with Separate Band

1. Prepare the collar by applying the interfacing to the upper collar and one band section. Stitch the upper collar to the collar facing.

Favor the collar by taking a smaller seam allowance in the upper collar. Grade, clip, and turn the collar right side out. Diagonally baste the outer edges and press. Topstitch the collar.

2. Pin the interfaced band to the under collar and the other band to the upper collar with right sides together. Stitch the seam, stopping at the neckline. Grade and clip the seam. Press the band sections toward the seam allowances.

3. Join the neckline seam by pinning the right side of the non-interfaced band to the wrong side of the garment. Stitch, grade, and press

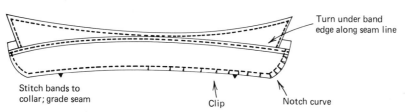

Turn under band
edge along seam line

Stitch bands to
collar; grade seam

Clip

Notch curve

the seam toward the collar. Turn under the interfaced band along the seam line; baste, overlapping the neckline seam slightly. Topstitch entire perimeter of band close to edge.

Application of Shawl-Collar

The shawl collar differs from other collars because the lapel and upper collar are cut in one piece with the garment. A shawl collar always has a center-back seam.

1. Stitch, trim, and press open the center-back seam of the under collar. Lap the center-back interfacing seam allowances, stitch twice, and trim.
2. Apply the interfacing to the under collar and to the garment front.
3. Pin the under collar to the garment, stretching the collar to fit and clipping the garment neck edge as needed. Stitch, trim to 6.0 mm (¼ in), and notch the under collar seam allowance. Press open the seam.
4. Stitch the center back seam of the upper col-

lar and press open. Stitch the back neck facing to the neck edge of the upper-collar facing section, carefully stitching the inset corners. Trim to 1.0 cm (⅜ in) and press open. Finish the facing edge.

5. Stitch the collar-facing unit to the corresponding edge with right sides together.

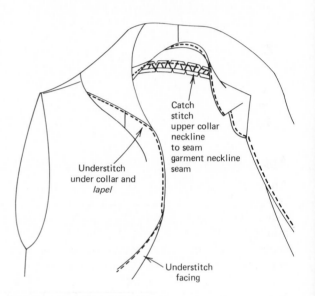

Catch stitch upper collar neckline to seam garment neckline seam

Understitch under collar and *lapel*

Understitch facing

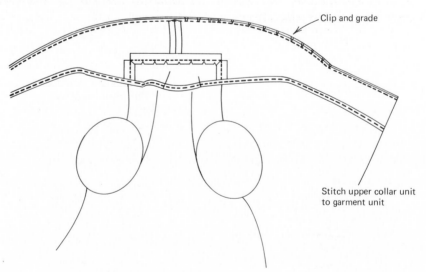

Clip and grade

Stitch upper collar unit to garment unit

Grade the seam, changing widths at the point where the lapel turns back. Press the collar seam toward the under collar and the front closure seam toward the facing. Understitch the under collar and lapel portion of the seam.

Favor the front closure edge of the garment, using the diagonal basting stitch. Press with the facings turned to the inside of the garment.

6. Try on the garment to establish the collar roll. Smooth the upper collar over the under collar; pin in position. Loosely catch-stitch the facing and garment seam allowances together as they fall.

Application of Notched-Collar

Although this method is used primarily to apply collars in garments made of bulky fabrics, it can be used for any medium-to-thick fabric to minimize bulk and create a smooth neckline seam. The under-collar pattern may be cut smaller.

1. Prepare the garment by stitching the facing shoulder seams together, trimming the seams to 1.0 cm (⅜ in) and pressing them open. Stay-stitch the garment and facing neckline seams.
2. Prepare the collar by applying the interfacing to the upper collar. Stitch the upper collar to the collar facing starting and stopping stitches 1.5 cm (⅝ in) from the neck edge.

Favor the collar by taking a smaller seam allowance in the upper collar. Grade, clip, and turn the collar right side out. Diagonally baste the outer edges and press.

3. Establish the collar roll line by shaping the collar until it rolls like the pattern illustration. Baste through all collar layers, following the roll line where the collar breaks. The neckline edges will not match. The upper collar will be larger than the under collar.
4. Pin the under collar to the garment, matching neckline seam lines and markings; clip the garment neckline where needed to release the seam. Stitch. Pin the upper collar to the facing, following the above procedures. Stitch.
5. Pin the facing to the garment, carefully pinning the edges together where the collar and lapel notch meet. If necessary, hand-baste to prevent the fabric layers from shifting as they are stitched. Stitch, reinforcing the notch point and being careful not to catch the collar seams.
6. Trim, grade, and clip the seams. The upper-collar–facing seam should be trimmed to 1.0 cm (⅜ in) and the under-collar–garment seam to 6 mm (¼ in). Press the neck seams open. Diagonally baste the front closure edges, favoring the upper lapel and outer garment edges; press.
7. Try on the garment to smooth the upper collar over the under collar. Pin the neckline seams as they are positioned and loosely catch-stitch together.

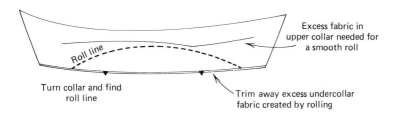

Roll line

Excess fabric in upper collar needed for a smooth roll

Turn collar and find roll line

Trim away excess undercollar fabric created by rolling

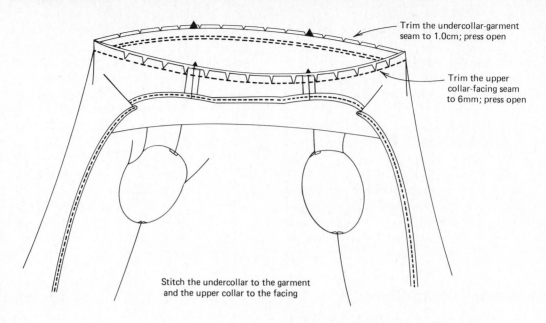

Trim the undercollar-garment seam to 1.0cm; press open

Trim the upper collar-facing seam to 6mm; press open

Stitch the undercollar to the garment and the upper collar to the facing

CRITERIA FOR EVALUATION

BANDS: CUFFS, WAISTBANDS, COLLARS

Check to ensure quality performance:

__ **1.** Harmonizes in scale with the total design.

__ **2.** Straight bands are even in width; shaped bands are symmetric from side to side.

__ **3.** Interfaced for support:

    __ a. Cut on straight lengthwise grain.

    __ b. Collar and cuff interfacings may be cut on bias for smooth roll.

__ **4.** Excess bulk minimized by grading and trimming; corners reinforced.

__ **5.** Enclosed seams fully turned and favored to right side.

__ **6.** Following the basic application, facings are securely and invisibly handstitched to the seamline.

__ **7.** Following the man-tailored application, band edges are evenly turned under and topstitched in position.

__ **8.** Bands with overlaps follow the overlap direction for sex of the wearer.

__ **9.** Band ends are evenly aligned at closure openings.

__ **10.** Any buttonholes are located on the overlap; buttons are located on the underlap.

In addition for *COLLARS:*

__ **11.** The facing (lower side) of the collar or lapel is understitched or decoratively topstitched.

__ **12.** The collar rolls smoothly around the neck without rippling; collar tips fall close to the body.

__ **13.** The back neckline seam is covered by the collar.

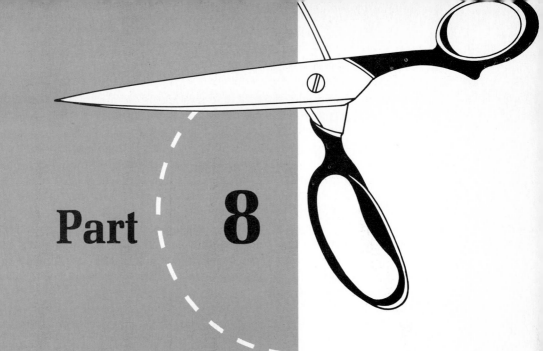

Part 8

Closure Systems and Pockets

Zippers, buttons and pockets may lend subtlety or dramatic detail to your garment's design, as well as provide functional services.

Zippers are subdued in appearance, yet they provide quick and easy access into any garment. Button closures, however, include a wide variation in button colors and sizes. They may be secured by buttonholes or loops in matching or contrasting colors or fabrics. As a result, button closures range from quiet to bold in design. Velcro closures are usually hidden in the fabric layers of the opening. Each closure type should be easy to operate. Buttons should be scaled to the total design, as well as to the age of the wearer and the function of the garment. Children require larger zipper pulls and buttons for easier manipulation by their small, inexperienced hands. Arthritic individuals will also find large-scaled zipper pulls and buttons easier to handle—or—they may prefer using Velcro to close their apparel. Active sportswear demands strong zippers and sturdily constructed button, snap, or Velcro closures. For most garments, zipper length or button diameter should be in scale with the wearer's body build and with the area of the garment where the closure will be located.

Pockets may be so subtle as to appear nonexistent (inseam pockets), or they may be the focal point of the design. In any case, their style lines and size should harmonize with the total design of the garment. They should be located so that they are easy to use and they should be stabilized so that they do not bag or stretch. If they are to be used for storage (e.g. back-packing jacket), the pockets should be large enough to hold typical items to be carried.

Because closures and pockets are such visible details, they must be carefully constructed and positioned. Precision is necessary. Markings and stitching must be accurate. Minor deviations such as a slightly longer buttonhole, a misplaced button, or an unevenly placed pocket are easily noticed. But—when beautifully constructed, they often provide styling details essential to the total garment composition and its function.

24 Major Closures

Garment access is gained through openings provided by zippers or button closures. Knit garments often have enough stretch so that a smaller opening can be used to don or remove them; some very stretchy knits permit access without even a placket opening.

Closures serve both functional and decorative purposes:

Zippers form subtle, convenient, and functional closures since they are inserted directly into the seam line. Decorative pull tabs or topstitching create design interest when desired.

Button closures are decorative as well as functional. They are almost always highly visible unless the buttons are purposely hidden.

Due to their visibility, buttons and buttonholes should be planned carefully in terms of size and location. Button scale, color, and spacing are critical to the design's balance. Using the recommended button diameter maintains the designer's intended scale. When the size of buttons is changed, test new arrangements within the relevant space. Smaller or larger buttons can sometimes be used if they are spaced closer or farther apart. When unusual or highly contrasting buttons are used, fewer of them may be needed because of their greater visibility.

Traditionally, closure locations and direction of overlap vary with the wearer's sex. Men's trousers zip only at center front; men's shirts and jackets button at center front unless they are double-breasted. The left side overlaps the right side. In contrast, women's closures can be located almost anywhere but are commonly found at the center front, center back, or left side. The right front overlaps the left, the front side overlaps the back side, and the left back overlaps the right back, as shown in the table below.

Fasteners are often used with zippers and buttons to help maintain a smooth, even closure. For instance, a hook-and-eye closure may be used to hold the neck of a dress together inconspicuously just above the zipper pull tab. Snaps also help to hold fabric layers together when there is no real strain involved.

Zipper Closures

OBJECTIVE

To select the application method most appropriate for the fabric weight and color and for the garment location and styling and to insert the zipper smoothly with even stitches.

Zippers are available in a variety of types and weights as well as in many lengths and colors. Therefore they can be used in many garments locations—the fly front of men's trousers, the center back of a dress, the side seam of a skirt, the center front of a tunic, or the underarm seam of an evening dress.

ZIPPER TYPES

There are three basic types of zippers: *conventional, invisible,* and *separating.* Conventional zippers closed at one end are used for skirts, necklines, and trousers. Those closed at both ends are used for dress side plackets. Invisible zippers can be inserted so that they are hidden in the seam line. Separating zippers, open at both ends, allow the garment seam to separate completely. They are used in jackets and sweaters.

All zippers are made of either a metal or plastic chain of teeth or a synthetic coil joined to fabric tapes. Chain and coil zippers are made in various weights and are about equal in performance and strength. Coil zippers tend to be lighter and more flexible. If jammed by thread or fabric, a coil zipper can be folded crosswise so that the coils are separated and the obstruction can be released. The zipper is reclosed simply by pulling the tab to the bottom stop and then up to the top stop.

The fabric tapes vary in fiber content, weight, and flexibility. All-cotton tapes tend to be

Sex	Closure Location	Overlap Direction
Male	Center front	Left over right
Female	Center front	Right over left
	Left side	Front over back
	Center back	Left over right

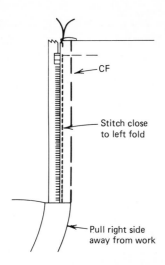

CF

Stitch close
to left fold

Pull right side
away from work

heavier and stiffer than cotton-polyester or synthetic tapes. Synthetic tapes can be very thin and flexible.

ZIPPER SELECTION

Choose the zipper type, weight, flex, and color to meet your garment's functional and esthetic needs. Use lightweight, flexible zippers for soft, lightweight, drapeable fabrics; use sturdier, heavier-weight zippers for sportswear, trousers, or jacket closures. Select a zipper color that matches or blends with your fabric color. Off-shades can be concealed by an inconspicuous application method. If your fabric includes several colors, choose a zipper in the predominant color or in a color that blends in value with the major color theme.

Although length is specified on your pattern envelope, you may have to deviate from the pattern company's specifications. Too long or too short a zipper length subtly influences garment proportion. Generally, women's skirt or pant zippers are best at 22-cm (9 in) unless hips are exceptionally broad. An 18-cm (7-in) zipper works best with shorter individuals and with shorter skirt or pants lengths. Men's trouser zip-

pers are available only in 28-cm (11-in) lengths, which are then shortened as needed. Women's dress openings usually require a 50- to 55-cm (20- to 22-in) zipper. However, if the wearer is quite short- or long-waisted, the zipper length should be adjusted. A 30- to 35-cm (12- to 14-in) zipper is generally suggested for dress side-seam plackets. In addition to being adjusted to suit the wearer's proportions, zipper length may also have to be adapted to the physical needs of the handicapped, the elderly, or the athletically active.

ZIPPER APPLICATIONS

Choice of zipper application varies with the sex of the wearer, the zipper's location, the weight of the fabric, and garment styling. Each type of application is described below.

Lapped Application

Used with conventional or separating zippers, the lapped application is commonly placed at the side, center-front, or center-back openings of women's apparel. Lapped separating zippers are also used at the center front of men's and

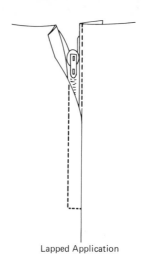

Lapped Application

women's outerwear. Only one row of stitches is visible; the chain or coil is well covered and the fabric lap is not likely to catch in the zipper. This method is generally preferred over the centered application for better-quality apparel, since it covers the zipper teeth without gaping.

Centered Application

This symmetric application of a conventional zipper is used where a balanced closure is desired at the center front or center back of women's clothing. It is also used at short neckline or sleeve openings and with separating zippers. Two parallel rows of stitching are visible, so they must be very straight in relation to one another. Since there is very little overlap, this method works well with bulkier fabrics. Extra care must be taken to see that the fabric flaps do not gap open, showing the zipper teeth.

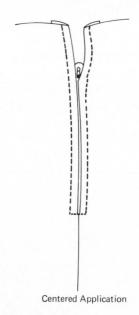

Centered Application

Fly-Front Application

Used with a skirt or trouser zipper, this conventional men's trouser application is also used

on women's pants or skirts. Women's apparel often uses the *mock fly application* without the extra thickness of the fly shield.

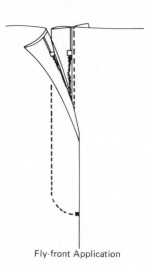

Fly-front Application

Invisible Application

This application can be detected only by the pull tab at the top of the seam. It is only possible

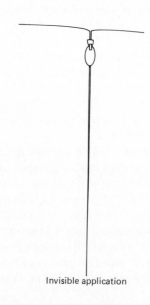

Invisible application

with an invisible zipper and substitutes for women's lapped and centered applications. It works well on pile fabrics, since there is no visible stitching to crush the fabric.

PRELIMINARY GUIDELINES

The following guidelines may help to simplify zipper insertion for you:

1. Preshrink the zipper by soaking it in hot tap water, rolling it in a towel to remove excess moisture, and air-drying it.
2. Check the length of the seam opening. It should equal the zipper length from top stop to bottom stop plus 6.0 mm (¼ in) plus any seam allowances.
3. Check the garment to be sure that the seam lines are of equal length and that any intersecting seams meet precisely. Make any necessary adjustments. Reduce bulk in cross seams (e.g., in waistlines or yokes) by trimming and pressing open the seam.
4. Stay-stitch the placket seam lines 6.0 mm (¼ in) from the edge to prevent them from stretching during zipper insertion.
5. Check the seam allowances. If they are less than 1.5 cm (⅝ in) or if the fabric frays easily, increase the seam allowances by stitching nonstretchy seam binding over each seam allowance 1.0 cm (⅜ in) from the seam line.
6. Sometimes you will need a zipper that is not of regulation length. For instance, your pattern may require an unusual length or your pattern length adjustments may necessitate an unavailable length. Purchase a zipper slightly longer than you will need and shorten it. To shorten from the bottom, determine the desired zipper length and mark with a pin on the zipper tape. Whip-stitch several times over the chain or coil 6.0 mm (¼ in) below the pin. Cut off the excess zipper about 2.5 cm (1 in) below the stitches.

  To shorten a zipper from the top (as for a fly-front zipper), insert the zipper as usual but with the excess length extending beyond the garment edge. Baste across the zipper tapes 1.3 cm (½ in) from the cutting line; trim excess zipper even with the raw edge of the garment. This method eliminates the top stops from the zipper. To form a new top stop, bend a straight eye in half and slip it over the zipper coil; sew securely.
7. Hand-basting provides better control than machine-basting when the zipper is being positioned during insertion. Use short, taut 6.0 mm (¼ in) stitches to set the zipper in place. To prevent the zipper foot from pushing the fabric out of alignment as the zipper is topstitched, stitch directionally from bottom to top. In addition, the diagonal basting stitch can be used to hold difficult fabrics in position.
8. Zippers can be inserted by machine or by hand. Application by machine requires a special zipper foot that makes it possible to stitch close to the ridge created by the zipper coil. The conventional zipper foot supplied with the machine is used to insert all zippers except the invisible zipper.

  The conventional zipper foot is adjustable to permit stitching on either side of the zipper coils. When the zipper is to the left of the machine needle, the zipper foot should be adjusted to the right, and vice versa. No part of the zipper foot should ride on the zipper chain or coils.

  The invisible zipper foot features two grooves at its base; the zipper coils pass through these during stitching. It also has an adjustable feature that enables stitching to be placed close to the zipper coils. To prevent puckering, pull the fabric and zipper tape taut as they are stitched.

Hand application includes all the machine application steps. Only the last topstitching step is performed by hand, using a variation of the backstitch.

9. It is easier to insert a zipper located at the center front or center back before other vertical seams are stitched. However, before inserting a zipper in the side seam (a fitting seam), you must be very sure of the garment fit.

10. Insert the zipper *before* applying facings, a waistband, a collar, or other bands. Refer to Chapter 22 for detailed instructions on finishing facings for a zipper closure.

11. Several stitching guides can be used to ensure even topstitching: (1) When basting the zipper tape to the garment for the final stitching, be sure that the basting line also forms an even stitching guideline. (2) Use a small hem gauge set at the desired placket width. As you stitch, run the adjustable tab along the garment seam line and the zipper foot next to the end of the gauge.

LAPPED ZIPPER APPLICATION: CLOSED METHOD

In the closed method, the garment seam is stitched prior to construction and most of the stitching is done from the wrong side of the garment.

Machine-baste the garment opening along the seam line. Press the seam open.

Attach the zipper foot to your machine. Turn the garment inside out with the left seam allowance extended. Open the zipper and place it face-down over the seam. With the coil next to the seam, position the left zipper tape over the extended seam allowance. The other seam allowance and the remainder of the garment should extend in the other direction. Hand- or machine-baste the tape to the extended seam allowance following the stitching guideline on the tape.

Close the zipper. With the seam allowance still extended, turn the zipper face up. Fold the left seam allowance close to the zipper coil so it forms a smooth, even fold. Adjust the zipper foot so it is to the left of the needle. Beginning at the base of the zipper, stitch close to the folded edge of the seam allowance, turning the pull tab out of the way.

Flip the zipper face down over the garment seam line. Two choices are now available: you may topstitch the zipper from the inside or the outside of the garment. Stitching from *inside* the garment allows you to follow the marked stitching guidelines on the zipper tape and prevents the fabric from slipping as it is stitched. Stitching from the *outside* of the garment enables you to see where you are stitching, thus ensuring that the topstitching will be even. The fabric can be basted in position to prevent it

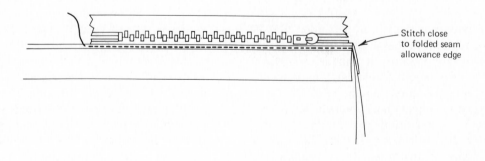

Stitch close to folded seam allowance edge

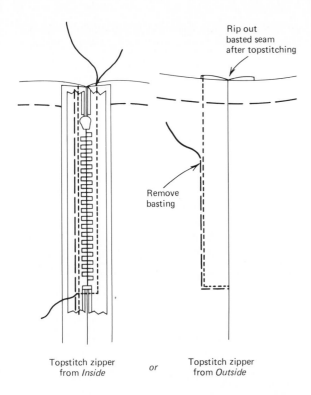

Rip out basted seam after topstitching

Remove basting

Topstitch zipper from *Inside*   or   Topstitch zipper from *Outside*

from slipping as you topstitch from the right side.

To topstitch from the inside, stitch across the base of the zipper tape and up the right side, following the stitching guideline on the tape. To topstitch from the outside, first hand-baste along the stitching line about 1.0 cm (⅜ in) from the garment seam line, matching stitches with the tape stitching guideline. Machine-stitch from the top left side of the zipper downward and across the base. Remove basting stitches from seam; press.

LAPPED ZIPPER APPLICATION: OPEN METHOD

The open method permits all topstitching to be done from the right side of the garment.

Turn under the underlap seam 1.3 cm (½ in) from the cut edge. Press. A small fold will form in the seam at the base. Turn under the overlap seam along the seam line 1.5 cm (⅝ in) from the cut edge; press.

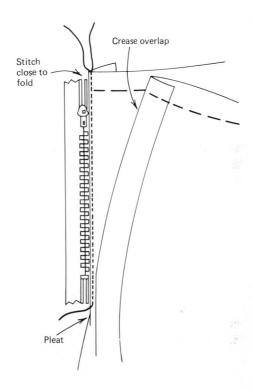

Stitch close to fold

Crease overlap

Pleat

Position the closed zipper under the underlap with the teeth next to the folded edge; baste in position. With the zipper foot to the left of the needle, stitch close to the fold from the base of the zipper tape to the top.

Position the overlap side over the zipper so it extends 3.0 mm (⅛ in) past the underlap fold. Garment seam lines will be matched. Baste along folded edge and along topstitching line. Machine-stitch from the right side across the base and up the left side of the zipper, keeping stitches parallel to the overlap fold (about 1.0 cm or ⅜ in from fold).

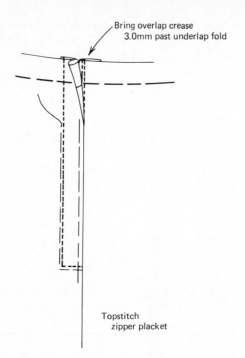

Bring overlap crease
3.0mm past underlap fold

Topstitch
zipper placket

CENTERED ZIPPER APPLICATION: CLOSED METHOD

As in applying the closed lapped zipper, all the topstitching can be done from the wrong side of the garment.

Machine-baste the garment opening along the seam line; press the seam open.

Open the zipper and place it face down on the extended seam allowance. Place the top stop 2.2 cm (⅞ in) below the cut edge and see that the coil edge is even with the seam line. Machine-baste from top to bottom along the tape guideline. Close the zipper.

Spread the garment flat with the zipper face down over both seam allowances. The final topstitching can be done on either the *inside* of the garment, following the zipper tape guidelines, or on the *outside* of the garment. To stitch on the outside, begin stitching at the top, 6.0 mm (¼ in) from the seam line. Continue stitch-

ing downward, across the base, and up the other side. Remove the seam-basting stitches and press.

CENTERED ZIPPER APPLICATION: OPEN METHOD

The open method allows for better coverage of the zipper teeth as well as generally more even topstitching, since this is done from the right side.

Turn under both seam allowances and press. Position the opened zipper under the garment opening. Align one coiled edge with the garment edge so that the teeth are just covered; baste in position. Repeat for the other side of the zipper.

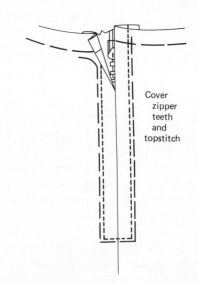

Cover
zipper
teeth
and
topstitch

Close the zipper to check coverage. The flaps should abut closely with one another but not buckle. Begin stitching at the top, 6.0 mm (¼ in) from the garment edge. Continue to stitch downward, pivoting at the base corners, and then up the other side. Remove basting and press.

INVISIBLE-ZIPPER APPLICATION

The invisible zipper should be inserted before you stitch the side seams of your garment.

Lay out the garment with the right side of the opening face up. Press the opened zipper tapes so that the coils fall away from the zipper tapes. Place the zipper face down on the right side of the fabric with the coil on the seam line and the zipper tape toward the cut edge of the fabric. Adjust the invisible zipper foot over the tape with the coil in the groove of the foot. The needle will pass through the hole next to the coil. Stitch from the top of the zipper tape to the pull tab. Backstitch to secure stitches.

Place the other side of the zipper on the remaining garment opening edge. Align as before. Adjust the zipper foot so that the coil is under the *other* groove. Stitch from the top of the zipper tape to the pull tab; backstitch. Finger-press

the fabric away from the zipper coil. Close the zipper. If the zipper tape shows, adjust the foot so that the needle stitches are closer to the coil and restitch.

Remove the zipper from the machine. Adjust the zipper foot to the left with the needle in the notch. With right sides together, stitch the seam below the base of the zipper. Begin the stitches 1.3 cm (½ in) *above* the zipper base. Stitch the lower portion of the zipper tape to each seam allowance.

ZIPPER APPLICATION BY HAND

The hand pick stitch may be used to complete the final topstitching of zippers inserted by either the lapped or the centered applications. Complete all steps of the zipper application by machine except for the last step. Hand pick-stitch the final topstitching through all fabric and zipper layers about 1.0 cm (⅜ in) from the garment seam line.

Right side

Stitch
close to coil

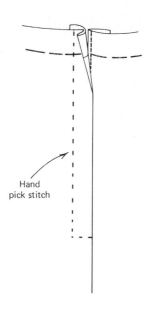

Hand
pick stitch

FLY-FRONT ZIPPER APPLICATION

The fly-front zipper is traditionally found in men's trousers as well as women's sportswear. Use the traditional lap direction for the sex of the wearer: right over left for women and left over right for men. Use a trouser zipper or other zipper type which will be shortened to fit the zipper placket.

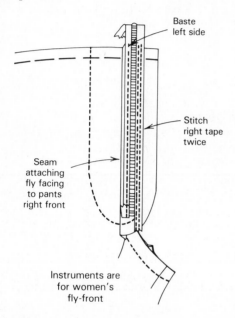

Baste left side

Stitch right tape twice

Seam attaching fly facing to pants right front

Instruments are for women's fly-front

Pin the right fly facing to the pants right front, matching markings. Stitch from the dot at the base of the fly to the upper edge. Grade the seam allowances and press them toward the facing.

Place the closed zipper face down on the right side of the facing. The edge of the left zipper tape should be next to the facing seam and the zipper stop should be 2.0 cm (¾ in) from the cut facing edge. The top of the zipper will extend beyond the upper facing edge. Baste the left zipper tape in place with the tape end turned up. Machine-stitch the right zipper tape twice: close to the coils and then close to the tape edge.

Turn the facing to the inside along the seam line; press. Baste the facing to the garment front, following the zipper topstitching guidelines. Machine-topstitch along basted lines without catching the left zipper tape in the stitching. Remove all basting.

Turn under the left front edge of the pants 6.0 mm (¼ in) from the seam line; press. Position the opened zipper with the coil next to the left front edge. Baste. Check the zipper position by closing the entire garment; adjust if necessary.

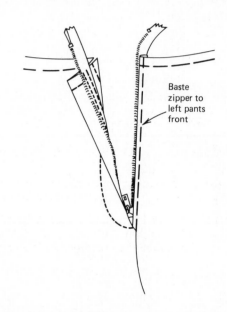

Baste zipper to left pants front

Prepare the fly shield. Stitch the outer curved edge of the fly shield and its facing. To minimize bulk, the fly-shield facing can be cut from lining-weight fabric. Trim, grade, and notch the seam. Turn right side out; press. Finish the long, straight edge of the fly shield by trimming 1.0 cm (⅜ in) from this edge. Turn the untrimmed facing edge over the raw edge and machine-stitch the hem.

Baste the fly shield over the back of the closed zipper, matching the curved shield edge to the curved topstitching; pin.

Open the zipper. Baste the fly shield to the

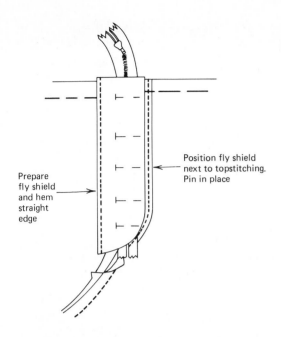

Prepare
fly shield
and hem
straight
edge

Position fly shield
next to topstitching.
Pin in place

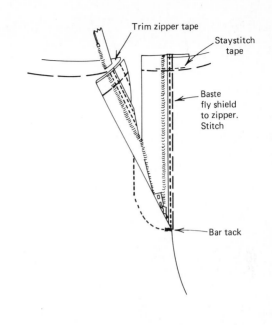

Trim zipper tape

Staystitch
tape

Baste
fly shield
to zipper.
Stitch

Bar tack

zipper. Stitch close to the zipper through all layers, including the garment, zipper tape, and fly shield. Remove basting. Stay-stitch across the opened zipper tapes at the waistline; trim away tape ends. Make a bar tack at the bottom of the topstitching, catching the fly shield. Press.

APPLICATION OF MOCK FLY-FRONT ZIPPER

The mock fly-front zipper is simpler to construct than a true fly-front zipper. The mock fly does not require construction of the underlying zipper flap commonly found on men's pants. Therefore it is less bulky yet looks the same from the outside of the garment.

Mark all fold lines related to zipper placement. Turn the front zipper extension to the wrong side along the fold lines.

Position the closed zipper, face up, under the left front fold line. Place the tab 6 mm (¼ in) below the waist seam line; place the coil close to the folded edge. Baste. Using the zipper foot,

stitch about 3 mm (scant ⅛ in) from the fabric edge.

Lap the right front over the left, matching the right-center-front folded edge with the basted left-center-front line. Baste the center lines together.

Hand-baste a guideline for topstitching the

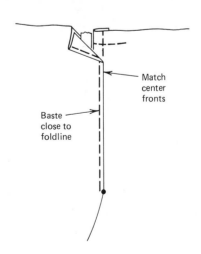

Match
center
fronts

Baste
close to
foldline

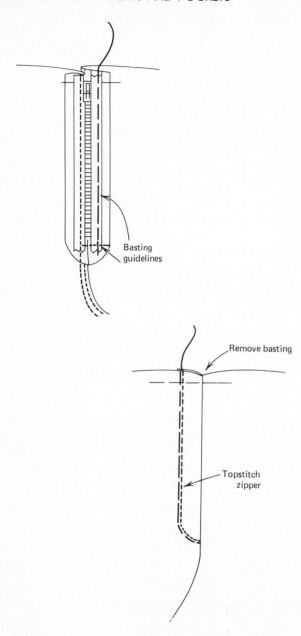

Basting guidelines

Remove basting

Topstitch zipper

zipper. Basting should run parallel to the center front and should catch all thicknesses.

With the right side up and using a zipper foot, machine stitch precisely along the basted guideline. Remove bastings and press.

CRITERIA FOR EVALUATION

ZIPPER CLOSURES

Check to ensure quality performance:

__ **1.** The zipper is inconspicuous, flat, and neat, with sufficient lap so it does not gap and so the zipper tape does not show.

__ **2.** The zipper color matches or blends with the garment fabric.

__ **3.** The zipper functions easily; no tugging is needed.

__ **4.** The zipper construction is durable—stitching is reinforced at both the top and the base.

__ **5.** The garment seam allowance is adequately caught in the topstitching so it does not fray out.

__ **6.** Stitching is straight and true. (Stitches may flare out slightly to cover the pull tab adequately.)

BUTTON CLOSURES

OBJECTIVE

1. To select the buttonhole length, position, and type most suitable for your button and garment styling.

2. To construct a buttonhole that lies smoothly and is balanced on the garment.

Whether used as the decorative feature of your garment or as a functional closing system, button closures are highly visible unless they are purposely hidden. Therefore it is essential that you mark and position the button and its closure accurately. Buttonholes or loops may be used with the buttons to form the closure.

The total closure design should be compatible with the garment styling. Button diameter should be in scale and each buttonhole should be equal in length with the others.

BUTTONHOLES

The three major types of buttonholes are the worked buttonhole, the bound buttonhole, and the split-seam buttonhole. Worked buttonholes may be machine- or hand-worked. *Machine-worked buttonholes* are suitable for sportswear, man-tailored jackets, children's apparel, and other casual wear. They consist of two parallel rows of zigzag stitches finished with additional reinforcement stitches at both ends. They can be made on a zigzag machine or with a special buttonholer attachment. *Hand-worked buttonholes* are used on soft, fine fabrics, men's jackets, and women's tailored garments. They are made by finishing a cut in the garment with handmade buttonhole stitches. All worked buttonholes are made after the garment is completed.

Bound buttonholes are generally reserved for high-quality tailored garments. The edges of the buttonhole slit are bound with self-fabric. Bound buttonholes are used with medium to large buttons to maintain a good proportion between length and width. They are rarely less than 2.0 to 2.5 cm (¾ to 1 inch) long. Bound buttonholes are made right after the interfacing is applied and before other details are constructed. Therefore all proportional fitting changes must be made before the buttonhole locations are established.

Split-seam buttonholes are formed by leaving unstitched a portion of the seam that is equal to the buttonhole length. When the seam is pressed open, the split remains, forming the buttonhole opening. The facing must also include a corresponding split in the seam. These buttonholes are formed during the seaming process.

PRELIMINARY GUIDELINES

Buttonhole Length

Buttonhole length is based on button size. If the buttonhole is too short, it will be difficult to button the garment without stretching the opening, and if it is too long, the button may slip out of the buttonhole.

Buttonhole length should equal the button diameter plus its thickness plus 3 mm (⅛ in) ease. To measure a ball button, wrap a strip of paper around the button. Mark where the ends meet, lay the strip out flat, and measure between the two ends. Add 3 mm (⅛ in) for ease. Measure the half-circumferences of a half-ball button and add 3 mm (⅛ in) ease to determine buttonhole length.

The Trial Buttonhole

Test buttonhole length by making a *trial buttonhole.* Use the same fabric layers, including interfacing, with which your garment is constructed. Insert the button through it to be sure that the length is correct.

Also, survey the trial buttonhole stitching to determine whether the machine or buttonhole-stitching mechanism needs adjustment. Check the tension, closeness of stitches, space between the two rows of stitches, and bight (stitch width). Buttonholes are difficult to remove without marring your fabric, so perfect your technique on the sample. Stitch around the buttonhole twice to improve its strength and prevent fraying. Practice cutting the buttonhole open with a pair of sharp-pointed scissors, being careful not to cut any stitches.

Buttonhole Placement

Buttonholes are made on the *right* side of women's garments and on the *left* side of men's garments. On other women's closure locations, the buttonholes are placed on the left side of the back closure and the front garment sections of side closures.

Placement always depends on the position of the button. Buttons are generally placed down the center front or back of the garment. When the garment is double-breasted, the buttons are spaced equidistant from the center front. Buttons should be located at these key points: (1) neck, (2) fullest level of bust, (3) waist area, and (4) above the bulk of a hem.

Once button positions are established, the buttonhole locations can be marked. Buttonholes are usually placed horizontally or vertically on the garment. *Horizontal placement* is most secure because the button pulls on the end of the buttonhole slit, making it less likely to pop open. Buttons are positioned to begin 3 mm (⅛ in) beyond the center front toward the garment edge. This permits the buttonhole to fit around the shank of the button while maintaining center-front alignment.

Vertical buttonholes are suitable for areas that receive little strain or have many closely spaced buttons and on garments with narrow vertical shirt bands. These buttonholes begin 3 mm (⅛ in) above the center of the button and are usually placed vertically down the center-front line.

Diagonally-angled buttonholes may be coordinated with the style lines of some garments. Note that because these buttonholes are on the bias, they are more likely to stretch.

If you adjusted your pattern for length, the buttonholes will have to be respaced. Divide the new distance between the top and bottom buttonholes by the number of spaces between buttonholes. Keep in mind the guidelines for positioning on the body. For large changes, it may be necessary to either eliminate or add a buttonhole.

Altering the suggested size of the button diameter may also necessitate buttonhole realignment. Larger buttons may indicate a need for fewer buttonholes to retain good proportions; using smaller buttons may mean adding an additional buttonhole. Space the buttonholes so that the button does *not* extend beyond the finished garment edge (at either the top or side). The distance between the button placement mark and the finished edge should roughly equal the button diameter. Adjust this distance to keep the garment lines in scale with one another.

MACHINE-WORKED BUTTONHOLES

Thoroughly construct and press the garment before making worked buttonholes. If possible, use interfacing in a color similar to that of your outer fabric, because it may show at the cut edges. Machine-worked buttonholes may be made using a buttonholer or the manual bartack method. The *buttonholer* is a special attachment used to make a variety of buttonhole types and lengths; it involves the insertion of differ-

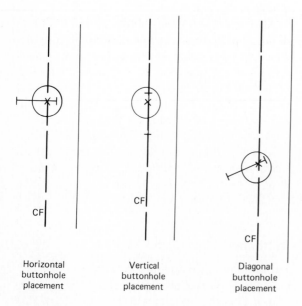

Horizontal buttonhole placement

Vertical buttonhole placement

Diagonal buttonhole placement

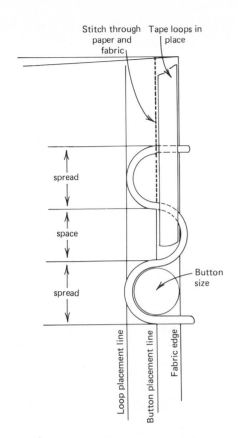

Stitch through paper and fabric

Tape loops in place

spread

space

spread

Loop placement line

Button placement line

Fabric edge

Button size

CRITERIA FOR EVALUATION

MACHINE-WORKED BUTTONHOLES:

Check to ensure quality performance:

__ **1.** The buttonhole length is adequate for the type of button.

__ **2.** The buttonhole is positioned as follows for:

__a. Horizontal Buttonholes: 3 mm (⅛ in) beyond the button position (usually center front) and toward the garment opening edge.

__b. Vertical Buttonholes: 3 mm (⅛ in) above the button position.

__ **3.** A series of buttonholes are uniform in length, width, and spacing.

__ **4.** The closure is functional—the button slips in and out of the buttonhole easily.

__ **5.** The buttonhole is made through all fabric layers.

__ **6.** The width of the bight is in scale with the buttonhole length and fabric thickness.

__ **7.** Each buttonhole has been stitched a second time, directly on top of the first buttonhole stitches.

HAND-WORKED BUTTONHOLES

Hand-worked buttonholes also are made after the garment is completed and pressed. They are made by slitting the garment and hand-working buttonhole stitches around the opening. Stitches must be close together and of uniform length, spacing, and tension. When positioned horizontally, the buttonholes are fan-shaped at the outside end to better accommodate the button shank. A bar tack is used at the opposite end. Vertically positioned button-

ent-length templates and adjustment of the bight (stitch width). Once the buttonholer has been adjusted for your fabric and the garment has been correctly positioned, the buttonholer takes over. The attachment automatically guides the fabric while the template controls the length. Refer to the instruction booklet included with your buttonholer for specific instructions.

Bar-tack buttonholes are made on zigzag machines only. The garment and machine are manually adjusted to form the buttonhole. Your machine may include a special buttonhole foot, or the general-purpose presser foot can be used. Follow your machine's instruction manual for the method.

holes are usually finished with a bar tack at each end. Keyhole buttonholes, used in tailored garments, leave a circular resting spot for the button. As a result, the buttonhole is not distorted.

Standard Hand-Worked Buttonholes

Mark the buttonhole placement on the right side of the garment, using a basting stitch. To reduce stretching, the placement lines should follow garment grain lines.

Machine-stitch a narrow rectangle 3 mm (⅛ in) wide around the marked line. Use very short reinforcement stitches and count the stitches across each end to ensure equal width at both ends. The rectangle will be used as a guide for the depth of the buttonhole stitches. Carefully slash the buttonhole exactly on the center line, using sharply pointed scissors.

Use a single strand of waxed buttonhole twist, heavy-duty thread, or regular thread long enough to complete the entire buttonhole. Two strands of regular thread can be used if care is taken to pull each strand evenly after taking a stitch. Begin on the back side at the upper corner of the buttonhole farthest from the center front. Hold the slit along the forefinger so that the buttonhole spreads slightly but without stretching. Secure the thread end by inserting the needle midway between the stitches and the slash. Take three or four short running stitches away from the center front, ending with a backstitch to fasten the thread securely. Hand-overcast the raw edges of the slit.

Working from the right side, insert the needle into the slash and bring the point up through the fabric just outside the machine-stitching line. Encircle the needle counterclockwise, with the thread passing the thread under the point of the needle.

Draw the needle through the fabric, pulling the thread away from the buttonhole at right

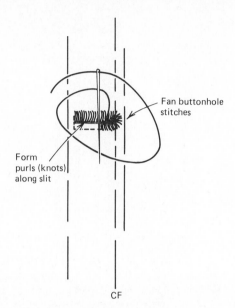

Fan buttonhole stitches

Form purls (knots) along slit

CF

angles to the slash until a purl (knot) forms on the cut edge of the slash. Pull the thread firmly but without creating puckers.

Insert the needle through the slash again and bring the point through exactly in line with the first stitch. Leave enough distance between the stitches so that they lie parallel to each other in orderly rows. The purls should touch like beads along the edge of the slash.

Continue making buttonhole stitches to the end of the slash nearest the center front. Circle the end in a fan pattern, keeping the stitches the same depth as along the edges. Space them equally but slightly further apart on the outside of the curve. This causes the purls to crowd a little, thus reinforcing the end of the buttonhole for the button shank. Turn the garment while proceeding around the end so that the needle will point down as it is inserted in the slash.

Continue stitching along the other side of the buttonhole toward the bar end. The last stitch should end exactly opposite the first one. Make a bar tack by taking several stitches across the end with each stitch right on top of the other.

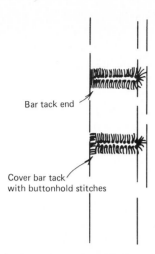

Bar tack end

Cover bar tack
with buttonhold stitches

of cord and place it loosely around the button-hole; secure with pins. Hand-overcast again to hold the cording in position.

Working from the right side, insert the needle through the slit at the end away from the eyelet hole. Bring the needle up through the fabric just outside the machine guideline. Encircle the needle counterclockwise with the thread passing under its tip.

To form a purl (knot) at edge of the slit, draw the needle through the fabric, pulling it taut and at right angles to the slit. Continue stitching until the edge is covered with purls. Space stitches right next to one another, keeping them the same length.

The bar stitches start and stop in line with the buttonhole stitches and lie parallel to them.

Catch the center of the bar to the fabric by taking several stitches over the bar in line with the opening.

Finish the bar tack by working over the end stitches with a buttonhole stitch. Fasten the thread on the wrong side by running the needle under the completed stitches for 1.3 cm (½ in); backstitch to secure. Clip threads close to the stitches.

Tailored Hand-Worked Buttonholes

Mark the buttonhole placement lines with basting stitches. Machine-stitch over these lines, using tiny reinforcement stitches. Form a round eyelet at the end closest to center front. Slash open the buttonhole along the centered placement line. Use an awl or short, flared slashes with a sharp scissor to open the eyelet hole.

Use a single strand of waxed buttonhole twist or heavy-duty thread. To secure the thread end, take several tiny running stitches, ending with a backstitch. Hand-overcast the edges of the slit and eyelet.

If the buttonhole will be corded, cut a length

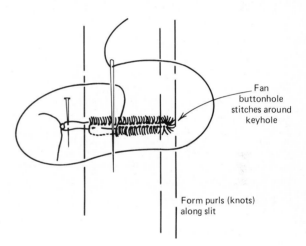

Fan buttonhole stitches around keyhole

Form purls (knots) along slit

When you reach the eyelet, continue the buttonhole stitch. Allow the stitches to radiate outward from the circle, but keep them close at the eyelet hole edge. The purls should be slightly crowded for greater strength. Turn the garment as you work around the eyelet; continue covering the other edge of the slit with buttonhole stitches. End the last stitch exactly opposite the first stitch. Pull the ends of the cording slightly to smooth out the buttonhole. Make a bar tack at the end with two or three long stitches taken directly on top of one another.

Work over the bar tack with buttonhole stitches. Fasten the thread on the wrong side by running the needle under the completed stitches; backstitch to secure. Tie the cording ends in a knot and tuck under the bar tack.

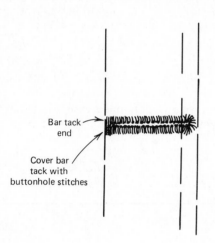

Bar tack end

Cover bar tack with buttonhole stitches

BOUND BUTTONHOLES

Bound buttonholes are made immediately after the interfacing is applied and before general seaming begins. The back of the buttonhole is completed after the facing is applied. The bound buttonhole includes two narrow "lips" that bind the edges of the buttonhole rectangle. Unless the fabric is very bulky, the rectangle should appear perfectly square at the corners and 6 mm (¼ in) wide. They should be a minimum of 2.0 to 2.5 cm (¾ to 1 in) in length. Each lip should be exactly 3 mm (⅛ in) wide. The lips may be cut on the lengthwise grain or on the true bias. Strips cut on the bias are less likely to fray. The bias direction also provides extra give for buttoning and unbuttoning, thus reducing strain at the corner, where there is some probability that the fabric may pull out. Bias strips also add an interesting design feature to plaid or striped fabrics and eliminate the need to match the fabric pattern.

CRITERIA FOR EVALUATION

HAND-WORKED BUTTONHOLES:

Check to ensure quality performance:

___ 1. The buttonhole length is adequate for the type of button.

2. The buttonhole is positioned as follows for:
   ___a. Horizontal Buttonholes: 3 mm (⅛ in) beyond the button position (usually center front) and toward the garment opening edge.
   ___b. Vertical Buttonholes: 3 mm (⅛ in) above the button position.

___ 3. A series of buttonholes are uniform in length, width, and spacing.

___ 4. The closure is functional—the button slips in and out of the buttonhole easily.

___ 5. The buttonhole stitches are worked through two or more fabric layers; all layers are caught in the stitches.

___ 6. Buttonhole stitches are closely spaced and uniform in length (3 mm or ⅛ inch), spacing, and tension.

___ 7. Bar stitches start and stop in line with the buttonhole stitches and are parallel to them.

___ 8. Stitches flare out evenly on fan-shaped ends; the purls are slightly crowded for greater strength.

Bound Buttonhole: Patch Method

Mark the buttonhole position lines with precise basting lines.

Cut a strip of fabric on the straight grain or true bias 5 cm (2 in) wide and 2.5 cm (1 in) longer than the buttonhole length. Mark the center of the patch. With right sides together, pin the patch to the garment, matching the patch's center line to the buttonhole placement line.

From the wrong side, machine-baste over the buttonhole position lines through all layers to indicate the exact width and location of the buttonholes on both sides.

Machine-baste 6 mm (¼ in) from both sides of the center line, extending stitching about 1.3 cm (½ in) beyond the buttonhole end marks. Halfway between the center buttonhole line and the basted lines, draw pencil lines the exact length of buttonhole.

On the right side of the garment, fold one edge of fabric strip back along the 6-mm (¼ in) basted line and toward the buttonhole center; press. Repeat on other side. Baste in position. Stitch 3 mm (⅛ in) from the folded edge, beginning and ending the stitches with the buttonhole length markings. Use very short reinforcement stitches (8 stitches per centimeter or

20 stitches per inch) and tie threads to secure. Remove basting.

From the wrong side, begin slashing from the center diagonally to each of the four corners, forming triangles. Stop slashing just short of the corners.

Turn the patch to the wrong side by slipping it through the slash. Press the patch away from the opening; baste the lip edges together. An inverted pleat will form at the ends with the folded edges meeting at the center of the buttonhole.

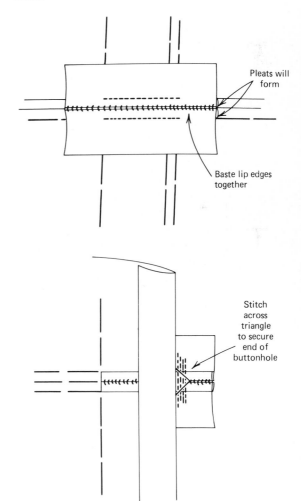

Stitch 3 mm from fold exact length of buttonholes

Pleats will form

Baste lip edges together

Stitch across triangle to secure end of buttonhole

Position the garment right side up on the machine. Fold the garment back so that the patch end and the triangular end of the buttonhole are exposed. Using 8 stitches per centimeter (set metric dial at 1; English at 20 stitches per inch), stitch back and forth across the base of the triangle and the inverted pleat. Repeat at other end.

Remove all basting guidelines except the center front line. Leave in the basting holding the lips together until the garment is completed. Press.

Bound Buttonholes: Two-Piece Piped Method

Machine-baste the buttonhole position lines on the interfacing through to the right side of the fabric. Continue the lines the length of the garment or about 2.5 cm (1 in) beyond the first and last buttonholes. Mark the (1) center front or center back line, (2) the buttonhole length lines *a* beginning 3 mm (⅛ in) beyond the center line and extending the length of the buttonhole *b*, and (3) the center placement lines of each buttonhole. Draw a line 3 mm (⅛ in) away from each side of center line *c*.

Cut a fabric strip 2.5 cm (1 in) wide. To determine its length, multiply *twice* the number of buttonholes by each buttonhole length plus 2.5

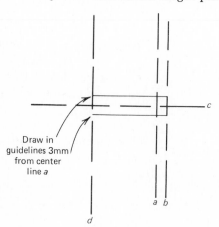

Draw in guidelines 3mm from center line *a*

cm (1 in). Fold the strip in half lengthwise with wrong sides together. Press. Machine-baste 3 mm (⅛ in) from the folded edge. Trim one edge to 3 mm (⅛ in) wide. Cut the strips into sections equal to the length of each buttonhole plus 2.5 cm (1 in).

Stitch strip 3mm from fold

Trim

Place the trimmed raw edge next to line *c* on the right side of the garment. The strip ends will extend 1.3 cm (½ in) beyond the length lines *b*. The long untrimmed edge will be on top. Hand-baste the strip to the garment, matching the stitching line on the strip to the penciled guidelines. Pull the stitches taut to hold the strip in place. Repeat for the other side.

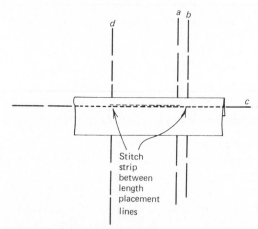

Stitch strip between length placement lines

Machine-stitch directly over the previous basting, using short reinforcement stitches (8 stitches per centimeter or 20 stitches per inch). Pull thread ends through to one side and tie. Slash from the center diagonally out to each of the four corners. Stop slashes just short of the corner stitching.

Pull the strips through the slash to the wrong side of the garment. Carefully pull the strip ends to square the corners. The strips should meet

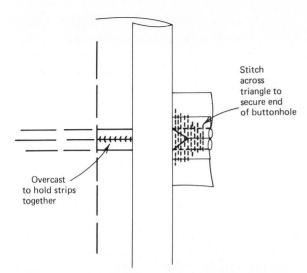

Stitch across triangle to secure end of buttonhole

Overcast to hold strips together

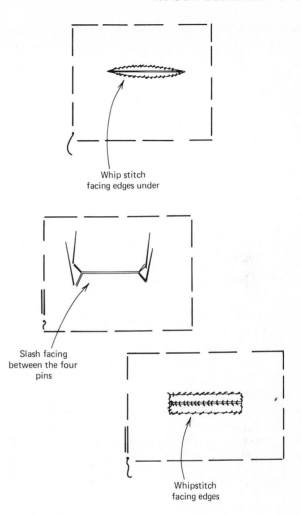

Whip stitch facing edges under

Slash facing between the four pins

Whipstitch facing edges

in the center of the buttonhole rectangle. Baste the strips together. With the garment right side up, fold back the fabric at the end of the buttonhole to reveal the strip ends and triangle. Stitch back and forth across the base of each triangle, using short reinforcement stitches. Repeat at other end. Remove all basting lines except center lines. Leave in basting holding strips together. Press.

Finishing the Back of the Bound Buttonhole

Two methods are illustrated which can be used to finish the back of the buttonhole. After the garment facing has been attached, the buttonholes can be finished from the back. Position the facing as it will be worn. Baste a box around each buttonhole to hold the fabric layers in alignment.

Procedures: Slash Method. Insert pins from the right side straight through the center of each buttonhole end to mark their length on the facing. Slash the facing between the pins and make a short clip at the center of each slash edge.

Turn in the raw edges of the facing, forming an oval. Hem securely, using short whip stitches.

The facing may also be slashed and clipped in the same manner as the garment was. Place marking pins at the four corners of the buttonholes. Turn in the long edges and triangular ends and hem securely with whip stitches to form a rectangle.

Procedures: Windowpane Method. This method is simpler and finishes the back off as nicely as the front.

Align garment facing. Mark the buttonhole location on the facing by inserting pins at the four corners.

Cut a piece of organza or other firm, light-weight fabric the same color as the garment 3.8 cm (1½ in) wide and 2.5 cm (1 in) longer than the buttonhole marking.

Center the strip and baste it over the button-hole marking on the right side of the facing. Using 8 stitches per centimeter (set metric dial at 1; English dial at 20 stitches per inch), stitch the rectangle indicated by the pins. Begin stitch-ing at center of the long buttonhole side and stitch to the end. Pivot at each corner, taking the same number of stitches across each end. Take about five overlapping stitches at the starting point.

Slash diagonally from the center to each cor-ner. A triangle will form at each end.

Slip the organza piece through the slash to the wrong side. Press the organza away from the opening, forming an open "window." This is the size of the finished buttonhole. Remove basting.

Securely whip-stitch the opening to the back of the buttonhole.

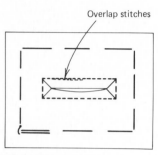

Stitch and slash patch

CRITERIA FOR EVALUATION

BOUND BUTTONHOLES

Check to ensure quality performance:

__1. The buttonhole length is adequate for the type of button.

__2. The buttonhole is positioned as follows for:

　　__a. Horizontal Buttonholes: 3 mm (⅛") beyond the button position (usually cen-ter front) and toward the garment open-ing edge.

　　__b. Vertical Buttonholes: 3 mm (⅛") above the button position.

__3. A series of buttonholes are uniform in length, width, and spacing.

__4. The closure is functional—the button slips in and out of the buttonhole easily.

__5. Lips are equal in size:

　　__a. Both lips are 3 mm (⅛ inch) wide.

　　__b. Lips are equal in length—a mini-mum of 2.0 to 2.5 cm (¾ to 1 inch) long.

__6. The lips form a perfect rectangle: cor-ners are square and no puckering or fraying are visible.

__7. Lips are cut on the true bias or length-wise grain.

__8. No stitches are visible.

__9. The back of the buttonhole is neatly fin-ished: the facing is securely handstitched to the wrong side covering any raw edges or stitches on the back of the buttonhole.

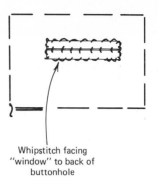

Whipstitch facing
"window" to back of
buttonhole

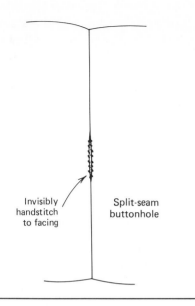

Invisibly
handstitch
to facing

Split-seam
buttonhole

SPLIT-SEAM BUTTONHOLES

Split-seam buttonholes are formed by finishing unstitched openings in a seam. Ties and sashes, as well as buttons, may be slipped through the split.

Mark the buttonhole end points on the seam line. Stitch the seams, backstitching at each end of the buttonhole to reinforce. Press open the seam.

Complete the facing seam in the same manner. Stitch the opening edges together, being careful not to pucker the opening and keeping the stitches hidden.

CRITERIA FOR EVALUATION

SPLIT-SEAM BUTTONHOLES

Check to ensure quality performance:

___ **1.** The buttonhole length is adequate for the type of button.

2. The buttonhole is positioned as follows for:
___a. Horizontal Buttonholes: 3 mm (⅛ in) beyond the button position (usually center front) and toward the garment opening edge.
___b. Vertical Buttonholes: 3 mm (⅛ in) above the button position.

___ **3.** A series of buttonholes are uniform in length, width, and spacing.

___ **4.** The closure is functional—the button slips in and out of the buttonhole easily.

___ **5.** Broken seams are reinforced at each buttonhole end.

___ **6.** The garment and facing seams are pressed open evenly.

___ **7.** The facing edges are securely attached to the garment edges without puckering or visible stitches.

FABRIC LOOPS

Button closures may be secured with fabric loops rather than with buttonholes. Loops may be both decorative and functional. They may be made from self-fabric tubing, corded fabric, or soutache. Prepare the loops first and then position them on the garment before attaching the facing.

Construction of Loops

Procedures: Self-Filled Loops. Cut a bias strip the desired length and four times the finished width of the loop. Lighter-weight fabrics may require wider seam allowances; heavier fabrics may need narrower ones. Experiment to find the best width for your fabric. Fold the bias strip in half lengthwise. Stretching slightly, stitch halfway between the fold and the raw edges. Leave both ends open but slant the stitching outward at one end to make turning easier.

To turn the loop, attach a large needle and heavy thread securely to the slanted end and pull them through the bias tube. Insert the eye of needle first so it does not catch in the fabric. Work the raw edges to the inside to get the tube started. Press.

Procedures: Cord-Filled Loops. Cut a bias strip the desired length and wide enough to encircle the cord plus 2.5 cm (1 in).

Cut the cord twice the desired length. Fold the bias strip around cord with the right side next to the cord. The long fabric edges should be even with one end and 1.3 (½ in) beyond the center of the cord.

Using the zipper foot, stitch across the end right at the center of the cording. Stitch next to the cording, being careful not to catch it in the stitches. Stretch the bias slightly as you sew.

Trim the seams to 6 mm (¼ in). Turn the loop by drawing the fabric out over the enclosed cording. Trim the excess cording away from the stitched end.

Loop Placement

The loops are sewn to the center line of the closure before the garment is faced. When adding loops to patterns with a centered-overlap closure, change the right front so that the center line becomes the seam line and the cutting line is 1.5 cm (⅝ in) away from it. The left front needs no adjustment.

Make a placement guide by marking a line the length of the closure seam line on a strip of lightweight paper. Draw lines for the spread

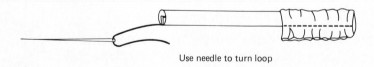

Use needle to turn loop

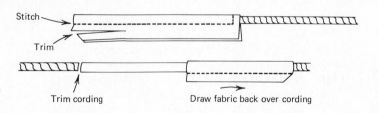

Stitch

Trim

Trim cording   Draw fabric back over cording

and depth of the finished loops, spacing them as needed. Flat buttons require more spreading and less depth than ball buttons do.

Procedures: Single-Loop Method. Determine the loop length by pinning the cording to the fabric edge. It should just be large enough for the button to pass through.

Cut each loop the correct length plus two seam allowances. Form loops on the paper guide markings, keeping their seams on top and to the inside of the curve; hold in place with masking tape. Machine-baste the loops to the paper with the ends in the seam allowance.

Pin the guide to the right half of the garment. Match the seam lines and remove the masking tape. Baste next to the previous basting. Baste carefully, checking to be sure your machine does not shift the loops. Tear the paper away. Attach the facing, stitching from the garment side next to the basting stitches.

Procedures: Continuous-Loop Method. Make small, closed loops on the paper guide as before, but this time use continuous tubing. Extend the small curved ends into the seam allowance. Trim the ends, tape in position, and machine-baste. Tear away the paper and attach the facing.

CRITERIA FOR EVALUATION
FABRIC LOOP CLOSURES:

Check to ensure quality performance:

___ **1.** The buttonhole length is adequate for the type of button.

___ **2.** The buttonhole is positioned as follows for:

___ a. Horizontal Buttonholes: 3 mm (⅛ in) beyond the button position (usually center front) and toward the garment opening edge.

___ b. Vertical Buttonholes: 3mm (⅛ in) above the button position.

___ **3.** A series of buttonholes are uniform in length, width, and spacing.

___ **4.** The closure is functional—the button slips in and out of the buttonhole easily.

___ **5.** Loops are even in width and smoothly formed.

___ **6.** Loops are just long enough for the button to slip through easily.

___ **7.** Loops extend from the garment centerline.

___ **8.** Continuous loops are equal in size and equidistant in spacing.

BUTTON APPLICATION

After the buttonholes have been made, the buttons can be attached. Special care should be taken to align the buttons exactly with the buttonholes so that the garment will hang evenly. Overlap the center fronts and mark the button location by inserting a pin through the button-hole slit. For a horizontal buttonhole, insert the pin at the end of the buttonhole nearest the finished garment edge; insert the pin 3 mm (⅛ in) below the top of a vertical buttonhole. The buttons should be positioned exactly on the *center-front line* at the correct level for each buttonhole.

Fabric weight and button type will determine

how a button should be attached. Any button that is to be inserted through a buttonhole should have a *shank*. The shank permits the button to lie over the buttonhole without pulling or puckering the fabric. The shank length should equal the thickness of the fabric layers at the buttonhole.

When a button has no natural shank, as with a flat button, or if the button shank is too short, you can make a thread shank.

Procedures: Thread Shank. Use a double thread, buttonhole twist, button-and-carpet thread, or heavy-duty thread drawn through beeswax. Take a few short stitches on the right side of the garment at the button marking. Slip

a heavy needle, pin, toothpick, or wooden match (use as many of each as is necessary) under the first stitch on top of the button. Stitch the button to the garment by inserting the needle through the other hole to the back of the garment. Repeat stitches through the holes until the button is secure.

Remove the object used and pull the button upward until the threads are taut. Wind the thread around the stem between the button and the fabric to create the shank. Secure stitches on the wrong side. The button will stand slightly above the fabric layers.

Procedures: Natural Shank. If the button has a *natural shank*, attach the button by taking short stitches through the shank opening. To prevent excessive wear, align the direction of the shank with the buttonhole.

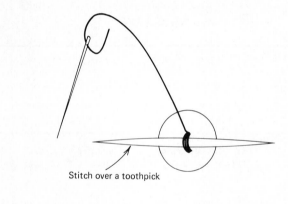

Stitch over a toothpick

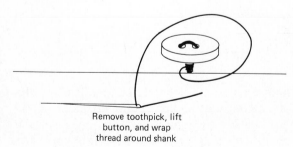

Remove toothpick, lift
button, and wrap
thread around shank

CRITERIA FOR EVALUATION

BUTTONS

Check to ensure quality performance:

__ **1.** The button size and placement are in scale with the garment styling and fabric texture.

__ **2.** Buttons are positioned on garment center lines (or equidistant from center if double-breasted) and in line with their corresponding buttonholes.

__ **3.** The button is securely attached.

__ **4.** The thread shank length is equal to the thickness of the buttonhole.

25 Fasteners

OBJECTIVES

1) To choose a fastener suited to the garment design, fabric, and color and to the degree of strain it will be expected to withstand.

2) To attach the fastener securely and inconspicuously to the garment, being careful to maintain garment alignment.

Inconspicuous small-scale fastening devices are necessary to finish garment closures. Included in the category of fasteners are snaps, hooks and eyes, thread loops, and Velcro fasteners. These fastening devices work alone or in conjunction with the major closure systems. Used alone, they perform the closure function in simply styled, loose-fitting garments made of lightweight fabrics. Their light weight and small scale make them inconspicuous. They do

Ball and socket snap   Hook   Straight eye   Round eye

HOOK AND EYES

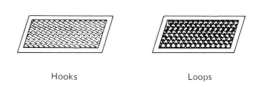

Hooks   Loops

VELCRO

not stiffen a soft crepe de chine as a zipper might, nor do they add the additional weight and need to manipulate a delicate fabric that a button-and-buttonhole closure would.

Fasteners also supplement the work of the major closure by holding free garment edges and corners in place or by holding the upper edges of a zipper closure together.

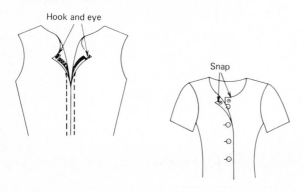

Hook and eye

Snap

When selecting any fastener, base your decision upon the garment's styling and fabric hand, the amount of strain the area will receive, and the degree of subtlety required. Generally, heavier fabrics require larger fasteners, areas of strain require stronger fasteners, and fine, smooth fabrics require smaller fasteners. To keep them subtle, cover them with matching fabric or keep the tone of the metal similar to that of your fabric color.

SNAPS

Snaps are used where there will be little strain on the fastener. Since they have less holding power than hooks and eyes, they are generally used to prevent the overlap of a button closure from gaping open. An extended snap can be used to hold abutted garment edges together. Snaps range in size from fine (size 4/0) to heavy (size 4) and may be purchased with either a

nickel or black finish. Clear nylon snaps are also available. A snap consists of two parts:
Ball section
Socket section

Ball   Socket

Procedures: Lapped Edges. Snaps are always positioned with the ball section on the underside of the overlap and the socket half on the underlap. Position the snap section about 3 mm (⅛ in) from the edge. With a double thread, secure the snap to the garment, using either whip stitches or the buttonhole stitch. Take four to five stitches through each hole, catching the interfacing for greater strength. Be sure that none of your stitches shows on the right side of the garment. Use a fastening stitch underneath the snap to secure the thread.

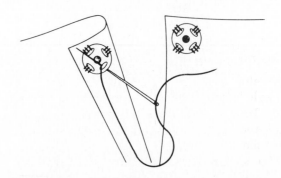

To position the socket portion accurately directly opposite the ball section, place the garment overlap over the underlap in the position desired. Insert a pin through the underlap and into the hole in the ball of the snap. Separate the overlap and underlap, being careful to leave the pin in the underlap. Slip the socket section of the snap over the pin and stitch it in place, using the same procedure as for the ball half of the snap. Remove the pin when you are finished.

Procedures: Abutted Edges. *Extended snaps* hold abutted edges together. They can be used to align the upper edges of a zipper closure when strain is minimal.

Attach the ball portion of the snap to the underside of the left garment edge. With the garment edges abutted, position the socket portion at the right garment edge; whip-stitch through one set of holes to hold in place.

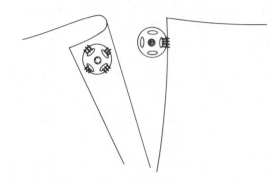

Covered Snaps

Sometimes it is necessary to use a snap in a visible location, such as a jacket or coat opening. To make them less conspicuous, purchase covered snaps or cover your own with color-matched, lightweight lining fabric. A larger snap, such as size 1 or 2, is easier to handle and will make the covering process much easier. The heavier size will also provide better security for a coat or jacket.

Procedures. To cover the snap, cut out two circles of fabric twice the diameter of the snap. Take small running stitches around the outer edge of each circle, leaving thread ends free. Place each snap section face down on the wrong side of a circle.

Place snap face down on wrong side of fabric circle

Draw fabric around snap

Draw up the threads to pull the fabric around the snaps, but do not fasten the threads yet.

Work the ball of the snap through the yarns of the fabric by snapping the sections together a few times.

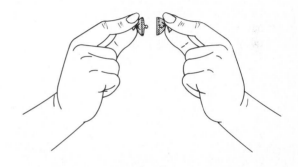

Draw up the threads tightly and secure. Attach the snap to the garment, following the procedures for a regular snap. Be sure that all raw fabric edges are tucked under before stitching. In addition, clear nail polish can be used on the raw edges to prevent the fabric from fraying.

Lingerie Strap Guards

Lingerie strap guards prevent shoulder seams from shifting and thus keep lingerie straps from showing.

Two types of guards may be used:
Thread chain
Seam binding

For each type, the socket section of the snap is sewn to the shoulder seam 2.0 cm (¾ in) from the center of the shoulder toward the neck edge.

Procedures: Thread-Chain Guard. Make a 3.8-cm (1½-in) thread chain beginning 3.8 cm (1½ in) away from the snap socket. Secure the ball section of the snap firmly to the free end of the thread chain.

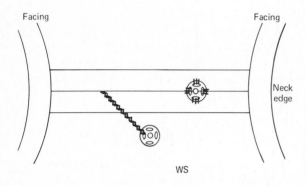

THREAD CHAIN GUARD

Procedures: Seam-Binding Guard. Cut a 5.6-cm (2½-in) length of seam binding. Turn under one end 6 mm (¼ in) and whip-stitch to the garment 3.8 cm (1½ in) from the socket section of the snap. Fold under 1.3 cm (½ in) at the other end and attach the ball section to the underside of the binding.

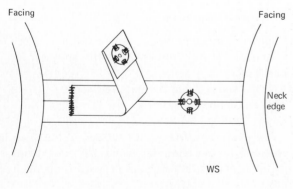

SEAM BINDING GUARD

CRITERIA FOR EVALUATION

SNAPS

Check to ensure quality performance:

__ **1.** Used in areas where there is minimal strain on the closure; size is coordinated with fabric weight and bulk.

__ **2.** Ball portion of snap is placed on the underside of the overlap; socket portion is placed on the upper side of the underlap.

__ **3.** A double thread is used to fasten the snap with whip or buttonhole stitches; no stitches show on the right side of the garment.

__ **4.** The ball and socket are positioned so that the garment is aligned when the snap is closed.

In addition, for **COVERED SNAPS:**

__ **5.** Visible snaps are smoothly covered with color coordinated lining fabric.

In addition, for **LINGERIE STRAP GUARDS:**

__ **6.** The guard length is slightly longer than the width of the lingerie straps.

HOOKS AND EYES

Hooks and eyes are used on garment areas subject to strain, such as necklines and waistlines. The size and number of hooks needed will vary with the degree of strain and fabric weight. Use a fine hook and eye (size 0) with delicate fabrics and a sturdier set (up to size 3) with heavier fabrics. Hooks and eyes can be purchased in either a nickel or black finish.

The *general-purpose hook and eye* consists of a hook that may be used with a straight eye on openings that overlap or a rounded eye on abutted openings.

| Hook | Straight eye | Round eye |

Procedures: Lapped Edges. First attach the *hook* to the underside of the overlap about 3 mm (⅛ in) from the edge. Secure with whip stitches or buttonhole stitches around each hook hole, being careful not to let any stitches show through to the right side. For greater security, catch the interfacing layer with stitches and use a double thread. After stitching around both holes, slip the needle *between* the fabric layers to the hooked end. Whip the thread around the hook end and through the fabric several times to hold it against the garment. Secure the thread under the hook with a fastening stitch.

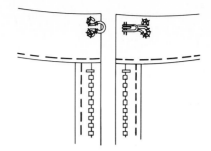

ABUTTED EDGES: ROUND EYE

joined. Sew on the eye, using the procedures used for attaching a straight eye. To hold the eye close to the garment, whip both sides of the loop down.

Special-purpose hooks and eyes are available in a nickel or black finish. These heavy-duty fasteners will withstand the strain placed on pants and skirt waistbands, since they are larger and are made from a solid piece of metal. Because the eye is straight, the pants hook and eye can be used for lapped edges only. Attach these hooks and eyes to the garment by following the procedures used to attach a general-purpose hook and eye.

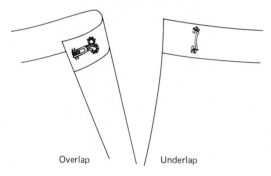

OVERLAPPED EDGES: STRAIGHT EYE

To position the *straight eye,* place it in the hook and close the garment as it will be worn. Insert two pins through the holes in the eye and unhook. Stitch around each end of the eye, using the same method used to secure the hook.

Procedures: Abutted Edges. Attach the *hook* to the underside of the overlap 1.5 mm (¹⁄₁₆ in) from the left garment edge, using the same procedures as for lapped edges.

Position the *round eye* so that the garment edges will abut when the hook and eye are

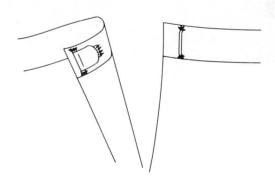

SPECIAL-PURPOSE HOOK AND EYE

Thread Loop

Thread loops are chains of matching thread used to make thread eyes, belt carriers, button loops, or lingerie strap guards. Two methods can be used to make a thread loop: the thread-chain method or the buttonhole-stitch method.

Procedures: Thread-Chain Method. Mark the thread loop's endpoint position on the garment with two pins. Using a double thread, bring the threaded needle up through one of the endpoints. Take two small stitches over this point and then take a third stitch, leaving a 10- to 12.5-cm (4- to 5-in) loop.

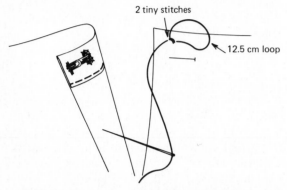

Hold the loop open with your left thumb and index finger. Hold the remaining "supply" thread taut with your right index finger and thumb.

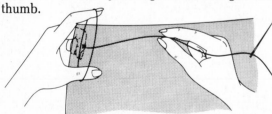

Pull the supply thread through the loop with the second finger of your left hand. Let the first

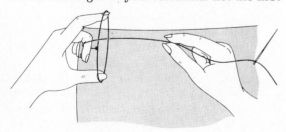

loop slide off your finger and be drawn down to the fabric.

Continue making loops until chain reaches the desired length.

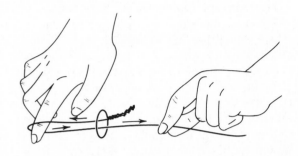

Note: If you are making a straight eye, the space between the marked endpoints and the chain length are equal. However, for a round eye, belt carrier, or button loop, the thread chain must be slightly longer than the space.

If you make the chain too long, pull the needle and the entire chain will come apart, so that you can start over.

Secure the last loop of the chain by bringing the needle and thread through it and pulling the thread taut. Use a fastening stitch to secure the free end of the chain to the second endpoint.

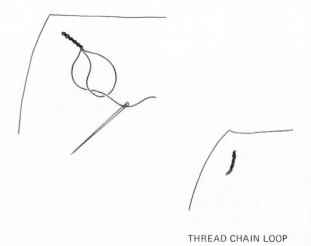

THREAD CHAIN LOOP

Procedures: Buttonhole-Stitch Method. Mark the thread loop endpoint positions with two pins. Secure the end of a double thread at one of the endpoints. Take a stitch by inserting the needle through the second endpoint and bringing it out at the first point. Repeat the stitch three or four times, making the stitch loose for a round eye, belt carrier, or button loop.

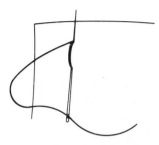

Completely cover these stitches with a closely spaced buttonhole stitch. Securely fasten the thread ends at each end of the eye.

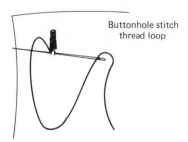

Buttonhole stitch
thread loop

CRITERIA FOR EVALUATION

HOOKS AND EYES

Check to ensure quality performance:

___ **1.** Used in areas subject to some strain; size and number are coordinated with fabric weight and estimated degree of strain.

___ **2.** The hook is placed on the underside of the overlap; the eye is placed on the upper side of the underlap.

     3. The type of eye is appropriate:
        ___a. The straight eye is used with lapped closures
        ___b. The round eye is used with abutted closures

___ **4.** A double thread is used to fasten the hook and eye with whip or buttonhole stitches; no stitches show on the right side of the garment.

___ **5.** Thread loop stitches are even; loop ends are securely attached to the garment.

___ **6.** The loop end of the hook is secured flat against the garment.

___ **7.** The hook and eye are positioned so that the garment is aligned when the hook and eye are closed.

___ **8.** A special-purpose hook and eye are used in areas that receive great strain (e.g. waistband).

VELCRO FASTENERS

Tape fasteners can be used for adjustable closures or removable trims. They are ideal for loose-fitting garments, children's clothes, garments worn by the physically handicapped, and sportswear. Avoid using tape fasteners on tight-fitting garments or lightweight fabrics or as zipper substitutes.

The Velcro fastener consists of two strips that lock together on contact. One strip is completely covered with tiny hooks; the other is covered with loops.

Procedures. Machine-stitch the *hook strip* to the garment underlap by edge-stitching around the entire strip. The *loop strip* is attached to the underside of the overlap. It can be visibly machine stitched through all layers, thus showing on the right side of the garment, or it can be machine stitched or hand-whipped to the garment facing section.

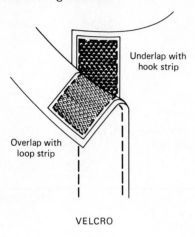

Underlap with hook strip

Overlap with loop strip

VELCRO

CRITERIA FOR EVALUATION

VELCRO FASTENERS

Check to ensure quality performance:

__ **1.** Used on loose-fitting garments and with fabrics medium to heavier in weight.

__ **2.** The loop strip is placed on the underside of the overlap; the hook strip is placed on the upperside of the underlap.

__ **3.** Visible machine stitching follows the edges of the Velcro, forming corners; hand stitches are invisible.

__ **4.** The Velcro strips are positioned so that the garment is aligned when they are closed.

26 POCKETS

To carefully prepare each pocket type and apply it symmetrically to the garment in a functional/decorative position.

Although the pocket is generally considered a functional structure that serves to carry small objects or to warm the hands, it may also be decorative. The classification of pockets is based on construction technique. They may be applied to the garment surface, integrated into seams, or set into the garment. Examples of various types of pockets are given below.

1. **Surface Application:**
   Patch Pockets

2. **Seam Pockets:**
Inseam Pockets
Side Hip Pockets

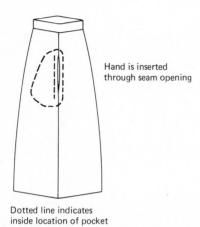

Hand is inserted
through seam opening

Dotted line indicates
inside location of pocket

3. **Set-in Pockets:**
Bound Pockets

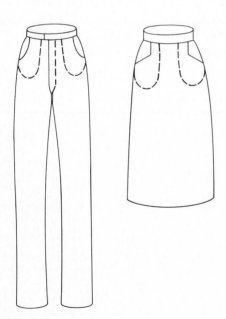

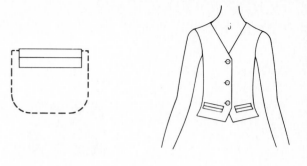

Welt and Flap Pockets

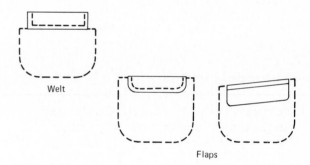

Welt

Flaps

[For all pockets, dotted lines indicate inside location of pocket.]

Pocket Checks. Before cutting out the pocket sections, check their shape, size, and location in relation to both the garment design and the wearer. Pocket shapes should repeat other shapes within the garment. The size of the pockets should be in scale with the wearer and with overall garment proportions.

Check the location of each pocket to be sure it is positioned where it can best be used. Functional pockets are generally located below the waist and decorative pockets above it. Functional pockets should be easily reached—neither too high nor too low. Any pocket may need to be relocated if the pattern has been adjusted or if the visual placement is not esthetically pleasing for a particular figure.

POCKET APPLICATION PROCEDURES

Because they are decorative as well as functional, pockets form a particularly visible portion of the garment. Skillful construction of enclosed seams, accurate positioning, and smooth application are each crucial to the final appearance.

SURFACE APPLICATION: PATCH POCKETS

Patch pockets consist of variously shaped fabric sections applied to the right side of the garment. The outer edges are finished before the pocket shape is secured to the garment, using hand or machine stitches. Patch pockets may be unlined or lined. Each type is attached to the garment following the same procedures.

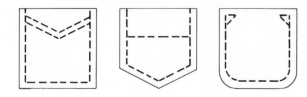

It is usually easier to attach the pockets to the garment before many seams are stitched and while the fabric sections are still flat. If, however, they have been basted to the constructed garment to check location, patch pockets may be attached permanently at a later stage.

To add a patch pocket to a pattern without pockets, first determine the desired size, shape, and location by using cut paper shapes. When designing the pocket shape, consider the garment's style lines. Are they primarily straight and angular, or are they curved? To relate the pocket styling to the garment, use similar style lines and shapes.

To construct the pattern shape in the finished size, add a 2.5-cm (1-in) hem facing to the *top* edge only. Add 1.5-cm (⅝-in) seam allowances to all edges. Grain lines should follow those of the garment in the area where it will be attached.

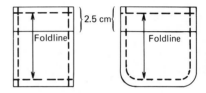

Unlined Patch Pocket

When a patch pocket is unlined, the raw edges are finished by turning the seam allowances and facing to the wrong side. The unlined pocket is used on casual clothing such as shirts and slacks.

Procedures
1. Cut out the pocket, using the pattern pieces provided.
2. Mark the *exact* location for the pocket on the garment if necessary. Thread-baste along placement lines to ensure accurate positioning.

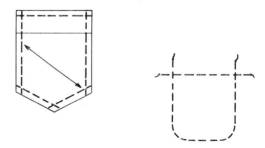

3. Clean-finish the hem facing edge by turning under 6 mm (¼ in) to the wrong side and edge-stitching.
4. Fold the hem facing to the right side of the pocket along the fold line; pin cut edges. Stitch from the folded edge to the hem edge, reinforcing the stitching at both ends. To minimize bulk, trim the corners diagonally and grade the seam.
5. Stay-stitch the remaining pocket edges 1.3 cm (½ in) from the cut edge.

   If the pocket corners are rounded, ease-stitch the corners 6 mm (¼ in) from the edges.

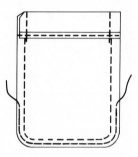

6. Turn the pocket hem facing to the back so that the right side of the pocket is facing outward. Shape the pocket corners.
   a. *To shape rounded corners:* Turn the same allowance to the wrong side, using the stay-stitching line as a guide; press in place. To distribute the fabric evenly around the curve, draw up the ease stitching around the pocket edge. Arrange the

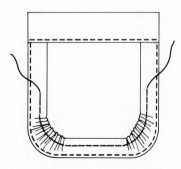

fullness smoothly and evenly around the curved edge. The two corners should be identical in shape.
   b. *To shape squared corners:* Finish the corner neatly by mitering. Press the seam allowances to the inside along the seam line. Open; fold each lower corner to the inside diagonally across the point, and press. Trim each corner to 9 mm (⅜ in) from the diagonal crease.

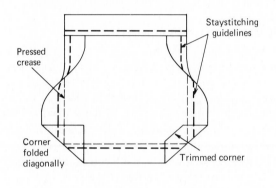

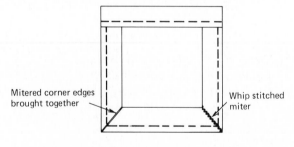

   Fold the seam allowances back to the inside and whip-stitch the edges of the corner miter together.
7. Attach the pocket to the garment following patch pocket application procedures on page 318.

Lined Patch Pocket

After construction, the lined patch pocket looks just like an unlined patch pocket. The lining, however, encloses the seam allowances and

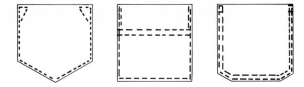

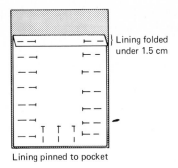

Lining folded
under 1.5 cm

Lining pinned to pocket

adds a custom finish to the garment. For sheer fabrics, opaqueness is provided. To line the pocket, you can use the garment fabric if it is lightweight. When the garment fabric is heavier, use a lining fabric.

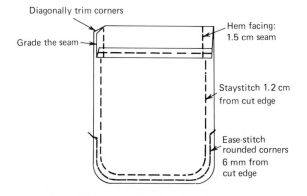

Diagonally trim corners

Grade the seam

Hem facing: 1.5 cm seam

Staystitch 1.2 cm from cut edge

Ease-stitch rounded corners 6 mm from cut edge

Procedures:

1. The pocket pattern may be used to make a lining pattern. Eliminate the hem facing from the pattern section and add 1.5 cm (⅝ in) to this edge.

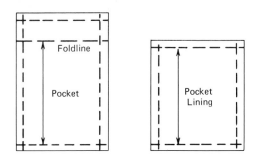

Foldline

Pocket

Pocket Lining

2. Press under the upper edge of the lining 1.5 cm (⅝ in). Pin the lining to the pocket with *right* sides together, keeping sides and bottom edges even.

3. With right sides together, turn the upper edge of the pocket down along the fold line and *over* the lining to form the *hem facing*. Begin stitching from the top and continue down the side, across the lower edge, and up the other side, checking to be sure the corners are smooth and identical. Grade the seams and trim the upper corner diagonally. Notch any curved edges.

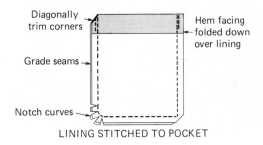

Diagonally trim corners

Hem facing folded down over lining

Grade seams

Notch curves

LINING STITCHED TO POCKET

4. Turn the pocket completely right side out; baste with a diagonal basting stitch, favoring the right side. Press.

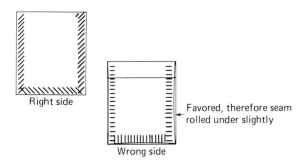

Right side

Wrong side

Favored, therefore seam rolled under slightly

5. Blind/slip-stitch the hem facing to the lining.
6. Attach the pocket to the garment following patch pocket application procedures below at right.

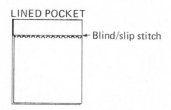

3. Turn pocket completely right side out, baste the edges diagonally, and press. Invisibly slip-stitch the opening closed.
4. Attach the pocket to the garment following patch pocket application procedures.

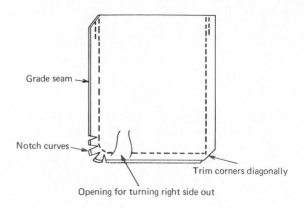

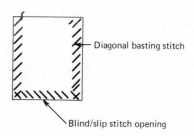

Self-lined Patch Pocket

A patch pocket may be self-lined with the fashion fabric if the fabric is not too bulky.

Procedures:

1. The pocket and lining are cut from one piece of fabric twice the length of the finished pocket.

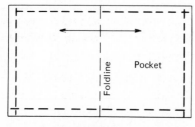

SELF-LINED POCKET PATTERN

2. Fold the pocket section in half with *right* sides together, cut edges even. Pin. Machine-stitch, leaving a 3.8-cm (1½-in) opening on one side, so the pocket can be turned right side out.

Grade the seam allowances and notch curves where necessary. If the corners are square, trim diagonally.

Patch Pocket Application Procedures

1. Thread or pin-baste the pocket in position on the garment.
2. The patch pocket may be secured to the garment by hand or by machine. The pocket is less likely to shift out of place during stitching when attached by hand. Therefore it is a relatively simple technique and is also very strong if the prick stitch is used.
   a. *To secure by hand:* Two hand stitches may be used. Use a blind/slip stitch to attach invisibly. Be careful not to pull the stitches too tight, as otherwise the pocket edges may pucker. The *prick stitch,* a se-

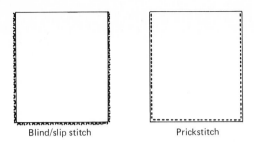

Blind/slip stitch   Prickstitch

cure and decorative variation of the back-stitch, can also be used. If desired, the rest of the garment may be prick-stitched by hand to match. Reinforce stitches at upper corners.

b. *To secure by machine:* To prevent the pocket from shifting, use the diagonal basting stitch to hold the pocket in position; machine-stitch close to the edge (3 mm or ⅛ in).

If the pocket is decoratively topstitched, one or more rows of stitching may be used. When the topstitching falls within the central portion of the pocket, it must be done before the pocket is basted to the garment. Various stitching patterns may be used. Some of these will incorporate the reinforcement stitching at the upper corners.

Pull all thread ends to the inside and tie.

3. Remove thread bastings and press.

CRITERIA FOR EVALUATION

SURFACE APPLICATION: PATCH POCKETS

Check to ensure quality performance:

___ **1.** Pockets are flat and smooth; matched in size or shaping.

___ **2.** Bulk is minimized: enclosed seams are graded, corners are trimmed diagonally, curves are notched.

___ **3.** Corners: square corners form 90-degree angles; curved corners are smooth and symmetric.

___ **4.** Pockets are accurately positioned.

___ **5.** Upper corners are reinforced.

___ **6.** Topstitching is perfectly even; it is placed 3 to 6 mm (⅛ to ¼ in) from edge.

In addition, for an *unlined patch pocket,* check that:

___ **7.** Faced edge is finished smoothly.

___ **8.** Seamed edges are turned under evenly and smoothly; visible seam allowances are not trimmed.

___ **9.** Corners: square corners are mitered; curved corners are smoothly rounded, with fullness drawn in evenly.

SEAM APPLICATIONS

Inseam Pocket

Inseam pockets are inconspicuous because they are concealed within the seams of the garment. They are generally made of lining fabric or lightweight self-fabric. An extended facing supports the opening and prevents the lining portion from being seen.

Procedures:

1. Stitch each pocket section to its corresponding garment-facing extension with right sides together. Press each seam toward the pocket.

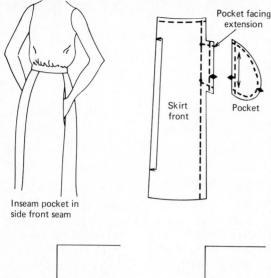

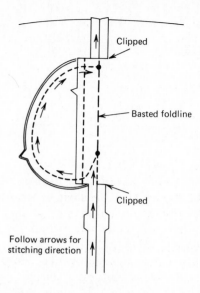

Pocket facing extension

Skirt front

Pocket

Inseam pocket in side front seam

Clipped

Basted foldline

Clipped

Follow arrows for stitching direction

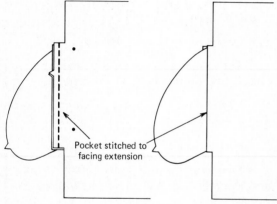

Pocket stitched to facing extension

2. Pin the garment sections with right sides together, dots matching, and pockets aligned with each other.

Stitch along the seam line, pivoting at the inner corner dot. Stitch around the pocket, pivot again at the upper corner dot, and continue stitching the side seam. Baste along the fold line between the dots.

2. Turn the pocket toward the garment *front* along the basted fold line. Clip the *back* seam allowance above and below the facing extension. Press the garment seams open; press the pocket flat. Remove the basting after the garment has been completed.

Side Hip Pocket

Front hip pockets angle or curve from the waistline seam to the side seam of pants or skirts. They form part of the structural design of the garment, since the shaping of the pocket opening often repeats other shapes within the garment. The pocket section itself is invisible, since it hangs inside the garment.

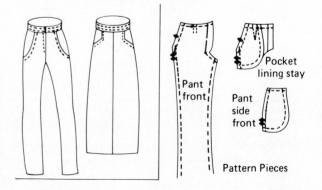

Pant front

Pocket lining stay

Pant side front

Pattern Pieces

Front hip pockets may gap or pop open if the pocket lining does not extend to the center front of the garment. An extension to the center front *stays* the side seam in position, preventing it from shifting to the back. If the garment has front pleats, the pocket stay will also hold them in position. Check the pattern pieces included with the pattern to see whether the pocket lining pattern extends to the center front of the garment. Study the shapes of the pattern pieces shown below.

Pocket Lining Stay Pattern. Notice that the pattern extends beyond the pocket portion to the center front. This type of pattern will usually have a dart at the waistline.

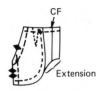

Pocket Lining Pattern. This pattern forms only the shape of the pocket. It does not extend to the center front. It is satisfactory for loosely fitted garments such as gathered skirts.

Pocket Lining Modification

To convert the pocket lining pattern to a stay, the pattern must be extended to the center front.

1. Working with the pants front pattern, partially fold out the pleat tucks to below the crotch level.
2. Place the pocket lining pattern over the pants front pattern, matching construction markings and seam lines. Pin the patterns together.

Pleat has been folded out

3. Cut a piece of tissue paper wider than the upper pants width and extending slightly below the pocket pattern.

   Place the tissue over the upper portion of the pants pattern. Cover the pocket pattern as well as the center front of the pants.

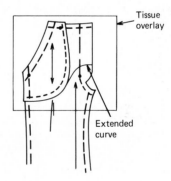

Tissue overlay

Extended curve

Trace the following:
   a. All cutting and stitching lines of the pocket pattern.
   b. The upper and center-front edges of the pants pattern, including all markings and dart locations.

   Extend the curve of the lower pocket edge to approximately 3 to 5 cm (1¼ to 2 in) above the zipper dot.

4. If the pants front has pleat tucks, one or two darts will have to be formed so that the pocket lining stay will fit smoothly over the stomach curve.

To make the darts, split the pattern beginning at the waistline tuck locations and ending at the lower edge of the traced pattern piece. Spread the pattern apart at the waist only. The width of the darts must correspond to the width of the tucks, so that the waistline seams will be the same length when they are stitched together.

 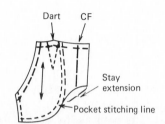

Pattern has been split. A dart 10-12 cm long has been drawn in.

Dart CF

Stay extension

Pocket stitching line

5. Trace the completed pattern onto clean tissue paper. Mark seam lines, darts, center front, dots, and pocket markings as shown.

Side Hip-Pocket Procedures:

1. Stitch tucks or darts in skirt or pants front. Press darts toward the center front; press tucks toward the side seam. Stitch darts in pocket lining stay. Press toward the center front.

2. To prevent the slanted pocket edge from stretching, stay the seam line with seam binding. Cut the seam binding, using the pattern tissue as a guide for length. Center the binding over the seam line and machine-baste 1.3 cm (½ in) from the edge.

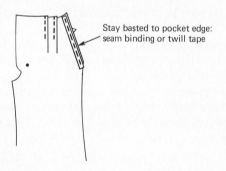

Stay basted to pocket edge: seam binding or twill tape

3. Stitch the pocket lining stay to the shaped upper side edge of the garment front. Trim the seam without cutting the seam binding.

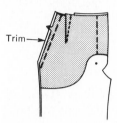

Trim

4. Turn the pocket lining stay to the inside; press. Topstitch 3 to 6 mm (⅛ to ¼ in) from the finished edge.

5. Stitch the side-front section to the pocket lining. Stay along the outer curved edge of the side front, following marked seam lines. Keep garment front free of stitching.

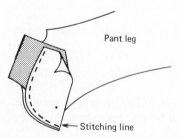

Pant leg

Stitching line

6. Turn the pocket section down next to the wrong side of the garment front. Match seam lines and center-front lines of the pocket lining stay and the garment; baste along center-front line, waistline, and side seam.

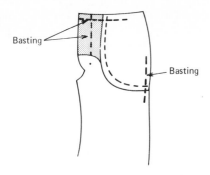

Basting

Basting

no center-front zipper, in the center-front seam. The side edges of the pocket will be caught in the side seam.

7. Finish garment construction. The pocket lining stay will be caught in the stitching of the zipper construction or, if the garment has

CRITERIA FOR EVALUATION

SEAMED POCKETS

Check to ensure quality performance:

Inseam pocket:

__ **1.** Seam line is smooth and unbroken at pocket opening.

__ **2.** Inside pocket is flat and smooth; lining-weight fabric has been used to reduce bulk.

Side hip pocket:

__ **1.** Pocket shaping is smooth and symmetric.

__ **2.** Pocket edges are stayed to prevent stretching.

__ **3.** Bulk is minimized: enclosed seams are handled smoothly.

__ **4.** Inside of pocket is flat and smooth; lining-weight fabric has been used to reduce bulk.

SET-IN POCKET APPLICATIONS

Set-in pockets are constructed much like a large bound buttonhole. The pocket is set into the garment through a narrow slash and hangs inside. Therefore there is little chance of correcting stitching errors. Precision marking, stitching, cutting, and pressing are particularly crucial to quality construction.

The *bound* and *welt* pockets are examples of set-in pockets. They are often found on tailored garments and menswear. The piping and welt are constructed from the garment or contrasting fabric; the inside pocket sections are

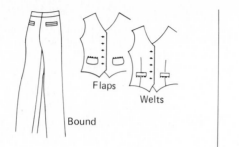

Flaps

Welts

Bound

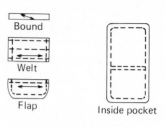

Bound

Welt

Flap

Inside pocket

TYPICAL PATTERN PIECES

constructed from firm pocketing or lining to reduce bulk. The piping or welts may be cut on the true bias to play up plaid or striped fabrics.

Marking. Precision construction of set-in pockets begins by the accurate transfer of placement lines onto the garment; this is done by thread basting. Check to be sure markings are *parallel* to one another.

} 1.3 cm

Construction. Techniques used to construct the bound and welt pockets are described separately. Since attachment of the inside pocket sections is the same for both types, it is described only once.

Bound Pockets

The *bound pocket* closely resembles an oversize bound buttonhole in both appearance and

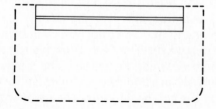

construction. Both edges of the pocket slash are finished with a narrow piping.

Preparation Procedures:

1. For each pocket, cut two piping strips 3.2 cm (1¼ in) wide and 2.5 cm (1 in) longer than the finished pocket length. The strips may be cut on the lengthwise or bias grain lines.

}3.2 cm{

2. Fold each strip in half lengthwise with the *wrong* sides together. Press. Machine-baste 4.5 mm (³⁄₁₆) from the fold.

} 4.5 cm

3. Working on the *right* side of the garment, position each piping strip over the pocket markings, matching stitching lines precisely. The folded edges will face outward and the

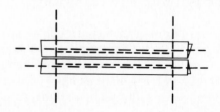

strip ends will extend 1.3 cm (½ in) beyond
the pocket end markings. Baste securely. The
set-in pocket lining application for bound,
welt, and flap pockets is the same. Instructions begin below at right.

Welt and Flap Pockets

A *welt pocket* looks very much like the *flap*
found on some pockets. The major distinction
between the two is that a flap hangs free and
in a downward direction. A welt stands up and
is securely attached along each side. With the
exception of one step, they are constructed the
same way.

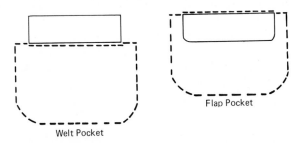

Welt Pocket   Flap Pocket

Procedures:

1. Interface the welt or flap section by trimming
   away interfacing seam allowances. Catch-
   stitch the interfacing to the wrong side along
   all edges.

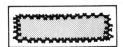

2. Pin the welt or flap to its corresponding facing with right sides together. Stitch around
   three sides, leaving the base edge unstitched

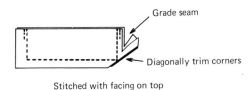

Grade seam

Diagonally trim corners

Stitched with facing on top

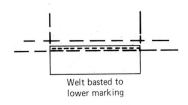

Trim to 6 mm

and reinforce stitches at the start and finish
of seams. Grade the seam. Trim square corners diagonally; notch rounded corners.

3. Turn the welt or flap right side out. Use the
   diagonal basting stitch to hold the turned
   edges in place; and press. Machine-baste
   long edges together and trim to 6 mm (¼
   in).

Welt basted to
lower marking

4. Pin the welt or flap section to the right side
   of the garment by placing the welt or flap
   seam line over the marked pocket stitching
   line. Baste securely.
   a. Pin the *welt* over the *lower* marked pocket
      stitching line.
   b. Pin the *flap* over the *upper* marked pocket
      stitching line.

Set-in Pocket Lining Application Procedures

The inside-pocket lining sections are applied
to both the bound and welt pockets with the
same construction techniques.

1. Position the pocket lining over the welt or
   flap with the *longer* pocket portion to the
   top of the garment. Match construction lines

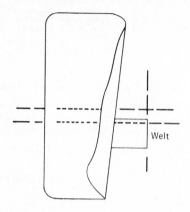

precisely and baste, using short running stitches exactly along the seam lines.

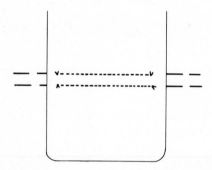

2. Stitch along the upper and lower stitching lines using *very short reinforcement stitches*. Tie thread ends securely.
3. Carefully slash between the two stitching lines to within 1.3 cm (½ in) of each end. Using the tip of the scissors, clip diagonally to each line.

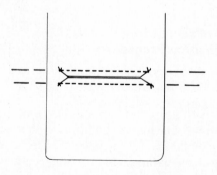

4. Turn pocket lining to the inside of the garment. Turn welt upward. Gently pull small triangles to inside at each end to square the corners.

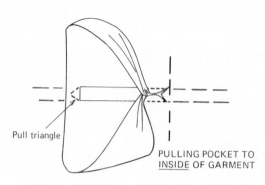

5. Press the triangles and seam allowances away from the opening. Stitch pocket edges together, catching the triangular ends in the stitching. Backstitch across triangles several times to secure. Stitch around pocket again 1.0 cm (⅜ in) from edges to strengthen.

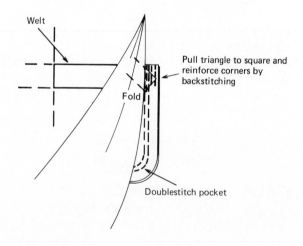

6. To finish:
   a. Slip-stitch the *welt* ends in place invisibly to hold the welt upright. Remove basting and press.
   b. Press the *flap* downward.

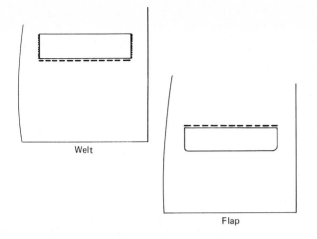

Welt

Flap

CRITERIA FOR EVALUATION

SET-IN POCKETS

Check to ensure quality performance:

__ **1.** Piping, welts, and flaps are even in width and symmetric.

__ **2.** Bulk is minimized; upper edges are favored.

__ **3.** Corners are square.

__ **4.** Reinforcement stitching has been used; ends are secure.

Metric Equivalency Chart Converting Inches to Centimeters and Yards to Meters

This chart gives the standard equivalents as approved by the Pattern Fashion Industry.

mm — millimetres   **cm — centimetres**   **m — metres**

INCHES TO MILLIMETRES AND CENTIMETRES
(SLIGHTLY ROUNDED FOR YOUR CONVENIENCE)

inches	mm		cm		inches	cm		inches	cm
⅛	3mm				7	18		29	73.5
¼	6mm				8	20.5		30	76
⅜	10mm	or	1cm		9	23		31	78.5
½	13mm	or	1.3cm		10	25.5		32	81.5
⅝	15mm	or	1.5cm		11	28		33	84
¾	20mm	or	2cm		12	30.5		34	86.5
⅞	22mm	or	2.2cm		13	33		35	89
1	25mm	or	2.5cm		14	35.5		36	91.5
1¼	32mm	or	3.2cm		15	38		37	94
1½	38mm	or	3.8cm		16	40.5		38	96.5
1¾	45mm	or	4.5cm		17	43		39	99
2	50mm	or	5cm		18	46		40	102
2½	63mm	or	6.3cm		19	48.5		41	104
3	75mm	or	7.5cm		20	51		42	107
3½	90mm	or	9cm		21	53.5		43	109
4	100mm	or	10cm		22	56		44	112
4½	115mm	or	11.5cm		23	58.5		45	115
5	125mm	or	12.5cm		24	61		46	117
5½	140mm	or	14cm		25	63.5		47	120
6	150mm	or	15cm		26	66		48	122
					27	68.5		49	125
					28	71		50	127

YARDS TO METRES

(SLIGHTLY ROUNDED FOR YOUR CONVENIENCE)

CHECK PATTERN ENVELOPE FOR MOST ACCURATE CONVERSIONS OF FABRIC REQUIREMENTS

YARDS	METRES	YARDS	METRES	YARDS	METRES	YARDS	METRES	YARDS	METRES
⅛	0.15	2⅛	1.95	4⅛	3.80	6⅛	5.60	8⅛	7.45
¼	0.25	2¼	2.10	4¼	3.90	6¼	5.75	8¼	7.55
⅜	0.35	2⅜	2.20	4⅜	4.00	6⅜	5.85	8⅜	7.70
½	0.50	2½	2.30	4½	4.15	6½	5.95	8½	7.80
⅝	0.60	2⅝	2.40	4⅝	4.25	6⅝	6.10	8⅝	7.90
¾	0.70	2¾	2.55	4¾	4.35	6¾	6.20	8¾	8.00
⅞	0.80	2⅞	2.65	4⅞	4.50	6⅞	6.30	8⅞	8.15
1	0.95	3	2.75	5	4.60	7	6.40	9	8.25
1⅛	1.05	3⅛	2.90	5⅛	4.70	7⅛	6.55	9⅛	8.35
1¼	1.15	3¼	3.00	5¼	4.80	7¼	6.65	9¼	8.50
1⅜	1.30	3⅜	3.10	5⅜	4.95	7⅜	6.75	9⅜	8.60
1½	1.40	3½	3.20	5½	5.05	7½	6.90	9½	8.70
1⅝	1.50	3⅝	3.35	5⅝	5.15	7⅝	7.00	9⅝	8.80
1¾	1.60	3¾	3.45	5¾	5.30	7¾	7.10	9¾	8.95
1⅞	1.75	3⅞	3.55	5⅞	5.40	7⅞	7.20	9⅞	9.05
2	1.85	4	3.70	6	5.50	8	7.35	10	9.15

AVAILABLE FABRIC WIDTHS

25″	64cm	50″	127cm
27″	70cm	54″/56″	140cm
35″/36″	90cm	58″/60″	150cm
39″	100cm	68″/70″	175cm
44″/45″	115cm	72″	180cm
48″	122cm	108″	275cm

AVAILABLE ZIPPER LENGTHS

4″	10cm	10″	25cm	22″	55cm
5″	12cm	11″	28cm	24″	60cm
6″	15cm	12″	30cm	26″	65cm
7″	18cm	14″	35cm	28″	70cm
8″	20cm	16″	40cm	30″	75cm
9″	23cm	18″	45cm	36″	90cm
		20″	50cm		

Bibliography

ALEXANDER, PATSY. TEXTILE PRODUCTS SELECTION, USE AND CARE. Boston: Houghton Mifflin Company, 1977.

BANE, ALLYNE. CREATIVE CLOTHING CONSTRUCTION. 3rd ed. New York: McGraw-Hill Book Company, 1973.

BERRY, THELMA. STRUCTURAL AND FUNCTIONAL FITTING OF TAPED PATTERNS ON THE FIGURE. Carbondale, Ill.: By the Author, Southern Illinois University, 1970.

DE LLOSA, MARTHA. "STRETCH FOR ALL SEASONS," *American Fabrics and Fashions,* Fall, 1980, Number 120.

ERWIN, MABEL D., LILA A. KINCHIN and KATHLEEN A. PETERS. CLOTHING FOR MODERNS. 6th ed. New York: Macmillan Publishing Company, Inc., 1979.

ERWIN, MABEL. PRACTICAL DRESS DESIGN. Rev. ed. New York: Macmillan Publishing Company, 1954.

EVANS, HELEN MARIE. MAN THE DESIGNER. New York: Macmillan Publishing Company, 1973.

GILES, ROSALIE. DRESSMAKING WITH SPECIAL FABRICS. London: Miles and Boon Limited, 1976.

HORN, MARILYN J. THE SECOND SKIN. 2nd. ed. Boston: Houghton Mifflin Company, 1968.

JOSEPH, MARJORY L. INTRODUCTORY TEXTILE SCIENCE. 3rd ed. New York: Holt, Rinehart and Winston, 1977.

KEFGEN, MARY and PHYLLIS TOUCHIE-SPECHT. INDIVIDUALITY IN CLOTHING SELECTION AND PERSONAL APPEARANCE. 2nd ed. New York: Macmillan Publishing Company, 1976.

LIPPMAN, GORDON and DOROTHY ERSKINE. SEW IT YOURSELF: HOW TO MAKE YOUR OWN FASHION CLASSICS. Englewood Cliffs, N.J.: Prentice-Hall, Inc., 1977.

MANSFIELD, EVELYN and ETHEL L. LUCAS. CLOTHING CONSTRUCTION. 2nd ed. Boston: Houghton Mifflin Company, 1974.

MESHKE, EDNA. TEXTILES AND CLOTHING ANALYSIS AND SYNTHESIS. Minneapolis: Burgess Publishing Company, 1961.

PALMER, PATI and SUSAN PLETSCH. PANTS FOR ANY BODY. Rev. ed. Portland, Oregon: By the Authors, P. O. Box 8422, 1976.

READER'S DIGEST COMPLETE GUIDE TO SEWING. Pleasantville, N.Y.: The Reader's Digest Association, Inc., 1976.

SINCLAIR, AMY. CONTOUR OF GARMENT VERSUS BODY CONTOUR WITHIN: A COMPARISON BETWEEN GARMENTS MADE BY DRAPING AND BY FLAT PATTERN TECHNIQUES. Unpublished Master's Thesis, Southern Illinois University, Carbondale, 1975.

"Stretch Clicks in Many Markets," AMERICAN FABRICS, Fall, 1972, Number 95.

TATE, SHARON LEE. INSIDE FASHION DESIGN. San Francisco: Canfield Press, 1977.

Time-Life Books, editors of. THE CLASSIC TECHNIQUES, THE CUSTOM LOOK, and DELICATE WEAR. In THE ART OF SEWING series. New York: Time-Life Books, 1975.

THE VOGUE SEWING BOOK. New York: Vogue Patterns, 1973.

WARDEN, JESSIE, MARTHA A. GOLDING, and JUDY STAM. PRINCIPLES FOR CREATING CLOTHING. New York: John Wiley and Sons, Inc., 1969.

Index

Abutted edges, 307, 309
Acetate, 17
Acrylic, 18
Adjustments, 93–104
Alteration lines, on pattern, 43
Alterations
  directly on body, 90, 93–104
  in fittings, 140–142
Antibacterial finishes, 22
Anticipated product life, of fabric, 27
Antistatic finishes, 22
Arm length, 30, 31, 32, 33, 88, 89
Armscye, 29
Armscye facing, 228

Back crotch length, 31, 32, 33
Back views, on pattern envelope, 40
Back waist length, 30, 88
Back width, 31, 32, 33, 88, 89
Backstitching, 149, 156–157
Balance, 140, 142
  fit and, 84–85, 105
Balance wheel, of sewing machine,
  56
Ball-point needles, 52, 53
Ball-point pins, 52
Bands, 255, 263–276
Bar-tack buttonholes, 293
Basic-weave, 27
Basting, 61, 150–152
Beeswax, 53, 147
Bent-handled shears, 121
Between needles, 52, 53

Bias, 21
Bias facings, 240, 253–254
Bias seams, 61, 190–191
Bias strip, 239
Biceps of sleeve, 204, 205
  measuring, 30, 31, 32, 33, 88, 89
Bindings, 228–229, 255–263
  see also Bands
Blind stitch, 153, 154–155
Bobbin, 58
Bobbin case, 58
Bobbin thread, 60
Bobbin-winding mechanism, 56
Bodkin, 54
Body-garment relationship, 5–13
Body measurements, 28–33, 86–89
Body proportions, 6–7, 8
Bolt-end label, 25
Border prints, pattern layout for, 120
Bound buttonholes, 291, 296–300
Bound finish, for raw edges, 219
Bound plackets, 260–262, 314, 323,
  324–327
Bound pockets, 260–262, 314, 323,
  324–327
Bracketed grain line, on pattern, 43
Brand name, of synthetic fibers, 17
Built-in stitch pattern system, for
  buttonholes, 60
Bulk, reduction techniques for, 231
Bust size, 30, 35, 36, 88
Button-closure edges, 24
Buttonhole foot, 58, 59

Buttonhole stitch, 158
Buttonhole stitch method, for thread
  loop, 311
Buttonholer, 59–60, 292–293
Buttonholes, 43, 290–303
Buttons, 10, 278, 279–280, 303–304
  on pattern, 43

Carbon tracing, for marking, 125,
  126–127
Care of fabric, 24–25
Care label, 25
Casings, 252–253
Catch stitch, 147, 153–154
Cellulose fibers, 16
Centered applications, for zippers,
  282, 286
Chain zipper, 280
Chalk, for marking, 125
Chalk pencils, 52
Checks, pattern layout for, 119
Chest measurement, 32, 33, 36, 89
Chevron, plaids cut creating, 115,
  117
Circumference measures, 29
Circumference seams, 83–84, 199–
  211
Clean finish, for raw edge, 218
Clipping, for marking, 125, 127–128
Closed construction procedure, 200,
  201
  for centered zipper application,
  286

for horizontal circumference
seams, 203–204
for lapped zipper application, 284–
285
for set-in sleeve, 206–207
Closure band, 229
Coil zippers, 280
Collars, 3
bands for, 67, 229, 270–276
facing for, 228, 271–272
Color, 8, 12
Combination curve, 50–51
Combined neck-armscye facing, 242
Comfort ease, 36
Complexity of garment, 3, 4
Compressing, inside curves bound
by, 260
Concave curved seams, 189–190
Concave darts, 184, 185
Continuous bound, 260–261
Continuous loop method, for fabric
loops, 303
Contour
dart and, 183, 184–185
dart-tuck and, 183, 185–186
tuck and, 183, 184, 185–186
strategies for, 161–177
Conventional zippers, 280
Convex curved seam, 190
Convex darts, 184–185
Corded seam, 226
Cording, in hem, 176
Corner hem, 249–250
Corner seams, 191–193, 233–234
Corners
binding, 259–260
turning a square, 63
Cotton, 16, 27
Covered snaps, 307
Crepe, pressing, 70
Crewel needles, 52, 53
Crosswise fold or cut, as pattern
layout, 112
Crosswise grain, of pattern, 42
Crotch
length, 30–31, 32, 33, 88, 89
level, 30, 31, 32, 33, 88, 89
seam, 211
Cuffs, 3, 24
man-tailored, 265
turned back, 251–252
Curved darts, 184–185
Curved hem facings, 248
Curved seams, 61, 64, 189–190, 235–
236
Curves, binding, 260
Cut pile, 19
Cutting line, on pattern, 43

Cutting a pattern, 43, 90, 121–122
fabric prepared for, 106–109
tools for, 51

Dart-tucks, 183, 185–186
Darts, 10, 183, 184–185
on pattern, 43
Decorative facing, 243–244
Decorative seams, 233–226
Decorative stitches, 144, 145, 146,
158–159
Design elements, 7, 8–13
Diagonal basting, 151, 237
Diagonal buttonhole, 292
Diagonal wrinkles, 82
Dimensional comparisons, fit and,
86–89
Directional stitching, for stay-stitch,
165
Disproportion, 74
Dots, 124
of sleeve, 205
Double binding, 258–259
Double knits, 20, 27
Double lengthwise fold, as pattern
layout, 112
Double-pointed darts, 185
Double-stitch finish, for raw edges,
216
Double welt seam, 224, 225
Dressmaker shears, 51
Dressmaker's carbon, 51–52
Dropped grain, 80
Dry-clean method, of preshrinking,
107–108
Durable-press finishes, 22

Ease, 140, 142
fit and, 80–81, 105
pattern, 29, 36–37, 75
Eased seam, 194–195
Easing
outside curves bound by, 260
by sewing machine, 61
Easing line, on pattern, 43
Edges, 3
protective finishes for, 215–222
stay stitching for, 164–165
Elastic, narrow lingerie, 50, 51
Elasticity, 27
Elbow darts, 205
Ellipse-shaped changes, as
alterations, 95
Embroidery needles, 52, 53
Embroidery scissors, 51
Enclosed seams, 180, 181, 231–238
Even basting, 150–151

Even feed foot, of sewing machine,
58–59
Even plaids
matching guidelines for, 116–117
yardage for, 114
Even stripes, layout for, 119
Exposed catch stitch, 153–154
Extended band facings, 264
Extended facings, 239, 240, 244–252
Extended lapped facings, 244–245
Extended snap, 306, 307

Fabric, 3, 4
care and maintenance, 24–25
contouring considering, 162
fiber content, 15
garment form and, 76
manipulation capabilities, 23
preparation, 106–109
quality, 25–27
quantity needed, 41
selection, 2, 14–27
structure, 15–20
texture, 12–13
Fabric conversion chart, 41
Fabric-garment compatibility, 22–24
Fabric garment form, 90–92
Fabric loops, 302–303
Fabric test garment, 85
Face plate, 56
Faced placket, 242–243
Facings, 228, 238–253
reducing, 237
zipper intersecting, 241–242
Fasteners, 305–312
Fastening stitch, 148
Favoring
of enclosed seams, 236–237
of perimeter seam, 231
Feed-cover throat plate, 59
Feed dog, 58
Felling stitch, 155–156
Figure type, 30, 33–35, 36
Filaments, 15
Filling yarn, 21, 108–109
Final fitting, 133, 135, 137, 138, 139,
140, 142
Finishes, functional, 21–22
First fitting, 133, 134, 138, 139, 140,
141
Fit, 3, 73–105
contouring considering, 162–163
Fitted sleeve, 205
Fitting
measurements for, 30–33
organization strategies for, 131–
140
tools, for 50–51

Flame-retardant fabrics, 22
Flap pockets, 314, 325–327
Flat-fell seam, 221
Flat knit, 21
Flattened cap sleeve, 206
Flexible spline, 50, 51
Flower accessory, 10
Fly-front application, for zippers, 282, 288–289
Folded-edge finish, 155
Form comparison, fit and, 89–92
French curve, 50–51
French seams, 220–221
Front closure facing, 228
Front crotch length, 30–31, 32, 33
Front hip pockets, 320–321
Front waist length, 30, 31, 88
Full corner seam, 234
Full hip, 30, 88
Full neck facing, collar with, 271
Full vertical circumference seams, 204–210
Functional finishes, 21–22
Fused interfacings, 169–170

Garment complexity, 3, 4
Garment description, on pattern envelope, 40
Gathered seam, 196–197
Gathering, by sewing machine, 61
Gathering lines, on pattern, 43
General purpose foot, 58, 59
General purpose hook and eye, 308–309
General purpose throat plate, 59
Generic name, of synthetic fibers, 17
Godets, 191, 192–193
Graded seam, 232
Grain, 21, 76, 140, 142
    fit and, 79–80, 105
Grain line, of pattern, 42–43
Gussets, 192–193

Half-corner seam, 234
Half-size figure type, 34
Hand, of fabric, 13, 76
Hand-basting, 150–152
Hand needles, 52, 53
Hand overcast finish, for raw edges, 216–217
Hand-pad-stitching method, for interfacing, 167–168
Hand-quilting, 175
Hand-rolled hem, 250
Hand stitching, 143, 144, 145–146, 146–149, 152–153
Hand-worked buttonholes, 291, 293–296

Heat-set fabrics, 26
Height, 30, 32, 88, 89
Hem fold line on pattern, 43
Hem marker, 50
Hems, 244–245
    binding for, 229
    facing for, 228, 246–257
    rolled, 247, 250
    softening, 176
    stitches for, 153, 154
high bust measurements, 30, 31, 35, 36, 88
Hip measurements, 30, 31, 32, 33, 35, 36, 88, 89
Hong Kong finish, for raw edge, 218–219
Hook and eyes, 305, 306, 308–311
Horizontal buttonholes, 292
Horizontal circumference seams, 199, 200, 201, 202–204
Horizontal ease, 75
Horizontal grain, 79–80
Horizontal reference lines, of pattern, 90
Horizontal seams, 10
Horizontal wrinkles, 81, 82
Hue, of color, 12

Ideal figure, 6
Inner supports, 3
Inseam, 32, 33, 89
Inseam pockets, 314, 319–320
Inset corner, 191
Inset wedges, 191–193
Inside corner seams, 233–234
Inside corners, bending, 259–260
Inside curved seam, 235
Intensity, of color, 12
Interfacing, 23, 24, 161, 163, 165–170, 176, 264–265
Intersecting seams, 189
Invisible application, for zippers, 282–283, 287
Invisible zipper foot, 58, 59
Invisible zippers, 280
Iron. See Steam iron
Ironing, 67
    see also Pressing
Ironing board, 66
Irregular ellipse-shaped changes, as alterations, 95

Jersey knit, 20
Junior figure type, 34
Junior petite figure type, 34

Knit bindings, 257
Knit stretch gauge, 40

Knitted fabrics, 20, 21, 24, 70, 109
Knotting, for securing machine stitching, 149–150

Lace fabrics, pressing, 70
Lamb's wool, in hem, 176
Lapped application, for zippers, 281–282, 284–285
Lapped edges, fastening, 306–307, 309
Lapped seam, 225
Large-scale prints, pattern layout for, 120
Length of garment, 9
Lengthwise fold pattern layout, for plaids, 112, 115
Lengthwise grain, of pattern, 42
Letting out seams, 94
Line, 8, 9, 10, 11, 105, 140, 142
Lined patched pocket, 316–318
Linen, 16
Lingerie strap guards, 307–308
Lining, 161
Location lines on pattern, 43, 124
London method, of preshrinking, 107
Loop pile, 19
Loop turner, 54
Loops
    for buttons, 302–303
    thread, 309–310
Looseness, 80–81
Lower thread, of sewing machine, 60
Lowered sleeve cap, 206

Machine-baste and trim method, for interfacing, 168
Machine-basting, 152
Machine-padding method, for interfacing, 168–169
Machine-quilting, 175
Machine stitching, 143, 144, 145, 149–150, 152, 157–158
    see also Stitching strategies
Machine topstitching, 159
Machine-worked buttonholes, 291, 292–293
Machine zigzag finish, 217
Man-tailored band application, 265
Man-tailored sleeve, 206, 208
Man-tailored waistbanding, 268–269
Marking
    techniques, 123–128
    tools for, 51–52
Matched fabrics, pattern layout for, 113–120
Matching points, on pattern, 43
Measurements
    body, 28–33

pattern, 29
tools for, 48–50
Men
  body measurement procedures for, 32–33
  ease allowance for garments for, 37
  figure type, 34, 36
  fit for, 86
  sizing and adjustment chart for, 89
Mercerized fabrics, 22
Metal gauge, 49–50
Meterstick, 50
Metric equivalency chart, 328
Micro-porous fabrics, 22
Mildew-resistant finishes, 22
Minimum care finishes, 22
Misfit. See Fit
Miss petite figure type, 34
Misses figure type, 33, 34, 35
Mitering, for binding corners, 259–260
Modacrylic, 18
Model figure, 6
Moisture, in pressing, 68
Mothproof fabrics, 22
Multiple fabric layers, concealing, 230

Napped fabrics, pattern layout for, 112–113
Narrow bindings, 228
Narrow lingerie elastic, 50, 51
Natural fibers, 16–17
Natural shank, of buttons, 304
Neck-base location, 29
Neck facing, 239
Neck plackets, 269–270
Neckband, 32, 33, 36, 89
Necklines, 23–24
Needle bar, 56
Needle board, 67
Needle position selector, 58
Needle thread, 60
Needles, 52, 53
  for hand stitching, 147
  selection of, 145–146
  for sewing machine, 56, 58, 64
No-fold layout, 112
Nonwashable fabrics, preshrinking, 107–108
Notched-collar, 275
Notches, 123–124
  on pattern, 43
  of sleeve, 205
Notions, 41–42
Numbers, on pattern, 43
Nylon, 19

Off grain, fabric as, 109
On grain, fabric as, 108
One-price bound plackets, 260–261
One-way printed fabrics, pattern layout for, 113
Open construction procedure, 200, 201
  for centered zipper application, 286
  for lapped zipper application, 285
  for man-tailored sleeve, 208
  for set-in sleeve, 209
  for small child's sleeve, 209
Organization strategies, 131–140
Outseam, for men, 32, 33, 89
Outside corner seams, 234
Outside corners, binding, 259
Outside curved seam, 235
Overedge foot, 58, 59
Overfitting, 99
Overlapped edges, hook and eye for, 309

Padded welt seam, 224, 225
Padding, 161, 163, 172–177
Padding stitch, 157–158
Pants
  length, 31, 32, 88
  size, 36
Partial-circumference seams, 202
Partial lengthwise fold, as pattern layout, 112
Partial neck facing, collar, with, 271–273
Partial underlining, 171
Partial vertical circumference seams, 210–211
Patch method, for bound buttonholes, 297–298
Patch pockets, 313, 315–319
Patching a seam, 63
Pattern, 2–4, 33–43, 76
  adjustments, 85, 86, 88–89, 93–104
  alterations, 85, 90, 93–104
  cutting, 120–121
  dimensions, 85
  layout, 42, 110–121
  refinement, 104–105
  repeat, 113
  reshaping perimeters, 94–95, 97
Pattern ease. See Ease
Pattern garment form, 90–92
Pen and chalk, for marking, 125–126
Pencil-dot, for marking, 124–125
Performance requirements, of fabric, 27

Perimeter edges, 3
  finishing, 229–237
  see also Bands; Bindings; Facings
Permanent stitches, 143, 144, 146, 152–158
Pick stitch, 158–159
Pile fabrics, 19–20, 69, 113
Pilling, 27
Pin-baste, 62
Pin-tucks, 185
Pinning, 52
  for marking, 125, 127
  pattern joined by, 91
Piped corded seam, 226
Piping, 10
Placket
  bound, 260–262
  faced, 242–243
  neckline or sleeve, 269–270
Plaids, pattern layout for, 113–119
Plain-knit, 27
Plain seam, 188–189
Plain weave, 15–16, 27
Pleated seam, 197–198
  hem with, 248–249
Plumb line, 50
Pockets, 278, 313–327
Point turner, 54
Polyester, 18–19, 27
Pounding block, 67
Prepared waistbanding, 268–269
Preshrinking, 22, 106, 107–108
  for fused interfacing, 169
Press cloth, 67, 69–70
Presser feet, 56, 58–59, 61
Presser-foot lever, 56
Pressing, 46–47, 66–72
Pressing hams, 67
Pressure regulator, 58
Prick stitch, 156–157
Primary colors, 12
Prints, pattern layout for, 120
Process construction plan, 133, 136–137, 139
Process method, of sewing instructions, 42
Proportion, 6–7, 8
  disproportion, 74
  see also Fit
Protective edge treatments, 215–222
Protein fibers, 16–17
Psychological comfort factors, 27
Purl knits, 20

Quality of fabric, 25–27
Quilter foot, 59
Quilting, 174–176

Raglan sleeve, 210–211
Raised grain, 80
Raised-surface fabrics, pressing, 69
Raschel knit, 20
Raw edges, protective treatments of, 215–222
Rayon, 19
Refinement
  of alterations, 90
  in pattern, 104–105
Residual shrinkage, 22
Resiliency, 26
Retention, contour and, 163
Reverse stitch regulator, 58
Reverse stitching, of sewing machine, 62
Rib knits, 20
Rolled hem, 247, 250
Roller foot, 59
Rounded cap sleeve, 205
Running stitch, 150–151

Saddle stitch, 158
Safety pin, 54
Sanforization, 22
Satin weave, 15, 16
Scalloped seams, 61
Seam allowances, 188
  enclosing, 230–238
  on pattern, 43
Seam binding guard, for lingerie straps, 308
Seam guide, of sewing machine, 60
Seam line, on pattern, 43
Seam pockets, 314
Seam ripper, 51
Seam roll, 67
Seamed pockets, 319–323
Seams, 9, 10, 83–84
  adjusting, 94
  decorative, 223–226
  enclosed, 180, 231–238
  of equal length, 187–193
  length, 163
  protective/decorative, 220–222
  by sewing machine, 61, 62–63, 64
  structural, 180, 181
  of unequal length, 195–198
Seat measurement, 32, 33, 36, 89
Second fitting, 133, 134, 136, 138, 139, 140, 141–142
Secondary colors, 12
Securing stitches, 143, 144, 147–150
Self-bound finish, for raw edge, 218
Self-filled loops, 302
Self-lined patched pocket, 318
Selvages, 21

Semi-closed construction procedure, 200, 201, 202
  for set-in sleeve, 209–210
Separating zippers, 280
Sequential analysis of fit, 77–85
Set, 140, 142
  fit and, 81–82, 105
Set-in pockets, 314, 323–327
Set-in sleeves, 204–210
Sewing machine, 46, 55–65
Sewing-machine needles, 53
Sewing tools, 49–54
Shaded fabrics, pattern layout for, 113
Shank, of button, 304
Shaped facings, 240, 241–243
Sharp needles, 52, 53
Shawl-collar, 274–275
Shiny-surfaced fabrics, pressing, 69
Shirt sleeve length, for men, 32, 33, 89
Shirt sleeve plackets, 269–270
Short naps, pattern layout for, 113
Shoulder, 30, 31, 32, 33, 88, 89
Shoulder to bust point, 30, 31, 88
Shoulder dot, 205
Shoulder pads, 173–174
Shrinkage, 22
  preshrinking and, 106, 107–108
Shrinkage test-check, 107
Side hip pockets, 314, 320–323
Silhouette, 3, 8, 9, 162
Silhouette seams, 83–84
Silk, 15, 16, 70
Silk pins, 52
Single bindings, 256–258
Single knits, 20
Single loop method, for fabric loops, 303
Single thickness layout, for plaids, 115
Single thread, 146–147
Size
  for men, 32, 33
  of pattern, 35–36, 39
  for women, 30, 31
Skirt length, for women, 31–32, 88
Slash method, for bound buttonhole, 299
Slashing and spreading, 98, 99, 100
Sleeve board, 67
Sleeve cap, 204, 205
Sleeve heads, 174
Sleeve roll, 67
Sleeve scye level, 30, 31, 32, 33
Sleeves, 3, 204–210
Slide plate, 58

Slip-basting, 151–152
Slip stitch, 153, 154–155
Slot seam, 225
Smooth, dull-surfaced fabrics, pressing, 69
Snaps, 306–307
Snugness, 80–81
Soil release finishes, 22
Spandex, 19
Special-purpose hooks and eyes, 309
Speed padding method, for fused interfacing, 169–170
Spline position, 30–31, 32, 33
Split-seam buttonhole, 291, 301
Spool pin, of sewing machine, 56
Square corner, turning a, 63
Stabilization finishes, 22
Stain-and-soil resistant finishes, 22
Standard body measurements, on patterns, 42
Standard figure, 6
Standard hand-worked buttonholes, 294–295
Standard size measurements, 85
Standard stitching, by sewing machine, 61
Standards of fit, 77–85
Staples, 15, 27
Stay stitching, 61, 163, 164–165
Stays, 161, 171–172
Steam iron, 66–67
Stitch pattern cams, 60
Stitch-width regulator, 58
Stitches
  classification table for, 144
  conversion chart for, 61
  on sewing machine, 58, 61–64, 65
  strategies for, 143–160
Stitching control dials, 58
Stitching guides, 60
Stop-motion knob, 56
Straight darts, 184
Straight-edge finish, 155
Straight hem facings, 247–248
Straight pins, 52
Straight seams, 188–189
Straight stitch foot, 58, 59
Straight stitch throat plate, 59
Straight topstitching, 159
Straight waistband with stiffener, 266–268
Straightening, 106–107, 108–109
Strapped seam, 221
Stretch fabrics, 70
Stretched seam, 196
Stripes, pattern layout for, 119–120
Structural seams, 180, 181

Structured garment, 162
Style ease, 36–37
Support, contour and, 163
Surface application, of pockets, 313
of patch pockets, 315–319
Synthetic fibers, 15, 17–19, 69, 70

Tailored hand-worked buttonholes,
295–296
Tailor's chalk, 52
Tailor's hemming stitch, 154
Tailor's tacks, for marking, 125, 126
Taking in seams, 94
Tape measure, 49, 50
Tautness, 82
Tearing, for straightening, 108
Teen boys' figure type, 34, 36
Temporary stitches, 143, 144, 146,
150–152
Tension, of sewing machine, 61–62
Tension discs, 58
Tentering quality, 26
Test check, for possible shrinking,
107
Test press, 68
Textile Fiber Products Identification
Act, 15
Texture, 8, 12–13
Thimble, 52–53
Third fitting. See Final fitting
Thread-chain guard, for lingerie
straps, 308
Thread-chain method, for thread
loop, 310–311
Thread guides, 56
Thread loop, 309–310
Thread shank, of buttons, 304
Thread takeup lever, 56
Threading, a sewing machine, 56, 60
Threads
selecting, 145, 146
sewing machine breaking, 64
synthetic, 147
Three-dimensional fitting, 76, 78–85,
86
Throat plate, 58, 59
Thumb test, 26–27
Topstitched seam, 223–224
Topstitching, 158–159
for single binding, 257–258
Tracing wheel, 51, 52, 126–127
Trade name, of synthetic fibers, 17
Trapunto, 175–176
Triacetate, 19
Trial buttonhole, 291

Tricot knit, 20
Trim-and catch-stitch method, for
interfacing, 167
Trim and hand-baste method, for
interfacing, 167
Trimming scissors, 51
Trims, 10
True bias, 21, 109
Trueing, 106–107, 109
Tubular knit, 21
Tucks, 93–94, 99, 100, 183, 184, 185–
186
Turn-and-stitch, for raw edge, 218
Turned-back cuff, 251–252
Turning
of enclosed seams, 236–237
of perimeter seams, 231
tools for, 54
Twill tape, 51
Twill weave, 15–16, 27
Two-dimensional approach, to fit,
86–87
Two-dimensional pattern
adjustments, 76, 78–83
Two-piece bound-seam-placket, 261–
262
Two-piece piped method, for bound
buttonholes, 298–299

Underarm seams, 204, 205
Underlining, 23, 24, 161, 163, 170–
171
Understitching, for turning and
favoring enclosed seams, 236
Uneven basting, 151
Uneven plaids
matching guidelines for, 118–119
yardage for, 114
Uneven stripes, layout for, 119
Unexposed catch stitch, 154
Unit construction plan, 132–133,
134–135, 138
Unit method, of sewing instructions,
42
Unlike curves, stitching, 236
Unlined patched pocket, 315–316
Unstructured garment, 162
Upper thread, of sewing machine, 60

Value, of color, 12
Velcro fasteners, 311–312
Vertical buttonholes, 292
Vertical circumference seams, 200,
201, 204–211
Vertical ease, 75

Vertical grain, 79–80
Vertical measures, 29
Vertical reference lines, of pattern,
90
Vertical seams, 9, 10
Visibility, stitching and, 147

Waist measurement, 29, 30, 31, 32,
33, 36, 88, 89
Waistband facing, self-facing and,
228
Waistbands, 23, 229, 266–269
Warp knits, 20
Warp yarns, 21
Washable fabrics, preshrinking, 107
Water-repellent finishes, 22
Waterproof finishes, 22
Wedges, as alterations, 95
Weft knits, 20, 27
Welt pockets, 314, 323–324, 325–327
Welt seam, 224–225
Western look, 10
Whipstitch, 156
Windowpane method, for bound
buttonholes, 299–300
With nap layout, 41, 115
Without nap layout, 41, 115, 118–
119
Women
body measurement procedures for,
30–32
ease allowance for garments for, 37
figure type of, 34
fit for, 86
pattern size for, 35–36
sizing and adjustment chart for, 88
Wool, 17, 69
Worked buttonholes, 291
Woven bindings, 256–257
Woven fabrics, 15–21, 24, 26–27, 108
Wrinkles, 81–82
Wrist pincushion, 52

Yarn structure
alignment, 108–109
structure of, 15
Young junior teen figure type, 33, 34

Zigzag finish, for raw edges, 217
Zipper, intersecting and facing, 241–
242
Zipper foot, 58, 59
Zippers, 43, 278, 279, 280–290